A DICTIONARY OF EDUCATION

About the Author

Derek Rowntree has a degree in Economics and a Certificate in Education. He has taught in secondary school, college of technology, college of education and university, and has been a visiting professor at Concordia University, Montreal, and at the Ontario Institute for Studies in Education, Toronto. He was for some time Chief Editor for a publishing company in the field of programmed learning, and led a team of writers working on industrial training topics and academic subjects. He has been with the Open University since 1970, and as Reader in Educational Development, he is chiefly concerned with the preparation and evaluation of courses and multimedia learning materials.

He is the author of *Learn How to Study, Educational Technology in Curriculum Development, Assessing Students : How Shall We Know Them?, Developing Courses for Students*, and *Statistics Without Tears*.

A DICTIONARY OF EDUCATION

Derek Rowntree

Reader in Educational Development
The Open University

Harper & Row, Publishers
London

Cambridge	San Francisco
Hagerstown	Mexico City
Philadelphia	Sao Paulo
New York	Sydney

First published 1981
Harper & Row Ltd
28 Tavistock Street
London WC2E 7PN

British Library Cataloguing in Publication Data
Rowntree, Derek
    A dictionary of education. – (Harper reference)
    1. Education – Dictionaries
    I. Title
    370'.3   LB15

    ISBN 0–06–318157–6

Typeset by Input Typesetting Ltd, London SW19 8DR
Printed and bound by The Pitman Press, Bath

INTRODUCTION

Like every profession, education has its own diction, its own special language consisting both of terms peculiar to itself and of everyday terms used in peculiar ways. Even people within the profession may be uneasy about terms used by specialists in branches other than their own; and the 'interested layman' can be completely flummoxed. This dictionary is meant to help anyone who needs to make sense of the diction of education – students and teachers, of course, but also administrators, employers and parents.

The book grew out of the various working glossaries I have compiled for my own benefit in studying many areas of education over the last twenty years or so. I was persuaded to fill these out so as to make a reasonably comprehensive dictionary: though I little appreciated then just how much educational diction I had yet to grapple with. There were times when I recalled some words from *Robinson Crusoe*: 'Now I saw, though too late, the Folly of beginning a Work before we count the Cost, and before we judge rightly of our Strength to go through with it'! Fortunately, the work took on an interest of its own that made the cost worthwhile; but I had cause to be grateful to a number of colleagues from two continents whose assiduous commenting and advising on a succession of drafts constantly renewed my strength to complete the project.

Contents

Deciding which terms to include in such a dictionary as this is always difficult. In general, I have concentrated on terms an

English-speaking person might be puzzled by in educational books or newspaper and journal articles, or in spoken discussions. Of course, readers on opposite sides of the Atlantic (not to mention those in Australasia) are likely to be puzzled by different terms. A UK reader is likely to question the inclusion of a term like 'lollipop lady/man' or 'rising fives' (which could, in fact, mystify a US or Australian reader); while terms like 'paddling' or 'school bond' might seem similarly redundant to the US reader but mean nothing to a reader in the UK.

In addition, however, I have included terms that the reader *ought* to be puzzled by, though perhaps he will not, because he is already familiar with them as everyday words and is unaware that they have special meanings in the rhetoric of education. Examples might be 'game', 'objectives' and 'reinforcement'. In extreme cases, the meaning may be the opposite of what the reader assumes. Thus, an American reader of a British text may wrongly assume 'grammar school' to refer to a school for children under 12; while the British reader of an American (or Scottish) text may wrongly assume 'public schools' to refer to fee-paying schools. Clearly, the danger here is that such terms simply will not be looked up in the dictionary; however, where such a term is used centrally or repeatedly, it does eventually dawn on most of us that we need to seek out a meaning other than the one we are familiar with.

I have omitted mention of all but a few of the numerous associations, committees, societies, councils, foundations, trusts etc that proliferate in education. Nor have I mentioned many of the educational credentials the countries of this world have to offer. To have included all such organisational and administrative items would have made the dictionary inordinately long, and probably more difficult to use. Besides, such information is already amply available elsewhere, usually in publications that are up-dated annually.

I have included references to a certain number of educational theorists and practitioners. Here I have chosen the sort of names many authors feel free to sprinkle unexplained in their texts as if assuming that all readers will have met them before (eg, Bruner, Montessori, Piaget). There is no room for professional biographies: but just an indication of such a person's main interest or contribution to education is often all the reader needs to make sense of the context in which the name is mentioned.

Treatment

Deciding how much, and what kind of thing to say about each

item is the other major difficulty in compiling a dictionary. Rarely has it seemed possible, let alone useful, to dispose of an idea in two or three words or even in a single sentence. On the other hand, I have had to restrain myself, on occasion, from producing brief essays that would be more appropriate to an encyclopedia.

In general, I have tried to imagine the contexts in which readers might have encountered the term whose meaning they are now querying. I have tried to say enough to help them survive in such contexts without suggesting that they will never need to know more about the topic. For example, a few lines can give a fair idea as to what 'behaviourism' or 'illuminative evaluation' are about; but volumes have been written on such topics and my few lines can scarcely hope even to hint at the complexity and diversity of viewpoints within them. Often, no doubt, I will have told some readers more, and others less, than they would wish to know about a topic.

When I have felt that a concept is best understood by comparison or contrast with another concept, I have referred the reader to that other concept also.

Presentation

The list of items runs in alphabetical order throughout. (That is, I have not grouped entries under common headings as is sometimes done.) When a term in the text is printed in SMALL CAPITALS then that term has an explanation of its own at the appropriate alphabetic point in the dictionary.

To help the reader rapidly locate a place in the alphabetic listing, I have followed the tradition of heading each page with the first term, if it is a left-hand page, or the last term, if a right-hand page.

I use the abbreviations 'US' and 'UK' (for United States and United Kingdom) to indicate that a term applies on one side of the Atlantic rather than on the other. However, US does not mean that the term necessarily applies throughout the United States (though it may well apply in Canada also). Similarly with UK terms, since education in Scotland is organised separately from that in England and Wales; so certain terms, as I make clear in the text, are peculiar to one system or the other.

As for the gender of my pronouns, I have, for want of an elegant alternative, reluctantly bowed to the tradition of allowing the male to embrace the female. That is, 'he' means 'he or she', 'his' means 'his or hers', and so on.

Using the Dictionary

For most purposes, readers will no doubt follow the basic rule –
if in doubt, look it up. This may or may not lead on to browsing
among adjacent items, a practice I would always be happy to
encourage. A few hardy souls may even set themselves the task of
scanning the entries right through from A to Z. As one who has
had to do this (several times) I can testify that it has no lasting
ill-effects, if spaced over a reasonable period of time. It certainly
leaves one with a fair picture of what is included and what is not.
It might also prove useful to students nearing the end of a programme of educational studies (eg, teacher-training) who want to
refresh their understanding of ideas they have (or should have)
encountered earlier.

Finally, readers may recognise the need to *contribute* to the dictionary themselves. No dictionary-compiler ever satisfied all his
readers. Some terms you look up will not have been included.
Others will be there, but not treated to your satisfaction. Hence,
I expect you will wish to add terms to the dictionary and to amend
or expand the explanations of many that I have included. (If you
do take exception to some of my omissions or find some of my
explanations unsatisfactory, please write to the publishers to let
me know what changes you would like to see in the next edition.)
Diction is alive and changing, in education as in every other field;
some parts of every dictionary will thus go out of date even while
it is being printed. This one can be no exception, so we have left
you a number of blank pages at the back of the book in which to
collect new terms and explanations of your own. In the end, I
believe, the most useful dictionary is always the one we compile
for ourselves!

A

AB (US) The DEGREE of Bachelor of Arts. Equivalent to BA in the UK.

ABD See ALL BUT DISSERTATION.

ability Strictly speaking, a person's ability is his present capacity to perform certain physical or mental operations. However, it is not uncommon to find the term being used for what might better be termed POTENTIAL ABILITY.

ability groups Sets of learners believed to be of common ability who are taught together (and differently from learners of supposedly greater or lesser ability) in the belief that this makes for easier teaching and ●learning. Ability grouping has in the past been used to separate children into different levels of school (SECONDARY MODERN, TECHNICAL and GRAMMAR) on the basis of a test of general ability. Similarly, within schools, it often still operates to sort children into STREAMS (A, B, C, etc) or TRACKS (US). It may even cut across streams (or across MIXED ABILITY classes) so as to bring together, for teaching purposes, sets of children who are at much the same level of ability in a particular subject like mathematics or French. (See SETTING). But even where children are in a mixed ability class, all working in the same room (eg in PRIMARY SCHOOL), the teacher may divide them into different ability groups and give them different teaching. (See also BANDING).

abitur The examinations-based school-leaving certificate on which depends entry to West German HIGHER EDUCATION. Similar to UK ADVANCED LEVEL GCE and French BACCALAURÉAT.

absenteeism See TRUANCY.

absolute standards Judgement of the quality of a student's work by comparison with some generally-acceptable criterion of what it means to be, say, a first-class chemist or a third-class geographer, rather than by comparison with how well other students in his group perform.

abstract A written summary, eg of a LEARNED ARTICLE.

abstracting journal The name tends to be used of any journal that specialises in listing LEARNED ARTICLES and other academic studies, whether or not it publishes abstracts as well as brief details of authors, subject matter, and places of publication.

abstraction **1** The process of mentally extracting the common quality or attribute from a variety of similar but different cases so as to form a concept, eg the quality of 'sweetness' from sugar, honey, fruit, etc. **2** The concept so formed, ie 'sweetness'.

academic **1** A scholarly teacher and/or researcher in HIGHER EDUCATION. **2** Adjective relating to scholarly activities, especially when concerning a DISCIPLINE or SUBJECT, not necessarily at higher education level.

academic board **1** Twelve or more staff members of a COLLEGE OF EDUCATION or POLYTECHNIC (with perhaps some students) elected to control its academic affairs and to nominate members for the more powerful body of GOVERNORS. **2** Generally, a senior committee in an educational institution.

academic dress The mediaevally-inspired gown, cap and hood worn by GRADUATES of a university on ceremonial occasions and intended to denote the nature of their degree and academic status.

academic freedom The right claimed by colleges and universities, as institutions, to decide their own teaching and research programmes without outside (eg governmental) direction. Similarly, the right claimed by individual teachers to teach and research without interference (even, or especially, from their institution) and to be free from victimisation on account of their political views.

academic registrar See REGISTRAR.

academic-related staff Administrative staff in UK universities whose salaries are related to academic salary-grades in pay negotiations.

academic standards The performance or attainment level required of students in return for a specific level of recognition, especially the award of a particular CREDENTIAL like an ADVANCED

LEVEL 'pass' or a second class DEGREE. If more degrees are awarded one year than another it may be because more people have reached the required standard or because a lower standard has been accepted. It is always difficult to tell whether standards are changing, especially when the content of a course changes with the years.

academic year   The period between one intake of students and the next in schools, colleges and universities. North of the equator it normally begins in the autumn, south of the equator it more or less coincides with the calendar year. It is normally divided into three TERMS or two SEMESTERS and concludes with a long vacation.

academy   1 A PRIVATE HIGH or SECONDARY SCHOOL. 2 In Scotland and Canada can be a private or a MAINTAINED SCHOOL. 3 Specialist type of TERTIARY EDUCATION establishment, such as a MILITARY ACADEMY. 4 An institution for the advancement of art, music, literature, or science, eg Royal Academy. 5 The SCHOOL of philosophy established by PLATO and named after the grove in which he taught. 6 (US) One of the many private schools or colleges established in the 18th and 19th centuries especially in Massachusetts and New York State. The first opened in Philadelphia, following a proposal by Benjamin Franklin in 1751 and eventually became the University of Philadelphia. In general, they provided a wider and more practical curriculum and catered for a wider range of pupil ability than did the earlier LATIN (GRAMMAR) SCHOOLS and they opened educational opportunities to girls. (Sometimes known as TUITION ACADEMIES because they were financed entirely from tuition fees.)

accelerated course/programme/studies   Means of enabling students of outstanding ability to progress faster and qualify earlier than less talented colleagues, eg by omitting one year of a course, or taking an examination earlier. (See ADVANCED PLACEMENT, ADVANCED STANDING.)

accommodation   Term used by PIAGET for the process whereby a learner absorbs a new concept but, in doing so, must alter his existing conceptual structure. (Contrast with ASSIMILATION.)

accountability   The watchword used by a movement to persuade administrators and academics in educational institutions (especially in the US) to justify their policies, procedures and expenditures in terms of the performance of their students and other measurable criteria.

accreditation   Recognition and approval of the ACADEMIC STAN-

DARDS of an educational institution by some external, impartial body of high public esteem.

acculturation The acquisition, conscious or unconscious, of the VALUES and customs of the social group into which a person has moved, eg children entering secondary school. (See SOCIALISATION.)

ACE See ADVISORY CENTRE FOR EDUCATION.

achievement quotient (**AQ**) A measure of a child's actual ATTAINMENT relative to his supposed potential ability. For example, we may express his READING AGE as a percentage of his MENTAL AGE (or of his CHRONOLOGICAL AGE) to indicate whether he is reading more or less fluently than the average child of that age.

achievement test See ATTAINMENT TEST.

action research The critical study of a particular (eg educational) situation with the purpose not simply of adding to the store of scientific knowledge (perhaps with the intention of applying it to some future situation) but of leading to the practical improvement of the situation being studied. May be called APPLIED RESEARCH. See also RESEARCH AND DEVELOPMENT.

active response A key feature of PROGRAMMED LEARNING. Active responses are thought to be vital to learning. So, it is not considered sufficient for the student to look and listen; in the process of learning, he must write, draw, make things, and solve problems, and generally come to grips with each new idea by using it.

active vocabulary The stock of words one uses in one's own speech and writing. Contrasts with the (larger) PASSIVE VOCABULARY of words one can recognise when other people use them.

activity learning/methods/teaching Learning that requires the learner to do something more than look at and listen to a teacher or PACKAGED teaching materials. He may, for example, be performing an experiment, making something, or carrying out a PROJECT. (See also ACTIVE RESPONSE and DISCOVERY LEARNING.)

adaptive programme Flexible type of PROGRAMMED INSTRUCTION in which the sequence of teaching material presented to the learner depends on his individual history of responses to previous materials in the PROGRAMME. Such 'memory-based' flexibility usually demands the use of a computer. The computer can, for example, monitor the learner's speed and accuracy so that, if he starts making too many mistakes, it presents him with easier tasks, or gives him more time to respond, or offers him highly specific remedial teaching. (See also BRANCHING PROGRAMME, COMPUTER-ASSISTED INSTRUCTION and SKIP-BRANCHING PROGRAMME.)

adjunctive programme   A self-testing/teaching approach pioneered by US psychologist, Sidney Pressey, and embodying learning materials whose distinguishing feature is a set of questions presented to the learner at the end of a text and designed to establish the extent to which he has learned and, where he has answered incorrectly, to direct him back to a particular point in the text to correct his error. The text itself is not necessarily structured in any special way. An ordinary TEXTBOOK can be used as the basis of an adjunctive programme.

Adler, Alfred Sigmund (1870–1937)   A Viennese psychoanalyst and contemporary of SIGMUND FREUD. He was specially concerned with the social influences on personality and his ideas were influential in CHILD GUIDANCE and in PROGRESSIVE EDUCATION. He introduced the term INFERIORITY COMPLEX. See his *The Education of Children* (1930).

admissions criteria/policy/procedures   The rules and arrangements determining which pupils or students may be enrolled in an educational institution.

adolescence   A period of human development (roughly the teenage years) in which the individual is passing from childhood through PUBERTY to adulthood. The adolescent has many personal problems to live through, not least being the coming to terms with his or her mature sexuality and the satisfactory resolution of the conflict between individuality and identification with others. (See IDENTITY CRISIS.) Different societies and CULTURES view adolescents in different ways and take different approaches (educational and otherwise) to helping them through this period.

adult education   The provision of largely non-vocational education for people who have left school and are not formally registered for college and university courses leading to certification. Day-time or evening tuition may be provided by an EXTRA-MURAL or EXTENSION DEPARTMENT of a college or university or by other institutions such as trade unions or the WORKERS' EDUCATIONAL ASSOCIATION. It may take place in college or secondary school premises and may cover a wide range of cultural, recreational, community and sporting activities. (See also ANDROGOGY/CONTINUING EDUCATION/PERMANENT EDUCATION/RECURRENT EDUCATION.)

advanced course Term used in UK FURTHER EDUCATION for courses leading to qualifications above the standard of GCE ADVANCED LEVEL or ORDINARY NATIONAL CERTIFICATE.

advanced further education (**AFE**) Term used in UK MAINTAINED COLLEGES and POLYTECHNICS for courses leading to qualifications above the level of GCE ADVANCED LEVEL and ORDINARY NATIONAL CERTIFICATE.

Advanced levels (**A levels**) Public examinations in the GENERAL CERTIFICATE OF EDUCATION, generally taken by SIXTH-FORM students in English and Welsh secondary schools or by students in colleges of FURTHER EDUCATION, at the age of about 18. They will have taken ORDINARY LEVEL examinations two years earlier. (The nearest Scottish equivalent is the CERTIFICATE OF SIXTH YEAR STUDIES.) 'Good' grades in two or three subjects at A level are normally required for entry to HIGHER EDUCATION to study for a DEGREE or similar qualification. During the 1970s, critics of sixth-form over-SPECIALISATION suggested two different alternatives to A-level. The first envisaged students taking Q-level (qualifying) examinations in five subjects one year after O-levels, followed by up to three F-level (further) examination subjects one year later. This idea met with little favour because it would have meant students facing annual public examining. The second proposal was for pupils to be examined in five subjects two years after O-levels – three at N-level (roughly half the standard of A-level) and two F-level (about three-quarters of an A-level). This proposal was strongly opposed by the universities and finally rejected by the Secretary of State in 1979.

advanced placement A US scheme whereby students leaving many HIGH SCHOOLS can take examinations to gain direct entrance to the second year of a four-year college course and omit some or all of the FRESHMAN YEAR. This results in ADVANCED STANDING. (See ACCELERATED COURSE.)

advanced standing Status of a student allowed to omit certain courses from a programme of studies (especially in the US) on grounds of demonstrable prior ability, and therefore expected to complete the programme more quickly than other students. (See ACCELERATED COURSE and ADVANCED PLACEMENT.)

advance organiser Any device used at the beginning of a learning experience, eg a LECTURE, a PROGRAMMED TEXT or a television lesson, that aims to alert the learner to what is to follow and help him organise his expectations so as to learn effectively from it. A summary or a list of contents or a set of OBJECTIVES might serve the purpose. Derives from the work of the US psychologist, David Ausubel.

adventure playground   A playground, usually in an urban area, in which children are provided not with the customary swings and roundabouts and slides, but with ropes, pipes, sand, building materials etc – a variety of equipment out of which they can invent and construct their own games, perhaps under the unobtrusive supervision of an adult.

adviser   A person employed by a LOCAL EDUCATION AUTHORITY to advise practising teachers on ways of teaching a particular subject or children of a certain age, to assist in the selection of new teachers and in the provision of IN-SERVICE TRAINING, and perhaps to act as INSPECTOR.

Advisory Centre for Education (**ACE**)   A non-profit making UK body founded in 1960 which publishes numerous pamphlets and reports and a regular magazine *Where?* Its main task is to help parents and other laymen with information and advice on educational issues.

advisory councils/committees   **1** The UK government has several such groups to advise it on matters like child care, social work, handicapped children, and adult and continuing education. **2** See also CENTRAL ADVISORY COUNCIL FOR EDUCATION. **3** See also REGIONAL ADVISORY COUNCILS.

aegrotat   A certificate given by British universities to a student who was too ill to take a particular examination but whom the examiners considered would have passed had he taken it. (Aegrotat is Latin for 'he is ill'.)

aesthetic subjects   A CURRICULUM term likely to embrace such subjects as art, music, dance, drama, and literature.

aetiology (or etiology)   **1** The study of causation. **2** The history of causes that led to a particular event or situation, eg a child's illness.

affective learning (**domain**)   Those aspects of learning that involve emotions, feelings, and attitudes. Contrasts with COGNITIVE LEARNING.

AFE   See ADVANCED FURTHER EDUCATION.

aftercare   The supervision of JUVENILE OFFENDERS discharged on licence from APPROVED SCHOOLS that is exercised by the probation service and by the social services departments of local authorities.

agraphia   Inability to write, supposedly caused by BRAIN DAMAGE.

age-participation rate   Term used in estimating the likely future demand for FURTHER and HIGHER EDUCATION by calculating the numbers of children likely to reach school-leaving age in future years and comparing with the proportion of such leavers who have wished to continue their education in previous years.

agreed syllabus   Each LOCAL EDUCATION AUTHORITY in England and Wales must, with the help of the various religious denominations and the teachers' associations, draw up and agree a non-denominational syllabus of RELIGIOUS EDUCATION for use in its COUNTY and CONTROLLED SCHOOLS.

agreement trial   A term used for a meeting of examiners at which common marking standards for ASSESSMENTS and EXAMINATIONS are agreed through discussion, usually by each person marking some sample scripts from candidates and comparing his marking with that of his colleagues.

agrégation   A French national EXAMINATION held annually to select teachers for the senior classes of the LYCÉES. About ten per cent of candidates are successful and become agrégés.

agro-botany evaluation   A term describing EVALUATION based on judging the extent to which several pre-determined criteria of educational success have been achieved. This approach is based largely on that of the physical sciences – agricultural research in particular; emphasises aspects of learning that are quantifiable; and makes considerable use of statistical techniques. Contrasts with ILLUMINATIVE EVALUATION.

AH 2/3/4   INTELLIGENCE TESTS devised by UK psychologist, Alice Heim, for adults and children over ten years of age.

AH 5/6   Two INTELLIGENCE TESTS devised by UK psychologist, Alice Heim, for use with highly intelligent people. AH5 contains verbal, numerical and diagrammatic sections. AH6 tests reasoning ability and was designed for use with candidates for PLACES in HIGHER EDUCATION.

aided places scheme   See ASSISTED PLACES SCHEME.

aided school   A type of VOLUNTARY SCHOOL in England and Wales (usually Church of England or Roman Catholic) whose GOVERNORS must meet 15% of the cost of providing/improving/ enlarging the school buildings, while the remainder is paid by the DEPARTMENT OF EDUCATION AND SCIENCE (DES). All running costs (including teacher salaries) are paid by the LOCAL EDUCATION AUTHORITY (LEA). The GOVERNORS (of whom the majority are appointed by the voluntary body and the minority by the

LEA) control the appointing of teachers and the nature of RE-
LIGIOUS EDUCATION in the school.

aides A US term (like AUXILIARY or the British HELPER) referring
to paid and unpaid PARAPROFESSIONALS who help teachers in the
classroom, usually by performing non-teaching support duties
like collecting lunch money or setting up equipment for teaching.
They may or may not have had some training. Often called
TEACHER AIDES.

aims Broad statements of educational intention, often expressing
what the teacher is intending to do for the learner, (eg 'to foster
the pupil's sense of social responsibility') in contrast to OBJEC-
TIVES which suggest more specifically what the learner might be
able to do as a result. In US, the term GOALS is used for aims.

Albemarle Report 1960 A UK REPORT on how the young
people (14–20 year olds) of England and Wales might be helped
to play their part in the life of the community. Its recommendations led to the establishment of a training college for YOUTH
LEADERS, and a committee for the negotiation of their salaries,
and to the founding of the Youth Service Development Council.

A levels See ADVANCED LEVELS.

algorithm Originally a recipe for performing a mathematical
computation; but the meaning has been extended to include any
set procedure for arriving at the most appropriate solution to a
(not necessarily mathematical) problem. The term applies particularly to FLOW CHARTS that take the user through a series of
yes/no questions until he reaches an outcome appropriate to the
situation he finds himself in. For example, one could use an
algorithm to track down the source of the trouble if a television
receiver failed to produce a picture.

alienation A term introduced by Karl MARX and used in various
SOCIAL SCIENCES to indicate the feeling, experienced by many
people in industrial society, that they are estranged from certain
key aspects of their social existence. For example, they cannot
affirm or express themselves in their work (maybe their school-
work if they are pupils) and they continue working not as a
satisfaction of a need but as the means of satisfying some need
external to it.

all-age school A school taking children of all ages from about
five to 14-plus. In UK used to be found mainly in rural areas
but scarcely any remain except in the INDEPENDENT sector.

all but dissertation (**ABD**) (US) Term used to indicate the

9

academic status of a DOCTORAL student who has completed all necessary courses and examinations and needs only to complete a DISSERTATION before graduation.

Allport, G W (1897–1967) US psychologist who taught at Harvard and is best known to educationists for his studies of PERSONALITY with their emphasis on the uniqueness of individuals. See his *Personality* (1937) and *Becoming* (1955).

all-rounder A student whose school performance is uniformly good (eg both academically and in sport) with no noticeable weak areas.

all-through school Either an ALL-AGE SCHOOL or a COMPREHENSIVE SCHOOL taking children from all ages between 11 and 18-plus.

Alma mater Latin for 'benign mother'. Rather sentimental way of referring to one's old school, college or university.

alternative education Ideological label for characterising (usually approvingly) any form of education other than what the user regards as 'traditional'. Often implies FREE SCHOOLS or the kind of informal, non-institutional, community-based learning associated with DESCHOOLING. When it takes place within regular schools then it is likely to feature strong PROGRESSIVE EDUCATION components.

alternative prospectus (or **catalogue**) Description of a college or university, and its courses and facilities, produced for the benefit of intending students by its existing students. Thus it is an alternative to the official prospectus produced by the college or university authorities, and many students would expect it to be more illuminating.

alumni (Latin plural of alumnus). The former pupils or students of a (usually US) school, college or university – especially, perhaps, those who continue to identify themselves with it (and think of it as their ALMA MATER).

alumni college (US) Programme of studies and/or recreational activity arranged by a COLLEGE or a UNIVERSITY for its ALUMNI, and usually lasting a week or so in the summer. May be seen as a fund-raising exercise or as a contribution to CONTINUING EDUCATION.

alumnus See ALUMNI.

American sign language (**Ameslan, ASL**) A means of physical communication for the deaf and dumb in which the emphasis is on using hand-movements to convey whole words and phrases rather than separate letters of the alphabet.

Ameslan   See AMERICAN SIGN LANGUAGE.

analysis of variance (ANOVA)   Statistical techniques using the VARIANCE within and between groups to determine whether those groups are or are not sufficiently similar to have come from the same POPULATION.

analytical marking   Method of marking students' written work (eg essays or reports), possibly using a MARKING SCHEME. The marker has a number of marks to award for each of several aspects that have been selected for his attention in advance of seeing the work (eg accuracy, style, logical argument, etc). He adds up the marks for each aspect to reach a total mark for the work. This contrasts with IMPRESSION MARKING.

Anderson Report 1960   This UK REPORT on grants to students, recommended that students admitted to universities to read for FIRST DEGREES should be given grants from public funds (provided they had two A LEVEL passes in GCE), that parents should not be expected to contribute, and that STATE SCHOLARSHIPS should be replaced with a single national award system.

androgogy   (US) The study of ADULT EDUCATION, and especially its methods of teaching and learning. (In contradistinction to PEDAGOGY.)

anecdote   See ANECDOTAL EVIDENCE.

anecdotal evidence   Narrative accounts of incidents or outcomes thought significant or revealing by someone reporting on his study of some situation (eg the introduction of a new CURRICULUM). Could recount how a particular pupil or teacher reacted in certain circumstances. Always an enriching supplement to statistical evidence, and crucial to ILLUMINATIVE EVALUATION.

animateur   See FACILITATOR.

anorexia nervosa   A condition, found especially among adolescent girls, in which the person loses appetite and eats little for fear of gaining weight. Sometimes fatal.

ANOVA   See ANALYSIS OF VARIANCE.

aphasia   Impaired ability to understand or to use speech (as opposed to written language). Supposedly caused by BRAIN DAMAGE rather than by deafness or by defects in vocal organs.

A posteriori   (Latin, 'from the latter' or from effect to cause.) Relates to reasoning by INDUCTION from observed facts to a general principle, or to the knowledge or conclusions reached by such reasoning. Such knowledge depends on EMPIRICAL evidence for its acceptability and remains open to challenge from new evidence. Contrasts with A PRIORI.

apple-polishing (US)   Term used of students who act in an unduly sycophantic or ingratiating way towards teachers. May also be called, more vulgarly, BROWN-NOSING. The UK equivalent is 'creeping' or 'toadying' or 'sucking up to'.

apprenticeship   A contractual arrangement lasting a specified period of time, in which an employer undertakes to employ a young person and see that he is systematically trained for a particular occupation or trade, usually by working alongside and under the guidance of an acknowledged expert (eg an experienced tradesman or professional).

approved school   See COMMUNITY SCHOOL.

apraxia   A disorder of the central nervous system characterized by loss of the ability to perform certain skilled movements.

A priori   (Latin, 'from the previous', or from cause to effect.) Term used of reasoning by DEDUCTION and of the knowledge or conclusions so reached. Such conclusions, derived from accepted principles or self-evident truths, are held to be true in advance of any further experience of the subject matter and to require no further proof in the way of evidence. Mathematics is built on such a priori reasoning. Contrasts with A POSTERIORI.

aptitude   An individual's ability to acquire a particular or general skill which he has not yet acquired, eg mathematical aptitude or mechanical aptitude. Indicates potential level (and or speed) of achievement, rather than present achievement.

aptitude test   Test used to establish a person's aptitude in a particular skill, usually with a view to deciding whether or not he will respond sufficiently readily to training.

APU   See ASSESSMENT OF PERFORMANCE UNIT.

AQ   See ACHIEVEMENT QUOTIENT.

area training organisations (ATO)   Regional organisations in England and Wales, based on University INSTITUTES OF EDUCATION, established in 1945 to control the PRE-SERVICE and IN-SERVICE TRAINING of teachers and examine candidates for a teaching qualification. Since the JAMES REPORT of 1972, the ATOs have been phased out, their duties being shared among other bodies. The recommendation to the DEPARTMENT OF EDUCATION AND SCIENCE that successful students be given the status of qualified teachers now comes from a university or from the COUNCIL FOR NATIONAL ACADEMIC AWARDS, whichever provides VALIDATION for the B Ed concerned.

Aristotle (384–322 BC) Greek philosopher, pupil of PLATO, whose main works touching on education are *Ethics* and *Politics*. Saw the purpose of education as being to prepare men for the exercise of reason, untainted by professional skills or menial distractions which he thought should be left to slaves and women.

arithmetic mean See MEAN.

Arnold, Matthew (1822–1888) English poet and literary critic, son of THOMAS ARNOLD and, for the last thirty years of his life, a government inspector of schools. He saw literature as the 'greatest power available in education' and was a great believer in the unifying possibilities of a national system of education. See his *Culture and Anarchy*.

Arnold, Thomas (1795–1842) Headmaster of Rugby School and pioneer of public school reform. His main concern was with raising the moral standard on the basis of Christianity but he is also remembered for modernising the curriculum (eg introducing French and mathematics) and for involving senior pupils in the management of the school.

articles **1** Similar to an APPRENTICESHIP insofar as the learner (usually a would-be accountant or lawyer) is contracted to serve in the office of a practising member of his chosen profession who, in return, provides him with relevant experience and the opportunity to study for professional qualifications. Formerly, the articled trainee would pay his employer a fee (premium); but nowadays he is more likely to receive a salary from his employer. **2** See ARTICLES OF GOVERNMENT.

articles of government A document describing the powers and responsibilities of the GOVERNORS of a MAINTAINED SCHOOL, COLLEGE, or POLYTECHNIC in the UK. Such articles are drawn up by the LOCAL EDUCATION AUTHORITY but must be approved by the SECRETARY OF STATE FOR EDUCATION AND SCIENCE. In PRIMARY SCHOOLS, prior to 1980, the document was called RULES OF MANAGEMENT. See also INSTRUMENT OF GOVERNMENT.

artificial language An invented language (as opposed to one that has developed naturally) either **1** as a means of communicating with computers or **2** as a WORLD LANGUAGE to aid communication among people from many countries (eg ESPERANTO).

arts-based discipline One of the DISCIPLINES, like literature, history and philosophy, in which the emphasis is on literary studies and creative reflection on experience leading to qualitative subjective interpretations, rather than on the controlled experiments, quantitative methods and concern with maximum objectivity of the SCIENCE-BASED disciplines. The SOCIAL SCIENCES (eg economics, sociology, psychology, geography) are often claimed to be science-based but would not usually be regarded as such by physicists, chemists, biologists and the like.

ascertainment The process of determining whether or not a child needs SPECIAL EDUCATION as defined by the UK EDUCATION ACT OF 1944.

Ascham, Roger (1515–1568) A brilliant scholar and Cambridge teacher (tutor to Elizabeth I as a girl). Author of *The Scholemaster*, a treatise on education that was extremely liberal for its time and advocated that children should be taught with sympathy and not be bullied into learning.

ASL See AMERICAN SIGN LANGUAGE.

aspiration level The standard of achievement which a learner is aiming for. May be higher or lower than what he is capable of.

assembly An official gathering of more than one class of pupils on school premises, usually during the school day, for educational, administrative, or recreational purposes. In England and Wales, the EDUCATION ACT OF 1944 requires all COUNTY and VOLUNTARY SCHOOLS to begin the day with an assembly whose purpose is 'collective worship on the part of all pupils'. Parents can have their children excused from such assemblies, but many schools, particularly those in multi-ethnic communities interpret the requirement rather loosely or ignore it altogether.

assessment The process whereby one person (usually a teacher or examiner) attempts to find out about the knowledge, attitudes or skills possessed by another (the learner). This may involve him in merely observing the student as he sets about normal learning activities; or he may need to create special assessment activities, eg quizzes, examinations, oral tests, etc. In the US, the term 'EVALUATION' is usually used instead of assessment. (See CONTINUOUS / CRITERION-REFERENCED / DIAGNOSTIC / EXTERNAL / CRITERION-REFERENCED / FORMATIVE / INFORMAL / NORM-REFERENCED/SELF/SUMMATIVE/TERMINAL/UNOBTRUSIVE ASSESSMENT.)

assessment centre 1 A type of UK institution staffed by teachers, psychologists and social workers to diagnose the needs of children with SPECIAL LEARNING DIFFICULTIES and/or BEHAVIOUR

PROBLEMS. **2** In the US, a location on a college or university CAMPUS where individuals come for testing, usually carried out with the aid of a computer or other electronic devices.

Assessment of Performance Unit (APU)   An organisation set up within the DEPARTMENT OF EDUCATION AND SCIENCE in 1974 to develop testing procedures that will enable it to monitor annually the performance of pupils at various ages in such key CURRICULUM areas as mathematics, English, languages and science. The possibility of carrying out surveys of attainment in other curriculum areas (even personal and social development) is being considered. Some teachers believe that the APU's activities could lead to increasing government intervention in deciding the curriculum.

assignment   A learning task (eg writing an essay or making notes on a chapter of a book) which a learner is expected to carry out without help from the teacher, possibly as HOMEWORK.

assimilation   **1** Term used by PIAGET to denote the learner's absorption of a new concept into an existing framework of concepts which remain unchanged by it. (See ACCOMMODATION.) **2** A policy of integrating a minority group (eg Asian immigrants in Britain) into the majority society through educational practices that make no concessions to the separate cultural and historical allegiances of that minority.

assistant   Usually refers to a foreign teacher spending at least one ACADEMIC YEAR in a UK school, perhaps as part of an EXCHANGE PROGRAMME, and helping with the teaching of his own language.

assistant professor   In North American universities, the academic rank lying above LECTURER or INSTRUCTOR but below ASSOCIATE PROFESSOR and roughly equivalent to SENIOR LECTURER in the UK.

assistant teacher   **1** In the US an assistant to a teacher. **2** In the UK, all members of staff other than the HEADTEACHER, DEPUTY HEAD, SECOND MASTER/MISTRESS and SENIOR TEACHER.

assisted places scheme   A scheme intended to enable 'bright children from less well off families' to attend certain INDEPENDENT (fee-paying) SCHOOLS with some or all of their fees being paid by the SECRETARY OF STATE out of public funds. The scheme was introduced for England and Wales in the EDUCATION ACT 1980, partly to take the place of the former DIRECT GRANT SCHEME.

associate professor   In North American universities, the academic rank above ASSISTANT PROFESSOR but below (full) PROFESSOR. Roughly equivalent to READER in UK.

association   Psychological term for a learned connection between ideas.

ataxia   Lack of muscular co-ordination.

ATO   See AREA TRAINING ORGANISATIONS.

attainment   Measured ability and achievement level of a learner in school subjects or particular skills.

attainment quotient   See ACHIEVEMENT QUOTIENT.

attainment test   Test for measuring learner's present ability in a particular subject area or skill – as opposed to his potential ability which is estimated by APTITUDE TESTS in specific skills or, in general, by INTELLIGENCE TESTS.

attendance area/zone   American term, equivalent to CATCHMENT AREA in the UK.

attendance officer   **1** (UK) See EDUCATIONAL WELFARE OFFICER. **2**(US) Another name for TRUANT OFFICER.

attendance order (UK)   **1** Served by a LOCAL EDUCATION AUTHORITY on parents to enforce them to send their children to school regularly or to satisfy the authority that acceptable alternative educational arrangements are being made. Failure to comply can lead to court proceedings resulting in a fine and/or imprisonment. (See TRUANCY.) **2** A different kind of attendance order may be placed by magistrates on a JUVENILE OFFENDER, eg on a 'football hooligan', requiring him to attend a particular venue on a number of Saturdays.

attention span   The length of time a learner can be expected to concentrate on some learning activity. Varies with age, fatigue, nature of activity, and so on.

attitude   A person's tendency to feel about and act towards certain people (or situations, objects, ideas, etc) in a particular manner. The development of 'positive' attitudes in pupils (eg towards a school SUBJECT or towards themselves) is sometimes spoken of as part of their AFFECTIVE education.

attitude test   A test designed to establish, or measure, a person's ATTITUDES, perhaps as part of a more general interest in PERSONALITY.

audio-tape   Magnetic tape used in REEL-TO-REEL or CASSETTE TAPE-RECORDERS (or tape-players) to record and reproduce sound. (Contrasts with VIDEO TAPE which carries pictures as well.)

audio-tutorial (course)   A form of SELF-INSTRUCTIONAL COURSE pioneered in the 1960s by Postlethwaite at Purdue University (US). Each student works individually in a study booth, with a tape player to listen to short recorded lectures and using other learning materials (texts, films, experiments, etc) under recorded guidance. Students all meet together with a tutor once or twice a week for tests or discussion of the week's work. Compare with KELLER PLAN.

audio-vision   A SELF-INSTRUCTIONAL PACKAGE based upon pictures or objects which the student examines individually under guidance from a recorded AUDIO-TAPE. (See RADIO-VISION.)

audio-visual   Term used of teaching methods and materials that involve the use of AUDIO-VISUAL AIDS.

audio-visual aids (AVA)   Equipment and devices for presenting recorded sound and/or visual images for educational purposes. Includes both the HARDWARE (presentation devices like film projectors, television receivers, tape players, etc) and the SOFTWARE (the films, video-tapes, audio-cassettes, etc) that carry the educational content. Sometimes extended to include software that needs no presentation device, eg a poster or a three-dimensional model, but books are not usually included. (See also RESOURCE MATERIALS.)

audit (US)   To attend classes at a college or university without intending to take any associated examination or seek a CREDIT.

aural training   Training designed to help partially-deaf learners to identify speech and music sounds. Usually involves the amplification of those sounds.

authoritarian teaching   The classroom style of the kind of teacher who characteristically makes all the decisions about what children should learn and how they should learn it; who conveys these decisions to the children as non-debatable orders; and who teaches largely by formal lecturing, allowing little or no discussion, and appraises students purely in terms of how well they give the answers he expects to his questions. Contrast this with DEMOCRATIC TEACHING.

authority   **1** Could refer to the local authority (eg a COUNTY OR DISTRICT COUNCIL) responsible for services, including perhaps education, in its area. **2** Could refer to such a body but, more

17

specifically, in its role of LOCAL EDUCATION AUTHORITY. (In Scotland, the term is EDUCATION AUTHORITY.)

autism A rare but often alarming state observable in children who, while perhaps of well above average intelligence, remain aloof from any kind of communication with other people (perhaps even their parents) and resist exposure to any new experience. Autistic children often suffer grave educational RETARDATION and have often been mistakenly diagnosed as mentally subnormal. The causes are not clearly established but some progress is being made in treating autistic children and helping them achieve academic success.

autodidact A somewhat dated term for a person who is self-taught.

autonomy **1** Many curriculum theorists speak of the pupil's autonomy as his freedom to make rational, informed choices, and see it as an important educational AIM. **2** More commonly in everyday education, however, the term is used by or of UK HEADTEACHERS with reference to their freedom to operate their schools with minimal direction from either the DEPARTMENT OF EDUCATION AND SCIENCE (or SCOTTISH EDUCATION DEPARTMENT) or the LOCAL EDUCATION AUTHORITIES. British teachers too (especially in SECONDARY EDUCATION) enjoy an autonomy (eg freedom from direction as to what and how they must teach) that would be envied by teachers in many other countries. (See ACADEMIC FREEDOM.)

auxiliary See AIDE.

AV See AUDIO-VISUAL.

AVA See AUDIO-VISUAL AIDS.

average Loosely speaking, the term applies to someone or something that has a medium amount of some attribute (eg weight or intelligence). In statistical terms, an average is quoted as a VALUE that is somehow typical of, or central to, a DISTRIBUTION of values. Usually, this will be the MODE (the most commonly-observed value); or the MEDIAN (the value that is bigger than half the observed values but smaller than the other half); or the MEAN (obtained by adding up the total of the values and dividing by the number involved.)

average pupil/ability/standard **1** May be used with any of the three meanings normally attached to AVERAGE (see above). Notice that, with two of those meanings (MEDIAN and MEAN), half the pupils will be below average. **2** The term is often used to refer to a RANGE of pupils (perhaps 40 to 50 per cent of all pupils) who are neither especially difficult nor especially easy to teach.

aversion therapy A technique (derived from CLASSICAL CONDITIONING) aiming to eliminate undesirable behaviour (eg smoking or sexual perversions) by causing the person to experience an unpleasant effect (eg electric shock or vomiting) while practising the habit.

B

Babbage, Charles (1792–1871) English mathematician who invented a mechanical computing device that anticipated the mode of operation of the modern electronic computer.

Baccalauréat French secondary school-leaving qualification based on examinations and necessary for admission to HIGHER EDUCATION. Similar to West German ABITUR and to British ADVANCED LEVEL GCE but including compulsory subjects. (See also INTERNATIONAL BACCALAURÉAT.)

Bachelor's degree Usually a FIRST DEGREE awarded by a university or other institution of HIGHER EDUCATION, after three or four years of study, eg Bachelor of Arts or Bachelor of Science. In some universities, a bachelor's degree in some subjects may be a HIGHER DEGREE, eg the Bachelor of Science at Oxford and the Bachelor of Philosophy in the OPEN UNIVERSITY.

Bachelor of Education (**B Ed**, **Ed B**) In the UK, a FIRST DEGREE and usually incorporating a teaching qualification awarded after a three or four year course involving study of education and other subjects, and periods of TEACHING PRACTICE.

backward Term used of children whose attainment in schoolwork falls noticeably below that of the AVERAGE child of their age (as determined either by the teacher's experience, or else by some kind of STANDARDISED TEST). Thus, we may say Johnny is socially backward (eg has not learned to share with other children) compared with the rest of his class. Or we may say 12-year-old Tom has a READING AGE of ten and is thus two years backward in reading.

backward chaining Strategy derived from work of B F SKINNER and suggested by US psychologist Tom Gilbert for teaching a sequence (or chain) of behaviour, like tying a shoelace. If the chain involves, say, five sequential steps from A through to E, start with step E. That is, put the learner in a position (eg give him partly-tied shoelaces) where all he needs to do is step E. Teach him to do it. Then put him in position where steps A to C are complete, teach him step D and let him complete E from memory. Then give him A and B, teach him C and let him complete D and E from memory, and so on. The advantage over 'forward' chaining is said to lie in the fact that the student has more frequent experience of successful completion and that knowledge of the outcome of each new step being learned acts as a powerful ADVANCE ORGANISER. The method has wide applications in industrial training but can also be applied in ACADEMIC areas.

backwardness   See BACKWARD.

Bacon, Francis (1561–1626)   Philosopher who greatly influenced educational thought with his insistence that knowledge gave man power over the environment and was only to be acquired by questioning pre-conceived ideas and adopting an experimental and analytical approach to inquiry.

Bains Report 1972   A UK REPORT on local government. It recommended changes in the committee structure of LOCAL AUTHORITIES which led to EDUCATION COMMITTEES (and others) losing some of their relative isolation and autonomy by being made subordinate to another committee of the authority (eg a policy and resources committee).

balanced intake   See BANDING.

Barnado's homes   See DR BARNADO'S HOMES.

banding   **1** A method of forming classes in school: pupils in a YEAR-GROUP may be split equally into two or more bands of higher or lower general ability; then, from within each of the two (or more) bands, two or more classes may be formed, each containing children of the highest and lowest ability within that band. (It represents a compromise between STREAMING and MIXED ABILITY grouping.) **2** The procedure adopted by some UK LOCAL EDUCATION AUTHORITIES to ensure that the pupils recruited each year to each of its COMPREHENSIVE SCHOOLS are a cross-section of the total range of ability.

Barlow Report 1946   A UK REPORT recommending that universities should double the output of science graduates; it greatly influenced both university and GRAMMAR SCHOOL policy in the post-war years.

BASIC (Beginner's all-purpose symbolic instruction code) A computer programming language which, since its development in the US in the 1960s, has become widely used in a variety of forms, especially in educational institutions. It is considered adequate for most non-professional computer users and excellent for beginners.

basic English An attempt in the 1940s by C K Ogden to identify about 850 commonly-used words capable of enabling international communication. It was never successful as a language but was influential in improving the teaching of English to foreigners and in the construction of a graded vocabulary for teaching young children.

basic research Long-term research into underlying assumptions and implications of (eg educational) theories and practices. (Contrasts with APPLIED or ACTION RESEARCH which is expected to have more immediately useable results.)

basic skill 1 The term is often used, loosely, to mean a skill essential to everyday living, eg the THREE Rs – reading, writing and arithmetic. (This is the sense that underlies the call for 'back to the basics' that arises periodically in education from people who are disenchanted with prevailing aims and standards.) 2 Strictly speaking, however, the term should apply to skills on which the mastery of further, related skills is to be built, eg addition and subtraction are basic skills without which a person cannot learn multiplication and division. 3 The term is also regularly used in FURTHER EDUCATION and INDUSTRIAL TRAINING to refer to practical abilities.

battery (of tests) An unfortunately aggressive collective noun used to denote a set of tests (eg of ability, personality, aptitude) administered to gain a more rounded picture of an individual than could be obtained from one test used alone.

BBC See BRITISH BROADCASTING CORPORATION.

Beale, Miss Dorothea (1831–1906) Miss Beale, who founded Cheltenham Ladies College in 1858, was (like MISS BUSS), one of the pioneers in SECONDARY EDUCATION for girls.

BEC See BUSINESS EDUCATION COUNCIL.

behaviour 1 In psychology this is the response made by any organism (eg a person) to a stimulus which may be internal (eg a thought) or external (eg someone else's question). The response may be external and observable – a body movement or a spoken comment; or it may be internal and unobservable – thinking,

21

experiencing, and emotion. **2** More loosely, the word 'behaviour' is often used in discussion of DISCIPLINE where certain kinds of pupil behaviour are labelled 'good' or 'bad'.

B Ed See BACHELOR OF EDUCATION.

behavioural objectives A statement of intent, much more precise than AIMS, and quite specific as to the learned BEHAVIOURS the student is expected to be able to exhibit as a result of the teaching, eg solve quadratic equations, distinguish between adjectives and adverbs, correctly mark on a map all the capital cities of South America, and so on. The objections should also indicate the conditions under which the behaviour is to be expected and the required standard of performance.

behavioural science(s) Those academic DISCIPLINES concerned with scientific analysis of human behaviour – especially psychology, sociology, ethnology, anthropology.

behaviourism A psychological theory (associated particularly with B F SKINNER) based on the analysis of observable BEHAVIOUR. Extreme proponents would insist that psychology should be concerned only with what is directly observable and that it can proceed quite adequately without attention to what might be going on in the respondent's 'mind'. Results in a theory of learning centred around CONDITIONING.

behaviourist A person whose approach to education or psychology is grounded in BEHAVIOURISM.

behaviour modification Techniques based on the BEHAVIOURIST concept of CONDITIONING and meant to eradicate an individual's unwanted behaviours such as stammering, classroom disruptiveness, fear of new places, etc, by the use of CONTINGENCY MANAGEMENT.

behaviour problem A pupil whose behaviour is disruptive or otherwise unacceptable to the teacher or others may be said to have (or present) a behaviour problem.

Bell, Andrew (1753–1832) Like Joseph Lancaster, Bell developed the monitorial system in ELEMENTARY EDUCATION, whereby older pupils taught younger ones.

Beloe Report 1960 This UK REPORT made recommendations leading to the setting up of the CERTIFICATE OF SECONDARY EDUCATION (**CSE**) examinations alongside the existing GENERAL CERTIFICATE OF EDUCATION (**GCE**) in England and Wales.

Bentham, Jeremy (1748–1832) A social philosopher who saw the pursuit of pleasure and the avoidance of pain as the chief determinants of human action, and universal ELEMENTARY EDU-CATION as the means by which a person might be persuaded to subordinate his own self-interest to that of the wider community.

Bernstein, Basil (Born 1925) British educational sociologist known particularly for his discussion of LANGUAGE CODES as a help or hindrance to a child's educational development. His major work is to be found with that of his colleagues in the monograph series of which he is editor: *Primary Socialization, Language and Education* (Routledge and Kegan Paul). For example, see his *Class, Codes and Control* (1973).

bias 1 Found in a statistical SAMPLE when it contains a much greater percentage of one type of item (eg retired female grammer school teachers) than does the POPULATION which it was assumed to represent. 2 The term is also used of a TEST when some of its questions result in lower overall scores among certain sub-groups (eg working class girls) of the people tested.

bilateral school A secondary school offering two separate kinds of education (eg academic and technical) within the same institution.

bilingual education An education in which a pupil is brought up to use two languages with equal competence, about half his school-work being done in each.

binary system (of higher education.) The practice in England and Wales of having colleges and polytechnics funded and con-trolled by the LOCAL EDUCATION AUTHORITIES while the univers-ities are autonomous and receive central government funds on the advice of the UNIVERSITY GRANTS COMMITTEE.

Binet, Alfred (1857–1911) French psychologist who made a major contribution to intelligence testing with the development of the Binet-Simon Scale which later developed into the STANFORD-BINET scale – one of the most widely used INTELLI-GENCE TESTS.

biofeedback Technique for achieving control over certain of one's bodily processes that are normally autonomous and invol-untary (eg blood-pressure or body-temperature) by obtaining instantaneous FEEDBACK from some kind of measuring instrument as to what is happening in one's body, moment by moment.

bipartite system Used to describe SECONDARY EDUCATION sys-tems like that of the UK which, prior to COMPREHENSIVE SCHOOLS, operated both SELECTIVE (GRAMMAR or TECHNICAL schools) and

NON-SELECTIVE (SECONDARY MODERN) schools. (See also TRIPARTITE SYSTEM.)

birth rate   The number of live births per year in a given area. Significant educationally because of its effects on estimates of the future need for schools, colleges, teachers, etc. See BULGE.

black college/university   See NEGRO COLLEGE/UNIVERSITY.

black list   1 In 1908, and again in 1924, the UK BOARD OF EDUCATION drew up a list of schools whose buildings were considered unacceptable and which they wished to persuade the LOCAL EDUCATIONAL AUTHORITIES to replace. **2** The term is also used of LIST 99.

black papers   Compilations of critical articles (the first in 1969) written by generally right-wing educationists and politicans, questioning or attacking various aspects of the UK educational system – especially aspects that might broadly be called 'modern' or 'PROGRESSIVE', eg COMPREHENSIVE SCHOOLS, DISCOVERY LEARNING, NON-STREAMING, CONTINUOUS ASSESSMENT etc – and suggesting that ACADEMIC STANDARDS are in decline. (The name serves to associate them with, and yet distinguish them from, the Government's official policy statements or 'White Papers'.)

black studies   Courses based on a study of the history and CULTURE of black peoples from their own viewpoint rather than from that of Europeans. Probably more common in US than in UK but particularly pertinent wherever ethnic minorities feel cut off from their cultural heritage.

block grant   An annual grant made by UK central government to local authorities to help them provide various public services (particularly education) and due to replace the RATE SUPPORT GRANT from 1981.

block practice   A way of enabling trainee teachers to spend extended periods of time (say a whole term) on TEACHING PRACTICE in schools, rather than short periods of three or four weeks.

block release   A UK system whereby employers release employees to attend full-time educational courses for blocks of several weeks each year without loss of pay. The amount of time allowed is greater than that implied by DAY RELEASE but less than that demanded by a SANDWICH COURSE.

block timetabling   Arranging for several classes in school to be studying the same subject at the same time. This facilitates the transfer of pupils from one teaching group to another. (See SETTING as well as TEAM TEACHING.)

Bloom, B S (Born 1911) A US psychologist best known for his efforts in classifying educational OBJECTIVES and in promoting MASTERY LEARNING. Major publications: *Taxonomy of Educational Objectives I* (McKay: New York 1956) and II (1969) with Krathwohl and Masia; and with Hastings and Madaus, *Handbook of Formative and Summative Evaluation of Student Learning* (McGraw-Hill: New York, 1971).

Bloom's taxonomy BLOOM and his colleagues produced two taxonomies (or classification schemes) for LEARNING OBJECTIVES, one for the AFFECTIVE DOMAIN and another for the COGNITIVE DOMAIN. The latter is the more discussed and it postulates six ascending levels of performance – from knowledge, through comprehension, application, analysis, and synthesis to evaluation – each of which incorporates and depends upon all those that go before it. The details are endlessly debatable, but the taxonomy has been influential in helping focus attention on the need for ASSESSMENT to ensure that a student acquires more than just a good MEMORY.

blue book **1** Official paper on education and other matters issued by the British government in the 19th century. **2** In US colleges, a booklet of lined paper in which students write their examination answers.

boarding school A residential school providing accommodation and meals for its pupils. Most of the UK's INDEPENDENT or PUBLIC (fee-paying) SCHOOLS are boarding schools, though many of them take 'day pupils' who live close enough to travel to school daily. LOCAL EDUCATION AUTHORITIES sometimes pay boarding fees to independent schools for children with special needs, and there are a few boarding schools maintained by local education authorities.

board of education Corporate body responsible for education at national, regional, or local level. For example, England and Wales had a Board of Education from 1900 to 1944 (when it was replaced by the Ministry of Education and subsequently by the DEPARTMENT OF EDUCATION AND SCIENCE). In the US, it is possible to find county boards of education, state boards, district boards, and so on.

board of governors/managers/regents See GOVERNORS, MANAGERS, REGENTS.

board schools UK ELEMENTARY SCHOOLS set up from 1870 by SCHOOL BOARDS in areas where no schools were provided by voluntary bodies.

25

body awareness/concept/sense   A person's consciousness of the space occupied by his body, the relationships between one part of his body and another, and between his body and the rest of his environment as he moves within it. Particularly relevant in PHYSICAL EDUCATION and in DANCE and MOVEMENT teaching.

body language   Non-verbal communication by means of body movements – postures, physical gestures, bodily contact, eye contact, facial expressions, etc. A person can use it consciously or unconsciously, either to reinforce or contradict what he is saying. An important factor to observe in the analysis of social interaction, eg a classroom lesson.

bond issue   (US)   SCHOOL DEBENTURE authorised by SCHOOL BOARD or by local voters to raise capital or even operating funds.

bookmobile   US term for a MOBILE LIBRARY.

booster training   Giving a person extra training in his present job in order to improve his performance. An industrial training equivalent of what, in professional areas like teaching or family medicine, is more commonly called REFRESHER or IN-SERVICE training.

borderline   Term used in MARKING for students near those CUT-OFF POINTS on a scale of marks at which students may be differently labelled according to which side of it they fall: pass/fail; credit/distinction; second class honours/first class honours, etc. Examiners are, by tradition, extra scrupulous about the fairness of the awarding of marks that put a student near a borderline.

borstals   Residential training establishments run by the UK Home Office for young offenders (age 15–21) convicted of offences for which older people could be sent to prison. Generally stricter and less open than what were once called APPROVED SCHOOLS and are now called COMMUNITY HOMES.

bowdlerise   To censor or expurgate by removing words and phrases regarded as indecent from a play or novel. Named after Dr Thomas Bowdler (1754–1825) who published an expurgated edition of Shakespeare, the forerunner of many such used in schools.

Bowlby, John   (Born 1907)   UK psychiatrist known particularly for his work on MATERNAL DEPRIVATION. See his *Child Care and the Growth of Love* (1953, with M Fry).

braille   A system developed by Louis Braille (1809–1852) to enable blind people to read by touching patterns of raised dots representing letters of the alphabet. The system also enables a blind person to write and even to type.

brain damage   A rather non-specific diagnosis referring to no necessarily observable physical lesion in the brain. Often used (without much justification) to account for specific learning difficulties in children of apparently normal INTELLIGENCE.

brain drain   Emigration of highly-educated professional people to countries where they can enjoy a higher standard of living or more interesting career prospects.

brainstorming   Technique for generating useable ideas or solutions to a problem. Members of a group are encouraged to meet together in a relaxed but purposeful atmosphere and let their suggestions flow, without self-censoring. No matter how unworkable or outrageous the ideas may seem to be, at first sight, they are not criticised or examined rationally until the end of the exercise, by which time it is hoped that a host of exciting possibilities will have emerged that might otherwise have remained hidden by inhibitions. Compare with SYNECTICS.

brains trust   A group of knowledgeable people discussing topical issues in public for the interest of an audience.

brainwashing   A form of INDOCTRINATION, involving a radical change in a person's beliefs and behaviour, especially if brought about by techniques involving, for example, CONDITIONING, IDENTIFICATION, SENSORY DEPRIVATION, living within a TOTAL INSTITUTION, etc.

branch   Point within a PROGRAMME or a course of studies where different learners are allowed, persuaded, or forced to embark on different learning experiences depending either on their own preferences and inclinations or on their differing learning needs as revealed perhaps by DIAGNOSTIC TESTS.

branching programme   A form of PROGRAMMED INSTRUCTION in which the student is presented with a series of FRAMES, each containing perhaps several paragraphs of information and posing a MULTIPLE-CHOICE QUESTION. After each question, the student is branched to one frame or another according to his choice of answer. His correct answer will be confirmed and he will be taken to the next step in the programme; or he will be given remedial help specific to the mistake he has made and will be helped to correct it before going on to the next step. (Contrast this with LINEAR PROGRAMME.) See also ADAPTIVE PROGRAMME.

break   UK term similar to RECESS (US), meaning free time between one set of lessons and the next in a school TIMETABLE. There may be one break mid-morning and another in mid-afternoon. Often known in PRIMARY SCHOOL as PLAY-TIME.

breaking up   A UK expression used to denote the end of a school term and the beginning of holidays.

British and Foreign School Society   This pioneering organisation in ELEMENTARY EDUCATION was founded in 1810 as the Royal Lancastrian Association to set up MONITORIAL SCHOOLS, as advocated by Joseph LANCASTER, and changed its name four years later. Though broadly non-conformist, these so called 'British schools' were open to children of all denominations and (unlike those run by the rival NATIONAL SOCIETY) gave no sectarian religious teaching. The society also pioneered TEACHER TRAINING.

British Broadcasting Corporation (BBC)   The major non-commercial UK producer and transmitter of television and radio programmes, funded entirely out of public money (from licence fees paid by users of television receivers) but independent of direct government control. Since its birth in 1922 it has had a firm commitment to educate, in a general sense, and was a pioneer in the development of directly educational programmes (for use in schools and colleges). In this area, as in others, it has a world reputation for quality.

British Education Index   A publication by the BRITISH LIBRARY giving an author and subject index to articles which have been published in UK educational journals. Equivalent to EDUCATION INDEX in US.

British Library, The   Created by merger in 1973, with the British Museum Library as its reference division and the NATIONAL CENTRAL LIBRARY and NATIONAL LENDING LIBRARY FOR SCIENCE AND TECHNOLOGY as its lending division.

British schools   ELEMENTARY SCHOOLS operated by the non-conformist BRITISH AND FOREIGN SCHOOL SOCIETY (founded 1810) of which there were some 1,500 (with 225,000 pupils) by the middle of the 19th century.

Brougham, Henry (1778–1868)   UK lawyer and politican who was a powerful advocate of ELEMENTARY EDUCATION and was instrumental in getting established a parliamentary enquiry into the 'education of the lower orders'. He tried, though unsuccessfully, to have a law passed in 1820 that would have caused parish schools to be built at the expense of manufacturers and supported by local rates, parental contributions and the redistribution of endowments which he claimed were being abused. He was also a supporter of MECHANICS' INSTITUTES and was influential in the foundation of London University in 1828 as a non-denominational teaching institution. His pamphlet, *Practical Observations on the Education of the People* (1825), was widely read and led to the founding of a SOCIETY FOR THE DIFFUSION OF USEFUL KNOWLEDGE.

Brown Decision (US) A 1954 Supreme Court decision that declared racial segregation in schools to be unconstitutional.

brownie-points (US) The imaginary marks of teacher approval assumed to have been obtained, or at least sought, by a student judged by his peers to be unduly sycophantic or ingratiating towards his teachers. (See BROWN-NOSING.)

brown-nosing (US) A graphic, scatological term used by students for behaviour among their peers that is more politely called APPLE-POLISHING – ie acting in an unduly sycophantic and ingratiating way towards a teacher. (See also BROWNIE-POINTS.)

Bruner, J S (Born 1915) A US psychologist with special interest in learning and CURRICULUM DEVELOPMENT. Best known for books like *The Process of Education* (1960), *On Knowing: Essays for the Left Hand* (1962), *Toward a Theory of Instruction* (1966), *The Relevance of Education* (1971). Famous for his much-quoted assertion that 'any subject can be taught effectively in some intellectually honest form to any child at any stage of development'. See also MACOS.

Bruner's modes In discussing children's intellectual development, BRUNER distinguishes three modes of representing experience that must be mastered in turn: the ENACTIVE mode (involving MOTOR responses); the ICONIC (involving models or pictorial images); and the SYMBOLIC (involving language or numbers). Thus, the concept of 'force' in physics might first be experienced physically as 'push and pull'; then represented in terms of acceleration, using graphs; and then represented algebraically.

Bryce Report 1895 The REPORT of a Royal Commission on the organisation of SECONDARY EDUCATION in England. Its recommendations (which have done much to shape UK education in this century) included: the setting up of a central authority for secondary education under a MINISTER OF EDUCATION (which led to the establishment of the BOARD OF EDUCATION in 1899); the establishment of an educational council to advise the Minister; and the creation of local authorities for SECONDARY EDUCATION (implemented in the EDUCATION ACT of 1902) with powers to supply, maintain and aid schools.

Brynmor Jones Report 1965   UK REPORT on AUDIO-VISUAL AIDS in higher scientific education. Its most influential recommendations were that institutions of higher education should set up central service units to promote the use of new audio-visual media and that a national COUNCIL FOR EDUCATIONAL TECHNOLOGY should be established.

BS (US)   The DEGREE of Bachelor of Science. Equivalent to BSc in UK.

Buckley Amendment (US)   An amendment to the ELEMENTARY AND SECONDARY EDUCATION ACT 1965 to the effect that students should have access to the files of information kept about them by their colleges and universities and that parents should have a similar right on behalf of school-children.

buddy system   A US term for an arrangement whereby a learner acquires experience from a colleague he is assigned to work with (similar to the British concept of 'sitting next to Nellie'); or, more commonly, where each member of the pair is meant to be responsible in some more general sense for the other's safety and well-being.

Buhler, Charlotte (1893–1975)   Austro-American psychologist who made important contributions to the psychology of CHILD DEVELOPMENT, especially in the areas of language and the value of play. See her *The First Year of Life* (1930), *From Birth to Maturity* (1939), and *Child Problems and the Teacher* (1952).

building superintendent (US)   Same as JANITOR or UK CARETAKER.

bulge, the   Sudden increase in the numbers of pupils reaching a certain stage of education, due to an earlier dramatic increase in the BIRTH-RATE. Term first applied in UK in consequence of sudden increase of birth-rate after second World War. A second bulge began in the late 1950s.

bulletin (US)   See CALENDAR.

bulletin board (US)   Same as notice-board in UK.

Bullock Report 1975   A UK REPORT called *A Language for Life* that made many recommendations concerning the teaching of reading and other aspects of English in schools. In particular, it recommended the regular SECONDMENT of teachers to full-time courses on reading, language and English; more stringent entry criteria for new teachers; a larger supply of fiction books in schools; secondary schools to receive detailed reports on the reading abilities of new pupils; and reading clinics or remedial centres in every LOCAL EDUCATION AUTHORITY.

bullying   The verbal and physical harrassment of pupils by other (usually older) pupils. This has always been a problem, especially for children new to a school, and in the very grandest schools downwards.

bunching   Occurs when the marks of students who have taken a test or examination are clustered close together rather than being spread out over a wide range. In traditional PSYCHOMETRICS, this might indicate a poor test (or insensitive marking) because it does not allow adequate distinctions to be made between the performance of different students.

burgh schools   Term once used for long-established GRAMMAR SCHOOLS in certain Scottish burghs (towns).

Burnham scale   Salary structure for teachers in England and Wales negotiated by the Burnham Committees (one for PRIMARY and SECONDARY EDUCATION, and one for FURTHER EDUCATION) comprising representatives of the SECRETARY OF STATE, the teachers, and the employers (THE LOCAL EDUCATION AUTHORITIES).

bursary   An award in cash or remission of fees to help certain favoured students take up places in a fee-paying school or in HIGHER EDUCATION. See also SCHOLARSHIP or FELLOWSHIP (US).

Burt, Sir Cyril (1883–1971)   Supposedly UK's first educational psychologist to be appointed to a local authority (London in 1913) and certainly a key pioneer in his field. His most influential work was in the area of INTELLIGENCE TESTING, not least in preparing the way for the SELECTIVE TRI-PARTITE system of SECONDARY EDUCATION. He did accept that an impoverished environment could help produce BACKWARD and/or delinquent children (for whom he showed much sympathy); nevertheless he firmly asserted that a child's intelligence was mainly determined by what he inherited from his parents rather than what was experienced after birth. During the 1970s his reputation was somewhat tarnished by allegations that he fabricated certain of his research data. Publications included *The Backward Child* (1937); *The Factors of the Mind* (1940); and *The Gifted Child* (1975).

Business Education Council (**BEC**)   UK body established in 1974 by the SECRETARY OF STATE FOR EDUCATION AND SCIENCE on the recommendation of the HASLEGRAVE REPORT, in order to establish in England and Wales a unified system of courses (below DEGREE level) in the broad area of business studies and public administration. It devises and approves suitable courses, establishes and assesses standards of performance, and awards certificates and diplomas to successful students. The equivalent in Scotland is the SCOTTISH BUSINESS EDUCATION COUNCIL (SCOTBEC).

Buss, Frances Mary (1827–1894) Miss Buss, who founded the North London Collegiate School in 1850, was (like MISS BEALE) one of the pioneers in SECONDARY EDUCATION for girls.

bussing The transporting of children from their home area to a school in another area so as to ensure that each school has an ethnic mix or a full range of pupil ability. (May also be used if the local school is over-crowded.)

busy work Disparaging (US) term for work that keeps children busy but has no educational justification.

Butler Act Another name for the EDUCATION ACT OF 1944, so-called after R A Butler (later Lord Butler of Saffron Walden) who was PRESIDENT of the BOARD OF EDUCATION at the time and piloted the legislation through Parliament.

Butler, Samuel (1774–1839) Grandfather of the Samuel Butler who wrote *Erewhon* and *The Way of All Flesh*, this Samuel became headmaster of Shrewsbury School at the age of 24. He carried through a series of innovations in TEACHING METHODS – simplifying the learning of Latin, introducing regular testing and promotion on merit, encouraging private reading, and developing a PREFECT system by giving some authority to senior boys (preposters).

buzz session (US) An informal discussion group, usually without any kind of agenda and consisting of people equal in status (eg all students or all teachers, but not a mixture).

buzz words (US) The JARGON of a particular trade or profession that practitioners use to communicate among themselves and, consciously or otherwise, to mystify outsiders.

C

cable television Television transmission system in which the signal is not broadcast but is delivered via a cable. Theoretically this allows a wider access to programme material, films and other stored data (see VIEWDATA) and also improves the quality of the picture received.

calendar Annual college or university publication listing key dates in the academic year and giving details of staffing, structure of government, rules and regulations, details of courses, and so on. Similar function to a PROSPECTUS but usually more detailed. The comparable US term is BULLETIN or CATALOG.

CAMOL (UK) Computer Assisted Management of Learning: a five year RESEARCH AND DEVELOPMENT project (1973–8) sponsored by the COUNCIL FOR EDUCATIONAL TECHNOLOGY.

camp counsellor (US) A vacation post taken by college and university students to act as general helpers at SUMMER CAMPS for school children.

campus The grounds (and often, by implication, the buildings also) of a school, college or university. Usually clearly distinguishable (by walls, fences, etc) from the surrounding environs. An institution with more than one site may be said to have a SPLIT CAMPUS.

campus school (US) See DEMONSTRATION SCHOOL.

cane A length of bamboo cane or other stick used for CORPORAL PUNISHMENT in some UK schools. The US equivalent is PADDLE.

Cantab Latin abbreviation representing Cambridge University.

capitation allowance In UK, the basic funds given annually by the LOCAL EDUCATION AUTHORITY to each of its schools for purchase of books, equipment, stationery, and other materials. The amount depends on the number of children in the school, and the amount 'per head' increases with the age of the children (being about twice as big for SECONDARY SCHOOL pupils as for PRIMARY pupils).

career grade In hierarchical organisations, the maximum salary or status level that the majority of staff will expect to reach by the time they retire, eg major for army officers and lecturer for academics in UK universities.

careers guidance (UK) Advice given to young people concerning the occupational or further educational opportunities that might be open to them on leaving school (or college). The advice may be given by a specialist careers advisory officer employed by the LOCAL EDUCATION AUTHORITY. Or the adviser may be a teacher in the student's school (careers tutor) who may or may not be a specialist and trained in this role. He may perform it in addition to, say, teaching English or social studies. The US equivalent is PLACEMENT GUIDANCE.

Careers (Advisory) Service (UK) A publicly-funded service (once called the Youth Employment Service) which exists to help young people (school-leavers especially) in finding suitable employment.

care order (UK) Court order whereby a child who, for some reason, cannot be properly looked after at home, is committed to the care of the LOCAL AUTHORITY. The child's parents or guardians may be expected to contribute to the costs. The equivalent US term is GUARDIANSHIP.

caretaker (UK) Person responsible for the cleaning and maintenance of school building and grounds. Being usually resident at the school, he may also serve as an important unofficial information channel between teaching staff and local people. The US equivalent may be called JANITOR (as may the Scottish) or CUSTODIAN.

Carnegie Foundation for the Advancement of Teaching (US) A foundation set up in 1905 to provide pensions for college teachers and sponsor educational research.

Carnegie unit (US) One year's study-time (at least 120 hours) of any one subject in secondary school – as defined by the Carnegie Foundation for the Advancement of Teaching to help clarify COLLEGE ENTRANCE requirements. The normal pattern is for secondary school students to complete 16 units in a four year period, which is the requirement for GRADUATION.

carrel A desk or work-space in a library, PRIVATE STUDY area or LANGUAGE LABORATORY, which may be enclosed on three sides by screens, allowing the individual student to work without being distracted by (or distracting) his colleagues. Such a carrel may well contain facilities for viewing educational film or television or for listening to AUDIO-TAPES or for using COMPUTER ASSISTED LEARNING.

cartridge recorder See CASSETTE RECORDER.

CASE (Campaign for the Advancement of State Education) A UK voluntary association of about 80 autonomous local groups which has no assistance from public funds and employs no paid staff. It campaigns for greater involvement of parents in education (eg through membership of EDUCATION COMMITTEES and as GOVERNORS) and for the improvement of school facilities and standards generally. It has always supported the COMPREHENSIVE principle and opposed selection for SECONDARY EDUCATION.

case conference A meeting of concerned professionals (eg teachers and social workers) to discuss the welfare of a person (eg a pupil) in whose 'case' they all have an interest.

case study   A teaching method, used particularly in MANAGEMENT EDUCATION, whereby a real or hypothetical situation is presented to students (eg in verbal description, film, facsimile documents, etc) so that they can discuss it and suggest possible solutions to the problems they identify within it.

cassette recorder   A machine for recording sound (or, on video cassette, sound and moving pictures) on magnetic tape that runs within a sealed container that can be removed from the machine intact. Contrasts with REEL-TO-REEL RECORDERS. Similar to CARTRIDGE RECORDERS except for the manner in which the tape is spooled within the container.

CAT   See COLLEGE OF ADVANCED TECHNOLOGY.

catalog   (US) See CALENDAR.

catalogue library   One in which only the librarians have access to the book-shelves and would-be readers must make their selection from the catalogue and wait for their chosen books to be brought to them (eg the British Museum library).

catchment area   UK term for the area from which a school draws its pupils. Catchment areas differ not simply in their size and geographical nature (eg town or country) but also in the life-style and affluence enjoyed by their inhabitants; such factors clearly influence the aspirations and achievements of the school. The US equivalent is ATTENDANCE AREA/ZONE.

Cattell, R B   (Born 1905)   A US psychologist renowned as an authority on PERSONALITY. His books include *Personality and Motivation* (1957) and *Scientific Analysis of Personality* (1965).

CCTV   See CLOSED CIRCUIT TELEVISION.

CEE   See CERTIFICATE OF EXTENDED EDUCATION.

Central Advisory Council for Education   (UK) Actually two advisory bodies (one for England and one for Wales) set up under the EDUCATION ACT 1944 to advise the SECRETARY OF STATE FOR EDUCATION AND SCIENCE. Membership varies according to the issues on which advice is sought. The group producing the PLOWDEN REPORT was quite different from that responsible for the CROWTHER REPORT. The councils have been very little used and not at all since 1967. See also ADVISORY COUNCILS/COMMITTEES.

Ceefax   The BBC's TELETEXT service, providing the owner of a suitably adapted television receiver with a choice from hundreds of pages of practical information (ranging from news and sport to food prices, recipes and the weather) that can be displayed on the TV screen.

central institutions Educational institutions in Scotland that are not universities but do offer DEGREE and DIPLOMA courses. They are funded directly by the SCOTTISH EDUCATION DEPARTMENT, except for three agricultural colleges which are financed by the relevant government department. They are roughly equivalent to POLYTECHNICS in England and Wales in the kind of courses they offer.

central schools These UK schools were forerunners of the SEC-ONDARY MODERN SCHOOLS and were established before World War I in the centre of certain large English towns (eg London and Manchester) to provide a four-year CURRICULUM (with a commercial or industrial bias but without being narrowly VOCA-TIONAL) for children from the age of 11 years as a kind of higher ELEMENTARY EDUCATION.

Certificate in Education A UK teaching qualification. Until the late 1970s, non-graduate students normally qualified as teachers by taking a three year certificate course in a COLLEGE OF EDUCATION or POLYTECHNIC. Such courses have now been largely replaced by BACHELOR OF EDUCATION courses. See also POSTGRADUATE CERTIFICATE OF EDUCATION.

Certificate of Extended Education (CEE) (UK) An experimental SCHOOL-BASED EXAMINATION intended chiefly for students of 17-plus in England and Wales who have stayed on at school for one year after taking CSE or GCE (ORDINARY LEVEL) examinations but who are not studying for GCE ADVANCED LEVEL. See KEOHANE REPORT 1979. There is some possibility that it may be replaced by a more vocationally oriented examination.

Certificate of Secondary Education (CSE) (UK) A SCHOOL-BASED EXAMINATION taken by pupils around the age of 15 or 16 years, and aimed at the 40% of the ability-range, in any given subject, who lie below the top 20% at whom GCE (ordinary level) is aimed. There are five grades of award, the top of which (Grade 1) is supposed to represent the same ACADEMIC STANDARD as a 'pass' in GCE ordinary level. Students may be examined in several separate subjects and will be awarded a certificate of the appropriate grade for each subject. The examination is administered by 14 regional boards in England and Wales. There is no equivalent in Scotland. There are three different modes of operation. Under Mode 1, the SYLLABUS and examination papers are set and marked by the Board's EXTERNAL EXAMINERS (teachers in the region). Under Mode 2, a school designs its own syllabus but the papers are set and marked by the Board. Under Mode 3, the school designs its own syllabus, and sets and marks its own papers with the approval and MODERATION of the Board's examiners. During the 1980s, the CSE system is to be combined with that of the GENERAL CERTIFICATE OF EDUCATION (GCE).

Certificate of Sixth Year Studies (CSYS)   Scottish examination taken at the end of the sixth year of SECONDARY SCHOOL (age 18–plus) by the most academically able students in one or two of the subjects in which they already hold H grade passes in the SCOTTISH CERTIFICATE OF EDUCATION. (Roughly equivalent to ADVANCED LEVEL GCE.)

CET   See COUNCIL FOR EDUCATIONAL TECHNOLOGY.

chaining   That type of learning in which the pupil links together a number of separate RESPONSES which must follow one another in a certain order. Each completed response serves as a STIMULUS for the next response. Thus, learning to tie one's shoe-laces or to recite a nursery rhyme can be seen as such a chain of linked responses. See also BACKWARD CHAINING.

chair   A highly-esteemed academic post in a university (or some other educational institution of comparable standing). The holder of the post will usually be called PROFESSOR. The chair may be a permanent one, for which a holder is always required; or it may be a 'personal' chair, specially created to honour the prestige in research (and perhaps teaching) of a particular individual and existing only while he or she remains with that institution.

'chalk-and-talk'   Can be descriptive but is usually a derogatory term for a TEACHING METHOD in which the teacher presents his subject without allowing for much student-participation. He talks 'at' them and writes or draws on the board. Of course this can be done effectively, and must be done sometimes; but the term is applied when teachers do it excessively, and to the exclusion of other, more appropriate methods.

chalk-board   Modern term for what earlier generations knew as a blackboard but which is as likely nowadays to be green or some other colour.

chancellor   **1** In UK universities, the chairman of the supreme decision-making group (eg COUNCIL). The role of chancellor is honorary and will be held by a person of eminence who has nothing to do with the day-to-day operations of the university. **2** In some US universities, an alternative title to PRESIDENT.

chancery script An ITALIC SCRIPT.

change agent A person who acts so as to bring about changes in the aims and/or activities of an institution, usually assuming that other people besides the agent himself will be involved (eg the head of an INFANTS SCHOOL, re-organising the teaching of reading).

charity schools UK ELEMENTARY SCHOOLS founded for poor pupils by such bodies as the SOCIETY FOR PROMOTING CHRISTIAN KNOWLEDGE (SPCK) from the end of the 17th century. The 'CURRICULUM' consisted chiefly of religious instruction, reading, the development of 'habits of industry' and acceptance of a lowly status in society. By the mid 18th century, some 30,000 children were in such schools.

chautauqua (US) A kind of travelling educational tent-show which evolved in late 19th century America from a summer educational and religious centre in New York State. It was based upon popular talks about subjects of the day, intended to enter-tain and edify and bring culture and enlightenment to people living away from the big cities.

chief education officer (or DIRECTOR OF EDUCATION) The sen-ior administrator in a UK LOCAL EDUCATION AUTHORITY. The nearest US equivalent is SUPERINTENDENT OF SCHOOLS.

child-centred approach/education/teaching Rather woolly slogan, but its main point is made by the teacher who claims 'I teach children, not subjects.' Implies care for the 'whole' child – his PERSONALITY, NEEDS and LEARNING STYLE and not just for his or her academic prowess. See also PROGRESSIVE EDUCATION.

child development The branch of EDUCATIONAL PSYCHOLOGY concerned with describing and explaining the physical, mental and social changes in children from conception to late adolescence.

child guidance clinic/centre A unit funded by a LOCAL EDU-CATION to diagnose and treat children with emotional or learning difficulties, who are usually referred to it by teachers or parents.

child minder Someone who, for a fee, looks after babies or children too young to go to school while their parents work. By law, child minders should be registered with the LOCAL AUTHOR-ITY and provide facilities of at least an agreed minimum standard. But many, perhaps most, are not, and consequently many chil-dren are left all day in over-crowded and unstimulating conditions.

children's department Formerly a branch of UK LOCAL AU-THORITIES whose duty was to provide care for children when parents or guardians are temporarily or permanently unable to look after them. This function is now carried out by the author-ities' social service departments. The children may be 'taken into care' and placed in CHILDREN'S HOMES or FOSTER HOMES.

children's home A residential institution for children who are taken into the care of a LOCAL AUTHORITY, temporarily or for a long period.

chip See MICROPROCESSOR.

Chips, Mr The model of a dedicated schoolmaster, created by James Hilton in his novel *Goodbye Mr Chips* which was a best-seller on both sides of the Atlantic in the 1930s and was twice filmed.

chi-square A statistical technique used to determine whether a difference between groups within a SAMPLE is likely to be found also in the POPULATION from which it came; eg if 20% of male school-leavers and 25% of female school-leavers in a sample were found to be still unemployed after 6 months, could we expect this difference between sexes to be found among school-leavers generally?

choir school Several Anglican cathedrals and colleges (eg King's College, Cambridge) have their own schools (often of very ancient foundation) whose pupils serve as choir boys and are given a general education (usually of the PREPARATORY SCHOOL type) as well as receiving intensive musical training.

Chomsky, Noam (Born 1928) Professor of Linguistics at Mas-sachusetts Institute of Technology, best known to educators for his interest in the relationship between language and the work-ings of the human mind, and the possibility that some aspects of language-use and understanding are INNATE (rather than ac-quired) and pertain to language as such rather than to whatever particular language is learned in one's youth. See *Chomsky : Selected Readings* by J P B Allen and P van Buren (1971).

chronological age What we ordinarily mean by a person's age (time elapsed since date of birth) which can be contrasted with, eg, his or her READING AGE or MENTAL AGE, allowing comparison with other children of the same chronological age. Thus a girl may have a chronological age of seven and a reading age of ten, indicating that she can read as well as an average ten-year-old.

church colleges UK COLLEGES OF EDUCATION operated by the

Church of England, the Methodist Church or the Roman Catholic Church.

church schools UK VOLUNTARY SCHOOLS operated by religious denominations.

circuit teacher See PERIPATETIC TEACHER.

circuit training PHYSICAL EDUCATION term for a method of high-pressure exercising in which a person tackles a circuit of individually prescribed activities or exercises, keeping to a strict time limit, and making continuous demands on heart and lungs and, supposedly, building up stamina.

circulars Statements of policy sent by the UK DEPARTMENT OF EDUCATION AND SCIENCE to LOCAL EDUCATION AUTHORITIES. They do not have the force of law; but they are highly influential.

Circular 10/65 A UK CIRCULAR from the DEPARTMENT OF EDUCATION AND SCIENCE in June 1965 requiring all LOCAL EDUCATION AUTHORITIES to submit plans for the re-organisation of their SECONDARY SCHOOLS along COMPREHENSIVE lines. An historic document in that it heralded the decline of the ELEVEN-PLUS selection examination and of the TRIPARTITE SYSTEM (of separate GRAMMAR, TECHNICAL, and MODERN secondary schools).

circulating schools Welsh ELEMENTARY SCHOOLS started in 1737, using PERIPATETIC TEACHERS to tour the country, stay a few months in each locality, teach poor children (and adults) to read the Bible and give religious instruction. The movement was supported by the SOCIETY FOR PROMOTING CHRISTIAN KNOWLEDGE (SPCK) and private donations but, despite initial success (more than 6,500 such schools by 1777), it died out towards the end of the century, giving way to the SUNDAY SCHOOL movement.

City and Guilds of London Institute A UK examining body founded in 1878 to 'provide and encourage' TECHNICAL EDUCATION and COMMERCIAL EDUCATION. It has arranged courses and assessment chiefly for craftsmen, skilled operatives, technicians and clerical workers being trained within industry or taking part-time courses at TECHNICAL COLLEGES. Some of its activity is now being taken over by the TECHNICIAN EDUCATION COUNCIL (TEC).

civics (US) The study of government and citizenship, usually starting with a strong emphasis on the student's position within his local community.

civic university (UK) Any of a number of universities created in the 19th and early 20th centuries in large provincial towns or cities (eg Liverpool, Exeter, Birmingham). Often called a RED-BRICK university.

Clarendon Report, 1864   The REPORT of a Royal Commission, enquiring into the nine chief PUBLIC SCHOOLS. The report praised the DISCIPLINE of the schools but criticised the CURRICULUM as lacking in breadth and flexibility, and found much of the teaching to be ineffective. Legislation followed, causing the schools to establish more representative governing bodies, but they were not made liable to government inspection.

class   **1** A group of (say, 20–40) pupils or students who are taught together and/or come together regularly for administrative purposes. **2** (US) All students at the same GRADE level in an institution, eg SOPHOMORE class. **3** (US) All students leaving an institution in a certain year, as in 'class of 1985'. **4** Category of HONOURS DEGREE awarded, eg first class honours. **5** As in SOCIAL CLASS.

classical conditioning   The process whereby people (or animals) learn to respond in a certain way to STIMULI which have not previously evoked those responses. For example, PAVLOV experimented with dogs who were seen to respond to the sight of food by the REFLEX of salivating. The presentation of food was then accompanied or preceded by a new stimulus – the ringing of a bell. Eventually, the dogs would salivate at the ringing of the bell, even though no food was presented. This salivation is a CONDITIONED REFLEX or RESPONSE, and the bell is a CONDITIONED STIMULUS. See also OPERANT CONDITIONING.

classical curriculum.   The liberal arts curriculum of mediaeval times, comprising the QUADRIVIUM of arithmetic, geometry, astronomy and music, and the TRIVIUM of grammar, rhetoric and logic.

classical studies   Studies relating to the language and literature (and perhaps other aspects of the culture) of ancient Greece and Rome.

classics   **1** The body of LITERATURE regarded as of enduring importance in a field or DISCIPLINE. **2** As CLASSICAL STUDIES.

class of 19—   (US) The group of students expected to leave a school or college in a particular year, having completed their studies.

clearing house   An organisation that exists to gather information from a variety of sources and distribute it to individuals and organisations according to their different needs. Thus, in the UK, the UNIVERSITIES CENTRAL COUNCIL ON ADMISSIONS

41

(UCCA) distributes details of intending students among the universities. In the US, the Educational Resources Information Centre (ERIC) collects, processes, and distributes educational information among teachers and educational researchers.

climbing frame   A piece of PRIMARY SCHOOL playground apparatus, usually of metal tubing, forming a cuboid framework several feet high, wide and long, encouraging children to practice MOTOR skills and develop physical confidence by clambering around it.

clinical approach/method   Within educational psychology, an approach to the understanding of intellectual and emotional functioning based upon detailed work (observation and discussion) with individual children.

clinical training   That part of a medical student's training that takes place in a TEACHING HOSPITAL in contact with patients. The term is sometimes used also when certain other professional students (eg law students) are learning while in contact with their future 'clients'.

closed circuit television (CCTV)   Television system used within education or training where the signal is not broadcast to the general public but is transmitted to a restricted number of receivers. (Radio also can be transmitted on closed circuit.)

closed scholarship   A SCHOLARSHIP at a university or other institution that is restricted to candidates with a special background, eg from a particular school or county.

closure   **1** A term from GESTALT PSYCHOLOGY referring to our tendency to perceive as a whole some incomplete thing that is presented to us. For example, even though we might be presented with six separate curved lines, we might see them as a circle. **2** The term used in the UK for the shutting down of a MAINTAINED SCHOOL by a LOCAL EDUCATIONAL AUTHORITY (eg because of FALLING ROLLS). In such cases, the authority has a legal obligation to publish its proposals (as it would also if it were to change the size or nature of the school) and allow two months for objections; and it may need the SECRETARY OF STATE's approval.

cloze procedure   Means of testing READABILITY of text by checking how well students can comprehend it even though a proportion of the words (say every third word) is deleted.

CMA   See COMPUTER MARKED ASSIGNMENT.

CNAA   See COUNCIL FOR NATIONAL ACADEMIC AWARDS.

coaching   Refers to training in sports and athletics, but also to the kind of intensive private tuition given to an individual child to improve his skill in a particular subject (or prepare him for an examination). Usually given in the child's or teacher's home and for a fee.

Cockcroft Committee A COMMITTEE OF ENQUIRY at present (1981) looking into the teaching of mathematics in primary and secondary schools, and due to publish a REPORT shortly

Cockerton Judgement A UK test case brought before the High Court in 1899 and establishing that SCHOOL BOARDS were not entitled to spend money from the rates on SECONDARY EDUCATION. Emergency legislation in 1901 legalised such spending, however, and it was firmly built into the EDUCATION ACT 1902 that certain LOCAL EDUCATION AUTHORITIES were now to be responsible for secondary education. (The case is not dissimilar from the US KALAMAZOO CASE, though the decision was different.)

codes in language The different ways in which words are chosen and put together in speech by different social groups. Differences in codes are accompanied by different ways of relating to the world and may make for difficulties in communication between one group and another, eg pupils and teachers. BERNSTEIN distinguished between RESTRICTED codes (relying on short, often illogical and ambiguous utterances) and ELABORATED codes which involve lengthier and more explicit statements allowing expression of logical nuances and shades of meaning. Part of the MIDDLE-CLASS child's advantage in education is held to arise from his being able to use the elaborated code (which is that used by his teachers) as well as the restricted code; while the WORKING CLASS child may have only the restricted code.

co-ed (US) A girl or woman educated at the same institution as boys or men. Derived from CO-EDUCATION.

co-education The education of males and females together in the same classes of the same institution.

coefficient of correlation In statistics, a measure of the strength (or closeness) of the CORRELATION between two VARIABLES. It is expressed as a decimal between 0 and 1; and carries a plus or minus sign to indicate POSITIVE or NEGATIVE CORRELATION.

cognitive development The progressive growth in a child's ability to understand concepts and explain relationships, which theorists like PIAGET believe to proceed through stages, each building on and transcending those that have gone before.

cognitive dissonance A concept developed by US psychologist,

Leon Festinger, and asserting that, when a person finds two or more of his beliefs or attitudes or behaviours to be in conflict with one another, he will be driven to reduce the incompatability in order to achieve consonance.

cognitive learning   Learning that emphasises thought (eg memorising, analysing, evaluating) rather than feeling or movement. Chiefly involves the learning of concepts and principles. Contrast with AFFECTIVE learning and PSYCHOMOTOR learning.

cognitive map   The mental picture a person has of his environment which differs according to each person's experience within it. For example, a teacher and a pupil are likely to have different cognitive maps of the same school because they will see different parts of it as having greater significance.

cognitive objectives   Learning OBJECTIVES that stipulate the expected knowledge or cognitive process (eg thinking, problem-solving), rather than externally observable behaviour or skill. See BEHAVIOURAL OBJECTIVES.

cognitive psychology   An influential school of psychology that embodies a marked shift away from BEHAVIOURISM towards a recognition of the complexities and individuality of intellectual life. It is concerned with complex perceptions, memory, language and thinking processes and is particularly responsible for the INFORMATION PROCESSING view of human learning and problem-solving.

cognitive set   A set is a tendency or disposition to perceive or respond to something in a pre-determined way, regardless of the properties the thing actually displays. For example, one may be set to expect difficulty in coping with mathematical problems.

cognitive style   A person's habitual approach to thinking or problem-solving, eg trying to get an overall grasp of the problem before probing separate aspects of it in detail, or vice versa. See HOLISTIC and SERIALIST.

cohort   A name often given to the SAMPLE in a LONGITUDINAL STUDY.

Colet, John (1467–1515)   A leading English humanist and Dean of St Paul's who (with ERASMUS) founded St Paul's School. He was far ahead of his time in advocating kindliness rather than harshness in teaching, and the encouragement of original thought and individual understanding rather than the prevailing ROTE LEARNING. He wrote a Latin GRAMMAR that enjoyed long popularity in schools.

college (From Latin, 'society, company, band of associates'.) The term is sometimes used of SECONDARY SCHOOLS (eg Eton college) but is more commonly associated with institutions of POST-SECONDARY education. In the UK, such colleges are either component bodies of a university (eg Merton College of Oxford or Royal Holloway College of London) or else are separate, funded by LOCAL EDUCATION AUTHORITIES, and of less than university status. In the US, colleges in the state-maintained sector are of lower status than universities (though even there, people are likely to speak informally of attendance at such universities as 'going to college'); but, in the private sector, 'college' and 'university' seem not to denote differences in status (eg one of the prestigious IVY LEAGUE institutions has retained its original name of Dartmouth College).

College Boards (US) Tests set by the COLLEGE EXTRANCE EXAMINATION BOARD.

College Entrance Examination Board (**CEEB**) (US) A national testing agency whose tests are taken by HIGH-SCHOOL leavers and used by colleges and universitites in considering applicants for admission.

college of advanced technology (**CAT**) (UK) Prior to 1966 there were ten such colleges offering courses in HIGHER EDUCATION with a technological and scientific emphasis. Subsequently they became TECHNOLOGICAL UNIVERSITIES or were absorbed by existing universities.

college of education The UK colleges of education, usually MAINTAINED by the LOCAL EDUCATION AUTHORITIES, were formerly known as TEACHER TRAINING COLLEGES, and their main course leads to the BACHELOR OF EDUCATION degree which is a teaching qualification. Many colleges of education were closed during the 1970s and all but a few of those remaining have expanded into COLLEGES or INSTITUTES OF HIGHER EDUCATION or have merged with POLYTECHNICS.

college of further education (UK) A college serving a primarily local CATCHMENT AREA and offering courses of FURTHER EDUCATION but little or no HIGHER EDUCATION. Usually MAINTAINED by a LOCAL EDUCATION AUTHORITY.

college of higher education (UK) One of several types of institutions in HIGHER EDUCATION offering DIPLOMA and DEGREE courses, usually in professional or vocational areas, probably including teacher training. MAINTAINED by a LOCAL EDUCATION AUTHORITY.

45

collegiate university A university composed of a number of partly or largely autonomous colleges (eg Oxford, Cambridge, Durham).

colour-factor apparatus Coloured wooden rods of between one and ten centimetres representing numbers, used in the teaching of basic mathematical concepts in primary school. Children learn by manipulating the apparatus on the basis of questions and set tasks as they do also with CUISENAIRE RODS and DIENES MULTI-BASE APPARATUS.

combined school An institution that is a combination of two or more schools that may also be found separately. For example, UK PRIMARY SCHOOLS are often combinations of INFANT and JUNIOR SCHOOLS.

come up (UK) We may say that a student has come up (or went up) to college or university when we mean that he has commenced upon his course of studies (or, more loosely, when he has resumed his studies after a vacation). At the end of his course(s) he 'goes down'.

Comenius, Johann Amos (1592–1670) A Polish bishop and educationalist whose ideas on CURRICULUM content and TEACHING METHOD were much ahead of his time. He advocated a wider curriculum and saw it as a means to universal brotherhood. The methods he proposed were gentler and more considerate of the child than were typical in his day and he suggested basing teaching on the concrete experiences of the child. His Latin textbook incorporated much of his new thinking and was used in several countries in Europe. Comenius worked in England, briefly, and in Sweden, as well as in Poland. See C H Dobinson (ed) *Comenius and Contemporary Education*, Unesco (1970).

commencement (US) Ceremony in educational institutions to celebrate GRADUATION.

commercial education Courses of study with a VOCATIONAL emphasis, ranging from subjects like shorthand and typing, book-keeping and elementary accounting to economics, company law and computer studies.

Commissioner of Education (US) The Chief Executive of the former US OFFICE OF EDUCATION.

committee of enquiry (UK) The SECRETARY OF STATE periodically appoints committees of enquiry to investigate and report on matters of educational concern. The committee will consist of a variety of people with an interest (professional or otherwise) in education and, like its eventual REPORT, will usually take the name of its chairman. Recent examples are the Rampton Committee on the education of children from ethnic minority groups and the Cockcroft Committee on the teaching of mathematics in primary and secondary schools.

common core   See CORE CURRICULUM.

common course   Term used in Scottish SECONDARY SCHOOLS where, for the first two years, all pupils follow essentially the same SYLLABUS, often in MIXED ABILITY classes.

Common Entrance Examination   (UK) An examination taken (chiefly) by PREPARATORY SCHOOL pupils at the age of 13 to qualify for entry to INDEPENDENT SCHOOLS. The examination is organised centrally for the schools by two separate boards (one for boys and one for girls) but each school makes its own appraisal of the candidates' efforts.

commoner   (UK) An undergraduate (especially at Oxford and Cambridge) who is not financed by a SCHOLARSHIP or EXHIBITION.

community college   1 (US) A local college serving students of wide ability range at post-secondary level and offering courses of FURTHER EDUCATION, usually of two-year duration and supposedly related closely to local needs. Many prepare students to transfer to degree studies in third and fourth years at STATE COLLEGE/UNIVERSITY. Also called JUNIOR COLLEGE and CITY COLLEGE. 2 (UK) Essentially a SECONDARY SCHOOL whose premises and facilities are also available to adults in the area as a cultural, educational and community centre. See also VILLAGE COLLEGES.

community education   Educational programmes that entail going outside of the school or college walls and involve other people in the community, either as learners or as teachers or as both. May well be intended to benefit the community generally (not just those people actively involved), eg by making the area a more interesting place to live.

community home   Residential institution for children IN CARE of a UK LOCAL AUTHORITY. Children may attend local schools or be taught on the premises.

community school   1 (UK) One that has a policy of being open to and helping promote activities with children and their parents, and perhaps other members of the community, outside of school hours. See also COMMUNITY COLLEGE. 2 (US) A school owned or controlled by a parents' association.

comparative education   A DISCIPLINE within EDUCATIONAL STUD-

IES concerned with the analysis of factors that account for similarities and differences in educational policies and practices in various countries as they have developed over time and as they are today. (HISTORY OF EDUCATION is often seen as a sub-discipline of comparative education.)

compensatory education Especially stimulating or well-resourced educational programmes or systems designed to overcome the academic or intellectual handicaps that certain children are believed to suffer as a result of their upbringing or environment and which prevent them obtaining maximum benefit from standard educational procedures.

competency-based teaching (US) The slogan of a movement within TEACHER EDUCATION whose proponents train teachers in specific skills of interacting with pupils in classrooms and who advocate that courses taken by prospective and in-service teachers should spell out very clearly the knowledge, skills and attitudes they are expected to acquire.

component objectives/behaviours/skills The set of more precise OBJECTIVES into which a broad objective may be broken down. For instance, the broad objective of being able to start a car is made up of such components as being able to depress the clutch pedal, operate the choke, check that the gear lever is in neutral, turn the ignition key, and so on.

composition 1 Rather out-dated term for an essay or lengthy piece of prose written by a student on some set theme. **2** Also used rather differently in art to mean the arrangement of shapes within a picture; and, in music, to refer to an original piece of music composed by a student or to the act or study of composing itself. **3** (US) A CURRICULUM activity concerned with the teaching of essay-writing and related skills.

comprehensive school (UK) A NON-SELECTIVE SECONDARY school catering for children of all abilities (apart from the EDUCATIONALLY SUB-NORMAL) from a local area. The organisation varies from area to area: eg ALL-THROUGH schools with an age-range of 11–18; TWO-TIER schools in which children may enter a junior comprehensive school (or JUNIOR HIGH SCHOOL) at 11 and transfer to a senior comprehensive school (or SENIOR HIGH SCHOOL) at 13 or 14; schools taking children from 11–16, transferring those who wish to go further to SIXTH-FORM COLLEGES at the age of 16 or so. Various combinations of these patterns are to be found. In areas that operate a MIDDLE SCHOOL system, pupils are 12 or 13 before they go to comprehensive school.

compressed speech A teaching technique whereby recorded speech is played back to the student at up to twice the speed it was originally spoken. Clearly this economises on tape but users claim that it also saves the student's time because people can usually comprehend speech at speeds considerably faster than normal.

compulsory education Whatever educational requirements are enforceable on a child by the laws of his country or state. For example, he may be required to attend school for a certain number of years and/or between certain ages, and/or to attain a certain standard.

computer-assisted (aided) instruction/learning (CAI/ CAL) The use of a computer to select and present instructional material to students and to react to students' responses. Students may work at separate TERMINALS linked to a central computer; but the computer can organise and pace the teaching individually for each student according to how he has responded to the teaching so far. See also COMPUTER-MANAGED INSTRUCTION.

computer-managed instruction/learning (CMI/CML) The use of the computer in administrative roles connected with teaching. Thus it may be involved with timetabling or scheduling, test-scoring and record-keeping, or even in diagnosing a student's learning needs and providing him with suitable materials or activities. May be used in conjunction with COMPUTER-ASSISTED LEARNING.

computer-mediated instruction. Same as COMPUTER-ASSISTED INSTRUCTION.

computer-marked assignment (CMA) A test consisting of various kinds of MULTIPLE-CHOICE QUESTIONS to which the student indicates his answers in a way that allows them to be marked by a computer.

concentric method (CURRICULUM) See SPIRAL CURRICULUM.

concept film (or TAPE) Very short sequence of moving pictures (often without sound commentary), intended to illustrate or demonstrate a single idea or process. See SINGLE CONCEPT FILM.

concept formation The process of discovering the distinguishing features which attach to a particular concept and whose recognition enables us to use that concept appropriately. See the writings of BRUNER, PIAGET and VYGOTSKY.

conceptual density A term relating to the degree of difficulty a student might experience with a text or spoken message according to the number and complexity of the concepts or principles he is presented with in a given number of words. Thus, three words like 'ontogeny recapitulates phylogeny' have greater conceptual density than, say, 'cats eat fish'.

concrete operations   The third stage postulated by PIAGET in the development of a child's ability to use concepts. Children of around seven to 11 years are said to operate at the concrete level. That is, their ability to organise the information available to them in an actual situation greatly exceeds their ability to generalise to hypothetical situations or to conceive of alternative hypotheses about the situation.

conditioned reflex   A REFLEX ACTION (eg an eye-blink) that a person has learned to make (through CONDITIONING) to a STIMULUS (eg a buzzer) that would not naturally elicit that RESPONSE.

conditioned response   A RESPONSE that a person has learned (through CONDITIONING) to make in response to a STIMULUS that did not previously elicit it.

conditioned stimulus   A stimulus to which a person has learned to make a CONDITIONED REFLEX or RESPONSE.

conditioning   Simple form of learning in which a person acquires the tendency to make a particular RESPONSE (eg an eye-blink) to a STIMULUS which has not previously evoked that response (eg a sound), or else the tendency to make that response more frequently. There are two main types – CLASSICAL CONDITIONING and OPERANT CONDITIONING.

conditions of service   The responsibilities and contractual obligations attached to a particular job. At present (1981), school teachers in England and Wales have some defined conditions of service but the LOCAL EDUCATION AUTHORITIES and teachers' associations are finding it difficult to agree on whether a contract should, for instance, oblige teachers to supervise school meals, specify how many hours per week they should spend with their classes, and indicate a maximum class-size.

conference call   The linking of several telephones so that each caller can be heard by all of the others at the same time. This allows for group discussion by telephone which can be valuable in DISTANCE EDUCATION.

conflation   The combining of two or more sets of marks to give an overall mark. For example, marks for practical work, theory, and examination might be conflated to give an overall mark for the course as a whole.

consciousness-raising   Any exercise of teaching (or learning without help from a teacher) in which a person becomes aware as never before of his or her own nature or relationship to others. Might be used especially if the person is rising above 'FALSE CONSCIOUSNESS' and coming to understand how he or she is exploited by others.

conservation   The concept that a given quantity of a substance stays the same even if its shape is altered. For example a quantity of water still has the same volume whether it is in a short, squat container or a tall, thin one. PIAGET observed that children achieve the concept of conservation of substance, weight, volume etc at different ages.

console   A desk or table containing the controls through which an electronic system with a number of separate, and perhaps distant, units (eg a LANGUAGE LABORATORY or a television studio) can be monitored and controlled.

consortia   (UK) Co-operative ventures between many LOCAL EDUCATION AUTHORITIES, sanctioned by the appropriate Government departments, to reduce costs and increase efficiency through co-ordinating their requirements in the design and construction of school buildings and furniture.

constructs   A term used in the REPERTORY GRID TECHNIQUE to refer to the concepts we use in categorising similarities and differences in our environment. For example, 'honest-dishonest' 'light-heavy', 'like me-different from me', 'lazy-industrious' are all constructs.

contact time/hours   The number of hours per week a teacher is expected to spend face-to-face with students.

contamination   Research term for the state of results or findings that have been affected to some unknown degree by a VARIABLE that was not anticipated (and therefore not controlled), making them difficult or impossible to interpret.

content analysis   A quantitative approach to the evaluation of such material as student writings, or textbooks, or radio and television programmes, eg by noting and tabulating the frequency of references that fall into various categories – racist, sexist, left-wing/right-wing, etc.

contingency management   An application of BEHAVIOURIST principles to classroom teaching in such a way that desired BEHAVIOURS in the pupil are systematically and explicitly rewarded. See also TOKEN ECONOMY.

continuing education   The availability of structured educational experience throughout a person's life. Related to ADULT EDUCATION, PERMANENT EDUCATION, and RECURRENT EDUCATION.

continuous assessment   The ASSESSMENT of a student's work at intervals during his course of study not only to obtain information that will help in teaching the student but also to use the results in arriving at an overall assessment for his work on the course as a whole.

continuous variable   A statistical VARIABLE such that between any two of its possible values there can, theoretically, be an infinite number of other values. For example, a child may be 100 cm tall this month and 101 cm tall next month; but, in the meantime, his height will have taken an infinite number of values. It is a continuous variable. Contrast with DISCRETE VARIABLE.

control group   Research term for a group of people who are as similar as possible to another group (the EXPERIMENTAL GROUP) who are being used in an experiment. The control group however, is not given the experimental treatment, so they provide a baseline against which the effect of the treatment can be judged. That is, any changes that take place in the experimental group but not in the control group can be attributed to the treatment.

controlled experiment   A research approach in which certain VARIABLES judged to be important are held constant (eg class-size, pupil age-range and sex) while another variable (eg teaching method) is varied in order to determine the differential effects.

controlled school   A type of VOLUNTARY SCHOOL in England and Wales (usually Church of England) for which the LOCAL EDUCATION AUTHORITY (LEA) is financially responsible and appoints two thirds of the GOVERNORS (the remainder being appointed by the voluntary body). The LEA also appoints all the teachers but must consult the managers or governors in appointing a HEAD TEACHER or teachers of RELIGIOUS EDUCATION (which follows the AGREED SYLLABUS).

convergent thinking   Thinking directed towards finding the one best, correct, or conventional solution to a problem. Contrasts with DIVERGENT THINKING.

converger   A person who tends to be better at dealing with problems that have a single correct solution than with more open-ended problems to which a variety of solutions are possible. Contrasts with DIVERGER. See CONVERGENT THINKING and DIVERGENT THINKING.

conversion training   See RETRAINING.

cookbook science/experiments   Derogatory term for 'experiments' in which the student simply follows all the instructions (a 'recipe') and has little need to think.

co-operating teacher   (US) The teacher who lends his class and/or offers supervision to a student teacher on TEACHING PRACTICE.

co-operative course/program   (US) A school or college VOCATIONAL EDUCATION course in which classroom work is alternated with periods of planned experience in appropriate industrial or commercial firms or other organisations. Similar to UK SANDWICH COURSES and some US WORK STUDY COURSES.

co-operative teaching   See TEAM TEACHING.

core curriculum   **1** The essential or basic parts of the CURRICULUM of an educational institution (or a department within it) that are studied by all its students even though each has a choice of optional subjects in addition. **2** SUBJECTS that must be taught by the teacher (eg in a PRIMARY SCHOOL) even though he is free to decide what else to teach in addition. **3** In 1980, the DEPARTMENT OF EDUCATION AND SCIENCE, together with the WELSH OFFICE, published *A Framework for the School Curriculum* as the basis of discussions towards some kind of nationally-agreed core of subjects or OBJECTIVES to be attained by all the pupils in the course of their school careers.

corporal punishment   Physical punishment inflicted upon the body of a schoolchild, usually by cane or leather strap on the hands or buttocks. The practice is now repugnant to a large proportion of teachers and, although still permitted by law in Britain, is much less used (especially in PRIMARY SCHOOLS) than it once was. The US equivalent is PADDLING.

correlation   The degree to which differences in one VARIABLE (eg people's heights) are related to differences in another variable (eg their weights). If, for example, tall people tend to be heavier and small people lighter, and vice versa, the correlation is said to be positive. If, on the other hand, big values of one variable tend to go with small values of the other, the correlation is negative.

correlation coefficient.   See COEFFICIENT OF CORRELATION.

correspondence colleges   Within the UK there are many institutions offering CORRESPONDENCE EDUCATION though only about thirty have gained ACCREDITATION. Such colleges prepare students for the GENERAL CERTIFICATE OF EDUCATION, for some EXTERNAL DEGREES of London University, and for many professional qualifications. The most prestigious correspondence institution is the OPEN UNIVERSITY which confers its own degrees.

correspondence course   One conducted by the tutor and student through exchange of written materials by post. See CORRESPONDENCE EDUCATION.

correspondence education   A type of DISTANCE EDUCATION based on exchange by post of written communications (eg course notes, student essays, tutor comments) between tutors and students. It may involve the study of specially printed materials, TEXTBOOKS, HOME EXPERIMENT KITS, audio-tapes, radio and television broadcasts; and it may be backed up by face-to-face meetings with tutors and by SUMMER SCHOOLS.

Cosford cube   A hand-held cube with each face a different colour that can be used by students in a classroom to indicate privately their choice from up to six possible answers to a MULTIPLE CHOICE QUESTION posed by their teacher. Developed as a low-cost form of FEEDBACK CLASSROOM at an RAF station in Cosford, England.

council   (UK) **1** The governing body of a university, composed largely of distinguished people from outside the institution. Normally, it has great influence over the administration and public image of the university but defers to the SENATE on academic issues. The Scottish equivalent is COURT. **2** The term often refers to a LOCAL AUTHORITY (eg a metropolitan district or county council) responsible for education and other services in its area.

Council for Educational Technology for the United Kingdom   Established in 1973 (in succession to the National Council for Educational Technology) to promote the understanding and the application, where appropriate, of EDUCATIONAL TECHNOLOGY in education and training. This it does by identifying possible beneficial applications and initiating the development work needed to establish the costs and benefits of innovations.

Council for National Academic Awards   An autonomous UK body established in 1964 to provide VALIDATION for courses offered by colleges and polytechnics and to supervise the ASSESSMENT of their students with a view to awarding DEGREES and DIPLOMAS.

counselling   Advising pupils or students on their educational progress, on career opportunities, on personal anxieties (eg regarding drugs or contraception), or on sudden crises in their lives. This may be partly the job of all teachers, but many institutions have specialist counsellors called, for example, PERSONAL TUTOR, MORAL TUTOR or PASTORAL TUTOR.

county schools (UK) PRIMARY SCHOOLS and SECONDARY SCHOOLS that are built, maintained, and staffed entirely out of public funds and administered by the LOCAL EDUCATION AUTHORITY. Of all the MAINTAINED SCHOOLS in England and Wales, about two thirds of the primary schools and four fifths of the secondary schools are of this type. The remainder are VOLUNTARY SCHOOLS.

course In North America, a series of class lessons during one SEMESTER, covering one distinct subject within the student's total programme of studies (which may comprise twenty or more such courses). The word is used similarly within the UK, but is also used to refer to a year's study (all subjects) or to the total study involved in obtaining a particular qualification. For example we speak of a degree or diploma course.

course team A group of academics and teachers (perhaps with the involvement of editors, administrators, designers, educational technologists, and others) responsible for developing and teaching a course. All OPEN UNIVERSITY courses are developed by such teams.

course work Work done by a pupil or student during a course, which may be assessed so as to count towards his overall grade for the course.

court The governing body of some UK universities, especially in Scotland.

Craik, Sir Henry (1846–1927) First Secretary of the Scottish Education Department (1885) who instituted many reforms in Scottish elementary, secondary and technical education and in the training of teachers.

crammer 1 A fee-paying school or college that exists not to educate but to get pupils or students through examinations. The name implies that it does so by stuffing them with facts, using much repetition, and relying on ROTE-LEARNING and memorisation rather than on understanding. 2 A book with the same aims and approach as in 1.

crash course A particularly intensive course designed to enable the student to acquire specified KNOWLEDGE and SKILLS considerably faster than he would in a normal course.

creaming (off) Term used for the practice of selecting those students who are believed to be most promising academically and educating them separately from the remainder (who are often thought to suffer thereby). Best-known example was selection for UK GRAMMAR SCHOOLS.

creative writing   Referring to writing ASSIGNMENTS given to pupils (especially in PRIMARY SCHOOLS) with a view to allowing them opportunity for greater self-expression than certain other writing assignments would do.

creativity tests   Unlike INTELLIGENCE TESTS which concentrate on questions that each have one correct answer, creativity tests are OPEN-ENDED and attempt to assess DIVERGENT THINKING. That is, they allow for many, and perhaps idiosyncratic, answers, eg by asking the pupil to list as many uses as he can think of for some everyday article like a house-brick or a paper-clip.

crèche   A DAY NURSERY for pre-school children. May be provided on the premises of a large educational institution or other organisation, for the convenience of employees with young children who might otherwise not be able to continue working.

credentials   Degrees, diplomas, certificates, references, testimonials, letters of recommendation and other statements (usually written) from which a person's general qualities or suitability for some specific situation might be estimated.

credit   The certification that a student has done acceptably well in a particular COURSE. In North American universities the student can obtain one or more credits for each course he takes and about 120 may be needed to obtain his DEGREE. In the UK, the OPEN UNIVERSITY operates a quite different credit system: only six (one for each year-long course the student takes) are needed for an ORDINARY degree; eight for an HONOURS degree.

credit exemption   A college or university may excuse a student from certain COURSES, and require him to obtain fewer CREDITS, because it recognises that experience he has had elsewhere, or qualifications he has earned, are equivalent alternatives to what it has to offer.

credit transfer   A form of CREDIT EXEMPTION in which two or more colleges or universities agree that students who move from one institution to another with certain specified CREDITS should be treated as if those credits had been earned in the institution to which they move.

cretin   A person whose mental and physical development has been retarded by the thyroid gland being under-active. The condition appears early in life and may be ameliorated if treated early enough with thyroid extract.

crib **1** Once referred to a baldly literal translation of a language text as used by pupils of Latin or Greek. **2** Now more commonly used as a verb to indicate cheating by copying from a text or from another pupil's work.

Crichton Vocabulary Scale A test designed to measure the ability of children, aged 11 years or less, to define a number of words: it is used with RAVEN'S PROGRESSIVE MATRICE as a measure of INTELLIGENCE.

criterion Refers to a test score or, more particularly, to the knowledge and abilities expected of a learner as the result of a planned sequence of teaching. See CRITERION BEHAVIOUR, CRITERION-REFERENCED TESTING and CRITERION TEST.

criterion behaviour The abilities a learner is expected to be able to demonstrate on successful completion of a planned sequence of teaching.

criterion-referenced testing Where a student's test performance is compared not with his own previous performances, nor with the performance of other students, but with some ABSOLUTE STANDARD or CRITERION performance. For example, a driving test is supposed to be criterion-referenced. (Contrast with NORM-REFERENCED TESTING.)

criterion test A test designed to allow the student's performance at the end of a sequence of teaching to be compared with some CRITERION of reasonable performance. (See also MASTERY LEARNING.)

critical incident technique A technique for the analysis of job-performance based on identification of those events occurring in the course of a job that are so crucial that they reveal the style and effectiveness with which the person does his job. Critical incidents in classroom teaching might arise when the teacher is faced with a pupil challenging his authority or when he realises that he has unjustly accused a pupil of some serious misdemeanour.

critical learning period A period of life during which people usually acquire a particular skill. If it is not acquired during that critical period it is supposedly very difficult or impossible to acquire later on.

critical path analysis A logical method of planning a complex project (eg the design and implementation of an innovatory CUR-

RICULUM) by analysing it into a sequence of contributory decisions and activities and then recording them on a FLOW CHART in such a way that potential hold-ups can be identified, along with the tasks that must be completed on time ('the critical path') if the project as a whole is not to be delayed. Originally derived from Program Evaluation and Review Technique (PERT).

Crombie code The regulations covering the financial compensation of staff made redundant by the closures of UK COLLEGES OF EDUCATION that began in the 1970s.

cross-cultural studies The seeking of understanding about a particular human activity (eg child-rearing) by comparing how it is carried out in quite different CULTURES.

Cross Report 1888 The UK REPORT of a Royal Commission appointed to enquire into the workings of ELEMENTARY EDUCATION since the EDUCATION ACT OF 1870. Its members disagreed on many issues (especially the status of VOLUNTARY SCHOOLS provided by religious denominations) but were unanimous that PAYMENTS BY RESULTS should be relaxed, that school buildings and facilities should be improved, that more emphasis should be given to science and to manual and technical education, and that there should be more provision for TEACHER-TRAINING. The report influenced subsequent legislation.

cross-sectional study A research technique in which information about a group of people or situations (eg primary school classrooms) is collected on one occasion only but may be compared with information gathered from a related cross-section at another time. Contrast with a LONGITUDINAL STUDY.

Crowther Report 1959 UK REPORT on the education of pupils between the ages of 15 and 18. It deployed statistical evidence to show that a great deal of talent was still being lost to the educational system and that opportunity depended on SOCIAL CLASS. It recommended that the school-leaving age be raised to 16 by 1968 and that county colleges should be created to provide compulsory part-time education up to age 18. It also recommended greater use of SANDWICH COURSES, less SPECIALISATION in SIXTH-FORMS, and an increase in the supply of teachers.

CSE (UK) See CERTIFICATE OF SECONDARY EDUCATION.

CSYS (UK) See CERTIFICATE OF SIXTH YEAR STUDIES (Scotland).

cue 1 Any stimulus that evokes a particular RESPONSE. A person may be unaware of the cues he is responding to. (See NON-VERBAL

COMMUNICATION.) **2** The word is also used in a more technical sense in PROGRAMMED LEARNING, (to mean extra information given to the student to help him make the correct response). **3** In the teaching of reading, a cue is anything in the overall meaning or structure of a text that might help a reader identify a word or phrase and understand its meaning.

Cuisenaire rods   Coloured wooden rods of lengths varying between one and ten centimetres, representing numbers, and used in the teaching of number concepts to children in PRIMARY SCHOOL. Children learn by manipulating the equipment on the basis of questions and set tasks as they do also with COLOUR-FACTOR APPARATUS and DIENES MULTI-BASE APPARATUS.

cultural deprivation   A condition we attribute to people who may be competent within their own social group or CULTURE but who seem intellectually or emotionally ill-prepared to enter some culture we wish them to aspire to.

culture   **1** In general, the VALUES, beliefs, customs and creations of a people who regard themselves as a coherent group (whether large or small). In this sense, the word carries no overtones of approval: the culture of a delinquent teenage gang is no less a culture than that of an OXBRIDGE college. **2** But the word is also used in the sense of 'high culture', generally meaning the arts and areas of scholarship approved of by the dominant group within society.

culture-free test   A test that, ideally, does not assume students are familiar with some particular cultural conventions in, for example, the use of language or pictures. Thus it can supposedly test for a quality like INTELLIGENCE without under-rating the performance of a candidate from a CULTURE different from that of the person who created the test. Really, no test can be completely culture-free but the ideal is an important one.

cum laude   (US) A Latin tag sometimes added when a DEGREE or other academic QUALIFICATION is awarded 'with praise'. It is the lowest of three such designations for academic performance above average. See also MAGNA CUM LAUDE and SUMMA CUM LAUDE.

cumulative record   (US) Files kept for each student in an educational institution and containing GRADES, psychometric test scores, teachers' reports, etc.

curricula   Plural of CURRICULUM.

curricular   Adjective relating to CURRICULUM.

curriculum   Can refer to the total structure of ideas and activities developed by an educational institution to meet the learning needs of students and to achieve desired educational AIMS. Some people use the term to refer simply to the content of what is taught. Others include also the teaching and learning methods involved, how students' attainment is assessed, and the underlying theory or philosophy of education. See also HIDDEN CURRICULUM.

curriculum development The deliberate process whereby an individual or a team identifies educational AIMS and OBJECTIVES for particular learners, designs an appropriate CURRICULUM (including the choice of content, teaching methods and MEDIA, ASSESSMENT techniques, etc), implements the curriculum with the learners, and improves it in the light of an EVALUATION of its effects and effectiveness. In the UK, curriculum development is very much the responsibility of individual schools, but the DEPARTMENT OF EDUCATION AND SCIENCE exercises considerable national influence through, for example, HER MAJESTY'S INSPECTORATE and the SCHOOLS COUNCIL.

curriculum laboratory Sometimes used of the facilities provided by an institution's RESOURCES UNIT or library, or by a TEACHERS' CENTRE, to help in locating or making teaching and learning materials for use in a CURRICULUM.

curriculum studies A SUB-DISCIPLINE within EDUCATIONAL STUDIES, with its own LEARNED JOURNALS, and concerned with the theory and practice of CURRICULUM DEVELOPMENT.

curriculum vitae A written outline of a person's educational and career history, used particularly when he seeks a new appointment. The US term is RESUMÉ.

cursive script 'Running script.' Handwriting in which the letters are joined rather than being left separate.

Curwen, John (1816–1880) A UK EDUCATIONALIST and follower of PESTALOZZI who developed the TONIC SOLFA system of learning to sing from written music.

custodian (US) Equivalent of CARETAKER. May also be called JANITOR.

cut-off point The point in a mark-list or a set of RANKINGS at which one intends to attach different labels to students falling either side of it. For example, students scoring less than 35 may be said to have 'failed', while all scoring 35 or more have 'passed'. Similarly, the students who rank 1st, 2nd, and 3rd may be deemed to have 'passed with distinction'. See also BORDER-LINE.

cybernetics The study of, and the body of theory relating to, communication and control within machines, human beings, and man-machine systems (eg aircraft plus pilot). Largely responsible for contributing the concept of FEEDBACK to education.

D

Dainton Report 1968 A UK REPORT that noted a swing away from science in education in England and Wales. It proposed that all pupils should study mathematics throughout their school lives, with special emphasis on its application in science; that more well-qualified science graduates should be attracted into teaching; and that both universities and employers should do more to draw young people into science and technology.

Dalton plan A learning plan introduced by Helen Parkhurst into Dalton High School, Massachusetts, in 1920, and imitated widely in the US and the UK. The plan required that pupils spend a large part of each day working individually, or in small groups, using libraries, WORKSHEETS, etc, and only occasionally conferring with a teacher; their work being based on monthly assignment cards which might differ from one pupil to another. A method combining independence with responsibility for the pupil and involving the teacher in considerable forward planning, production of materials and monitoring. See H Parkhurst, *Education in the Dalton Plan* (1926). (Compare with KELLER PLAN.)

dame schools Common in the 18th and 19th centuries, these schools were run by elderly women in their own homes and, for a small weekly fee, provided young children with a rudimentary introduction to reading, writing and, perhaps, arithmetic.

dance in education Folk-dancing, EURHYTHMICS, and even classical ballet have had their advocates in British schools, but the modern approach to dance (or 'movement') stems largely from the ideas of Rudolf LABAN who settled in England in 1938. He saw dance as a form of human expression through which pupils could extend the emotional and intellectual, as well as the physical, aspects of their personalities.

day boy/girl/pupil Pupil attending a BOARDING SCHOOL but living at home.

day care (US) A system for providing CHILD-MINDERS for children too young to go to school and whose parents are working.

day continuation schools A form of evening institute providing continued ELEMENTARY EDUCATION for UK pupils leaving school at 14. Such schools were advocated in the Education Act of 1918 but their development was curbed by financial crisis and the GEDDES AXE.

day nursery A place where children too young to go to school may be left to be cared for while their parents are working or studying. Also known as CRÈCHE. Day nurseries are sometimes organised by educational institutions and by large employers. One maintained by a LOCAL EDUCATION AUTHORITY will be known as a NURSERY SCHOOL.

day release (UK) Time off allowed to young employees from their jobs (normally without loss of pay), perhaps one day a week, to take part in job-related courses at FURTHER EDUCATION institutions. See also BLOCK RELEASE.

day school Historically, rather like a DAME SCHOOL (18th century, fee-paying and rudimentary), but run for older children and usually by a man. Nowadays might be applied to any school that is *not* a BOARDING SCHOOL.

day training colleges (UK) TEACHER TRAINING institutions established as a result of the CROSS REPORT OF 1888. They were non-residential non-denominational institutions attached to universities and university colleges and enabled their students to read for degrees as well as pursue professional training.

dean A senior member of a college or university whose concern is primarily with discipline or administration rather than with scholarship or teaching.

decoding The process of extracting the meaning from any set of words, pictures, symbols, gestures etc. (See ENCODING).

decomposition method One of two basic methods of subtraction. For example, instead of $55 - 17 = ?$, we may think of it as $(40 + 15) - 17 = ?$ The 55 has been decomposed into 40 and 15. We can now subtract 17 from 40 and add the result to 15. See also EQUAL ADDITION METHOD.

deduction An approach to reasoning, much used in logic and mathematics, in which a pair of propositions lead us to an inescapable conclusion about a particular example. For instance: 'All university students are over 18 years old; Bob is a student at university, so he must be over 18.' The conclusion can only be false if one or both of the original propositions is incorrect (eg if some university students are not over 18, and/or if Bob is not a university student). Contrasts with INDUCTION.

deep level processing Term used in discussion of STUDY SKILLS for the kind of reading done by a student who is penetrating beneath the surface details of an author's text to seek out the main ideas and lines of argument, examining them critically in relation both to the evidence presented and to his own ideas and experience. Contrasts with SURFACE LEVEL PROCESSING.

defence mechanisms Unconscious techniques (identified by SIGMUND FREUD) for protecting oneself against stressful experiences, eg through RATIONALISATION or REPRESSION.

deficit Certain children (eg from WORKING CLASS homes or from THIRD WORLD races) may be said to have cultural deficits which cause them to fail in school. BERNSTEIN offers an alternative model – that schools have deficits which cause them to fail such children.

degree A QUALIFICATION awarded to a student by a COLLEGE or POLYTECHNIC or UNIVERSITY, or by some body charged with the ACCREDITATION of other institutions' qualifications. A FIRST DEGREE (usually a bachelor's degree, BA, BSc etc) signifies the successful completion of perhaps three or four years of successful studies. A HIGHER DEGREE or POST-GRADUATE degree (eg a master's degree, MA, MSc, etc, or a doctorate, PhD, D Phil) is awarded after further years of study (course-work or research or both). Distinguished people in public life are often awarded HONORARY degrees on account of their achievements rather than because of any studies they may or may not have pursued.

degree factory (or DIPLOMA FACTORY) An institution with no academic reputation in the field of higher education and possibly not even offering courses but, nevertheless, profiting from the issue of certificates and 'qualifications' that misrepresent a person's educational attainments.

delegacy A body of people within a COLLEGE or UNIVERSITY to whom a particular responsibility (eg for CONTINUING EDUCATION) has been delegated.

Delphi technique An approach to forecasting or problem-solving in which each of a group of experts is independently asked for his prediction or solution. The several answers are then circulated among the experts so that they can appraise them and, if necessary, offer new ones.

63

democratic teaching   Classroom style in which teacher shares decisions with his pupils about who should learn what and how they should learn it and how their progress should be judged. Typically the teacher will issue suggestions rather than orders and will expect the pupils to take a good deal of responsibility for their own learning and for helping one another. (Contrast with AUTHORITARIAN TEACHING.)

demonstration school   A school attached to a teacher-training establishment in order to allow students to observe experienced teachers at work and to undertake TEACHING PRACTICE themselves. The idea of basing teacher-training on such model schools is no longer in favour in the UK, but a few such schools still survive in the US as CAMPUS or LABORATORY SCHOOLS.

demonstrator   A junior teaching post in a university and usually concerned with guiding students in laboratory or other practical work.

denominational school   One established and operated by a religious body.

density of information   A concept developed in PROGRAMMED LEARNING but relevant to many teaching methods; it indicates the 'difficulty' of a sequence of learning by referring to the amount of new ideas presented to the learner before he gets an opportunity to make a response that will obtain him FEEDBACK as to how well he has mastered them. Compare with CONCEPTUAL DENSITY.

Department of Education   (US) A cabinet-level department, with its own Secretary of Education, created in 1979 to take over the federal responsibilities in education formerly exercised by the DEPARTMENT OF HEALTH, EDUCATION AND WELFARE through its OFFICE OF EDUCATION. However, each state (like each province in Canada) remains responsible for its own educational system.

Department of Education and Science (**DES**)   (UK) Government department responsible, since 1964, for the educational system in England (as well as for science and libraries) and for POST-SECONDARY education in Wales. It also allocates funds to UK universities through the UNIVERSITY GRANTS COMMITTEE. (Primary and secondary education in Wales are the responsibility of the SECRETARY OF STATE FOR WALES; the whole of Scottish non-university education is that of the SECRETARY OF STATE FOR SCOTLAND; and there is a separate Department of Education in Northern Ireland.)

The DES is headed by a SECRETARY OF STATE supported by

a Minister of State and two Parliamentary Under-Secretaries of State. It formulates general policy and controls the broad allocation of resources for education but does not administer schools or colleges and has little direct influence on CURRICULUM. It works in co-operation with the LOCAL EDUCATION AUTHORITIES which control about 85% of the total public expenditure on education, though they can recover about two-thirds of this from the government.

Department of Health, Education and Welfare (US) Former government department with federal responsibility for education through OFFICE OF EDUCATION. Replaced by a cabinet-level DEPARTMENT OF EDUCATION, with its own Secretary of Education, in 1979.

dependent variable In a statistical study, the VARIABLE in whose VALUES we are expecting to see changes as a result of changes we have made or observed in the values of some other variable (the INDEPENDENT VARIABLE). For instance, we might ask how the amount of pocket-money children get (the dependent variable) varies with their age (the independent variable).

deprogramming (US) Techniques used on teenage children, on behalf of parents who believe they have been subjected to BRAIN-WASHING by some unacceptable religious or mystical cult. The intention is to rid them of their new-found beliefs.

depth psychology Forms of psychology related to PSYCHOANALYSIS that centre around the understanding and unconscious motivations and feelings.

deputy head A senior teacher who deputises for the HEAD-TEACHER in a school and to whom certain administrative reponsibilities may be delegated, eg for PASTORAL CARE or for CURRICULUM matters. A large school may have more than one deputy.

DES See DEPARTMENT OF EDUCATION AND SCIENCE.

deschooling The slogan of a movement initiated in the US, and spreading to the UK and elsewhere, which disapproves of organised education (ineffective, undemocratic, too expensive) and advocates its replacement by independent and co-operative learning in the community, using libraries and networks of tutors who are not necessarily trained teachers. The term and concept originated with Ivan ILLICH in his book *Deschooling Society* (1971).

descriptor Term used in INFORMATION SCIENCE for one of a small group of 'key-words' likely to occur to a student trying to seek out books or articles on a given topic. All such materials will then be listed under all such headings so as to enable the student to find them easily. (Suggested descriptors are nowadays often listed on the reverse of a book's title page.)

desegregation (US) The process of arranging for students of different race to be educated together where previously they have been in separate schools. Often called INTEGRATED EDUCATION. (Could also apply to students of different class, sex, religious faith, etc.) Can be a strongly contested process. See also BROWN DECISION.

detention Form of school punishment in which the offending pupil is required to remain at school when others are free to go home.

detention centre/home A UK establishment where young people may be detained for a short period by order of a court.

developmental tasks Term used by US psychologist, ERIK ERIKSON, for the various demands and expectations that a person must satisfy at various stages of his development through childhood to maturity. For example: learning to walk, achieving a sense of identity, and developing satisfactory relations with a PEER GROUP.

developmental testing The process of trying out teaching materials and methods on students of the type for whom they are intended. The students' responses and comments are used in detecting and rectifying unduly difficult or confusing areas in the teaching for the benefit of future students. Especially useful where the materials can be tried out cheaply before making a large investment in material that might later prove to need substantial modification. See also FORMATIVE EVALUATION.

deviance A term one might use to describe the behaviour of another person when that behaviour is significantly different from what one would expect from people of that kind (or of one's own kind).

Dewey decimal system A system for classifying books, developed in the US by Melvil Dewey and used in the majority of libraries in the US and the UK. Dewey's system divides knowledge into nine major classes (philosophy, religion, sociology, natural science, useful arts, etc) plus a tenth class for general works. Each class is then sub-divided into ten sub-divisions and the sub-divisions into a further ten, and so on. See also LIBRARY OF CONGRESS SYSTEM.

Dewey, John (1859–1952) American philosopher and EDUCA-TIONALIST who argued that education should prepare children to participate in democratic life – by basing itself on existing, real-life interests that can be seen as problematic and worthy of inquiry – using the 'scientific method' of formulating and testing and revising a hypothesis, and so enhance the wisdom and thinking ability of children. Among his books are *How We Think* (1910) and *Democracy and Education* (1916).

dextrality Preference for using the right hand (or foot, eye, ear, etc) rather than the left. Special case of LATERALITY. Contrasts with SINISTRALITY.

diagnostic teaching Teaching based on and incorporating DIAGNOSTIC TESTING.

diagnostic testing Testing a pupil's strengths and weaknesses, especially in reading and NUMBER SKILLS, with a view to providing teaching that will concentrate on what he has found difficult.

diascope The original 'magic lantern' – a device for projecting an enlarged picture on to a screen by shining light through a transparent slide.

didactic An adjective usually applied perjoratively to teaching that is thought to be excessively concerned with rather authoritarian instruction – telling students everything they are expected to know in a way that does not allow them opportunity for DISCOVERY or for making their own approach to the subject.

Dienes multi-base apparatus Wooden blocks used in the teaching of basic mathematical concepts (especially place-value) in PRIMARY SCHOOL. Children learn from manipulating the equipment on the basis of questions and set tasks, as they do also with CUISENAIRE RODS and COLOUR-FACTOR APPARATUS.

differential staffing (US) Staffing policy adopted by some large schools whereby teaching staff are expected to specialise not just in teaching a particular subject but perhaps also in just one activity among those that are normally all practised by a teacher (eg diagnosis of learning difficulties, preparation of materials, presenting of lessons, assessment of student work, etc). Intended to capitalise on the individual strengths of teachers and justify differentials in salary.

differentiation 1 A term used by US psychologist, Witkin, to refer to a DIMENSION in a person's COGNITIVE STYLE. The greater a person's tendency to notice variegation and differences in his experience (rather than seeing only amorphous wholes), the

67

higher he scores on differentiation. **2** The term may also be used in connection with attempts to individualise teaching by taking account of pupils' different needs and skills.

difficulty index   A measure of the difficulty of any particular ITEM in a test or examination, eg the percentage of candidates answering correctly or the average mark. Also known as a FACILITY INDEX. In traditional test construction an item with a very low or very high difficulty index would be omitted from revised versions of the text.

dilution   Seen by many as the inevitable consequence of employing comparatively unskilled or untrained people (dilutees) to work in a professional situation (but at comparatively low wages) and letting them do at least some of the work formerly done by skilled professionals who are consequently employed in smaller numbers. Some teachers have felt that the employment of AIDES or HELPERS might lead to the dilution of the profession.

dimension   Any attribute of PERSONALITY that may be describable, and preferably measurable, on a scale. The extremes of the scale will usually be described by opposites like: convergent/ divergent or impulsive/reflective or introvert/extrovert.

diorama   A kind of VISUAL AID made by teachers and pupils, and often seen in museums, to illustrate a scene in, eg history, geography, or natural history. It may consist of three-dimensional objects displayed against a painted background and will be viewed through a glass screen or aperture and may incorporate special lighting.

Dip HE   See   DIPLOMA OF HIGHER EDUCATION.

diploma   **1** (UK) A qualification awarded on the basis of one or two years' successful study. Usually it is at less than DEGREE level, but some diplomas are at POST-GRADUATE level. **2** (US) Students graduating from HIGH SCHOOL and from certain colleges receive a diploma.

diploma factory   See DEGREE FACTORY.

Diploma of Higher Education (**DIP HE**)   A UK qualification introduced in 1974 on the recommendation of the JAMES REPORT and awarded after a two-year course (especially to students in COLLEGES OF HIGHER EDUCATION). For some students it is a TERMINAL qualification but many are using it as a stepping stone towards a DEGREE.

direct grant school   Type of UK school not maintained by a LOCAL EDUCATION AUTHORITY but receiving funds direct from the

DEPARTMENT OF EDUCATION AND SCIENCE or from the WELSH OFFICE in return for a proportion of its places being allocated free to local children. (The Scottish equivalent is a GRANT-AIDED school.) Since 1976 the direct grant system is being phased out, the schools having to decide whether to become fully INDEPENDENT, fully MAINTAINED or to close.

direct grant system   See DIRECT GRANT SCHOOLS.

direct method   Method of foreign language teaching in which the teacher aims to use only the foreign language throughout the course. The emphasis is on pupils learning conversational skills rather than literary skill in the language.

director of education   See **chief education officer**.

discipline   **1** Pupil behaviour acceptable to teachers, and the arrangements that promote it: through rules and example, reward and punishment and/or through the fostering of mutually respectful and productive relationships. **2** A formal area of human knowledge and enquiry (eg geography, biology, engineering) systematically investigated and taught, with its own LEARNED JOURNALS, professional associations, and, no doubt, a healthy brood of SUB-DISCIPLINES.

discovery learning   Instead of being given verbal descriptions of a concept or principle, the learner is put in a position whereby he can develop the concept or arrive at the principle himself out of LEARNING EXPERIENCES that have been structured, to a greater or lesser extent, by his teacher. Advocates claim that things we find out for ourselves are usually better understood and remembered longer than things we are simply told by others. The discovery approach was recommended long ago by EDUCATIONALISTS like QUINTILIAN and underlies much work in PRIMARY SCHOOL today. Also called INQUIRY LEARNING. (Contrast with EXPOSITORY TEACHING and RECEPTION LEARNING.)

discrete variable   A statistical VARIABLE in which there is a gap (usually of 1) between one possible VALUE and the next. For example, the number of children in a class, or the number of days late for school, or the number of examinations passed. That is, there may be 32 or 33 children in a class but there cannot be any value in between (eg 32½). Contrast with CONTINUOUS VARIABLE.

discretionary grant   A grant that may be given according to the judgement of a LOCAL EDUCATION AUTHORITY (eg to students following non-degree courses at COLLEGES OF FURTHER and of HIGHER EDUCATION.) Contrasts with MANDATORY GRANT.

discrimination index A measure of the extent to which any particular ITEM in a test or examination is tackled more or less successfully by (and therefore discriminates between) candidates who do well or poorly on the test as a whole. In traditional PSYCHOMETRICS, items that did not discriminate would be omitted from revised versions of the test.

discussant (US) A person who has been nominated to initiate discussion of a speaker's formal PRESENTATION at a conference by immediately afterwards making a formal response to it.

discussion A teaching/learning approach that capitalises on the fact that a student can learn not just on his own or by listening to a teacher, but also by putting a point of view to his fellow-students and by listening to what they have to say from their experience.

dispersion Statistical term for the extent to which the observed VALUES of a VARIABLE differ in size. For example, are the examination scores dispersed over a range from 10 to 90 or did nearly all students get a score between 45 and 52?

disputation Originally developed as a form of verbal combat between philosophers in ancient Greece with two or more disputants arguing different points of view. In the mediaeval university it became a kind of ASSESSMENT technique with the student seeking academic acceptance being expected to present a prepared DISSERTATION and defend it in oral argument with prestigious scholars. The practice survives in the modern 'VIVA' or ORAL EXAMINATION.

dissenting academies (UK) Schools or colleges staffed largely by non-conformist clergymen who had lost their livings as a result of the Act of Uniformity in 1662 which demanded loyalty to the official Anglican faith. At first, the academies were clandestine and often short-lived. But, with increasing religious tolerance, they became well-established during the 18th century and many had an outstanding reputation for their broad, liberal CURRICULUM and thorough teaching.

dissertation A written report of an original investigation, usually submitted as an item for ASSESSMENT in studying for a HIGHER DEGREE, especially in the US. Although the term is used at this level in the UK also, it is used more commonly in undergraduate work. The more usual term at higher degree level is THESIS, especially in the case of a RESEARCH DEGREE.

dissonance The uncomfortable experience when two or more of a person's beliefs or attitudes are in conflict with one another. See also COGNITIVE DISSONANCE.

distance education/learning/teaching Where students and teachers meet face-to-face rarely, if at all, and communicate with one another by such means as correspondence, radio, and television. Examples of this approach are CORRESPONDENCE COLLEGES, the UK's OPEN UNIVERSITY, and Australia's radio classes for isolated children.

distractors Incorrect answer to a MULTIPLE-CHOICE QUESTION that will nevertheless seem plausible to students who do not know the correct answer (and so will distract them from it).

distributed (spaced) practice The learning of a new skill by practice spaced out over a period of time with other activities intervening. Sometimes thought preferable to MASSED PRACTICE – the same total amount of practice but done at once with no breaks for other activity.

distribution Statistical term for the pattern of values obtained in measuring or recording some VARIABLE, eg the heights of children in a class, or the number of children in each class in a school.

divergent thinking Thinking or learning style capable of producing many solutions to open-ended problems that have no single correct answers. (Contrasts with CONVERGENT THINKING.)

diverger A person who tends to be better at producing many solutions to open-ended problems than at solving problems that have a single correct answer. (Contrasts with CONVERGER.)

divisional education officer (UK) The education official responsible for implementing the policies of the LOCAL EDUCATION AUTHORITY within a DIVISION.)

divisions (UK) Some of the larger LOCAL EDUCATION AUTHORITIES divide their geographical region into areas or divisions for administrative convenience.

doctorate or doctor's degree A HIGHER DEGREE ranking above the MASTER's degree and normally awarded after two or three years' research reported in a doctoral DISSERTATION or THESIS. The most common doctorate is the Ph D (Doctor of Philosophy), which can be awarded for research in any subject (not just philosophy). Sometimes doctorates are awarded as HONORARY DEGREES or on the basis of distinguished scholarly publications. See also HIGHER DOCTORATE.

domestic science See HOME ECONOMICS.

dominative teaching   Similar to AUTHORITARIAN TEACHING.

don   (UK) Derived from the Spanish title of rank, the term has been applied to FELLOWS of OXBRIDGE colleges since the mid-17th century and is often used nowadays (in the popular press at least) to refer to any university teacher.

dormitory   **1** In the UK, a room within which several pupils or students sleep. **2** In the US, not a room but a building (like a hall of residence or hostel) in which students sleep, though not necessarily more than one or two to a room.

Dotheboys Hall   The PRIVATE SCHOOL, run by Mr Squeers, portrayed by Charles Dickens in *Nicholas Nickleby*, whose name is now used (generically) to characterise any such fee-paying school that exploits its pupils and their parents' purses, by providing a worthless form of education, together perhaps with insufficient food and comfort.

double first   A UK HONOURS DEGREE in which the graduate has studied two main subjects and been graded first class in each.

double period   Two adjacent PERIODS on the school TIMETABLE allocated to the same subject so that pupils can spend longer on it, without interruption, than they do on the majority of subjects. Especially useful when much of the time may be taken up with pupils changing clothes or moving equipment at the beginning and end of the LESSON (as in, for example, art, drama and games).

Down's syndrome   An abnormal physical and mental condition, more common in the children of older rather than younger mothers, and characterised by flattened features, stubby fingers and mental RETARDATION. The condition is named after the 19th century physician who first described it, but is also known (offensively to many people) as mongolism. It is now thought to be associated with chromosomal abnormalities.

drama in education   The emphasis has shifted from the public performance of published plays by a small group of children (largely for the prestige of the school) towards the general participation by all children in the classroom dramatisation of scenes and incidents and ideas in various subjects as a means of creative expression and imaginative growth through role-playing and identification with others.

Draw-a-man Test   A test of intellectual maturity for 3 – 18 year olds in which the child is asked to draw human figures and his results compared with NORMS for children of his age.

Dr Barnardo's Homes   (UK) A child-care organisation established in the second half of the 19th century and now providing residential homes for children who are orphaned or otherwise in need.

dress code   (US) School regulations governing personal appearance of students, eg acceptable hair-length, clothing, etc.

drill   The name once used for PHYSICAL EDUCATION and still used (especially in military circles) for repetitive practice of some physical or mental operation that has to become automatic, eg rifle-drill or the multiplication tables.

drive   Seen by some psychologists (eg HULL) as a motivational force impelling a person to act. Primary drives (like hunger and sex) are basic to survival. Secondary drives (eg the drive to acquire money or power) are acquired by learning – that is, by learning that they enable one to satisfy primary drives. (See MOTIVATION.)

drive reduction theory   Proposed by the psychologist HULL, it suggests that all behaviour is motivated by primary or secondary DRIVES towards certain goals. Reaching the goal causes the drive to be reduced and the behaviour ceases.

drop-out   A person drops out, and becomes a drop-out, by failing to complete a course of study (or, by extension, some other social obligation).

dual system   The system of UK education that was established by the EDUCATION ACT OF 1870 and consisted of two types of school: the secular, non-denominational schools provided by the SCHOOL BOARDS (now the LOCAL EDUCATION AUTHORITIES) and the VOLUNTARY SCHOOLS, usually operated by denominational bodies.

Duke of Edinburgh's Award   A scheme that has been in operation since 1956 to encourage a wide variety of leisure activities among young people between the ages of 15 and 18 years of age. It originated in the UK but has since been adopted in more than 40 other countries. The aim is to encourage serious sustained effort in developing and using talents in the areas of public service, pursuits or interests, expeditions, and physical fitness.

dull   Term used of a child who is not only slow to learn but also so limited in INTELLIGENCE that even special teaching will not help him become a normally bright adult

dunce   Referring to a child who has failed abysmally in schoolwork, the word is rarely used in school nowadays but is still seen in newspaper cartoons and the like where the unfortunate child is depicted standing 'in the corner' facing away from his class-mates and wearing the dunce's cap.

Dunelm Latin abbreviation representing Durham University, England.

Dunning Report 1977 A UK REPORT on ASSESSMENT at 16-plus in Scotland; it recommended a revision of the SCOTTISH CERTIFICATE OF EDUCATION to allow an overlapping system incorporating both INTERNAL and EXTERNAL ASSESSMENT for pupils of all abilities. See also MUNN AND DUNNING PROPOSALS.

Durkheim, Emile (1858–1917) French sociologist and EDUCATIONALIST and originator of what is now the DISCIPLINE of sociology of education. Major books include *Moral Education* and *Education and Sociology*.

dyad Two people capable of communicating with one another, eg parent and child, or tutor and student.

dyslexia A modern term associated with the problem once known as 'word blindness', that occurs in children with no apparent physical or mental intellectual handicap, yet who have severe learning difficulties, especially in reading and spelling. Dyslexic children (and adults) may, for instance, confuse the order of letters in a simple word or words in a sentence, and may be prone to MIRROR-WRITING. Experts differ as to how widely dyslexia is spread among school-children (or whether it even exists as a condition!) and most would caution against using the term for learning difficulties that may well be attributable to other causes.

E

early adolescence The period at the beginning of ADOLESCENCE (about 11–16 years) in which the individual develops mature sexual features and becomes capable of procreation. Compare with LATE ADOLESCENCE.

earth sciences Modern term for geology and related subjects.

echolalia The name of a normal stage in a child's development when he echoes, with or without understanding, the speech of people around him. The term is also used when older children do so involuntarily to an excessive degree.

ecology   The complex system of interdependence by which the plants, animals, (and humans) in a given locality interact with their environment and one another. (Also the name of the academic DISCIPLINE concerned with such systems.)

econometrics   The application of measurement approaches (especially statistical and other mathematical concepts and techniques) to the study of economic phenomena. Plays an important role in the ECONOMICS OF EDUCATION.

economics of education   Study of the allocation of resources among educational institutions and activities, and of the returns obtained both by individuals and nations.

EDU   See EDUCATIONAL DISADVANTAGE UNIT.

education   The process of successful LEARNING (usually, but not necessarily, aided by teaching) of KNOWLEDGE, SKILLS and ATTITUDES, where what is learned is worthwhile to the learner (in the view of whoever is using the term) and usually (in contrast with TRAINING) where it is learned in such a way that the learner can express his own individuality through what he learns and can subsequently apply it, and adapt it flexibly, to situations and problems other than those he considered in learning it. Also, 'education' is used to refer to the product of the above process, and to the academic DISCIPLINE studying the nature of the process and its outcomes.

Education Act 1870   (UK) The great Elementary Education Act which first made ELEMENTARY EDUCATION compulsory for all young children in England and Wales. It set up SCHOOL BOARDS and allowed for school-building to be financed out of local rates. An equivalent act for Scotland followed in 1872.

Education Act 1902   (UK) The Act that introduced a coordinated national system of education for England and Wales. It abolished the SCHOOL BOARDS and laid upon the elected councils of local government the responsibility of acting as LOCAL EDUCATION AUTHORITIES in providing ELEMENTARY EDUCATION or, in the case of the larger authorities, ELEMENTARY, SECONDARY and POST-SECONDARY EDUCATION (including TECHNICAL EDUCATION and TEACHER-TRAINING).

Education Act 1944   (UK) Some thirty education acts had been passed in England and Wales since the EDUCATION ACT OF 1870, but the 1944 Act (the Butler Act) was perhaps the most important. The Act established the three-part system of PRIMARY, SECONDARY and FURTHER EDUCATION, and laid the duty on parents to ensure that their children received an 'efficient' education, though not necessarily in schools. The school-leaving age was raised from 14 to 15, and the Act stipulated that LOCAL EDUCATION AUTHORITIES should pay the teachers salaries to be recommended by an independent committee and approved by a new Minister who would be directing national policy on education with powers to compel reluctant authorities. The Scottish equivalent followed in 1945.

Education Act 1980   (UK) Among other provisions, this Act: requires all MAINTAINED SCHOOLS to have GOVERNING BODIES, each with at least one teacher and one parent as GOVERNORS; strengthens parents' right to have their choice of school for their children respected by their LOCAL EDUCATION AUTHORITY (LEA); provides for an appeals procedure on ADMISSIONS; requires LEAs and schools to publish detailed information to help parents exercise their choice; provides for an ASSISTED PLACES SCHEME; removes the obligation of LEAs to provide school meals at a standard charge except for needy children; and makes the education of children under five (in NURSERY SCHOOLS or elsewhere) discretionary for the LEAs.

educational development   Referring to some kind of planned change (for the better, of course) within an educational system or institution. Many institutions in FURTHER and HIGHER EDUCATION have set up educational development groups comprising professional staff to engage in STAFF DEVELOPMENT, to offer advice to teaching staff on CURRICULUM DEVELOPMENT or to provide EDUCATIONAL TECHNOLOGY support, and so on.

Educational Disadvantage Unit (EDU)   Unit set up within the UK DEPARTMENT OF EDUCATION AND SCIENCE in 1971 to help investigate the needs of children thought to be educationally disadvantaged, and to ensure appropriate allocation of resources.

Educational Institute of Scotland (**EIS**)   Scotland's largest professional body and TRADE UNION for teachers.

educationalist   A term used synonymously with EDUCATIONIST to mean someone who is known in the field of education as a researcher or theoretician and enjoying greater prestige than if he were simply a teacher (which he may no longer be, or even never have been). Contrasts with EDUCATOR.

educationally subnormal (**ESN**)   In official terms, this label refers to 'pupils who, by reason of limited ability or other conditions resulting in educational retardation, require some specialised form of education wholly or partly in substitution for the education normally given in ordinary schools.' When children are considered ESN (perhaps with IQs from about 50–85) some will be given special (remedial) classes in ordinary schools while others will attend SPECIAL SCHOOLS (some of them BOARDING SCHOOLS). If the subnormality of such a child is considered 'moderate' he will be labelled ESN(M); if severe, ESN(S).

educational measurement The attempt to quantify a person's attributes or attainments or potential abilities in any area that is relevant to education, eg his intelligence, creativity, subject-matter knowledge, manual co-ordination, etc. One aspect of ASSESSMENT and of EVALUATION.

educational park (US) An arrangement suggested in the 1960s (though few have been set up) whereby a complex of schools ranging from KINDERGARTEN up to HIGH SCHOOL or JUNIOR COLLEGE, draw in students from a wider than usual area and so minimise the racial segregation and inequality of resources often associated with NEIGHBOURHOOD SCHOOLS.

educational philosophy See PHILOSOPHY OF EDUCATION.

education priority area (EPA) The PLOWDEN REPORT (1967) identified certain urban areas in the UK where education struggles under adverse conditions and recommended that such areas (EPAs) be given extra funds to help offset the deprivation suffered by pupils. An example of POSITIVE DISCRIMINATION.

educational psychology The study of children's and adolescents' individual differences (intellectual, emotional, social and physical) insofar as they have influence on a child's education; and a concern with understanding the processes of learning and with developing effective teaching approaches. The subject is researched and taught as an academic DISCIPLINE in educational institutions and is applied practically (especially in the diagnosis and remedial treatment of special learning difficulties) by educational psychologists working for LOCAL EDUCATION AUTHORITIES in schools and CHILD GUIDANCE CLINICS.

educational sociology See SOCIOLOGY OF EDUCATION.

educational technology For many people this term suggests the use of AUDIO-VISUAL AIDS in education; but, since the late 1960s, the term has referred also to the systematic design and evaluation of CURRICULA and LEARNING EXPERIENCES to suit the needs of particular groups or individual learners (probably but not necessarily involving new media). It has become the banner of a movement committed to a more rational approach to CURRICULUM DEVELOPMENT.

educational television (ETV) A term used chiefly in the US and referring to the production and transmission (by broadcasting or via closed circuit) of television programmes that are intended to be, or can be seen to be, educational, however broadly (eg documentary films). See also INSTRUCTIONAL TELEVISION.

Educational Testing Service (ETS) (US) A commercial organisation in Princeton, New Jersey enjoying a national (and world-wide) reputation for its research and practical activities in EDUCATIONAL MEASUREMENT. It provides tests and counselling services for a variety of educational and government institutions.

educational theory See **theory.**

education authority The Scottish equivalent of a LOCAL EDUCATION AUTHORITY in England and Wales.

education committee (UK) Each LOCAL EDUCATION AUTHORITY is required to set up an education committee to which it may delegate all its powers relating to education (eg the organising and administering of MAINTAINED SCHOOLS), apart from the power to borrow money or levy rates. The majority of members are elected councillors.

Education Index (US) A publication indexing subjects, authors and titles of articles published in journals in education and related areas. Equivalent of BRITISH EDUCATION INDEX.

educationist See EDUCATIONALIST.

education officer (UK) An administrator working for a LOCAL EDUCATION AUTHORITY under the direction of the CHIEF EDUCATION OFFICER or director of education. Roughly equivalent to the US assistant SUPERINTENDENT OF SCHOOLS. (The term may also be used elsewhere, eg in industry or commerce, for an executive with responsibility for educational and training matters.)

education permanente See CONTINUING EDUCATION and PERMANENT EDUCATION.

education shop A kind of citizen's advice bureau catering for parents, and giving advice on schools and educational problems from an ordinary shop-front in local high streets. The idea is that parents should be able to pop in casually for advice while doing the shopping.

education voucher See VOUCHER SYSTEM.

education(al) welfare officer Once known as the truant-catcher, or attendance officer, this person is employed by a LOCAL EDUCATION AUTHORITY to oversee the general welfare of school children (of which persistent TRUANCY will be simply one aspect).

He is a kind of educational social worker responsible for a group of schools. The nearest US equivalent is the ATTENDANCE OFFICER.

educator Someone active in education who may or may not carry out research and make public pronouncements on the subject but who regards himself primarily as, and still practices as, a teacher. Contrast with EDUCATIONALIST/EDUCATIONIST.

effect, law of See LAW OF EFFECT.

EFL The abbreviation used by people teaching 'English as a foreign language' – either to foreign students in the UK or in overseas countries. In the US, ESL is used (English as a Second Language). See TESL and TEFL.

Eg-rul The abbreviation for 'examples followed by rule' – a teaching approach advocated by some practitioners of PROGRAMMED LEARNING, suggesting that the student should be presented with examples (egs) of the rule (rul) or principle he is expected to learn before he encounters a verbalisation of the principle itself. (An INDUCTIVE approach.) Contrast with RUL-EG.

eidetic imagery The recall of a very detailed 'picture' of some sensory experience. Sometimes called 'photographic memory'. Rarely found after adolescence.

elaborated code Term used by BERNSTEIN to refer to one of his two LANGUAGE CODES. The elaborated code is richer, more logical, and more explicit than the RESTRICTED CODE and allows for the learning of more complex relationships among concepts. Bernstein suggests that MIDDLE-CLASS children learn both codes while WORKING-CLASS children suffer by learning only the restricted code.

elective course (or **optional course**) A course chosen freely by the student from among a number of alternatives. Contrasts with a REQUIRED COURSE.

Elementary and Secondary Education Act 1965 (US) Very important legislation which, among other provision, initiated the largest ever programme aimed at the educational development of children from low-income families by distribution of government funds to areas with high proportions of such families. (An example of POSITIVE DISCRIMINATION.)

elementary education **1** A term once used in the UK to describe the patchwork of educational provision, of a rather basic and inferior kind, for children of poor parents (some provided by voluntary bodies, some funded out of local rates) that had developed over the centuries (particularly the 18th and 19th) and, by the time of the EDUCATION ACT OF 1870, catered for pupils between the age of 5 and 13 years. The concept became obsolescent with the EDUCATION ACT OF 1944 which distinguished between PRIMARY EDUCATION (up to the age of about eleven) and SECONDARY EDUCATION which the Act introduced for all older pupils. **2** In the US, the term continues in use for what is called PRIMARY EDUCATION in the UK.

Elementary Education Act 1870   See EDUCATION ACT 1870.

elementary school   In the US, a GRADE SCHOOL, for pupils between 6 and 12 years – roughly equivalent to a UK PRIMARY SCHOOL. (The term was used in the UK, prior to the EDUCATION ACT OF 1944, for a school taking children between the ages of 5 and 13.)

Eleven-plus   (UK) The examination taken by children at about the age of 11, the results of which were used in allocating children between secondary GRAMMAR SCHOOLS (about 20–25% of the age-group) and SECONDARY TECHNICAL or SECONDARY MODERN schools. With the spread of COMPREHENSIVE schools, the examination is now almost defunct. In Scotland, prior to the establishment of a comprehensive system, the equivalent was twelve-plus.

elitist education   Education based on the assumption (whether explicit or not) that a minority group within society, usually with specially acclaimed academic talents, should attract a disproportionately large share of educational expenditure – either because they are intrinsically more worthy or because greater returns to the community can be expected by the enhancement of such special talents and the leadership and innovation that will ensue.

elocution   See SPEECH TRAINING.

embedded figures test   Test of a person's ability to make visual discrimination between geometrical shapes and the backgrounds that camouflage them.

emergency training   (UK) The intensive one-year training of teachers (about 35,000) between 1945 and 1951 made necessary by the effects of war and the raising of the school-leaving age in the EDUCATION ACT OF 1944.

emeritus professor (or **professor emeritus**)   From the Latin, merere, 'to merit'. The honorary title awarded to certain senior academics who have retired from salaried teaching and research.

empirical knowledge/methods   Relating to knowledge gained solely through trial, experiment and practical experience, and INDUCTION therefrom. Contrasts with A PRIORI knowledge.

Employment and Training Act 1973   This UK Act established the MANPOWER SERVICES COMMISSION, with what are now its Employment Services Division and TRAINING SERVICES DIVISION. The Act amended the INDUSTRIAL TRAINING ACT 1964 by bringing the INDUSTRIAL TRAINING BOARDS under the Training Services Division but giving it responsibility for more industries than had been covered by the boards.

enabling objectives/skills   OBJECTIVES that must be attained by a student to enable him to achieve certain subsequent objectives. For example, a pupil cannot attain the objective of being able to divide one number by another without having first mastered the ability to subtract.

enactive (mode of) representation   See BRUNER'S MODES.

encoding   Any process whereby one form of behaviour or experience is transformed into words, pictures, symbols, gestures, etc, from which other people can extract a meaning. (See DECODING.)

encounter group   A group activity intended to expose each participant to how he is perceived by others and to provide release from various inhibitions such as fear of bodily contact and verbal disclosure.

endowed schools   UK schools (chiefly GRAMMAR SCHOOLS) founded by benefactors since early times. Winchester (1382) and Eton (1440) are two of the earliest. Most of the famous PUBLIC SCHOOLS began life as endowed grammar schools catering for a local population.

endowment   The flow of private or commercial funds into the establishment or maintenance of educational institutions. In the UK, such funds largely went into schools prior to the last quarter of the 19th century but, since then, the bulk has gone to FURTHER and HIGHER EDUCATION (eg to the CIVIC UNIVERSITIES).

enquiry-based course/activity   Studies centred around students' attempts to solve a particular problem or investigate a real problem, usually through some kind of individual or group research PROJECT.

enquiry/inquiry learning   See DISCOVERY LEARNING.

enrichment programme   Activity designed to provide a more stimulating environment for children considered to be CULTURALLY DEPRIVED or, in general, more stimulating or stretching activities for *any* children (perhaps even for particularly bright, rapid learners).

enrolment The process of registering as a student at a school, college or university or the total number of students enrolled.

entry behaviour/knowledge/skills **1** Whatever pre-requisite knowledge or abilities the teacher expects students to have prior to starting a particular course or LEARNING EXPERIENCE if they are to be able to profit from it. **2** The knowledge and abilities they actually do have on starting it.

entry qualifications/requirements Whatever is required of a would-be student by selective educational institutions as a condition of entry, eg age, sex, PRE-REQUISITE ABILITIES, relevant experience, and, especially, academic CREDENTIALS acquired through prior courses.

entry test A test that students might be expected to take prior to embarking on a course or other learning experience, and designed to ascertain whether they have the prerequisite ENTRY BEHAVIOUR.

environment A term much used in educational discussion (eg in talk of a child's intellectual growth through interaction with his environment). It refers to things, events and people in the real world around the child that he might perceive or that might have some effect on him.

environmental studies/science An INTER-DISCIPLINARY study of man's social and physical surroundings which seeks to determine his relationships with them. It may utilise concepts and METHODOLOGIES from, eg history, geography, biology, literature, architecture, town planning, medicine, and so on.

environment-based learning A loosely-used term most likely referring to going out of school to learn (eg local history from examining buildings, or botany by studying an area of local woodland).

EPA See EDUCATIONAL PRIORITY AREA.

epidiascope A projector combining the capabilities of both DIASCOPE and EPISCOPE.

episcope Also called the OPAQUE PROJECTOR, this is a device for projecting an enlarged picture onto a screen by reflecting light off an object (rather than through a transparent slide); so paper diagrams or maps or photographs and three-dimensional objects such as plant specimens or fossils can be magnified for class discussion.

equal addition method One of two basic methods of subtraction. It works by adding an equal amount to both the numbers concerned. For example, instead of 55 − 17 = ?, we may think of (50 + 15) − (20 + 7) = ? See also DECOMPOSITION METHOD.

equalisation (US) A principle of subsidies embodying the belief that funds for education should be collected from communities that can best afford them and spent in whichever communities have children and schools in most need.

Erasmus (1466–1536) RENAISSANCE scholar who travelled widely in Europe, teaching and writing. His works on education embody the HUMANIST spirit of his time and are chiefly concerned with the duties of parents and tutors.

Erhard Seminar Training (**est**) A commercially-promoted form of GROUP THERAPY, arising out of the HUMAN POTENTIAL MOVEMENT. A group of people confined together for several hours are supposed to achieve significant new understanding of themselves through being humiliated by the seminar-leader.

ERIC (US) Abbreviation for Educational Resources Information Centres. A system of clearing houses for information relating to all aspects of education, sited mainly in universities around the US, and allowing LITERATURE SEARCHES via computer.

Erikson, Erik (Born 1902). A US psychologist known especially for his theories of IDENTITY FORMATION in young people. See his *Identity, Youth and Crisis* (1968) and *Childhood and Society* (1965).

error analysis An examination of where, how and why errors commonly occur in the performance of a particular task or activity (eg long division or logical argumentation) with a view to teaching in such a way that the student avoids making those errors.

error rate Term used in PROGRAMMED LEARNING for the percentage of a student's responses that are incorrect over a given sequence of questions; or, similarly, the percentage of students making incorrect responses to any given question.

Esalen Training (or **courses**) Training directed towards SELF-ACTUALISATION (involving ENCOUNTER GROUPS and the like), as developed at the Esalen Institute in California in the 1960s – part of the HUMAN POTENTIAL MOVEMENT.

ESL Abbreviation used by teachers of English as a second language. See also TEFL and TESL.

ESN See EDUCATIONALLY SUBNORMAL.

Esperanto An ARTIFICIAL LANGUAGE created from words common to the chief European languages by the Polish philologist,

Zamenhof (1859–1917), as a means to international communication and understanding. (The word means 'one who hopes'.)

essay An extended piece of non-fictional student writing – several hundred words or more – usually on a topic or question set by a teacher or examiner and calling upon the writer to show his ability at analysing the topic, organising his ideas on it, and conducting an argument or explaining matters clearly. Also called a COMPOSITION, or in the US, a THEME or TERM PAPER. Essay questions are easy to set, and test important skills; but they are difficult to assess fairly because different teachers can have quite different opinions of the merits of any given essay. (See RELIABILITY.)

essentialism A doctrine in education that maintains there is an essential body of knowledge and skill that all pupils should learn, through hard work and rigorous mental discipline, and to a high standard of attainment.

est See ERHARD SEMINAR TRAINING.

ethnocentric Indicates an approach or viewpoint in which other cultures are appraised by comparison with one's own. Can militate against objectivity, especially if applied unconsciously.

ethnology The comparative study of human CULTURES including, in the work of some modern ethnologists, the culture of a school or other educational organisations.

ethnomethodology A branch of sociology concentrating on the routine activities of everyday social life (eg classroom interactions or conversations between friends) and laying prime stress on the way the participants interpret the situation and convey explicit or implicit meanings and messages to one another.

ethos The prevailing spirit (tone, sentiments, mood) of an institution. For example, the POLYTECHNIC ethos may be thought to differ in significant ways from the OXBRIDGE ethos; and even within an institution, two departments may differ markedly in ethos.

etiology See AETIOLOGY.

ETV See EDUCATIONAL TELEVISION.

eurhythmics A combination of physical and musical education developed in the late 19th century by Emile Jacques-Dalcroze, uniting the appreciation and interpretation of music (especially where it involves complex rhythms) with bodily movement intended to help the learner experience the music physically.

evaluation In the UK, this term tends to mean identifying the effects and judging the effectiveness of some LEARNING EXPERIENCE (eg a lesson) or of a course, or of a complete CURRICULUM. In the US, the term is also used for what we in the UK call ASSESSMENT (of student attainment). Assessing student attainment before and after the learning experience might be an important part of evaluation but so too are interviews with teachers, administrators, students, parents and other people in the community, critical analysis of teaching materials, observation of teaching and learning activity, and so on. Some evaluators incline more towards a quantitative approach while others emphasise the qualitative aspects. Some will combine the two approaches. See AGRO-BOTANY EVALUATION and ILLUMINATIVE EVALUATION.

evening classes Informal term for courses of FURTHER EDUCATION attended mainly by adults in the evenings. See EVENING INSTITUTE.

evening institute Institution supported by LOCAL EDUCATION AUTHORITY and providing EVENING CLASSES in FURTHER EDUCATION for people of POST-SECONDARY age, usually using the premises of a school or college.

examination A formal ASSESSMENT of a student's learning, used particularly at the end of a course. Although many teachers bemoan the distorting influence exams can have on teaching and learning, when used wisely they can assess student qualities that would otherwise go unobserved. An examination usually involves one or more of the following features: all students are given the same task to perform (perhaps with some degree of choice); its precise nature will not be made clear until the moment they begin upon it; they will be given a time-limit and they will not be allowed to consult references or one another; they will perform in the presence of an INVIGILATOR or PROCTOR; and they will be expected to experience some sense of urgency or stress. Nowadays, many examinations relax one or more of these restrictions (eg students may be given advance notice of the questions or may be allowed to use certain reference materials), but the last-mentioned feature usually remains.

exceptional children (US) Pupils with unusual educational needs – eg because they are specially GIFTED or because they are mentally or physically handicapped.

exchange programme Arrangements for the temporary exchange of students or teachers between one country and another.

exclusion A term used in UK MAINTAINED SCHOOL for the temporary barring of a pupil from school, sometimes as a form of disciplinary action that might elsewhere be called SUSPENSION and sometimes for other reasons (eg because the child has an infectious disease).

exeat Permit granted to a pupil to allow him to be absent from school at a time when he would normally be expected to be there (eg for an overnight absence from a BOARDING SCHOOL).

exercise A task designed to encourage a student to develop or apply a new concept or principle or to practice a new skill. Traditional TEXTBOOKS have lengthy passages of EXPOSITORY TEACHING followed by a block of exercises based on the preceding material. More recent approaches apply the SELF-INSTRUCTIONAL approaches developed in PROGRAMMED LEARNING, and build the exercises one at a time into the teaching passages of the text.

exercise book A book of lined paper in which a pupil writes his EXERCISES (essays, calculations, etc).

exercise, law of See LAW OF EXERCISE.

exhibition **1** Display of items which may have educational significance. **2** A SCHOLARSHIP (not of the greatest monetary value) awarded to students attending certain colleges or universities (or some fee-paying schools).

Exon Latin abbreviation representing Exeter University, England.

expectancy The type and level of performance expected by a teacher from a child on the basis of that teacher's experience of that child or of others whom he believes (rightly or wrongly) to be similar. Such predictions, even when ill-founded, can influence the way the child actually does perform. See PYGMALIAN EFFECT and SELF-FULFILLING PROPHECY.

experiential learning It is not, of course, possible to learn except from experience of some kind, but the kind referred to here is usually that of work and everyday life rather than academic study. Used particularly in the US in awarding a student LIFE EXPERIENCE CREDITS.

experimental group The group in an experiment for whom the experimental VARIABLE is manipulated (eg members of the group may be given a drug). The results are compared with what has happened to a comparable CONTROL GROUP who were not given the experimental treatment.

experimental psychology An approach to psychology using laboratory techniques to investigate various aspects of human behaviour such as perception, learning and memory. Plays a considerable part in EDUCATIONAL PSYCHOLOGY.

expository teaching When the teacher relies on telling his pupils or students all he believes they need to know – leading to RECEPTION LEARNING.

expository writing EXPOSITORY TEACHING in print.

expressive objectives The US art educator, Eliot Eisner, distinguishes between *instructional* OBJECTIVES (the immediate goals of teaching) and *expressive* OBJECTIVES (the diverse ways in which different students will be able to express themselves as a result of having attained the basic instructional objectives.) Thus we might distinguish between learning to speak Swahili and being able to say something interesting in it.

expressive attitudes Displayed in actions and decisions taken with a view to satisfying emotional needs rather than gaining some EXTRINSIC REWARDS. Contrasts with INSTRUMENTAL ATTITUDES.

expulsion The permanent casting out from an educational institution of a pupil or student whose conduct is unacceptable. To be expelled (or, in the universities, SENT DOWN), is the ultimate punishment and milder breaches of DISCIPLINE are likely to be punished more mildly by SUSPENSION (known in some universities as RUSTICATION). In the UK MAINTAINED SCHOOL system, the term expulsion is not officially used (except for pupils beyond the school leaving age) since, if one school objects to keeping a certain pupil any longer, the LOCAL EDUCATION AUTHORITY has a legal duty to find another school in the district that is willing to take him. See also EXCLUSION and SUSPENSION.

extended day Experimental scheme introduced by ILEA and some other LOCAL EDUCATION AUTHORITIES whereby, in some SECONDARY SCHOOLS, pupils can stay on after normal school hours to continue their studies or engage in leisure activities, under supervision of members of the school's teaching staff (who may receive additional payment).

extension services/courses (US) The extension of teaching by a college or university to adults other than its students following UNDERGRADUATE and GRADUATE courses, and usually away from the CAMPUS. Comparable to EXTRA-MURAL teaching in the UK.

external degree A degree obtained by a student who has not prepared for it at the university whose ASSESSMENT procedure he has satisfied, but who has studied on his own (perhaps with the help of a CORRESPONDENCE COLLEGE or at another institution). In the UK, only London University awards external FIRST DEGREES, but HIGHER DEGREES are awarded by many institutions without the requirement of studying in them.

external examination An examination either set or marked (or both) by an institution other than those preparing students for it. For example, the EXTERNAL DEGREE examinations of London University, the examining boards for GCE and CSE and (in the US) the COLLEGE ENTRANCE EXAMINATION BOARD.

external examiner/assessor An examiner or assessor who is not on the staff of the institution whose students are being assessed.

external study Study through a course organised via correspondence or some other means by a college or university.

extinction The process through which, after a period during which no reinforcement has been given, a learned response ceases to be elicited by a stimulus that once elicited it.

extra-curricular activities Activities of a generally educational nature that are not thought to merit a slot in the official school TIMETABLE but which teachers have nevertheless traditionally been willing to spend time on with interested pupils out of school hours, eg drama, music, minority-interest sports, chess, stamp-collecting, photography, etc.

extra-district pupils Pupils living in the area of one LOCAL EDUCATION AUTHORITY but, for some reason, attending school in that of another authority. Authorities reimburse one another in such cases.

extra-mural teaching Teaching organised by a special department of a college or university for adults who are not its regular undergraduate or post-graduate students.

extrinsic motivation The motivation to perform some task, or to engage in some activity, not for its own sake but in order to gain some reward that depends on it, eg money, the approval of a teacher, or a valued CREDENTIAL. (Contrast with INTRINSIC MOTIVATION.)

extroversion A personality DIMENSION investigated by UK psycholigst H J EYSENCK, in which a person is characterised as outgoing, sociable, uninhibited, carefree and impulsive, with interests directed chiefly towards the outside world of things and events. Contrast with INTROVERSION.

Eysenck H J (Born 1916) A British psychologist who is an authority on INTELLIGENCE and PERSONALITY, has developed many psychological tests, and has a special interest in racial and genetic differences in intelligence. See his *The Structure of Human Personality* (1970). He is also a considerable populariser, eg see his *Know Your Own Personality* (1975).

F

facilitator   A person whose task it is to encourage the productive interaction of other people in a group situation, eg a discussion group or a CURRICULUM DEVELOPMENT team. His role is not to provide the expertise but to channel and enhance the expertise of others. (Similar meaning to the French term ANIMATEUR.)

facility index   See DIFFICULTY INDEX.

factor analysis   Statistical technique for extracting a few basic factors that underlie a larger number of VARIABLES, starting from the CORRELATION between those variables. Factor analysis can suggest answers to questions like: do examination markers make quite separate assessments of different aspects of their candidates' essays or are all their assessments coloured by their assessment of one aspect only (eg of handwriting or political bias)?

faculty   **1** A college, polytechnic or university department or group of departments, eg Faculty of Law or of Science. **2** In the US, the teaching staff of a school, college or university.

faculty evaluation   (US) Appraisal of the professional performance of teaching staff in a college or university by senior staff and/or students, and/or a specially appointed evaluator.

faculty psychology   An outmoded school of thought in psychology which sought to explain mental phenomena by postulating the existence of agencies or faculties (such as memory or imagination) as if they were entities capable of being made more effective through specific exercise.

faculty-student ratio   US equivalent of STAFF-STUDENT RATIO.

fading   **1** A term from PROGRAMMED LEARNING (but applicable to many teaching situations) meaning the systematic cutting down on the amount of help given to a student in the form of CUES and PROMPTS until he is able to solve the relevant problem unaided. **2** The weakening of the association between a STIMULUS and its related RESPONSE due to insufficient REINFORCEMENT.

fagging   A dying PUBLIC SCHOOL practice whereby the young boys (usually first year pupils) are expected to perform menial tasks (like making tea and cleaning shoes) for the seniors.

failure rate   The percentage of students who fail to pass an examination or otherwise do not perform satisfactorily in the overall ASSESSMENT for a course. Often taken by the unwary as an indicator of the level of ACADEMIC STANDARDS in an institution: however, it may have ensured a low failure rate by seeing that only candidates who are virtually certain to succeed are allowed to get as far as taking the examination.

falling rolls   Because of falling birth-rates in earlier years, the number of children 'on roll' in UK SECONDARY SCHOOLS is expected to fall by one-third in the decade beginning in 1980. Already, falling rolls (allied with spending cuts) are resulting in schools shrinking in size, are squeezing certain subjects out of the CURRICULUM, and are leading to CLOSURES and amalgamations between schools.

fall semester   (US) The first half of the ACADEMIC YEAR, beginning in the fall (autumn).

false consciousness   Term used by KARL MARX to denote the ideas and beliefs held by people who are exploited by others. These ideas and beliefs are said to hide their true situation from them and to be manipulated by the exploiters in support of an IDEOLOGY that enables them to maintain their power.

family day care   (US) See DAY CARE.

family grouping   An alternative term for VERTICAL GROUPING – an arrangement whereby children in many PRIMARY SCHOOLS (especially in the INFANT years) are placed in classes with perhaps a two or three year age-range. The idea is that just as younger children in a family will learn from their older siblings, so the younger pupils will learn faster (socially as well as academically) in the company of more experienced pupils.

father-figure   A term borrowed from PSYCHOANALYSIS to mean a person (or, by extension, a group or movement or school of thought) to whom someone looks with respect and perhaps dependency (sometimes tinged with awe or fear), acknowledging him as an authority and as a source of wisdom and inspiration.

farm institute   A FURTHER EDUCATION college offering courses in agriculture, horticulture and related subjects.

feasibility study   A preliminary study undertaken prior to some intended project, to help determine whether that project is practicable or worth attempting.

FE UK abbreviation for FURTHER EDUCATION. (Like HE for HIGHER EDUCATION and as in 'FE/HE colleges'.)

federal university A university in which academic and financial issues involving the whole institution are managed centrally, by a SENATE or ACADEMIC BOARD and by a COURT or COUNCIL, but with constituent colleges which are otherwise virtually autonomous. The University of London and the University of Wales are two UK examples. (In the US, the term might mean a university controlled by central, federal government, rather than by the states; but, at present, there are none.)

feedback A term borrowed from CYBERNETICS which, in an educational context, means 'knowledge of results' or the information which a person receives about the consequences of his actions. If he is not satisfied with those consequences he may take new action. Thus the student receives feedback, for example, when he has an ESSAY marked. The teacher receives feedback when he listens to the comments of his students or considers their test results. Either can decide to study or teach differently as a result.

feedback classroom A classroom or LECTURE THEATRE electrically wired up in such a way that each student can immediately inform the teacher of his answer to a MULTIPLE-CHOICE QUESTION. The idea behind this is that a lecturer can improve the quality of his presentations by inserting occasional questions that test students' grasp of what he has said so far and then decide whether to review, digress or go on to the next main point on the basis of the pattern of answers which he reads off the display unit on his CONSOLE. See also COSFORD CUBE.

fellow **1** Originally (and still) a senior member of an OXBRIDGE college in which he has rooms and dining rights and with a paid teaching role in the college and perhaps another in the university. **2** The term is now also used by many colleges and universities to designate a member of the teaching or research staff whose post is financed by an outside body or who has been employed for a limited period, eg SCHOOL-TEACHER FELLOWSHIP.

fellowship **1** In the UK, the post held by a FELLOW. **2** In the US, a financial award to assist a GRADUATE STUDENT with the costs of study.

field centre/station Building with special equipment or facilities established by an educational institution or LOCAL EDUCATIONAL AUTHORITY in an area suitable for pursuing FIELD STUDIES.

field day   A day on which the pupils of one or more schools come together to compete in athletic (track and field) events.

field dependence v. independence   A DIMENSION of PERSONAL-ITY described by Witkin, measuring differences in the ability to separate parts of the perceptual field from the whole. People who 'can't see the wood for the trees' are field-dependent.

field studies/work   **1** Learning and teaching conducted in the environment outside of an educational institution (eg a geological visit to a quarry or a visit to examine local architecture). **2** The empirical information-gathering stage of a research project or survey. **3** In the US, practical experience anywhere outside the institution (eg in a lawyer's office or in a factory). A lengthy attachment might be known as an INTERNSHIP.

field trial/test   The DEVELOPMENTAL TESTING of teaching ma-terials or methods in conditions similar to those in which they will be used in their eventual, improved form. Might also be called a PILOT STUDY.

finals   **1** (UK) The examination at the end of a three or four year college or university degree course. **2** (US) The examina-tions taken at the end of each term (or semester) for the courses studied during that period.

finger painting   A technique used by young children, especially in NURSERY and INFANT SCHOOL, where they apply paint directly with their fingers to mark out shapes and patterns in wet paint that has already been spread upon the paper.

finishing school   A school or college concerned with developing in the student (probably a genteel young lady of no great intel-lectual ambitions) sufficient of what count as accomplishments in her circle to make her an acceptable marriage partner. Essen-tially a nineteenth century phenomenon, but one that is not yet totally obsolete.

Finniston Report 1980   A UK REPORT on the training and professional opportunities of engineers in industry. Made rec-ommendations for improving the quality, and making better use, of engineers through the creation of a new body to control train-ing and professional standards.

first degree   A DEGREE (eg BA or BSc) taken by a student after three or four years' study and without which (or some equivalent evidence of scholarship or relevant experience) he could not go on to study for a HIGHER (or FURTHER) DEGREE.

first school 1 The name frequently used for the first school a child goes to between the ages of five and eight or nine years, in UK areas that operate a three-stage system where the first school is followed by a MIDDLE SCHOOL and that by SECONDARY school. 2 In UK areas that do not operate a middle school system, the term may be used to mean PRIMARY SCHOOL (5 – 11 years).

fixation 1 In psychology, a person's strong attachment to a particular individual, object, erroneous belief or behaviour pattern. 2 In reading, the moments when the eyes pause while moving along a line of print and register what is written there. Poor readers need to make many more fixations per line than do good readers.

fit person order A court order (in England and Wales) committing a child to the care and protection of some fit person (which can also be the LOCAL AUTHORITY) perhaps because he has committed an offence or is beyond the control of his parents.

five point scale A commonly-used grading scale, used in ASSESSMENT of students' work, (or in tests of PERSONALITY or ATTITUDE), running from A (the top grade), through B, C and D, down to E (the lowest grade). The five points are sometimes turned into 15 by markers who think they can identify subtler distinctions among students' work and so add pluses and minuses (A+, C+, etc).

'five steps' See HERBART,

Flander's interaction analysis A system developed by US psychologist Ned Flanders for observing and classifying verbal behaviour in the classroom, using ten categories: seven for teacher-talk, two for student-talk and one for silence or confusion. Essentially it covers teacher-pupil interactions only, and is not designed to analyse communications between other pairs or within groups.

flannel board/graph A VISUAL AID consisting of a board covered with flannel or felt. When pieces of card (carrying pictures or words, for example) are backed with strips of similar material or sandpaper they will adhere to it.

flashcards A VISUAL AID used in teaching word recognition or number facts (like $7 \times 5 = 35$). Each card will have on it one word or number fact and will be displayed briefly to a pupil or group in order that they can rapidly identify and pronounce the word or complete the number statement.

Fleming Report 1944   The UK REPORT of an enquiry into how the PUBLIC SCHOOLS in England and Wales might be more closely integrated with the state system of education. It made various recommendations, including the suggestion that ASSISTED PLACES should be made available in public schools for children from MAINTAINED SCHOOLS who might benefit but whose parents would not be able to afford the full fees. However, its recommendations were not implemented.

F-level   See ADVANCED LEVEL.

flexible scheduling   An arrangement whereby class PERIODS can be lengthened, shortened, combined, or moved to other parts of the week in order to adapt to the ongoing and emerging needs and activities of a class of students.

flexi-study   A form of DISTANCE EDUCATION for part-time students organised by certain UK FURTHER EDUCATION colleges, often based on reading materials published by the NATIONAL EXTENSION COLLEGE, but using their own staff to mark students' ASSIGNMENTS and give occasional face-to-face tutorials.

flipchart   A VISUAL AID for use in teaching a group. It consists of a pad of very large sheets of paper which can be drawn or written on with a felt-tip pen or a crayon and then (because the pad is hung on an easel) each used page can be flipped-over to reveal a clean one.

flogging   Term for flagellation (or CORPORAL PUNISHMENT), much practised in PUBLIC SCHOOLS during the 19th century and still to be found (though in milder forms and under many constraints) in some UK schools today.

flow chart/diagram   A VISUAL AID showing the sequence (or sequences) of logical steps in a programme or plan of action. (See also ALGORITHM and NETWORK DIAGRAM.)

flunking   (US) Failing a course or examination. The most-used UK equivalent is PLOUGHING.

flunking out   (US) Being forced to leave an educational institution because of academic failure.

flying university   Term used of a programme of lectures and seminars arranged by academics banned from university posts in certain 'iron curtain' countries (especially Poland and Czechoslovakia). The teaching and discussion groups meet in the homes of participants and, because of official harassment, are constantly 'flying' to new venues. Also known as an underground university.

Ford Foundation (US) A foundation established in 1936 to support research and other activities in education.

form 1 The term used chiefly in SECONDARY SCHOOLS (less so in PRIMARY SCHOOLS) for a group (CLASS) of 30–40 pupils who do most or all of their work together as a group, though they may be split up by SETTING and mixed with members of other forms for certain activities (eg mathematics or foreign languages). 2 Used also to mean the whole YEAR-GROUP (eg the 3rd form or 5th form) made up of several classes. Similar to US GRADE.

formal approach/methods/teaching, etc The adjective 'formal' is likely to be applied pejoratively to teachers and systems regarded as too inflexible, authoritarian, subject- and teacher-centred, examination-bound, insensitive to pupil-contributions, and so on. Contrasts with INFORMAL APPROACH and PROGRESSIVE EDUCATION.

formal education 1 The EDUCATION a pupil or student receives under the aegis of an educational institution, as opposed to that which he acquires on his own. 2 An education in which a FORMAL APPROACH predominates.

formal operations The final stage in concept development postulated by PIAGET, and following the stage of CONCRETE OPERATIONS. It involves the ability to reason abstractly and logically about hypothetical situations. It begins around the age of 12 years and continues to develop for about three years, but is not attained to the same degree by everyone.

formal prompt A PROGRAMMED LEARNING term for a clue or hint that tells the student about the form of a RESPONSE expected from him, thereby reducing the likelihood of error. For instance, he may be told the initial letter of a word he is to provide, or how many letters it contains. Such prompting, unfortunately, tends to divert the student's attention from the meaning of what he is reading. Contrasts with THEMATIC PROMPT.

formative assessment Judging and commenting on a student's work with the prime aim of helping him to improve in his future attainments. Contrasts with SUMMATIVE ASSESSMENT where the emphasis is on recording (or reporting to other people) the student's present attainments.

formative evaluation Analysing the effects and effectiveness of new teaching materials (or a new CURRICULUM, etc) with a view to improving them for present and future students, eg through DEVELOPMENTAL TESTING. Contrasts with SUMMATIVE EVALUATION where the prime emphasis is on explaining what has happened rather than on considering how it might be improved. (In the US, formative evaluation would also include what is described above as FORMATIVE ASSESSMENT).

– form entry   As in 'four-form entry' or 'six-form entry'. A way of indicating the size of a SECONDARY SCHOOL by the number of FORMS or classes (eg of 30 pupils per form) admitted each year.

form board   A device used to test INTELLIGENCE in very young children, or in people with poor verbal skills, by requiring them to fit variously-shaped pegs or blocks into correspondingly shaped holes in a board.

form-room   (UK) The class-room which a FORM of pupils regards as its base and where it registers attendance, stores personal belongings, and so on. The US equivalent is HOME ROOM.

form teacher (or MASTER or MISTRESS)   The teacher responsible for administrative and PASTORAL matters with a particular class. In SECONDARY SCHOOLS, the FORM TEACHER may or may not be one of the class's SUBJECT-TEACHERS. (Equivalent to US HOME ROOM TEACHER.)

Forster Act 1870   See EDUCATION ACT 1870.

foster home   The home provided for a child (or children) by foster parents – adults who accept parental responsibilities for other people's children but without legal adoption.

foundation course (or **studies**)   A basic course (or set of courses), perhaps designed to prepare students for subsequent courses.

foundation governors   Members of the GOVERNING BODY of a UK VOLUNTARY SCHOOL appointed by the religious or other organisation that founded the school in order to ensure that its religious or special character is preserved.

four Rs   In addition to the generally agreed-upon 'THREE Rs' (reading, (w)riting, and (a)rithmetic) many US schools once sought to add religion as a fourth. In the UK, nowadays, (o)RACY is suggested as the fourth R. (However, in 1967, *The Fourth R* was used as the title of the Durham Report on religious education.)

four year college   (US) A college providing all four years of undergraduate teaching towards a FIRST DEGREE.

four-year junior college   (US) A JUNIOR-COLLEGE providing not only the FRESHMAN and SOPHOMORE college years but also the equivalent of the final two years in HIGH SCHOOL.

frame   **1** A unit of teaching in PROGRAMMED LEARNING, generally the stimulus material to which a student is exposed between making one response and the next. Each frame (which may consist of a few words or several paragraphs) normally confirms or comments on the student's previous response, takes the argument one step further, and calls for another response. **2** In the SOCIOLOGY OF EDUCATION, a frame is the set of constraints determining or limiting what can happen in a particular teaching situation, eg at one level the frame may include class size and availability of equipment; at a higher level it may include examinations, curriculum, and staffing policy; and at a national level it will include legal and political constraints.

fraternity   (US) Type of society or club in colleges and universities to which male students may be elected, usually in recognition of social acceptability rather than academic qualities. Their function is largely social and they often provide eating and sleeping facilities. (The equivalent organisation for women students is the SORORITY.) See also HONORARY SOCIETY.

fraternity house   (US) A building owned by a FRATERNITY and containing the eating and sleeping facilities.

free activity period/session/time   Time regularly scheduled within the PRIMARY SCHOOL day when the pupils, perhaps after having completed some set assignments, are free to choose what to do from a variety of individual or group activities.

free association   A psychoanalytic technique for uncovering conflicts and fears by having the patient report continuously on the ideas that come into his head, without censoring them. (Differs from WORD ASSOCIATION where the patient responds to a set list of words.)

free period   **1** A space on the pupil's TIMETABLE where he is not being taught and is expected, instead, to organise his own learning (eg in the library). **2** A space on the teacher's timetable where he is not scheduled to be with a class and is free to mark students' work, prepare future lessons, and catch up on administrative chores.

free place   A place awarded to a student in a fee-paying school, or in a college or university, without his having to pay any fees.

free school   Historically, a free school was simply one that did not charge fees. In the 1970s, however, in the wake of the DE-

SCHOOLING movement, the term began to refer to schools that are free from some constraint of CURRICULUM, TEACHING METHOD, social relationships, etc, that are found objectionable by their advocates. Many free schools have been set up in large towns in the UK as in other countries, and a few have lasted, usually with financial help from the LOCAL EDUCATION AUTHORITY, and cater for children who habitually TRUANT from, or otherwise show their disaffection with conventional schools. Generally, the free schools aim to be INFORMAL and PROGRESSIVE in CURRICULUM and teaching methods, and DEMOCRATIC in relationships between teachers and pupils.

free university   (US) The name chosen by disaffected students in the late 1960s and early 1970s to refer to the informal (and usually short-lived) programmes of seminars and TEACH-INS they organised for themselves in protest against, and as an alternative to, what they saw as the aridity and irrelevance of their conventional university CURRICULUM.

Freire, Paolo   (Born 1921) A Brazilian educator whose ideas, developed in teaching reading and writing to the illiterate poor people of Latin America and, at the same time, bringing them to a new awareness of themselves and their social situation and ways of transforming it, have been widely seen as relevant to the education of under-privileged groups in any culture. See his *Pedagogy of the Oppressed* (1970) and *Education for Critical Consciousness* (1975).

frequency distribution   Statistical term referring to the number of times (the frequency) each VALUE (or range of values) of a VARIABLE was recorded, eg, 3 children with IQs between 80 and 85, 6 with IQs between 85 and 90, 11 with IQs between 90 and 95, 15 between 95 and 100, 14 between 100 and 105, and so on.

fresher   A first year student at many colleges and universities. Compare the US FRESHMAN.

freshman   (US) A first year student (man or woman) at a college or university (and sometimes also in HIGH SCHOOL). In the second, third and fourth years of the typical four-year US course, the student is known as a SOPHOMORE, a JUNIOR, and a SENIOR.

Freud, Anna   (Born 1895) Daughter of SIGMUND FREUD and herself a psychoanalyst working in London since 1939. Interested in application of psychoanalytical ideas in education (see her *Introduction to Psychoanalysis for Teachers*, 1931) and in the care of very young children, especially such homeless children as those cared for in her residential day nursery during the 1939–45 war (see her *Infants without Families*, 2nd ed, 1965).

Freud, Sigmund (1856–1939) Founder of PSYCHOANALYSIS. Worked in Vienna most of his life but spent his last years in England. Freud's emphasis on the power of unconscious motivation, on its emotional rather than rational basis, and on the great importance of early childhood experience in shaping it, have all had enormous influence on child care and education during this last half century. For an outline of Freud's thinking, see David Stafford-Clark's *What Freud Really Said*, 1967, or Chapter 2 of J A C Brown's *Freud and the Post-Freudians* (1961).

Friends' schools INDEPENDENT, fee-paying SECONDARY SCHOOLS run by the Society of Friends (Quakers). There are nine such in the UK, all BOARDING SCHOOLS and all but two of them CO-EDUCATIONAL. Quaker principles lead them to express more interest in children's personal development (as compared with academic attainment) than do most schools.

frieze A wall painting or decoration running along a classroom wall (or walls) – usually a group painting, depicting themes the class is currently working on and to which each child will have contributed some of his handiwork.

Froebel, Friedrich (1782–1852) German EDUCATIONALIST who fathered the KINDERGARTEN movement. He and his followers had immense influence on the development of INFANT SCHOOLS in the UK, especially in his emphasis on encouragement rather than repression of children, on the need to build on the child's own interests and desires, and on the central importance of child activity and creative PLAY. See Evelyn Lawrence's *Friedrich Froebel and English Education* (1969).

FTEs See FULL-TIME EQUIVALENTS.

Fulbright Exchange Program (US) A system of government awards available to help US citizens studying or teaching abroad, or foreign citizens studying or teaching in the US.

full professor See PROFESSOR.

full-time equivalent (FTEs) A term used in expressing the size of the STUDENT BODY (or of the teaching staff) of an educational institution, taking into account the fact that some students (or staff) may be part-timers. Thus, if a full-time student were expected to be given 25 hours of teaching per week, and a college had 100 part-time students who, between them, received 500 hours of teaching per week, those 100 students would count as

$^{500}/_{25}$ = 20 full-time equivalents. Similarly, the total CONTACT HOURS of part-time staff can be divided by the number of contact hours expected of a full-timer, to calculate how many full-timers they are the equivalent of.

functionalism   See STRUCTURAL-FUNCTIONALISM.

functional literacy   Whatever level of skills in reading (and writing) a person needs in order to cope with everyday life. Opinions differ as to how much skill is needed, but it has been estimated that at least one million adults in the UK can read less well than the average nine-year old.

further education   The term is used in three ways in the UK and the meanings overlap: **1** Least commonly, it is used to cover all POST-SECONDARY EDUCATION; ie, same as TERTIARY EDUCATION. **2** A widely-assumed definition views further education as all post-secondary education below the academic level of HIGHER EDUCATION and leading to CERTIFICATES and DIPLOMAS rather than to DEGREES. It is chiefly technical and vocational but does include provision for continuing general education and for cultural and recreational interests. The courses are provided chiefly in colleges of FURTHER EDUCATION, TECHNICAL COLLEGES, and TERTIARY COLLEGES. **3** The 'official' view (that of the DEPARTMENT OF EDUCATION AND SCIENCE and the LOCAL EDUCATION AUTHORITIES) is that further education includes all post-secondary education other than that provided in universities, ie, broadly the MAINTAINED sector. The courses provided range from lower-level technical work to professional training (eg TEACHER EDUCATION) to degree-level work and even POST-GRADUATE studies. That is, it includes higher education as provided in POLYTECHNICS, COLLEGES/INSTITUTES OF HIGHER EDUCATION and the remaining COLLEGES OF EDUCATION, as well as the education provided by the kinds of college mentioned in **2** above.

G

g (or **g factor**)   This is the name given by the psychologist, Charles Spearman, to a postulated common factor of *general* ability which contributes to all intellectual activity and which accounts for part of a person's score on any tests of intellectual activity, be it verbal, spatial or social. (See S FACTOR).

Gagné, R. M. (Born 1916) US psychologist and an authority on types of LEARNING and the means by which they may be facilitated. See his *Conditions of Learning* (1965) and *Learning and Individual Differences* (1966).

gain score (or **ratio**) A measure of the extent to which students have benefited from a course or other learning experience. Usually calculated by subtracting the students' average score on a PRE-TEST from the average score on a POST-TEST. If this actual gain score is expressed as a fraction of the maximum gain that would have been possible, it is a GAIN RATIO.

Galton, Sir Francis (1822–1911) A British medical scientist and statistician who pioneered the measurement of individual differences among children. In doing so he fathered PSYCHOMETRICS and developed many statistical concepts still used today (in education and elsewhere). His explanation of differences in ability, however, were largely in terms of what a child had inherited from his parents; he credited far less influence to environmental factors (eg the child's diet and upbringing) than we would today.

game A teaching/learning technique in which students learn (or practice what they have already learned) by trying to achieve certain goals within the rules and structure of a game specially devised to embody the appropriate kind of learning. Students may compete with one another (either individually or in groups) or simply within the constraints of the game itself. A special variety is the SIMULATION game in which students play out a working MODEL of some real-world, human situation, eg negotiating the siting of a new airport or coping with a period of unemployment. They will be provided with background data, and with new information as the game proceeds. The game may also involve them in ROLE PLAYING.

games, organised The playing of athletic games and sports as a regular activity in the school timetable. Schools still concentrate on the major team games of football, cricket, hockey and netball, but the variety of activities (eg table-tennis, rock-climbing, cycling, rowing, squash, etc) has increased greatly in recent years.

games period A slot on the school timetable scheduled for the playing of organised GAMES.

games teacher (or **master** or **mistress**) Member of PHYSICAL EDUCATION staff responsible for supervising organised GAMES and providing coaching.

gate-keeper function 1 Examiners and assessors of students are sometimes seen as keeping (guarding) the gates leading to various desirable statuses or professions that must be denied to 'unsuitable' candidates. **2** The term is also used in MASS-MEDIA research, where editors are seen as gate-keepers controlling access to information.

gang A set of children, usually of much the same age, who think of themselves as a stable, cohesive group, probably with an acknowledged hierarchy and implicit rules for relating to one another and to other groups. An important vehicle for learning about social relationships which we tend to notice only when the NORMS of a particular gang are delinquent or otherwise run contrary to the school CULTURE.

gating Academic (particularly OXBRIDGE) equivalent of 'confined to barracks' – a disciplinary measure forbidding students to be out of their college after a certain hour in the evening.

guardianship (US) See CARE ORDER.

Gaussian curve The shape of a graph of the NORMAL DISTRIBUTION.

GCE See GENERAL CERTIFICATE OF EDUCATION.

GCSE See GENERAL CERTIFICATE OF SECONDARY EDUCATION.

Geddes axe (UK) The swingeing cuts in educational spending (including reducing teacher salaries and reducing school attendance) proposed by a committee under Sir Eric Geddes in 1922. Many of the so-called 'economies' turned out to be both counter-productive and expensive. The Geddes Axe had a pernicious effect on educational development in the UK and is still referred to, by people who recall the inter-war years, whenever education is threatened with financial cuts.

General Aptitude Test Battery (US) Battery of twelve tests designed to measure APTITUDE for various occupations or vocations. A person's results are recorded as a PROFILE and compared with standard profiles typical of people in many different occupations.

General Certificate of Education (GCE) (UK) A certificate of educational attainment which replaced the previous SCHOOL CERTIFICATE and HIGHER SCHOOL CERTIFICATE in 1951 and controls entry to FURTHER and HIGHER EDUCATION and to prestigious employment in England and Wales. Certificates are awarded on the basis of examinations aimed chiefly at school-pupils in the top 20% of the ability-range in any given subject but also taken by adults. Candidates can obtain a certificate in one or more of a wide variety of subjects. The examinations are organised by nine separate examining boards and are at two levels: ORDINARY LEVEL and ADVANCED LEVEL. An alternative examination system for rather less academic school-leavers is that of the CERTIFICATE OF SECONDARY EDUCATION. The two systems are to be combined during the 1980s.

general degree (UK) A degree awarded by a university (or some other institution of HIGHER EDUCATION) to students who have studied several subjects but only at a level which (sometimes) precludes their being awarded an HONOURS DEGREE.

genetic potential A person's inherited characteristics that set a limit to, eg, the maximum height he can reach or the level of intelligence he can attain. The extent to which he will realise his genetic potential in such areas depends on environmental factors such as diet and education.

General Certificate of Secondary Education (GCSE) One of the names proposed for a new examination for children of 16–plus in England and Wales, combining the present GENERAL CERTIFICATE OF EDUCATION and CERTIFICATE OF SECONDARY EDUCATION.

generalist A person whose interests and knowledge span a wide range of subjects. If this wide knowledge commands exceptional respect in educational circles he may be called a POLYMATH or even a RENAISSANCE MAN.

generalisation 1 Tendency for a RESPONSE learned in association with one STIMULUS to become associated with a similar stimulus (eg becoming alarmed by all snakes, or even all animals, not just the type that bit you). Similarly, one stimulus can become associated with several related responses. 2 In educational research, the act of arguing that what has been found true in one situation that has been investigated may also hold true in certain other situations (eg can teachers in other schools be expected to react to a certain CURRICULUM change in similar ways to teachers in the schools investigated?).

general science Title of a course often taught in SECONDARY SCHOOL and consisting of elements from physics, chemistry and biology.

general semantics A school of thought initiated by Alfred KORZYBSKI in *Science and Sanity* (1933) and particularly active in the US. Adherents stress the arbitrary nature of language and other symbol systems and argue that the misuse of language is a major cause of human conflict.

103

General Teaching Council for Scotland (GTC)   All teachers in Scottish MAINTAINED SCHOOLS must be registered with the Council which consists of representatives of teachers, of EDUCATION AUTHORITIES, of the churches, and nominees of the SECRETARY OF STATE FOR SCOTLAND. The Council controls conditions for entry to and training for teaching in Scotland. (Salaries and conditions of service are negotiated separately.) There is no equivalent in England and Wales.

generation gap   The difference in outlook and values sometimes found to hinder communication between people of one generation and those that precede and follow it.

Geneva School, the   A name sometimes used to indicate PIAGET and his colleagues.

genius   Usually taken to be an extremely GIFTED person of high intellectual ability who has made a uniquely creative contribution in some field of study or in some scientific or artistic activity. Some psychologists have suggested that anyone with an IQ over 140 should be considered a genius.

gentleman's degree   A 19th century OXBRIDGE term for the standard of DEGREE that might be aimed at by a gentleman – one who put most of his energies into social activities and only the necessary minimum into his studies.

Gesell, Arnold (1880–1961)   A US psychologist and pioneer of CHILD DEVELOPMENT as an observational study. See his *The First Five Years of Life* (1940) and *The Child from Five to Ten* (1946).

geoboard   A piece of learning apparatus consisting of a flat board into which is hammered a pattern of nails. Elastic bands can be stretched over the nails in various configurations, allowing the pupil experience of the properties of different geometrical shapes.

gestalt psychology   A SCHOOL of psychology originating in Germany in the early years of this century. Its central thesis is that the human brain has an in-built tendency to organise bits of experience into patterned wholes or configurations. ('Gestalt' is German for 'configuration'.) Hence, followers of the school advise against any approach to teaching that concentrates the student's attention on parts at the expense of his chance of seeing the whole. For example, in the teaching of reading they could be expected to prefer LOOK AND SAY or even SENTENCE METHODS to PHONIC METHODS. They would also warn against analysing a person's mental activities without considering how they relate to one another and to the person's whole PERSONALITY.

gestalt therapy This is a form of PSYCHOTHERAPY, sharing with GESTALT PSYCHOLOGY a commitment to wholeness of PERSONALITY. Its central concept is growth – out of the stagnation that breeds symptoms commonly regarded as neurosis and mental illness – towards an awareness of the world that results in wholeness and integrity of personality.

gifted child Usually taken to be a child of exceptional performance in academic studies or creative arts like music, painting or acting. (An exceptional soccer player would not usually qualify.) Sometimes the label is awarded on the basis of high IQ, even in the absence of exceptional performance – perhaps even in the presence of apathetic or disruptive attitudes, suggesting to some observers that the child is bored and not being sufficiently challenged. Opinion is divided as to whether or not gifted children should be educated separately from the others (the ungifted?).

Gittins Report 1967 A UK REPORT on PRIMARY EDUCATION in Wales. Many of its conclusions and recommendations were similar to those of the PLOWDEN REPORT but it differed chiefly in emphasising IN-SERVICE TRAINING for teachers, in arguing for freedom from the compulsion to include RELIGIOUS EDUCATION in the school CURRICULUM, and in favouring a fully BILINGUAL EDUCATION.

goals See AIMS.

go down, to To go down is the opposite of COMING UP and is the term used when a student leaves university on completing his studies. See also SENT DOWN.

Goodenough Draw-a-man Test See DRAW-A-MAN TEST.

Gottschaldt Figures Test Test of person's ability to sort out spatial patterns and his general cognitive insight and flexibility, especially when working under stress.

go up, to See COME UP.

governess Usually a woman of genteel upbringing but little private income who was employed to live with a wealthy family and instruct its young children in some basic skills (eg the THREE Rs) and in the social graces. Largely a nineteenth century phenomenon.

government school 1 School set up by government representatives (eg an embassy) in a foreign country for the children of its staff. 2 In many countries, simply a STATE SCHOOL funded by rates or taxes.

Government Training Centres See SKILL CENTRES.

governing body (UK) **1** The group of people (the GOVERNORS) appointed (unpaid) by a LOCAL EDUCATION AUTHORITY in England and Wales to oversee the 'general conduct and curriculum' of each of its MAINTAINED SCHOOLS (and also its maintained colleges and polytechnics). All governors are appointed by the authority (except for some, in the case of a VOLUNTARY SCHOOL, who are appointed by the foundation concerned), but must include parents and teachers (and some add senior pupils) as well as councillors and representatives of local interests. The governing body's role is to question, comment, advise and support, in close co-operation with the headteacher. In Scotland, a comparable body is a SCHOOL COUNCIL. **2** As GOVERNORS 1.

governors **1** The GOVERNING BODY of a UK MAINTAINED SCHOOL or institution of further or higher education. **2** The trustees or managers of an INDEPENDENT SCHOOL or college.

GPA See GRADE POINT AVERAGE.

grade (or **group**) **of a school** (UK) A figure, based on the number of pupils of various ages in the school, that determines not only how many teachers it may have earning the higher SCALE POST salaries, but also the size of the HEADTEACHER'S salary.

grade **1** A letter (usually from the FIVE-POINT SCALE) used after ASSESSMENT to indicate a student's level of achievement in COURSE WORK or an EXAMINATION. **2** In the US, the YEAR-GROUP of children working together at the same stage of the CURRICULUM. First grade starts at six-plus years, second grade at seven-plus and so on. Normally, grades 1–6 are in ELEMENTARY SCHOOL, grades 7–12 in the HIGH SCHOOL, (though some variation is possible). The two years of JUNIOR COLLEGE are sometimes known as grades 13 and 14. Pupils can skip a grade or be held back according to whether they reach an expected level of attainment (compare with UK STANDARDS). **3** In Scotland, the SCOTTISH CERTIFICATE OF EDUCATION has two levels, O grade and H grade.

grade card (US) Record card or report card on which student's grades are indicated at the end of a TERM, SEMESTER or ACADEMIC YEAR.

graded post (UK) Formerly a post in a school in England or Wales carrying additional salary for a teacher with some special responsibility (eg for the library). A teacher with special responsibilities might now be rewarded with a SCALE POST.

graded reader A book intended to help the pupil learn to read and aimed at a particular level (grade) of difficulty.

grade point average (GPA) (US) The average GRADE obtained over a number of school or college courses. Each letter grade has a numerical value (ie A=4, B=3, C=2, D=1, F=0); and a certain minimum GPA (eg 2.0) must be obtained in order to progress through the system and, eventually, to GRADUATE.

grade school (US) Another name for ELEMENTARY SCHOOL (age range 6–11). Compare with UK PRIMARY SCHOOL.

gradient of difficulty See INCLINE OF DIFFICULTY.

'grading on the curve' Grading system whereby teachers allocate GRADES or MARKS roughly according to the NORMAL DISTRIBUTION. That is, only a few pupils will do very badly or very well, rather more will do fairly badly or fairly well, and so on, with the majority (the 'hump' in the middle) doing moderately. See NORM-REFERENCED TESTING.

graduand Student who has succeeded in degree examinations but has not yet officially become a GRADUATE by having his DEGREE conferred upon him.

graduate 1 A person who has been awarded a DEGREE after a period of study or research under the aegis of an institution of HIGHER EDUCATION. **2** In the US, a student who has satisfactorily completed his course of studies, but not necessarily in higher education – perhaps only in ELEMENTARY, JUNIOR HIGH, or SENIOR HIGH SCHOOL.

graduate assistant (US) A person who already holds a FIRST DEGREE and is acting as a RESEARCH ASSISTANT or TEACHING ASSISTANT in an institution of HIGHER EDUCATION.

Graduate Certificate of Education See POSTGRADUATE CERTIFICATE OF EDUCATION.

graduate equivalent A person who is not a graduate but who possesses some qualification accepted by one or more institutions as being equivalent to a degree.

Graduate Record Examination (GRE) (US) National examination used in predicting likely success of graduates who wish to undertake POST GRADUATE studies in GRADUATE SCHOOL. One of several selection criteria.

graduate school (US) A teaching and research institution for GRADUATE STUDENTS, normally attached to a university.

graduate student (US) A college or university GRADUATE who is now studying for a HIGHER DEGREE. The UK equivalent is POST-GRADUATE STUDENT.

107

graduate teacher A qualified teacher who holds a DEGREE or is considered a GRADUATE EQUIVALENT and is therefore entitled to a higher salary than a non-graduate teacher (other things being equal).

graduation 1 Being awarded a DEGREE. 2 (US) Successfully completing the course of studies in school, college or university. 3 (US) The actual ceremony at which degrees are conferred (like COMMENCEMENT).

grammar 1 The system of rules in terms of which the usages of a particular language can be described and explained. 2 A book describing the grammar of a language, especially for the benefit of students attempting to learn that language.

grammar school 1 In the UK, one of the SECONDARY SCHOOLS which catered for the academically able children (perhaps 20% of the YEAR-GROUP in any area) who had passed the ELEVEN-PLUS examination and who were being prepared for entry to HIGHER EDUCATION and the professions. Grammar schools have almost all been replaced by COMPREHENSIVE schools. (Between 1965 and 1975 their number fell from 1285 to 261.) Most grammar schools were MAINTAINED by LOCAL EDUCATION AUTHORITIES but many were DIRECT GRANT SCHOOLS. 2 In the US, another name for ELEMENTARY SCHOOLS.

grammar-technical school (UK) A BILATERAL SCHOOL incorporating both GRAMMAR SCHOOL and TECHNICAL SCHOOL wings. Rare since SECONDARY RE-ORGANISATION began.

grand tour (UK) The 18th century tradition of the children (especially the sons) of wealthy families completing their education with an extended and leisurely tour of Europe. The tradition has been revived and democratised in recent years, thanks to hitchhiking and transit vans.

grandes écoles The pinnacle of the French system of HIGHER EDUCATION, catering for highly academic students expected to go beyond FIRST DEGREES.

grant-aided school A school receiving funds from local or central government but not fully MAINTAINED by it. The term could have been applied (as indeed it was in Scotland) to the former DIRECT GRANT SCHOOLS.

graphicacy The ability to think visually and spatially. Compare with LITERACY, NUMERACY, ORACY.

graphics terminal A type of VISUAL DISPLAY UNIT (VDU). A computer TERMINAL incorporating a TV-tape screen that can display words and digits and line drawings and other graphics. It may also allow for the use of a LIGHT-PEN.

great books course (US) An approach used in some institutions of HIGHER EDUCATION, especially between the two world wars, based on the belief that a LIBERAL EDUCATION can be built around the study of certain 'great books' (of philosophy, literature, history, science, etc). Teachers, of course, may well disagree as to which books should count as 'great'.

Great Debate, The (UK) Collective name for a number of meetings and speeches discussing the implications of a speech in 1976 by the Prime Minister, James Callaghan, in which he called for higher educational STANDARDS, the development of a CORE CURRICULUM, and more attention to be paid to how pupils and students were being prepared for a working life in industry and commerce. The reverberations are still (in 1981) to be heard.

greats or **literae humaniores** An undergraduate CLASSICS course at Oxford University.

group dynamics 1 The complex system of social interactions expressed in people's individual behaviour in groups. 2 The label of the SUB-DISCIPLINE of SOCIAL PSYCHOLOGY that systematically studies such group behaviour.

grouping The allocation of pupils or students into groups of a size and nature thought to facilitate teaching and learning. See BANDING, SETTING, AND STREAMING.

group therapy Form of PSYCHOTHERAPY in which a number of people with related needs or problems discuss them in a group under the supervision of a skilled FACILITATOR (probably a professional therapist).

group training scheme Where a number of small or specialist firms, none of which could provide complete training for its APPRENTICES or other trainees on its own, join together to ensure full training by rotation of trainees among firms and/or by joint employment of training staff and resources.

group work Tasks performed by small groups of pupils or students from within a class, perhaps in connection with TOPIC WORK, PROJECTS, or a practical exercise. Membership of a group and its goals and methods may sometimes be decided by the pupils or students, sometimes by the teacher.

guided reading Books and journal articles and the like that students are expected to read as part of a university course, perhaps with some advice from their teachers on what to look for, or how to approach the task.

Guilford, J P (Born 1897) US psychologist and authority on PSYCHOMETRICS in the investigation of PERSONALITY and INTELLIGENCE. See his *Psychometric Methods* (1954).

Gulbenkian Foundation A charitable foundation, based in Lisbon, which makes funds available for educational (and other) research and innovation in the UK and other parts of the world.

guru A Hindu or Sikh religious teacher who gives spiritual guidance to his disciples. Sometimes used facetiously, even disparagingly, of the FATHER-FIGURE or leader of any movement with mystical or ideological overtones.

Guttman scale An approach to the construction of ATTITUDE TESTS that can be seen in the device of asking a person to indicate how far he agrees with a succession of statements, each expressing a more and more extreme viewpoint on the issues about which his attitude is being measured.

gymnasium **1** A hall designed for PHYSICAL EDUCATION activities. **2** The name of the highly academic SECONDARY SCHOOLS found in Germany and some other European countries. (Compare with UK GRAMMAR SCHOOL and French LYCÉE.)

H

Hadow Report 1926 A UK REPORT on 'Education of the Adolescent', it proposed that the period of education ending around the age of 11 should be called PRIMARY; that post-primary education (which should preferably take place in a separate school) should be called SECONDARY; and that secondary schools should be of two main types – GRAMMAR and MODERN.

Hadow Report 1931 A UK REPORT on 'The Primary School'. It proposed two stages in PRIMARY EDUCATION – up to age 7 and 7 – 11. Further suggested that the curriculum be thought of 'in terms of activity and experience, rather than of knowledge to be acquired or facts to be stored'.

Hadow Report 1933 UK REPORT on 'Infant and Nursery Schools'. Argued the case for NURSERY SCHOOLS for children from the age of two and drew attention to the need for suitable buildings with adequate fresh air and sunlight, and suitable furniture.

half Term once used where an institution's ACADEMIC YEAR was divided into two terms (each being a 'half') rather than into three. Equivalent to a US SEMESTER.

half-term (break) A few days' holiday in the middle of a term.

half-timers (UK) The name given to pupils who, in the period up to 1927 (when the law was changed) were allowed to spend half of the school week in school and the other half in work.

hall of residence A residential building (incorporating study-bedrooms, common rooms, eating facilities, etc) for students belonging to an institution of FURTHER or (more usually) HIGHER EDUCATION. Equivalent to the US HOSTEL DORMITORY.

halo effect A phenomenon in ASSESSMENT (noted by THORNDIKE) whereby an assessor's judgments of several of a person's qualities or abilities are biased by a previous assessment of some other quality or ability. (For example, the GRADE for an ESSAY may be unduly influenced by the legibility of the candidate's handwriting.)

handbook A MANUAL of advice or instructions, perhaps intended to accompany a course or a piece of equipment.

handedness The tendency to use one hand rather than the other in a one-handed task (eg writing) or to place them habitually in one of two possible (and opposite) positions in a two-handed activity (eg using a spade). Special case of LATERALITY.

handicapped children Children who require special educational facilities because of disability (ie those who are blind, partially-sighted, deaf, partially-hearing, EDUCATIONALLY SUBNORMAL, epileptic, maladjusted, physically handicapped, delicate, defective in speech, autistic, or dyslexic).

handicraft A name that has been applied to many school subjects or activities, particularly woodwork and metalwork, but including several others like pottery, book-binding, weaving, etc.

hands-on training Training that involves the trainee in actual physical contact with the environment (especially the equipment and materials) in which he will work on completing training.

Hans, Nicholas (1888–1969) British pioneer of the study of COMPARATIVE EDUCATION. See especially his *Comparative Education: a Study of Educational Factors and Traditions* (3rd ed, 1958).

hard money Term used in CURRICULUM DEVELOPMENT and other projects for money that must be found to support the project from the funds of the institution in which the project is based. Contrasts with SOFT MONEY which comes from outside funding bodies, usually as PUMP-PRIMING or SEED FUNDING meant to get the project started. The availability or otherwise of hard money is often taken to indicate the extent to which a new project has achieved INSTITUTIONALISATION.

hardware   One or more pieces of equipment (eg tape-recorders, film-projectors, computer terminals) that can be used in education. See also SOFTWARE.

Harkness Fellowships   Fellowships awarded by a US foundation to encourage study and travel in the US by people between 21–30 years old from the UK, the Commonwealth and certain European countries.

Harris-Goodenough Draw-a-man test   See DRAW-A-MAN TEST.

Harris, William T   (1835–1909) As SUPERINTENDENT OF SCHOOLS in St Louis (1868–1880), as the general editor of a major series of books on education, and as the United States COMMISSIONER OF EDUCATION (1889–1906), Dr Harris was acclaimed as one of the most distinguished US educators of the 19th Century. He was an active and practical innovator in schools and, as a philosopher, emphasised the transmission of the cultural heritage as education's main contribution to helping children mature mentally and morally.

Haslegrave Report 1970   A UK REPORT on the education and training of technicians which led to the setting up of the TECHNICIAN EDUCATION COUNCIL (TEC) and the BUSINESS EDUCATION COUNCIL (BEC).

Hawthorne effect   Used to describe what happens when a new approach (eg a new teaching method) has been introduced and the people involved are performing better (eg learning more) *not* because of the new approach itself but simply because it *is* new. That is, their attitude has changed: they have been stimulated to better performance (perhaps only temporarily) because of the novelty or because of the extra attention they are getting. See also PLACEBO EFFECT.

Hayes Pegboard Test   A brief US test for measuring manual coordination.

hazing   (US) Mild form of BULLYING of students (especially new ones) by their elders, sometimes as a form of ritual INITIATION (eg to a FRATERNITY).

HE   UK abbreviation for HIGHER EDUCATION. (Like FE for FURTHER EDUCATION and as in 'FE/HE colleges'.)

head   Short for HEADMASTER/MISTRESS or HEADTEACHER.

head boy (or **girl**)   The name given to the boy or girl sometimes chosen in a UK SECONDARY SCHOOL (possibly by election among senior pupils), to represent the pupils, to lead the PREFECTS, or to fulfil various functions on formal or public occasions.

headmaster/mistress   See HEADTEACHER.

Head Masters' Conference (**HMC**)   (UK) An association (holding annual conferences) involving the headmasters of the most prestigious INDEPENDENT SCHOOLS only. The schools are sometimes spoken of as HMC schools.

headmistress   See HEADTEACHER.

head resident   (US) Member of staff responsible for a DORMITORY (or HALL OF RESIDENCE). Similar to WARDEN in UK.

Head Start   (US) A programme for three–five year-old children from low-income families, intending to provide medical, nutritional and social benefits and, by pre-school enrichment activity, to enable them to learn more effectively once they reach school. Largely financed by federal government.

headteacher   The administrative and academic leader of a school who has considerable autonomy in deciding its organisation, curriculum and staffing. He or she is, however, constrained by the checks and balances exercised by the GOVERNING BODY, the attitudes of his staff, the feelings of parents, and the overall policy of his LOCAL EDUCATION AUTHORITY. Equivalent to US PRINCIPAL in a PUBLIC SCHOOL (US meaning); though headmaster/mistress/teacher is sometimes used in private (fee-paying) schools in the US.

health service   See SCHOOL HEALTH SERVICE.

health education   A CURRICULUM subject whose concern is with studying the development and maintenance of mental and physical health. Includes such topics as nutrition, hygiene, smoking, drugs, sex, exercise, and so on.

hearing-impaired   Term used for children who are partially deaf.

Hebb D O   (Born 1904) Canadian psychologist whose theory of mental behaviour seeks neurological as well as psychological explanations. He is responsible for the concepts of INTELLIGENCE A AND B. See his *Organisation of Behaviour* (1949) and *A Textbook of Psychology* (1966).

hectograph   An early type of REPROGRAPHY machine allowing the copying of type, manuscript or drawings from a glycerin-

113

coated gelatin surface to which the material to be copied had been transferred.

helper In British PRIMARY SCHOOL this term refers to paid staff who are not trained TEACHERS but who help teachers in the classroom by performing non-teaching support duties like making teaching materials. They may or may not have had special training. (The US equivalent is called an AIDE or AUXILIARY.)

Herbart, Johann Friedrich (1776–1841) A German philosopher with an interest in the psychology of teaching and learning. Best known for his advocacy of planned, systematic teaching, following the 'five steps' of preparation, presentation, association, generalisation, and application.

heredity-environment controversy See NATURE-NURTURE CONTROVERSY.

Her Majesty's Inspectorate (HMI) More than 500 INSPECTORS are employed by the DEPARTMENT OF EDUCATION AND SCIENCE and the SCOTTISH EDUCATION DEPARTMENT to inspect schools (both MAINTAINED and INDEPENDENT) and those institutions dealing with FURTHER and HIGHER EDUCATION that are maintained by the LOCAL EDUCATION AUTHORITIES. The inspectors (each known as an HMI) monitor CURRICULUM and TEACHING METHODS; give advice to teachers; run IN-SERVICE TRAINING courses; publish many survey reports, advisory booklets, and discussion papers on educational issues; and represent their Department on many national educational bodies. (The local education authorities also have their own, quite separate, teams of inspectors – or ADVISERS.)

hermeneutics A body of approaches to analysing, explaining and interpreting textual material that developed from the work of German Biblical scholars in the late 18th century and is now of influence in history, the social sciences and literary criticism.

heterogeneous group/class (US) Usually refers to a group of children of widely differing academic abilities, interests and attainments who are, nevertheless, being taught as a group (and not formed into sub-groups or re-groupings through STREAMING or SETTING which would give HOMOGENEOUS groups). Similar to MIXED ABILITY GROUP.

heuristic approach/method Teaching strategy in which the pupils are helped to carry out investigations and discover the essential ideas and principles for themselves. See also DISCOVERY LEARNING.

heuristic learning   See DISCOVERY LEARNING.

H grades   The higher level, termed the HIGHER GRADE, in the SCOTTISH CERTIFICATE OF EDUCATION.

HEW   The former US DEPARTMENT OF HEALTH, EDUCATION AND WELFARE.

hidden curriculum   All the beliefs and VALUES and understandings that are passed on to the student in an educational institution, not through formal teaching but, unconsciously, through what the institution implicitly demands of the student (eg regularity of work, deference to authority, respect for EXTRINSIC MOTIVATION etc). See B R Snyder's *The Hidden Curriculum* (1971).

hierarchy of needs   Part of a theory of human MOTIVATION proposed by ABRAHAM MASLOW, suggesting that human beings are motivated initially by basic physiological needs, then, when those have been satisfied, by needs relating to safety, then by needs for love and affection and belongingness, and, ultimately, by the need for SELF-ACTUALISATION.

high culture   The CULTURE, and especially the arts, music and literature, subscribed to by those members of society who believe themselves to be preserving and advancing the finest traditions of that society.

higher criticism   The use of 'scientific' techniques of literary criticism to establish the sources of the books of the Bible.

higher degree   A POST GRADUATE DEGREE, eg a MASTER'S DEGREE or a DOCTORATE, normally taken after having obtained a FIRST DEGREE and awarded on the basis of more advanced study which may revolve largely or wholly around individual research.

higher doctorate   Degree awarded by some universities for contributions to scholarship (usually through published works rather than supervised research) beyond the level of a normal DOCTORATE. (The title could be Doctor of Letters/Science/Music/ Theology, etc).

higher education   This term is sometimes used rather loosely to refer to all POST-SECONDARY (or TERTIARY) education, including what is usually identified as FURTHER EDUCATION. (Conversely, and confusingly, 'further education' is sometimes used so as to include much of higher education). More specifically, the term applies only to education leading to the award of a DIPLOMA, or DEGREE or other advanced qualification, and usually demanding more stringent ENTRANCE QUALIFICATIONS from intending stu-

115

dents than would be needed for entry to further education. But see also FURTHER EDUCATION.

higher grade   The equivalent, in the SCOTTISH CERTIFICATE OF EDUCATION, of ADVANCED LEVEL GCE (but awarded with A, B or C grades) and used as a criterion for entry to HIGHER EDUCATION. Usually taken in more subjects and only one year after ORDINARY GRADE.

higher grade schools   During the second half of the 19th century a demand arose for education beyond ELEMENTARY SCHOOL for particularly able pupils. From 1870, many higher grade schools were set up by the SCHOOL BOARDS to meet this demand and eventually became MAINTAINED SECONDARY SCHOOLS.

Higher National Certificate (HNC)   A widely-recognised UK qualification, below DEGREE level, in some aspects of science, technology, agriculture or business studies, usually acquired after two years' part-time study. It is now being replaced by the qualifications of the TECHNICIAN EDUCATION COUNCIL (TEC) and the BUSINESS EDUCATION COUNCIL (BEC), and of the Scottish equivalents, SCOTEC and SCOTBEC.

Higher National Diploma (HND)   A qualification in the same general subject areas as HIGHER NATIONAL CERTIFICATE (HNC) but at a higher level (approximately equal to PASS DEGREE standard, and requiring two years of full-time study.) Now being replaced by the qualifications of the TECHNICIAN EDUCATION COUNCIL (TEC) and the BUSINESS EDUCATION COUNCIL (BEC), and of the Scottish equivalents, SCOTEC and SCOTBEC.

Higher School Certificate   From 1917 until 1951, when it was replaced by GCE ADVANCED LEVEL, this was the public examination (in three principal subjects or in two principal subjects supported by two subsidiary subjects) taken by SECONDARY SCHOOL pupils at the age of about 18 years, not least as an ENTRY QUALIFICATION to HIGHER EDUCATION.

'higher tops'   Term used in late 19th century ELEMENTARY SCHOOLS for pupils who had passed through Standard VII and were staying on for more advanced work in a HIGHER GRADE SCHOOL.

high flier   A pupil or student of outstandingly high ability and/ or aspirations.

high master   The HEADMASTER of certain (usually INDEPENDENT) schools.

high school   A SECONDARY SCHOOL. In the UK, the term is often used by GRAMMAR SCHOOLS and by INDEPENDENT girls' schools; but it is also used by some COMPREHENSIVE schools. In the US, some high schools take children from age 12 to 18 years; while in other cases the pupils move from JUNIOR to SENIOR HIGH SCHOOL at the age of about 15 years.

high school degree/diploma (US) The qualification earned by a HIGH SCHOOL student who has successfully completed his grade 12 year.

High School Equivalency Examination (US) A test taken by people who left HIGH SCHOOL without obtaining a HIGH SCHOOL DEGREE or diploma and who now wish to demonstrate that they merit certification at that level. Also known as a General Educational Development Test.

high school graduate (US) Student who has successfully completed the requirements for GRADE 12 in high school.

high table The table at one end of the REFECTORY in a tradition-conscious school or college, perhaps raised on a dais, and at which the teachers or DONS and their favoured guests will dine.

Hilary term The TERM between Christmas and Easter at Oxford University and some other educational institutions.

histogram A statistical chart for representing a FREQUENCY DISTRIBUTION by a row of columns. The width of each column varies with the width of the range of values of the VARIABLE concerned (eg IQs of 80–84, 85–95, etc) and the height varies to show the number of times a value in each range is recorded.

historigram A now almost-defunct term (but still capable of getting confused with HISTOGRAM), referring to a TIME-SERIES graph in which a line connects up points showing the VALUE of some VARIABLE (eg school attendance) at various intervals of time (eg first school day of every month).

history of education Often seen as a SUB-DISCIPLINE of COMPARATIVE EDUCATION with the emphasis here on the study of how particular educational institutions, systems or theories developed.

HMC See HEAD MASTERS' CONFERENCE.

HMI See HER MAJESTY'S INSPECTORATE.

HNC See HIGHER NATIONAL CERTIFICATE.

HND See HIGHER NATIONAL DIPLOMA.

holidays According to the EDUCATION ACT 1944, UK schools must operate for a total of 200 days per year (which can be reduced to 190 by OCCASIONAL CLOSURES). The remainder is holiday to be taken at times decided by the LOCAL EDUCATION AUTHORITIES.

holist   Person who uses a HOLIST(IC) APPROACH.

holist(ic) approach/method/strategy   An approach to learning or problem-solving adopted when the learner seeks to obtain an overview of the material to be learned or problem to be solved, before he starts to attend to details. (Contrasts with SERIALIST approach.)

Home and Colonial Infant School Society   Founded in 1836 to train INFANT SCHOOL teachers in the methods of PESTALOZZI.

homecoming   (US) The annual programme of social and sporting activities traditionally mounted in a college or university for the benefit of returning ALUMNI.

home economics   Formerly called DOMESTIC SCIENCE. The study in school or in colleges of FURTHER EDUCATION of the knowledge and skills involved in running a home – planning and budgeting, mortgages and finance, buying, cooking and preserving food, making and repairing clothes, house maintenance and repairs, etc. Nowadays available to boys as well as girls.

home education/teaching   For various reasons, a LOCAL EDUCATION AUTHORITY will sometimes agree to a child being educated at home by a qualified tutor (who may be a parent), provided it is satisfied that the teaching is appropriate and sufficient. It may, in fact, provide a HOME TUTOR.

home experiment kit   Materials specially designed to enable students to carry out scientific tests and experiments at home under guidance from a CORRESPONDENCE COURSE. Much used in science and technology courses of the OPEN UNIVERSITY.

home tutor   A teacher employed by a LOCAL EDUCATION AUTHORITY to give part-time teaching in their homes to children who are unable to attend school.

home visiting   Visits by teachers or social workers to children's homes, either simply to strengthen relationships between home and school or, more specifically, to help parents take on an active role in the educational development of their children (particularly in the pre-school years). An EDUCATION WELFARE OFFICER is especially likely to make such visits.

homework   Work set by teachers (usually only in SECONDARY schools) for pupils to do at home in the evenings or at weekends. In private schools may be called prep.

homogeneous group/class   (US) A group of pupils similar in academic ability, interests, attainment, etc. May be achieved by what we in UK call streaming or setting. Contrasts with heterogeneous group.

honorary degree   An academic title given to a person by a university not for success in academic courses but to reward an outstanding contribution to academic or public life.

honorary society   (US) A society to which academically able students in high school, college or university can be elected. Some societies recognise general scholarship, others excellence in a specific discipline. Their names are usually combinations of three Greek letters, eg Alpha Phi Sigma (scholarship), Kappa Delta Pi (education).

honors class   (US) A class working faster and/or at a higher level than other classes in an institution. (Such classes, similarly named, are also to be found in Scottish universities.)

honors curriculum/program   (US) Studies undertaken by students in honors class.

honor system/code   (US) Supposed code of behaviour whereby students in certain educational institutions act to discourage cheating and stealing.

honors degree   1 (UK) A degree at higher than pass degree level and awarded in one of the classes: 'first class', 'second class' (which may be divided into 'upper second' and 'lower second') and 'third class'. 2 (US) A degree earned with an outstandingly high grade point average and/or as a result of following an honors curriculum.

hooky (or **hookey**)   To 'play hookey' is to play truant.

horn book   An early teaching aid, much used in dame schools and day schools, consisting of a board on which letters of the alphabet or other material was written and covered with a thin layer of transparent horn as a protection.

HORSA huts   After World War II and the raising of the school-leaving age, the increased number of children in UK schools meant that temporary accommodation had to be erected in school grounds as the 'Hut Operation for Raising School-leaving Age'.

Houghton Award   A major UK salary award to teachers in 1975, increasing the average pay of a teacher by 25%, (head

TEACHERS getting a 50% increase). The award followed a period of considerable militancy among teachers who were protesting, with some sympathy from the general public, about the way in which inflation had been allowed to erode their salaries (and educational standards).

Houghton Report 1974   A UK REPORT on salary structures in PRIMARY, SECONDARY and MAINTAINED FURTHER and HIGHER EDUCATION teaching that led to rapid improvement in teachers' salaries. See HOUGHTON AWARD.

house   1 UK PUBLIC SCHOOLS commonly divide their boarding pupils among several different buildings in which they eat, sleep, and spend their leisure time. Each of these 'houses' is supposed to command the loyalty of its denizens. 2 Other (non-boarding) schools use the idea of houses as a convenient means of dividing their pupils into a few large groups for sporting and other competitive purposes.

house master/mistress   The teacher responsible in terms of DISCIPLINE and/or PASTORAL CARE for the pupils allocated to a particular HOUSE in a school.

house mother/father   People who perform, as far as possible, the role of parents in a residential home or school for delinquent, deprived or handicapped children.

house points   Marks of approval awarded to pupils for academic or other achievements and credited to their HOUSE, which will be in competition with other houses in the school.

house system   As described in HOUSE 2 above.

howler   A glaring and ludicrous blunder found in a student's written work. Some UK teachers perpetuate a long but not too noble tradition of pouncing on and gleefully publishing such howlers – especially during the examination season.

Hull, C L (1884–1952)   US psychologist well known for his theory of learning centred on the idea of DRIVE REDUCTION. See his *Principles of Behaviour* (1943).

humanism   A label applied subsequently to the 15th century movement to rediscover the language, literature and thought of classical antiquity which powered the RENAISSANCE and led to an increasing educational concern with teaching 'the HUMANITIES'. More recently, 'humanism' has come to denote a belief which rejects the idea of a god, exalts mankind, and regards the human spirit as worthy of the utmost veneration.

humanistic education   A movement within education (chiefly in the US) embodying the emphases and approaches of HUMAN-ISTIC PSYCHOLOGY.

humanistic psychology   An approach to psychology deriving from the writings of such US psychologists as ABRAHAM MASLOW and CARL ROGERS, emphasising the inner states of mind and emotion in human beings (rather than their observable BEHAV-IOUR), especially with a view to helping them achieve SELF-AC-TUALISATION. Also called THIRD FORCE PSYCHOLOGY.

Humanities Curriculum Project   Sponsored in the late 1960s by the UK SCHOOLS COUNCIL for older pupils in SECONDARY SCHOOLS, and meant to help them explore, and reach their own informed opinions on, some of the controversial issues in modern society (eg race relations, war, living in cities). The project was distinctive in refusing to pre-specify learning outcomes or OBJEC-TIVES and in insisting on the teacher acting as a neutral chairman in class discussions.

humanities   Studies in which mankind is the central concern. Originally involving Greek and Latin literature only, the term broadened to include any literature, history and philosophy, and some aspects of the social sciences are sometimes included under this heading in a CURRICULUM.

human potential movement   Composite term for a host of tech-niques and ideologies, chiefly of US origin, concerned with en-abling individuals to fulfil themselves and, in some way function more effectively and efficiently than they could otherwise expect.

Huxley T H   (1825–95)   A biologist and Fellow of the Royal Society, he greatly influenced the new national education system in the 1870s through his advocacy of PROGRESSIVE teaching meth-ods and of the need for PHYSICAL EDUCATION, science, and AES-THETIC SUBJECTS in the CURRICULUM.

hyperactivity   This is a notional condition from which many US and UK children are said to be 'suffering' when they behave too disruptively or rebelliously for their teachers, and for which they can then be 'treated' by being sedated with drugs.

hypothesis   An untested statement put forward as explaining some phenomena in the physical world or in social interactions. In research, a hypothesis needs to be worded explicitly enough for it to be testable by observation or experiment. See also NULL HYPOTHESIS.

I

iconic (mode of) representation   See BRUNER'S MODES.

ideal self   A person's image of how he would like to be. Contrasts with PERCEIVED SELF.

identification   An important process in FREUD'S theory of PERSONALITY formation, it is the act of 'putting oneself into another person's shoes', seeing things 'through his eyes' and, in so doing, incorporating aspects of that other person into one's own personality.

identity-crisis   A theory of the US psychologist ERIK ERIKSON that adolescents search for a sense of self-assuredness about the nature of their goals and VALUES in life and the means of achieving them; and that they experiment with a variety of possible ROLES or identities until they find a satisfactory synthesis they can be committed to. It involves also the establishment of an internal authority, independent of external figures of authority (parental or otherwise).

ideographic approach   See IDIOGRAPHIC APPROACH.

ideology   A body of belief or doctrine, which may be held and acted on by a social group, perhaps in ignorance or even defiance of evidence that might throw doubt on its validity – usually because it is believed to be socially or politically useful or else to be morally undeniable.

idiographic approach   An approach to the ASSESSMENT of PERSONALITY that concentrates on describing and understanding a particular individual in his or her uniqueness (rather than on comparing him with others or seeking generalizable explanations of human personality). Contrast with NOMOTHETIC APPROACH.

idiot savant   (French for 'a knowing or wise idiot'.) A person of very low mental ability generally but with an outstanding facility in some mental skill (eg remembering numbers).

ILEA   See INNER LONDON EDUCATION AUTHORITY.

Illich, Ivan   (Born 1926) Austrian priest, educationist and social critic who has spent much of his working life in US and Latin America. He was one of the chief exponents of the DESCHOOLING movement – see his *Deschooling Society* (1971).

illiteracy   A person's inability to read (or write) as well as he or she ought to be able to do (in the opinion of the person using the term).

illuminati A 19th century term (but still potent, especially when used satirically) for people claiming to possess special enlightenment on a particular subject.

illuminative curriculum planning An approach to CURRICULUM DEVELOPMENT that avoids the emphasis placed on pre-determined OBJECTIVES by the RATIONAL CURRICULUM PLANNING approach. Instead, it concentrates more on the traditions or inherent logic of the subject being taught and, above all, on responding to insights and illuminations obtained through discussions with participants, once the curriculum is under way. See also ILLUMINATIVE EVALUATION.

illuminative evaluation An approach to EVALUATION, pioneered in the UK by Parlett and Hamilton, and by Stake in the US. It avoids the quantitative emphasis of the so-called AGRO-BOTANY approach and concentrates more on ascertaining how participants in the CURRICULUM feel about the experience. The chief means of collecting data are observation, conversation, discussions, CONTENT ANALYSIS of student writings, and so on, and the overall strategy is meant to be flexible enough to develop along with the situation being investigated.

image 1 In psychology, the mental experience of something that is not immediately present in the senses. 2 With AUDIO-VISUAL MEDIA, the picture on a screen.

imaginary playmate Young children often imagine a regular fantasy companion with whom they converse about their play.

imagination The ability to form mental images of sounds, sights, tastes, smells and movements for which there is no immediate sensory stimulus.

imaginative play Term used by CHARLOTTE BUHLER in her theory of PLAY and referring to a child's ability to act and talk in his play as if he is someone else, doing something other than what he is doing, and perhaps in the company of people who are not actually with him.

imitation Copying the speech or behaviour of another person. A crucial part of learning, eg in learning to talk.

immediate memory span The amount of information a person can recall (eg the number of digits) immediately after it has been presented to him.

immersion course An INTENSIVE COURSE that occupies the learner so totally with what is to be learned that, during the course, he has little time to think of anything else. Particularly used in the teaching of a foreign language, where the learner may be placed for a period with people who communicate with him in the foreign language only.

immigrant education   A special problem-area within UK education with large numbers of children from Asia and the West Indies who suffer acute language and other learning difficulties exacerbated by racial prejudice, the stress of inner-city life, and the predominantly low SOCIO-ECONOMIC STATUS of their parents. The problem is largely one of ACCULTURATION and needs sensitive handling if children (and their parents) are not to become alienated and confirmed in a second-class status within society. See RAMPTON REPORT.

immigrant language centres   Facilities set up in various parts of the UK to provide intensive courses in English language for immigrants – both adults and children.

imperial system/units   The British units of measurement (feet, pounds, pints, etc) from which the US CUSTOMARY SYSTEM was derived. Both systems are now gradually being superseded by the METRIC SYSTEM and, in scientific work and technology, by the INTERNATIONAL SYSTEM (or SI UNITS).

impression marking   An approach to ASSESSMENT in which the examiner or assessor forms a general impression of a piece of the student's work (eg an essay) and gives a GRADE for its overall quality, rather than making separate assessments for content, style, presentation, etc, and combining them to get an overall grade as with ANALYTIC MARKING.

imposition   A piece of work (eg the writing of LINES) which a teacher may demand from a pupil in his spare time as a punishment for some minor breach of DISCIPLINE.

imprinting   A presumably instinctive survival mechanism whereby young animals (eg newly hatched geese) follow the first moving object they see. Normally this would be their mother but they would be equally likely to follow a human being or a clockwork toy.

improvement curve   Same as LEARNING CURVE.

impulsive v. reflective   A DIMENSION of PERSONALITY recognised by the US psychologist, Kagan. The impulsive person is likely to suggest solutions to problems quickly and without much thought, whereas the reflective person wants to be sure he has thought out the most reasonable answer before committing himself.

in absentia (Latin: 'in his absence') A student, unable to attend the graduation ceremony may be awarded his degree '*in absentia*'.

inaugural lecture 1 The first public lecture given by a new PROFESSOR to mark the fact that has taken up the CHAIR. 2 A lecture intended to commence a conference or to mark the opening of a new building, etc.

in-basket exercise See IN-TRAY EXERCISE.

in care When children are neglected by their parents, or get beyond their control, they may be placed under the protection of the LOCAL AUTHORITY. Such children 'in care' may be looked after in, for example, COMMUNITY HOMES or in FOSTER HOMES.

incidental learning The kind of knowledge (or skill) that we can acquire, without consciously trying while in pursuit of other knowledge; eg while conscious only of acquiring subject-matter knowledge from our teacher, we may also be acquiring some of his attitudes. 'More is caught than is taught' as someone once said.

incline of difficulty A series of questions or test ITEMS that get progressively more difficult (eg as in a POWER TEST).

in-company training Training for the staff of an organisation, conducted on that organisation's premises, usually by other members of staff. Contrasts with a GROUP TRAINING SCHEME, DAY-RELEASE, SANDWICH COURSE, etc.

inconsequential behaviour (or **child**) A behaviour disturbance described by the psychologist STOTT, consisting in the child being very easily distracted by any momentary STIMULUS and therefore appearing to be incapable of concentrating on any purposeful activity. He or she is weak in concept development and his or her INTELLIGENCE may be under-estimated.

incubation period After first thinking around a problem we may put it aside for a time in order to allow the UNCONSCIOUS to work on it and, with luck, incubate a creative solution.

indenture(s) A deed or contract or agreement between two parties (at one time having two copies, each with identically indented edges for security). Especially an agreement between an APPRENTICE and his master.

independent learning/study A term applied, usually approvingly, to a situation where the student is freed from some constraint that might otherwise inhibit his learning. For example, he may be independent of other students (and therefore free to learn at his own pace) and/or free of some of the constraints a teacher might impose. The student may be free to decide not only his own pace of work, but also the method of learning, and even what is to be learned – the OBJECTIVES. The term is often used (ill-advisedly) of INDIVIDUALISED LEARNING, where the student may be free to work at his own pace but may be highly dependent on a teacher's decision as to the content and sequence of his learning.

independent schools   Schools that are not MAINTAINED from public funds, though they may choose (in the UK) to satisfy HER MAJESTY'S INSPECTORS that they offer a satisfactory education. In the UK the main categories of independent schools are the PREPARATORY SCHOOLS and the PUBLIC SCHOOLS. The US has PAROCHIAL SCHOOLS and PRIVATE SCHOOLS.

independent sector   Schools and colleges that operate without support from public funds.

independent university   A university that receives no grants from public funds but relies on student fees, endowments, and other private sources. Only one such exists in the UK, University College, Buckingham, but such PRIVATE UNIVERSITIES are common in the US.

independent variable   In a statistical study, the VARIABLE whose VALUES are going to be deliberately changed (or natural differences observed) in order to see how this influences the values of another variable (the DEPENDENT variable). For instance, we might examine how far the age of children (the independent variable) influences the amount of pocket-money they get.

index numbers   A statistical device enabling easy comparison of the VALUES of a VARIABLE (eg prices, wages, number of examination candidates) as they vary over time. For example, the value in a 'base-year' may be regarded as 100, with each subsequent value being expressed as a percentage of the base-year value. Thus, if a school entered 60 candidates for an examination in the base-year and 90 in some subsequent year, the index number representing examination candidates in that later year would be 150.

individual differences   What psychologists are looking for in tests of PERSONALITY, INTELLIGENCE, ATTAINMENT, ATTITUDE, etc – that is, the ways in which people differ on these and other characteristics that can be measured.

individualised instruction/learning   Some attempt to tailor the teaching and learning to the individual needs of each learner.

Often this means no more than enabling the learner to learn at his own individual pace (perhaps using SELF-INSTRUCTIONAL MATERIALS) but it can also allow for the learner to choose his own approach to learning (drawing perhaps on a variety of RESOURCES) and even to decide on his own individual OBJECTIVES. Though the two terms are often used synonymously, INDIVIDUALISED LEARNING is not necessarily INDEPENDENT LEARNING. Nor does individualised learning necessarily imply individual, solitary learning – students may sometimes need to work with others to meet certain individual learning needs. (SEE DALTON PLAN, IPI, KELLER PLAN, PLAN.)

individually prescribed instruction   See IPI.

indoctrination   Teaching a particular doctrine or belief in such a way that the learner has no opportunity to consider it critically or compare it with alternative doctrines or beliefs.

induction   An approach to reasoning (much used in the generation of scientific HYPOTHESES) in which we propose a general law or principle on the basis of a number of particular examples. For instance: 'All children so far that have been taught by the new method have learned more than those taught by the old method; so the new method seems to be more effective.' Such propositions can be disproved by further (contrary) evidence. Contrasts with DEDUCTION.

induction course/training   Training, usually of brief duration, intended to familarise a new employee with the work he will be doing and the systems and people he will be interacting with.

induction year   Proposal made by the UK JAMES REPORT 1972 that, during his first year in school, the newly-qualified teacher should be given a light enough teaching load to be able to spend one fifth of the total time in further training, and should be supported and guided by a specially appointed PROFESSIONAL TUTOR.

industrial archaeology   The historical and technical study of the factories, warehouses, machinery, transport etc, used in the industry of earlier times.

industrial arts   (US) Subjects such as metalwork, woodwork, technical drawing, and technology taught in HIGH SCHOOL but not specifically as VOCATIONAL TRAINING.

industrial schools   **1** (UK) Schools set up during the industrial revolution by industrialists like ROBERT OWEN, often on factory premises, for the workers and/or their children. **2** (US) Residential schools (similar to the UK BORSTALS) for the rehabilitation of delinquent youths.

industrial training The training of employees in industry, usually with the intention of making them more productive in their work.

Industrial Training Act 1964 This UK Act aimed to increase the quantity and quality of INDUSTRIAL TRAINING and to share the cost of training more evenly among the companies who would benefit from it. The Act, which set up the INDUSTRIAL TRAINING BOARDS, was later amended by the EMPLOYMENT AND TRAINING ACT 1973.

industrial training boards Statutory UK bodies, established under the INDUSTRIAL TRAINING ACT 1964, each one being responsible for encouraging better training in a different industry. There are 24 boards, covering about 55% of the nation's workforce. They operate by raising a training levy from the firms in their industry and paying this revenue back in grants to firms who provide satisfactory training.

Industry, Schools of See SCHOOLS OF INDUSTRY.

infant(s) school MAINTAINED PRIMARY SCHOOL for UK children between the ages of five and seven, after which they transfer to a JUNIOR SCHOOL. A PRIMARY SCHOOL often has both an infant and a junior department. A school attended by infants will sometimes be referred to as a FIRST SCHOOL and, indeed, that will be its official designation in a LOCAL EDUCATION AUTHORITY that operates a MIDDLE SCHOOL system.

ineducable child Mentally SUBNORMAL children were once regarded as incapable of profiting from education and hence were regarded as the responsibility of the local health authority rather than that of the education authority. Since education is now seen as embracing more than the achievement of competence in school SUBJECTS, and, in particular, since social, emotional and moral development have been recognised as educational, and essential to such children, the responsibility for most subnormal children has reverted to the LOCAL EDUCATION AUTHORITIES.

inference Process of coming to a conclusion on the basis of accepted propositions (DEDUCTION) or on the basis of observed evidence (INDUCTION).

inferiority complex A PERSONALITY trait named by psychoanalyst ALFRED ADLER that arises out of conflict between the desire to impress others and a fear of humiliation and is associated with

128

withdrawal and/or agression. The term tends also to be used rather loosely to refer to a person's sense of inadequacy.

informal approach/methods/teaching   An approach in which the teacher tends to be flexible, STUDENT-CENTRED and DEMO-CRATIC in classroom relationships, to be sensitive to individual needs and differences in LEARNING STYLE, and to put emphasis on the students' learning (eg through individual study, small group discussion, and excursions outside of the school, rather than on the teacher teaching (eg by giving lectures and demonstrations). Likely approach in PROGRESSIVE EDUCATION.

informal education   The acquisition of knowledge, skills and attitudes by following personal needs and interests in reading, conversation and other experiences in life, without taking courses or looking for help from teachers. Not the same as NON-FORMAL EDUCATION.

information explosion   The unprecedented growth of knowledge (especially scientific and technical) that is characteristic of the last few decades. Of all the people in the world's history who have been scientists, we are told, the great majority are still living at this moment – and producing knowledge. Hence the increasing concern with efficient ways of communicating, storing and retrieving knowledge (see INFORMATION SCIENCE) and, in the educational CURRICULUM, with teaching young people how to create and get access to knowledge as they need it, rather than to attempt the hopeless task of learning all they'll ever need to know during the years of formal education.

information mapping   An approach to the design of SELF-STUDY MATERIALS, developed by US psychologist Robert Horn, in which different kinds of information are presented in different formats and are identified by marginal labels so as to enable the reader to scan and process the information as efficiently as possible.

information-processing   A view of learning and problem-solving associated with COGNITIVE PSYCHOLOGY, in which the learner is seen as being actively at work on processing information – translating it into his own terms, organising it in his mind, storing it in meaningful patterns that allow him to retrieve it satisfactorily – rather than being seen (as in BEHAVIOURISM) merely as a passive receiver of stimuli and one who emits responses.

information retrieval   The art and technology of organising information (especially books and journal articles but also an increasing array of paper materials, film, magnetic tape, etc) so that people who might need the information are able to establish its existence, trace its whereabouts and obtain the opportunity to view it. A central concern of INFORMATION SCIENCE.

information science The systematic study of the nature and properties of human communication and information systems. It is concerned with the collection, evaluation (see CONTENT ANALYSIS), organisation (see INFORMATION RETRIEVAL) and dissemination of information – often using computerised approaches. (A development of, but now a far cry from, what was once studied under the heading of 'librarianship'.)

information theory A collection of mathematical methods (based on statistics) of coding, communicating, storing, retrieving and decoding data.

infrastructure The underlying structure of an organisation or system. The word means little more than 'structure', but writers often seem to use it because it sounds grander or suggests they have special knowledge of a covert structure that lies below the apparent one.

in-group Any collection of people who share a common bond (eg, of religion or shared social life) that makes them feel different from (and perhaps superior to) other people around them and which maybe leads to resentment from those others.

inhibition **1** In everyday parlance, an individual is said to 'suffer from' inhibition when he holds back from a social interaction out of fear of the other person's response. **2** The term is also used in STIMULUS-RESPONSE psychology, to account for the fact that an individual has not responded with the learned response to the stimulus that has hitherto evoked it. This may well be because the stimulus has now changed, perhaps being associated with punishment or having been confused by similarity with a more recently-learned stimulus. See RETRO-ACTIVE INHIBITION.

initial ability level See ENTRY BEHAVIOUR (KNOWLEDGE/SKILLS).

Initial Teaching Alphabet (ita) An alphabet consisting of 43 symbols instead of 26, invented by Sir James Pitman to overcome the difficulties caused by the irregularities of the traditional system when children are learning to read. The alphabet ensures a close relationship between visual symbol and spoken sound and, despite early suspicions, is now widely used in the beginning stages of teaching children to read. Children seem to make the transition to TRADITIONAL ORTHOGRAPHY without difficulty.

initial training Training undertaken before commencing upon a profession (eg teaching) ie pre-service as opposed to IN-SERVICE TRAINING.

initiation 1 The acceptance of a person into a new social or working group, perhaps accompanied by ceremony and LEARN-ING EXPERIENCES intended to break the ties with previous groups and/or impress upon him/her the nature of the new role and the relationships attached thereto. 2 A view of CURRICULUM expressed by R S PETERS in which education is seen as the initiation of children into 'worthwhile activities', these being the pursuits in which the rationality and spirituality of mankind has found its highest expression – the arts, science, religion, etc.

ink-blot test See RORSCHACH INK-BLOT TEST.

in loco parentis (Latin, 'in place of the parent'.) Refers to legal nature of the rights and responsibilities of a teacher towards his pupils. He is expected to act as a caring and responsible parent could reasonably be expected to do. (Seen by some teachers, for example, as an argument for their being able to administer CORPORAL PUNISHMENT; and by some parents who do not hit their children as an argument against.)

innate factors/tendencies/mechanisms Behavioural charac-teristics assumed to be in-born in the individual rather than acquired since birth through learning.

inner-city school A school situated near the centre of a large town or city, perhaps catering for children whose parents are of low SOCIO-ECONOMIC status, and perhaps carrying out the bulk of IMMIGRANT EDUCATION.

inner directed See OTHER-DIRECTED.

Inner London Education Authority (ILEA) The largest LO-CAL EDUCATION AUTHORITY in England and Wales, with respon-sibility for close on half a million pupils and students in the twelve Inner London boroughs and the City. (Scotland, however, has an even larger EDUCATION AUTHORITY – Strathclyde.)

inner space The idea of the human mind being as unknown or as rich with possibilities as outer space.

innovation The promotion of new ideas and methods within education – especially in respect of CURRICULUM. .

Inns of Court Four private societies or colleges (Lincoln's Inn, Gray's Inn, Inner Temple, Middle Temple), that function as a law school, organise examinations, and control the professional recognition (through 'calling to the Bar') of newly-qualified bar-risters in England.

131

inquiry-based See ENQUIRY-BASED.

inquiry learning See DISCOVERY LEARNING.

in-service education of teachers (INSET) The provision of professional education and training activities for teachers once they have embarked upon their careers, eg evening sessions at TEACHERS' CENTRES, short courses run by the DEPARTMENT OF EDUCATION AND SCIENCE, SECONDMENT to study for a HIGHER DEGREE, etc. THE JAMES REPORT OF 1972 helped shift attention from INITIAL TRAINING towards INSET.

in-service training See IN-SERVICE EDUCATION OF TEACHERS.

INSET See IN-SERVICE EDUCATION OF TEACHERS.

insight Term used in GESTALT PSYCHOLOGY for a person's sudden perception of the solution to a problem.

inspector An official, appointed to visit educational institutions and ensure that reasonable standards are being maintained. See also ADVISER and HER MAJESTY'S INSPECTORATE.

Inspectorate, The See HER MAJESTY'S INSPECTORATE.

in statu pupillari (Latin, 'in the state of being a pupil'.) This phrase describes the student's relationship to the teacher who is IN LOCO PARENTIS.

instinct theories Attempts to explain human BEHAVIOUR and MOTIVATION in terms not of learning and experience but of innate or inherited tendencies. The major 'instinct theorist' was McDOUGALL who postulated a number of such tendencies as being 'the essential springs or motive powers of all thought and action'. Such theories are still discussed but are no longer influential.

institute of education Usually a body within a UK university that has responsibility not only for educational research but also perhaps for TEACHER EDUCATION. In the latter connection it may offer one-year courses for new graduates and IN-SERVICE TRAINING for practising teachers and may provide VALIDATION for the INITIAL TRAINING courses mounted by COLLEGES OF EDUCATION and COLLEGES/INSTITUTES OF HIGHER EDUCATION.

institutionalisation **1** The process whereby a new idea or method may be incorporated into the accepted way of doing things within a group and so come to be regarded as beyond debate. **2** The process whereby inmates of such self-contained institutions as prisons, hospitals and BOARDING SCHOOLS may become so imbued with the mores and values peculiar to the institution that they find difficulty in adjusting later to life outside.

instruction Often used (especially in the US) as a synonym for TEACHING or even for EDUCATION, but generally used in the UK to refer to TRAINING that enables the learner to carry out some fairly routine skill.

instructional design (US) The planning and development of instructional courses and materials. A form of systematic CURRICULUM DEVELOPMENT directed towards the attainment of INSTRUCTIONAL OBJECTIVES.

instructional development (US) Term used synonymously with INSTRUCTIONAL DESIGN.

instructional materials centre (US) A LEARNING RESOURCES CENTRE (especially for INDIVIDUALISED LEARNING).

instructional media (US) Same as AUDIO-VISUAL AIDS.

instructional technology (US) A synonym for EDUCATIONAL TECHNOLOGY, usually implying systematic design and testing of instructional materials directed towards specific INSTRUCTIONAL OBJECTIVES.

instructional television (US) The production and distribution (usually through CLOSED-CIRCUIT) of programmes directed towards helping students achieve specific INSTRUCTIONAL OBJECTIVES. Contrast with EDUCATIONAL TELEVISION.

instructional objectives May be used to refer to OBJECTIVES that seem concerned with INSTRUCTION or TRAINING rather than with education. See also EXPRESSIVE OBJECTIVES with which instructional objectives are sometimes contrasted.

instructor This term is often used loosely of any kind of teacher. More specifically it refers to **1** A teacher of crafts and PSYCHOMOTOR SKILLS, eg in sports or in INDUSTRIAL TRAINING. **2** The most junior level of teacher (below ASSISTANT PROFESSOR) in US colleges and universities.

instrumental attitude/approach/behaviour An attitude with which the person engages in an activity or exercise not to enjoy that activity for its own sake but to achieve, thereby, some goal external to it. Contrasts with EXPRESSIVE ATTITUDE.

instrumental conditioning Similar to OPERANT CONDITIONING.

instrumental teacher One who teaches the playing of a musical instrument.

instrument of government A written statement of the constitution and rules of procedure for GOVERNORS of schools and colleges. See also ARTICLES OF GOVERNMENT.

integrated course/curriculum/studies/training   Course in which normally separate subjects or components (eg theory and practical work, or college classes and industrial experience) have been brought together in a coherent way. Often the term appears to be used to seek approval for a course or curriculum on the grounds simply that it has been carefully planned.

integrated day   An approach to the organisation of teaching and learning, especially in PRIMARY SCHOOLS, in which there is little use of a formal TIMETABLE. Instead, the emphasis is on individual and small group work on TOPICS and PROJECTS, in which SUBJECTS as such are avoided and a kind of INTER-DISCIPLINARY approach may be encouraged instead. However, some work on BASIC SKILLS (eg language and mathematics) is likely to be done on most days.

integrated education   (US) System in which all children attend the same schools, regardless of differences in sex, religion, ability and (especially) race.

integrative teaching   Similar to DEMOCRATIC TEACHING.

intelligence   Intelligence is a widely disputed term. It may be used to refer to: the capacity to think; general mental ability; the ability to learn from experience or to respond appropriately to new situations; abstract reasoning; the ability to see relationships and make predictions, and so on. Many psychologists play safe by saying that 'intelligence is what INTELLIGENCE TESTS measure'. Even in this sense, tests appear to recognise that intelligence has many different aspects – verbal skill, memory, and so on. The extent to which intelligence is inherited rather than acquired (and whether some races inherit more than others) is a matter of perennial controversy. See INTELLIGENCE A, B AND C.

intelligence, A, B and C   Intelligence A and B were suggested by the psychologist HEBB. Intelligence A represents an individual's innate potential INTELLIGENCE, inherited in his genetic make up. Intelligence B is the result of the interaction between intelligence A and the person's environment and is what he expresses in his behaviour. Professor VERNON then suggested intelligence C to indicate what INTELLIGENCE TESTS are measuring – they give some indication of intelligence B but the accuracy of the result depends on the VALIDITY and comprehensiveness of the test.

intelligence quotient (IQ)   A measure of how a person scores on an INTELLIGENCE TEST. With children, the IQ used to be defined as the ratio of mental age to chronological age, expressed as a percentage. General purpose intelligence tests are so constructed that the mean IQ score for the POPULATION as a whole will be 100 and about two-thirds of the population will score IQs between 85 and 115.

intelligence test One of many different STANDARDISED TESTS used to obtain a person's IQ which is assumed to give an indication of his INTELLIGENCE.

intelligentsia, the The group of people in society who are both well-educated and intelligent and who tend to regard themselves as the protectors of what is best in that society's CULTURE.

intensive course A CRASH COURSE; one covering a great deal in a short time – found especially in the teaching of foreign languages.

interaction analysis An approach from GROUP DYNAMICS involving the systematic recording of how members of a group react to one another in a situation, and the analysis of the results with a view to interpretation. For one of the many applications to educational group situations, see FLANDERS INTERACTION ANALYSIS.

interactive device Usually a computer TERMINAL allowing the user to communicate directly with the computer and obtain immediate answers to his questions – perhaps as part of a developing dialogue.

interdisciplinary approach/course/enquiry/method One in which two or more DISCIPLINES are brought together (eg medicine and architecture in the study of a problem in public health), preferably in such a way that the disciplines interact with one another and have some effect on one another's perspectives. Contrasts with a UNI-DISCIPLINARY APPROACH (in which only one discipline is concerned) and also with a MULTI-DISCIPLINARY APPROACH (in which several disciplines are involved but do not interact with one another in coming to their conclusions).

interface The boundary through which communication is possible between one entity and another, eg a keyboard may be the interface between a student and a computer.

interference Term used in the psychology of learning and MEMORY to describe a person's inability to remember a piece of knowledge or demonstrate a skill because of something contradictory or confusing he has also learned. For example, one's

135

recall of a Spanish word may be interfered with by recall of the French or Italian equivalents.

interlibrary loan   Most college and university libraries operate a scheme whereby books they do not possess can be obtained for borrowers for a short period of time from other libraries, notably from the BRITISH LIBRARY.

intermittent reinforcement   See REINFORCEMENT SCHEDULE.

intern   See INTERNSHIP.

internal degree   Term relating particularly to London University whose FIRST DEGREE examinations may be taken by students of its own colleges (internal degrees) but also by certain students who have studied in certain other colleges or by correspondence courses (external degrees).

internal examination/assessment   ASSESSMENT of pupils or students by an INTERNAL EXAMINER/ASSESSOR.

internal examiner/assessor   An examiner who is on the staff of the institution whose students are being assessed. (Contrasts with an EXTERNAL EXAMINER who is from another institution.)

internalisation   The process of making 'part of oneself' the ATTITUDES, VALUES and ideas that one has heard from others or thought out for oneself.

internal truancy   Term sometimes used in connection with pupils who are in school but are missing lessons.

International Baccalaureate   Qualification established in 1967 to be worked towards by students attending a school catering for a variety of nationalities (perhaps as a result of their parents' temporary residence in the country). It is meant to serve as an ENTRY QUALIFICATION acceptable to institutions of HIGHER EDUCATION whether they return to their own country or move on to another one.

International Standard Book Number (ISBN)   Since 1967, the growing use of computers in the book trade has led to books being identified by a system of standard book numbers. Each book has its distinctive number, usually found on the reverse of the title page: the first set of digits identifies the publisher, the second set identifies the book and the particular volume or edition, and the final digit provides a means for the computer to check the rest of the number. The purpose of standard book numbers is to facilitate the ordering, storage and supplying of books. (See also INTERNATIONAL STANDARD SERIAL NUMBER.)

International Standard Serial Number (ISSN)   The equivalent of the INTERNATIONAL STANDARD BOOK NUMBER but used for serials; that is, journals and periodicals.

international system (SI units) A measuring system (système international d'unites) that is being adopted in many countries (usually at the expense of the IMPERIAL SYSTEM or the US CUSTOMARY SYSTEM), especially for scientific and technical purposes. It has seven basic units: the metre, kilogramme, second, ampere, kelvin, candela and mole – all other units being derived from these by multiplication or division.

internship (**US**) **1** Equivalent to the UK PROBATIONARY YEAR – a period of probation served by the newly-qualified schoolteacher who is known as an intern. (Other professions, eg doctors, use the same term for the same purpose.) **2** Sometimes a probationary or practice period that forms part of the degree programme (as in a UK SANDWICH COURSE).

interpolation The process of estimating the VALUE of the DEPENDENT VARIABLE associated with a particular value of the INDEPENDENT VARIABLE on the basis of two or more known values of the dependent variable. For example, if the temperature at 12 noon was 10°C and at 12.30 was 12°C, one might interpolate the temperature at 12.05 as having been about 11°C.

interpretative reading 'Reading aloud' when the reader is expected not simply to convey the literal meaning of what is written but also to 'put expression into it'.

intersession (US) Short break between academic TERMS, which may be used simply as vacation or in which extra, short courses may be available, optional for some students perhaps but required for others.

interval scale See SCALES OF MEASUREMENT.

interview **1** A form of ASSESSMENT in which two or more people meet face to face. Usually we think of one or more people interviewing a candidate to decide whether or not to offer him a particular job or educational opportunity. But we might usefully think also of the candidate interviewing them to decide whether he really wants what they have to offer. Either way, such an interview is often thought to be a rather ineffective means of getting reliable information. **2** A research technique, much used in SOCIAL SURVEYS and ILLUMINATIVE EVALUATION, in which the researcher asks questions of the interviewee (often in a pre-determined sequence) to ascertain his habits, opinions, history, etc.

interviewer bias Where the opinion or reactions of the interviewer intrude on an INTERVIEW to the extent that the person being interviewed gives different answers than he otherwise would.

in-tray/in-basket exercise A form of SIMULATION training in which realistic work conditions and tasks are simulated by requiring the learner to make appropriate decisions and implement appropriate actions in response to a sequence of letters, memos and other problem-posing documents supposedly reaching him in his in-tray. Originated in MANAGEMENT EDUCATION.

intrinsic programme Another name for a BRANCHING PROGRAMME.

intrinsic motivation The motivation to perform some task or engage in some activity for its own sake, not the sake of some external reward (eg the praise of a teacher). Contrasts with EXTRINSIC MOTIVATION.

introjection The process whereby **1** a person adopts into his SELF-IMAGE the perceptions and attitudes of other people towards him; or **2** directs towards himself any feelings towards another person that he is unable to express (for example, hostility to others can supposedly be repressed and turned inward as a suicidal impulse).

introspection The conscious examination of one's own feelings and thought processes. One early and influential school of psychology depended heavily on introspection for its insights, but criticisms of the subjective nature of such an approach caused it to fall out of fashion.

introversion The PERSONALITY state of an individual who is withdrawn, inhibited, serious, pre-occupied with his own thoughts and feelings and more interested in ideas and subjective processes than in social interaction and the outside world. Contrasts with EXTROVERSION.

intuit To know or apprehend by intuition, without conscious reasoning.

intuitive stage A stage in Piaget's theory of COGNITIVE DEVELOPMENT in which the child (aged around four to seven years) relies on impressionistic, superficial perceptions of the world (eg his undeveloped sense of CONSERVATION). Precedes the stage of CONCRETE OPERATIONS.

inventory A form of QUESTIONNAIRE, often used in the assessment of PERSONALITY. It commonly contains a number of statements, some of which a person may indicate as applying to him;

his particular selection enables the researcher to identify him as belonging to one or another of several pre-determined categories.

inverse correlation See NEGATIVE CORRELATION.

invigilator A person responsible for supervising and ensuring the proper conduct of candidates while an EXAMINATION is in progress. (In the US might be called MONITOR or PROCTOR).

invisible college **1** In general, the wider community of scholars to which many ACADEMICS feel they belong, sharing values and aims and standards with an international body of 'seekers after truth', most of whom they will never meet but whose existence helps give purpose and validity to their own activities. **2** More restrictively, the closely linked network of researchers and scholars in a specific subject or problem area, who read and criticise one another's work and who exchange regular and frequent visits, and who debate with one another at conferences.

IPI (US) Individually Prescribed Instruction, a scheme covering the teaching of the LANGUAGE ARTS, mathematics and science from the KINDERGARTEN to sixth grade of ELEMENTARY SCHOOL, developed in 1964 by staff of the University of Pittsburgh. It incorporates BATTERIES of tests used to assess where each child needs to start in each subject, and to assess his progress. On the basis of the tests, the teacher develops a 'prescription' which involves the learner in working through an appropriate sequence of pre-prepared learning materials and exercises – chiefly in print but with some AUDIO-TAPE material. Similar to, though less elaborate than, the PLAN project.

IQ See INTELLIGENCE QUOTIENT.

Isaacs, Susan (1885–1945) British psychologist and teacher who wrote of her observations of child development in the Malting House School, Cambridge. Her influential books included: *The Intellectual Growth of Young Children* (1930); *The Children We Teach* (1932); and *The Social Development of Young Children* (1937).

'isation and 'ism Endings added to words like urban or egalitarian or instrumental or ritual (usually by sociologists or historians), and usually in order to suggest that some apparently ordinary feature of everyday life is, in reality, a force or trend within society.

ISBN INTERNATIONAL STANDARD BOOK NUMBER.

isolate, an Term used in SOCIOMETRY to describe a person who chooses to make a relationship with no-one in his social group and with whom no-one in the group chooses to make a relationship either.

isotype chart   A form of PICTOGRAM developed by Otto and Marie Neurath in Vienna in the 1920s in which statistical data is represented not by figures (or not only by figures) but by little pictures which illustrate the item and quantity concerned. Thus, if one country builds four hundred ships a year and another country only one hundred, then the first country would have four ship symbols against its name (each representing one hundred ships) and the second country would have only one such symbol.

ISSN   International Standard Serial Number.

ita   See INITIAL TEACHING ALPHABET.

italic script   A style of handwriting, using a broad-nibbed pen, based upon informal writing of the Italian RENAISSANCE. It has been popular in the UK since the 1940s (especially with artists and designers) and is taught to children in many PRIMARY SCHOOLS in the belief that it can combine speed, beauty and individuality. It is sometimes called CHANCERY SCRIPT.

item   The name given to each question or problem in PSYCHOLOGICAL TESTS.

item analysis   The study of students' responses to each ITEM in a test with a view to improving the test, perhaps by removing items that are too difficult or too easy or that students answer equally well regardless of how well they do on the test as a whole.

item bank   A large collection of test questions, in a particular subject-matter and at a particular level, that is constantly being added to and from which can be drawn new combinations of questions to make up new tests.

itinerant teacher   (US) Same as PERIPATETIC TEACHER.

ITV   In US contexts ITV means INSTRUCTIONAL TELEVISION – rather than the UK meaning of independent (ie commercial) television.

ivory tower   Intellectuals and scholars, and especially ACADEMICS in universities, are sometimes accused of shutting themselves up in an 'ivory tower' and isolating themselves from the problems and practicalities of real life.

Ivy League   (US) Term referring to eight universities in the north-eastern states (Harvard, Yale, Princeton, Cornell, Dartmouth, Pennsylvania, Brown and Columbia), enjoying there the same kind of academic and social prestige as Oxford and Cambridge in the UK. The term arose out of intercollegiate sports but is now used to label the attitudes, clothes, standards etc, associated with students of those institutions. (Similar to UK talk of 'OXBRIDGE attitudes'.)

J

'jackdaw' Trade-name for a UK publication consisting of a wallet containing facsimile documents (letters, maps, diary pages, drawings, posters, proclamations, etc) for use in a RESOURCE-BASED approach to history teaching.

James Report 1972 The UK REPORT of an enquiry into the EDUCATION and TRAINING of teachers in England and Wales. It made far-reaching recommendations, particularly for a new qualification, the DIPLOMA OF HIGHER EDUCATION, that could be used either as a qualification in its own right or as a stepping stone towards a DEGREE (eg in education); for an intending teacher's INITIAL TRAINING to conclude with a year in which he teaches for four fifths of his time and spends the remainder following courses at special centres; and for much greater emphasis to be placed on IN-SERVICE EDUCATION and training, with PROFESSIONAL TUTORS on the staff of schools and centres for in-service education; and paid leave at intervals for teachers wishing to pursue further professional studies.

James, William (1842-1910) US philosopher and psychologist (and brother of novelist, Henry James). He taught at Harvard, established the world's first experimental psychology laboratory and confirmed his reputation with his book, *The Principles of Psychology* (1890), which indirectly influenced generations of students, as did his subsequent book *Talks to Teachers* (1899).

janitor US and Scottish equivalent of CARETAKER. May also be called CUSTODIAN in US.

jargon The specialised language used by people involved in a particular trade or profession or academic DISCIPLINE. It may consist of vocabulary peculiar to that pursuit and/or it may incorporate words and phrases drawn from other contexts but use them in peculiar ways. People familiar with the jargon see it as a kind of shorthand way of communicating among themselves. But outsiders (eg students new to the area) often regard it with some hostility, believing it (justifiably, on occasions) to be a barrier erected to keep them out or a smoke screen meant to distract attention from the fact that its user has nothing very original or significant to say.

Jaques-Dalcroze, Emile (1865–1950) A Swiss composer who developed EURHYTHMICS as a union of music and physical movement in education.

JCR See JUNIOR COMMON ROOM.

Jesuit education As carried on in the schools and colleges staffed by members of the Society of Jesus (founded by Ignatius Loyola in 1534) which have long been major institutions for education and scholarship, producing many of the INTELLIGENT-SIA of the Roman Catholic Church.

job analysis The study of a job with a view to determining its component tasks and the circumstances in which each is carried out. The type of analysis may vary according to whether it is intended to aid in TRAINING, personnel selection, JOB ENGINEER-ING, etc.

job centre One of the many new 'employment exchanges' set up on the main shopping streets of UK towns since 1973. They are operated by the Employment Service Division and provide informal surroundings in which people seeking jobs can discover what vacancies are available, obtain advice about particular jobs, and even obtain general OCCUPATIONAL GUIDANCE.

job corps (US) A federal organisation established in 1964 to provide general education and VOCATIONAL TRAINING for unemployed youths or school DROPOUTS in order that they might more easily find work.

job description The description of a job, its component tasks and the circumstances in which they are performed, such as might result from a JOB ANALYSIS.

job engineering Altering a job, by changing the duties and responsibilities, or methods and materials, or the amount or kind of skill required, so that it can be done by the person who is available to do it. In effect, job engineering adapts the job to the worker while TRAINING, on the other hand, adapts the worker to the job.

job enrichment The process of restructuring a job (or, more likely, a group of related jobs) so as to increase the level of initiative required in each job and so offer more JOB SATISFACTION to the worker.

job evaluation The process of determining the relative demands of a number of related jobs (but not the effectiveness of the workers currently occupying them), with a view perhaps to attaching an appropriate salary grade to each job.

job instruction breakdown   A term used in TRAINING WITHIN INDUSTRY courses for the instructor's analysis of the stages of a job to be presented to a trainee together with notes relating to safety and quality at each stage.

job/labour market   The demand for workers, either school leavers or more experienced people, in general or in particular categories. Beliefs as to the nature of the likely job market may influence decisions made in schools and colleges.

job mobile   (US) Van staffed by social workers touring around to give information about job opportunities to DROPOUTS and other unemployed people.

job rotation   Systematic transfer of people from one job to another within a group of jobs. Meant to widen each one's experience and expertise and/or to divide the burden of responsibility or irksome duties.

job satisfaction   The extent to which each person in an organisation obtains satisfaction from the processes and context of his work. Maximising job satisfaction and minimising the frustrations and dissatisfactions is widely recognised as one of the important goals in modern management.

jock   (US) As in 'a campus jock'. Somewhat contemptuous term for a college student who pursues athletic rather than ACADEMIC success. (Presumably derived from 'jock-strap'.)

joint (honours) degree   An HONOURS DEGREE resulting from the study of two or more subjects to the same level.

Jung, Carl Gustav   (1875–1961) Swiss psychoanalyst and SIGMUND FREUD's prized disciple who broke with Freud over the latter's emphasis on the sexual causation of neurosis. He went on to establish his own school of analytical psychology, developing the concepts of collective unconscious (a 'race-memory' inherited from our ancestors) and of the introvert and extrovert as the two main psychological types. See M Fordham's, *An Introduction to Jung's Psychology*. Penguin (1966).

junior college   (US) Local college (sometimes called a city or COMMUNITY COLLEGE) offering a wide range of two-year courses to HIGH SCHOOL GRADUATES. The two years may be known as GRADES 13 and 14 and the ACADEMIC work done therein may sometimes be regarded as equivalent to the first two years in another college or university, allowing some students to transfer to such an institution for the final two years of a BACHELOR'S DEGREE programme.

junior common room (JCR)   Phrase used in college or university to describe the meeting room(s) used by students and sometimes, by extension, to refer to the STUDENT BODY itself.

Junior Eysenck Personality Inventory   Test of PERSONALITY for school-children designed to measure the dimensions EXTROVERSION-INTROVERSION and NEUROTICISM-STABILITY.

junior high school   (US) A HIGH SCHOOL for children between the ages of 12 and 14 years (GRADES 7, 8 and perhaps 9). Originally developed to help pupils make the transition from ELEMENTARY SCHOOLS.

junior school   One of the several schools maintained by each UK LOCAL EDUCATION AUTHORITY for children aged between about 7 and 11 years. Younger children attend an INFANT(S) SCHOOL which may be quite separate or may, with the junior school, be part of a combined PRIMARY SCHOOL under one HEADTEACHER.

junior secondary school   Type of Scottish school broadly equivalent to the SECONDARY MODERN SCHOOL in England and Wales. (See also SENIOR SECONDARY SCHOOL.)

junior-senior high school   (US) A HIGH SCHOOL providing for all children of HIGH SCHOOL age (12 to 18 years) but usually with a junior and senior division within it.

junior technical college (or school)   Prior to the EDUCATION ACT 1944, a UK institution offering TECHNICAL and VOCATIONAL EDUCATION to pupils between the ages of 13 and 16/17 years.

junior year   (US) The third year of a four year degree course at college or university. The first two years (the FRESHMAN and SOPHOMORE years) may be omitted by students transferring from JUNIOR COLLEGE. The fourth year is the SENIOR YEAR.

juvenile   In legal terms, a person not considered as an adult and therefore not capable of criminal responsibility in a court of law. The age of criminal responsibility varies from country to country, just as it has changed over time.

juvenile court   **1** (UK) A special magistrates' court dealing with criminal charges against young people between 10 and 17 years or with applications to the effect that they are in need of care and protection. A juvenile court is informal and excludes the press and public. **2** (US) A children's court that deals both with juvenile offenders and with adults accused of causing juveniles to commit offences.

junior training centres Institutions set up to enable severely subnormal children (once thought to be ineducable) to acquire whatever skills each is capable of; formerly operated by the UK Department of Health and Social Security but, since 1971, absorbed into the system of SPECIAL SCHOOLS provided by LOCAL EDUCATION AUTHORITIES.

K

Kalamazoo case (US) This was a test case brought to the Michigan Supreme Court in 1874 (as were similar cases in other states) to determine whether the city of Kalamazoo had the legal right to establish a HIGH SCHOOL, to employ a SUPERINTENDENT OF SCHOOLS, and to collect local taxes to pay for these services. As in several other states, it was decided that high schools were a legitimate expenditure in that they were needed to complete the path from ELEMENTARY SCHOOL to STATE UNIVERSITY. (The case is somewhat similar to that giving rise to the COCKERTON JUDGEMENT in the UK, though the decision was different.)

Kant, Immanuel (1724–1804) German philosopher whose chief works of educational relevance are *Groundwork of The Metaphysics of Morals* and *On Education*. He saw the function of education as being to awaken individuals to a realisation of their autonomy as rational beings capable of moral action for its own sake, not for hope of external (eg heavenly) reward.

Kay-Shuttleworth, Sir James (1804–77) As a physician working among the poor cotton workers in Manchester during the cholera epidemic of 1832, and later as an administrator of the system for providing relief and support for the poor from public funds, he came to believe in education as a means of fighting poverty. In 1839, he became First Secretary to the Committee of the Council on Education and promoted many of the distinctive features that emerged with the rise of popular education in the 19th century, eg PUPIL-TEACHERS, teacher-training, and inspection of schools.

Keate, John (1773–1852) Keate's claim to fame rests largely on his 'reign of terror' as headmaster (1809–1832) of Eton College which, like most famous PUBLIC SCHOOLS of the day, was notorious for its brutality, disorder and rebellion. Although he pioneered no educational innovations, he did impose order on the school – largely through severe corporal punishment. On one day alone, in 1832, he flogged 80 boys.

Keller, Helen (1880–1968)   US author and lecturer who became deaf, blind and mute in her infancy, but who learned to read, write and speak thanks to an extra-ordinary relationship with Miss A M Sullivan who began teaching her from the age of seven years. Helen Keller herself went on to work for the handicapped and wrote *The Story of My Life* (1951).

Keller Plan   An INDIVIDUAL LEARNING system in university teaching, where the student works through a sequence of (largely printed) SELF-INSTRUCTIONAL MATERIALS, being allowed to pass from one unit to the next only when his POST-TEST results are satisfactory. Lectures and seminars may be added for motivational purposes. The system was developed in the US, but is now to be found in many countries. See *The Keller Plan Handbook: Essays on a Personalised System of Instruction* (1974) by Keller and Sherman.

Kellogg Foundation   (US) An educational trust founded in 1930 to narrow the gap between the creation of knowledge and its application for the public good. It is influential in promoting CONTINUING EDUCATION through the universities.

Kelly G A (1905–1967)   US psychologist with a special interest in PERSONALITY; creator of PERSONAL CONSTRUCT THEORY. See his *Theory of Personal Constructs* (1955).

Kennedy scholarships   (US) Awards named after President Kennedy and enabling UK students to study in certain US universities.

Keohane Report 1979   A UK report recommending the establishment of a CERTIFICATE OF EXTENDED EDUCATION (CEE) to be taken by students at 17-plus. The CEE would be a one-year full-time course designed to help prepare young people for employment and would contain proficiency tests in basic language and numerical skills. Despite promising trial runs of the proposed course, the Government seems likely to back instead a new, even more vocationally oriented course.

keynote lecture/speech   The introductory lecture at a conference or gathering, usually given by a person of eminence in the relevant field and intended to set the tone and/or outline some themes for the subsequent proceedings.

key words 1 Words revealed by the analysis of children's literature (eg by Dolch in the US and Murray and McNally in the UK) to appear with the greatest frequency, and therefore needing to be taught early and effectively. For example, it has been suggested that the following twelve words – a, and, he, I, in, is, it, of, that, the, to, was – make up about one quarter of all words read. 2 In INFORMATION SCIENCE the term may be used to refer to any single words within a document that can be picked out to give people an idea of its content.

K-factor The spatial factor in INTELLIGENCE – the ability to perceive size and spatial relationships correctly.

kinaesthetic method A method of teaching reading and number concepts by having the child trace the form of a written letter or numeral with his finger at the same time as he is saying its name.

kinaesthetic perception The sensation of movement, weight, resistance, muscle tension and bodily position.

Kilpatrick, William H (1871–1965) US EDUCATIONIST, professor of education at Columbia University, who stressed the educational value of life experiences for children and defined learning as living. See his *The Project Method* (1918), *Foundations of Method* (1925) and *Remaking the Curriculum* (1936).

kindergarten A school for children of about two to five years. The name, which was invented by FROEBEL, is more commonly used in the US than in the UK, where NURSERY SCHOOL is the more common name. In Australia, the first year of INFANT SCHOOL may be called the kindergarten year.

kinetographic notation/symbols Systems of symbols used by choreographers, sportsmen, physical educationalists, etc, to illustrate complex movements of the human body.

kit Set of educational materials (perhaps a MULTI-MEDIA PACKAGE) from which a student can learn, alone or in a small group, but probably without a teacher being present. See HOME-EXPERIMENT KIT.

Klein, Melanie (1882–1960) German psychoanalyst who settled in England in 1926 and became leader of one of two British groups of psychoanalysts following SIGMUND FREUD, the other being led by his daughter, ANNA FREUD. The Klein group worked with children as young as three years and claimed to interpret their play in terms of the underlying conflicts. See her *The Psycho-analysis of Children* (1959).

knowledge   The body of information and understanding which individuals acquire through life-experience and through education. Educational institutions are so powerful in determining and rewarding what is to count as worthwhile knowledge that people from a CULTURE other than that embodied in those institutions often come to have little awareness of, or respect for, their own undoubted knowledge and their capacity to learn.

knowledge structure   The notion that a body of specialist knowledge is organised within the minds and thinking processes of the practitioners of a profession or academic DISCIPLINE in such a way that it can be described (perhaps even diagrammatically) in terms of hierarchies and networks of related concepts and principles.

knowledge of results   A form of FEEDBACK important in learning. A learner will be encouraged in a good performance if he is told how well he has done. Of course, if the results of his performance are poor, knowledge of them may be discouraging, but may still be necessary if he is to make progress.

Kohler, Wolfgang   (1887–1967) German psychologist and leading exponent of the GESTALT school who researched into learning and problem-solving among apes. See his *Principles of Gestalt Psychology* (1935).

Koh's Block Design Test   A non-verbal test in which a person has to reproduce from a number of blocks with differently-coloured sides certain patterns presented to him on test cards.

Kuder preference record   Test used in VOCATIONAL GUIDANCE in which the individual indicates his most preferred and least preferred activity in each of several sets of activities.

L

lab   Short for laboratory.

Laban, Rudolf (1879–1958)   German innovator in free dance who settled in England in 1938 and became instrumental in developing the modern approach to DANCE IN EDUCATION – based on his idea of movement as a form of human expression that is capable of drawing on all aspects of the personality (not just the physical) and enriching it. See his book *Modern Educational Dance* (1948).

labelling Sociological term for the familiar but dangerous habit of classifying a person or a thing as a member of this or that or the other category (eg rebel, slow learner, racist, deprived child, etc) and then endowing him in one's mind with all the attributes associated with our STEREOTYPE of that category, regardless of whether there is evidence of them all in this particular case. This may result in a HALO EFFECT and amount to a SELF-FULFILLING PROPHECY.

laboratory 1 A room equipped for scientific experiments or demonstrations. 2 A room equipped for practical work in non-scientific subjects, eg a LANGUAGE LABORATORY. 3 The term is also sometimes used (especially in the US) as an alternative to 'WORKSHOP' when describing not a room but a course or SEMINAR. For example, 'a two-day human relations laboratory'.

laboratory course One centred around work in a LABORATORY and probably emphasising practical and experimental techniques.

labour market See JOB MARKET.

laddering A technique in PERSONALITY-testing developed by Hinkle in which the person being tested is asked to explain his preferences on each DIMENSION of personality revealed as important to him, and which leads to even more important dimensions being revealed.

laissez-faire (French, 'let do'). Usually refers to a government policy of non-interference in the economic activities of business and commerce but, in education, is sometimes applied to the style of the kind of teacher who gives no direction to his pupils, allowing them to work or not as the fancy takes them.

Lancaster, Joseph (1778–1833) Like ANDREW BELL, Lancaster developed the MONITORIAL SYSTEM in ELEMENTARY EDUCATION whereby older pupils taught younger ones. Lancaster exported his version to Canada in 1818 and his book, *Improvements in Education* (1803), promoted world-wide interest in the so-called LANCASTRIAN SYSTEM.

Lancastrian system The version of the MONITORIAL SYSTEM (whereby older pupils teach younger ones) developed by JOSEPH LANCASTER.

land grant college (US) A Federal Government Act of 1862 granted public land to the states so that colleges and universities might be established to promote the study of agriculture, engineering and other 'practical' subjects. Most land grant institutions have long since offered a wider range of subjects.

Lane, Homer (1875–1925) A US pioneer in the educational treatment of disturbed and delinquent children. He first made his mark by introducing a considerable measure of self-government into a school for such children in Detroit and in 1913 came to England to take charge of a similar institution in Dorset, called the LITTLE COMMONWEALTH. Lane's central emphasis was on winning the trust of children, even at the risk of teachers having to put up with anti-social and aggressive behaviour. He was also an early advocate of PSYCHOANALYSIS in dealing with disturbed children. Such ideas were ahead of their time and LITTLE COMMONWEALTH closed in 1918. Lane's ideas, however, continued to have influence. See David Wills's *Homer Lane: A Biography* (1964).

language Any system of conventional signs and symbols (eg written or spoken words, gestures, pictures, numerals, etc), whereby a human being (or, in a more limited sense, an animal or even a computer) can interpret his/her/its experience and communicate thoughts and/or feelings to another person (or creature or machine) capable of extracting an appropriate meaning. The acquisition of language skills, and the psychological and social roles of language, are active and controversial areas of research in EDUCATIONAL PSYCHOLOGY and the SOCIOLOGY OF EDUCATION.

language arts (US) A CURRICULUM SUBJECT concerned with the skills involved in expressing ideas in writing and in speech, and in understanding the written and spoken ideas of other people. (The term is also used in Scottish primary schools.)

language codes Usages of LANGUAGE peculiar to particular groups of people, or particular circumstances; the term was suggested by BERNSTEIN who identified ELABORATED CODE and RESTRICTED CODE.

language deficit/handicap Suffered by a person (eg a child or an adult immigrant) whose language skills are inadequate to cope with the demands made by the CULTURE.

language development/growth The growth of a person's skill in using language (usually his native language) in reading, writing, and speech. May be influenced by age, INTELLIGENCE, MOTIVATION, prior knowledge of LANGUAGE(s), and the MODELS of language provided by his companion, parents, teachers, etc.

language laboratory A classroom for language teaching, with equipment enabling each student to listen to words or phrases played back from a pre-recorded tape on his individual TAPE-RECORDER and to record and compare his own repetitions or responses. The teacher, at a central monitoring CONSOLE can 'listen in' on any individual student's efforts, and advise him, without the rest of the class hearing.

large type books Books (and other reading materials) printed in unusually large, clear letters (eg lower case letters at least seven millimetres in height) for the benefit of people with poor sight.

latch-key child Child who carries a doorkey to let himself into the house on return from school because the parents are out at work. Often assumed to be a child suffering from neglect or even CULTURAL DEPRIVATION.

late adolescence The period of adolescence from about 16 to 20 years when the physical changes of puberty have usually taken place but the individual is still facing and resolving questions about his role in relation to others. (See IDENTITY CRISIS.)

late bloomer (US) See LATE DEVELOPER.

late developer A person who achieves certain standards (eg in academic work or sport) at a later age than most people are expected to and/or who achieves higher standards than were predicted from his earlier achievements. In academic work, the late development may apply generally or just to one or two subjects. (A common US equivalent is late bloomer.)

latent learning Knowledge that is acquired (perhaps as INCIDENTAL LEARNING) rather than INNATE, but which is not displayed until some time after its acquisition.

lateral dominance See LATERALITY.

laterality A person's preference for using a limb or muscle or organ on one side of his body rather than its counterpart on the other. Thus a person may be right-handed or left-footed, or may prefer to use his right ear or left eye. In 'cross-laterality' the person chooses different sides for different purposes, eg the person who is left-handed but whose right eye is dominant.

lateral thinking A kind of DIVERGENT THINKING, where one looks at a problem from a variety of view-points instead of committing oneself exhaustively to one immediately promising line of enquiry. Recommended as a creative approach to problem-solving by Edward de Bono in *The Use of Lateral Thinking* (Penguin, 1971).

Latin (grammar) school (US) Schools established in the British

Colonies before the Revolution, usually religious in ethos, and existing primarily to help boys acquire the familiarity with Latin (and to a much lesser extent, Greek) required for entry to COLLEGE.

laurea   A FIRST DEGREE from an Italian university giving its holder the title of 'dottore'.

law of effect   A simple generalisation about LEARNING formulated by THORNDIKE suggesting, in essence, that, given a certain STIMULUS, a person is more likely to make RESPONSES of a kind that gave rise to feelings of satisfaction on past occasions than to make responses of a kind that were accompanied by discomfort.

law of exercise   A generalisation about LEARNING, formulated by THORNDIKE, and suggesting that the likelihood of a person (or animal) making a particular RESPONSE to a given STIMULUS is a function of the frequency with which the stimulus and response have been associated in the past.

lay teacher   Teacher in a school run by the clergy of a religious persuasion but who is not himself a member of that clergy.

LEA   See LOCAL EDUCATION AUTHORITY.

leading question   A question so phrased as to suggest the desired answer, eg 'Is it not a fact that . . . .?'

learned goal   A GOAL or purpose that is acquired (eg through social interaction and increased knowledge) rather than INNATE or physiological, eg the desire for a balanced diet rather than for as much food as possible.

learned journal   (Pronounced 'learn-ed) rather than 'learnd'.' Any regular and prestigious publication, perhaps associated with a LEARNED SOCIETY, in which appear papers setting forth the latest thinking or research findings of leading scholars in a particular academic DISCIPLINE.

learned society   (Pronounced 'learn-ed' rather than 'learnd'.) An association of scholars in a particular academic DISCIPLINE, devoted to the advancement of knowledge in that discipline through research and publication.

learner-centred approach/teaching/education   An approach to teaching in which the teacher purports to be guided more by the needs and interests of the individual child than by the dictates of a SYLLABUS or the demands of other members of society. This is a key element in PROGRESSIVE education and teachers who advocate it commonly voice the slogan: 'I teach children, not subjects'.

learner-controlled   education/approach/teaching/instruction   A situation in which the learner has some control over the ends and/or means of his learning. See INDEPENDENT LEARNING.

learner verification and revision (LVR)   A US slogan used in urging that educational materials should not be subject to DEVELOPMENTAL TESTING only prior to publication: that, in addition, data showing learners' reactions to the materials should constantly be collected and used for regular improvement of the materials as long as they continue to be published.

learning   A long-lasting change in KNOWLEDGE, ATTITUDE or SKILL, acquired through experience (rather than, say, through MATURATION). This experience may take the form of CONDITIONING, EDUCATION, INCIDENTAL LEARNING, INSTRUCTION, TRAINING, and so on.

learning activity package   See PACKAGE.

learning block   A difficulty in mastering a particular SUBJECT, or, more likely, part of a subject. May be due to lack of PRE-REQUISITE knowledge or to INTERFERENCE.

learning-by-appointment   Scheme in which students have access to SELF-INSTRUCTIONAL MATERIALS at pre-arranged times, probably in a specially-equipped room and with advice available, if needed, from a teacher.

learning curve   A graph showing how a learner improves with practice in a new SKILL he is learning. Quality or speed of performance will be measured along the vertical axis and time, or number of repetitions, along the horizontal axis. The curve may, for example, show that the student improves in skill very slowly at first; then big improvements come very quickly; then the rate of improvement slows right down to almost nothing.

learning difficulty   **1** The extent to which a given SUBJECT or topic seems hard to learn for most pupils in a given group. **2** The extent to which a given pupil finds a particular subject or topic (or maybe all subjects) hard to learn. Such difficulties may be due, for example, to lack of certain PRE-REQUISITE learning among pupils, to INTERFERENCE from what they know already, to mental or physical handicaps, and, of course, to weaknesses in the teaching or ambiguities or inconsistencies in the subject itself.

learning experience   Any event, created, for example, by a course, lesson, book, discussion or whatever else, that was intended to help a pupil learn, or that results in his doing so whether intended to or not.

153

learning hierarchy The KNOWLEDGE and SKILLS to be learned in a certain SUBJECT-area analysed into separate elements and ordered according to which elements need to be learned before certain others become learnable. For example, the learning may be analysed in terms of COMPONENT OBJECTIVES and ENABLING OBJECTIVES.

learning laboratory Room(s) equipped with SELF-INSTRUCTIONAL MATERIALS and all appropriate audio-visual HARDWARE for INDIVIDUALISED LEARNING, whether by individuals or small groups of students.

learning materials Anything in the world could be learning material in that it might help the student learn. But the term is usually applied to books, worksheets, tapes, films, etc, on which some educational content has been pre-recorded, or to some natural object (eg a rock specimen or prepared microscope slide) whose educational content is brought out by the teacher or by other accompanying materials.

learning network The kind of informal association of people willing to teach and learn from one another that IVAN ILLICH envisaged as part of his DE-SCHOOLED society. (See his *Deschooling Society*, 1971.)

learning objectives See OBJECTIVES.

learning outcomes The KNOWLEDGE, ATTITUDES, SKILLS etc, that the student acquires as a result of some LEARNING EXPERIENCE. These include any unintended (and perhaps undesirable) results of learning as well as those that were intended (eg the OBJECTIVES). Thus, for instance, the learning outcomes of a course on simultaneous and quadratic equations may be not only that the student has become capable of solving such equations but also that he has come to hate algebra.

learning package See PACKAGE.

learning plateau A flat section on a learner's LEARNING CURVE, showing that he has reached a stage in learning a new skill at which (perhaps temporarily) additional practice or extra time devoted to the SKILL is resulting in no measurable improvement in performance.

learning programme Can refer to any systematic sequence of LEARNING EXPERIENCE, whether arranged by a teacher or by the student himself; or it may refer, more specifically, to the kind of structured LEARNING MATERIALS produced by practitioners of PROGRAMMED LEARNING.

154

learning resources   Not only the LEARNING MATERIALS, but also the human beings (teachers, other students, SKILL-MODELS, and other people knowledgeable in a certain subject) from whom students might learn.

learning resources centre   See RESOURCES CENTRE.

learning skills   See STUDY SKILLS.

learning strategy   This term may be used like LEARNING STYLE to refer to the student's general approach to a variety of learning tasks or it may refer to his chosen way of tackling a particular task, See DEEP LEVEL and SURFACE LEVEL PROCESSING for descriptions of two different learning strategies.

learning style   A student's habitual manner of problem-solving or thinking or learning, eg SERIALIST or HOLIST, REFLECTIVE or IMPULSIVE. The student may not be conscious of his style and may adopt different styles for different learning tasks or circumstances. See also LEARNING STRATEGY.

learning system   The organised means whereby students are helped to learn. Includes the planning of CURRICULUM, the provision of LEARNING RESOURCES (including human beings) in appropriate places and at appropriate times, and facilities whereby students can obtain FEEDBACK regarding their progress and ultimate attainment.

learning techniques   See STUDY SKILLS.

learning theory   The body of theory (or, rather, theories – often conflicting) produced by different schools of psychology to explain what comprises learning and/or how it takes place or fails to take place. See also THEORY.

learning web   Same as LEARNING NETWORK.

leaving certificate   See SCHOOL LEAVING CERTIFICATE.

lecture agency/bureau   (US) One of several organisations arranging financially-rewarding lecture tours of colleges, women's clubs, etc, for celebrities (eg sportspersons, authors and ex-astronauts).

lecture method   Teaching method in which the teacher presents a stream of ideas orally to a group of students without much opportunity for them to participate other than by listening and taking notes. It is still the central teaching method in HIGHER EDUCATION. Done well, it can be valuable in introducing students to a field of study and they can be enthused by seeing how an expert thinks and talks about his speciality. However, it can be over-used and the lecture method needs to be properly balanced with SELF-TEACHING MATERIALS (eg books) and SEMINARS and other methods that take more account of individual differences among students and/or allow for more active participation.

lecturer   The term can be used of any person who teaches using the LECTURE METHOD. More specifically it appears in the academic titles of most staff in UK institutions of FURTHER and HIGHER EDUCATION, viz, assistant lecturer, lecturer, senior lecturer, principal lecturer (some of whom may choose not to use the lecture method at all). In UK universities, lecturer is the CAREER GRADE and often compares with ASSISTANT PROFESSOR in similar US institutions.

lecture theatre   A room specially designed for the LECTURE METHOD of teaching, usually with AUDIO-VISUAL facilities and rows of banked seats and desks allowing a large number of students (perhaps several hundred) a clear view of the teacher.

Leicestershire   An English county whose LOCAL EDUCATION AUTHORITY gained a name for innovation in the 1950s with a pioneering TWO-TIER SYSTEM of COMPREHENSIVE SCHOOLS. Its fame spread to the US in the 1960s on account of its OPEN-PLAN INFANT SCHOOLS which served as models to the US advocates of OPEN CLASSROOMS.

Lent term   The term between Christmas and Easter at Cambridge University and some other educational institutions.

lesson   An individual session (eg a PERIOD or a DOUBLE PERIOD) within a course, during which teacher and pupils concentrate on a particular topic. The term may also be used of each section, concerning a separate topic, within a SELF-INSTRUCTIONAL COURSE.

lesson plan   A teacher's outline of what he hopes to accomplish with the pupils during a particular lesson. It may list AIMS and OBJECTIVES, main TEACHING POINTS, MEDIA and RESOURCES, TEACHING METHODS, method of ASSESSMENT, and so on.

letter grade   A GRADE expressed as a letter of the alphabet, usually on a FIVE-POINT SCALE, eg A, B, C, D and E.

letters   As in 'Doctor of Letters' or 'Faculty of Letters', referring to literary culture in a fairly wide sense (literature, history, philosophy, musicology, etc).

level of significance   See SIGNIFICANCE.

Leverhulme Foundation   A UK educational foundation set up in 1933 to sponsor educational research.

Lewin, Kurt   (1880–1947) German-born US GESTALT psychologist much of whose work is of relevance in education, especially that concerned with AUTHORITARIAN, DEMOCRATIC and LAISSEZ-FAIRE 'social climates' (all of which can be seen in classrooms) and his ideas on GROUP DYNAMICS and the mechanisms of social INNOVATION. See his *Resolving Social Conflict* (1945).

Lewis Report, 1968   The UK REPORT of an enquiry into the education of deaf children which recommended a range of research activities to improve teaching methods.

liberal arts   In the Middle Ages the *artes liberales* (studies fit for free men) were those of the TRIVIUM (grammar, logic, and rhetoric) and QUADRIVIUM (arithmetic, geometry, music, and astronomy). Nowadays, the liberal arts are any subjects (including some science) that fit in with modern conceptions of a LIBERAL EDUCATION.

liberal arts college   (US) A college, or department within a university, offering NON-VOCATIONAL four-year degree courses in a variety of subjects (usually including science). Sometimes called a college of arts and sciences.

liberal education   Education that is intended to free the mind and spirit, avoiding narrow specialisation, and *not* intended as vocational preparation. Its goal is 'preparation for living' rather than for earning a living. It is to be seen as satisfying EXPRESSIVE rather than INSTRUMENTAL needs.

liberal studies   More or less the same as LIBERAL ARTS but appearing under this title in the CURRICULUM of FURTHER EDUCATION COLLEGES as a minor, but hopefully 'broadening', relief from the mainly VOCATIONAL studies of technicians.

libido   A term from PSYCHOANALYSIS indicating some kind of psychic energy in the individual. For FREUD it was PSYCHOSEXUAL energy, but JUNG and others have seen it as a more basic and general psychic force.

library classification systems   Systems devised for labelling books, periodicals, and other materials so that they can be arranged in a logical way on library shelves and easily located by would-be readers. See DEWEY DECIMAL SYSTEM and LIBRARY OF CONGRESS SYSTEM.

Library of Congress system   A LIBRARY CLASSIFICATION SYSTEM developed by the staff of the major national library in the US. The scheme divides books among twenty-one main classes of knowledge, each identified by a letter of the alphabet, and into divisions or sub-divisions of those by adding a further letter and up to four numerals.

library period   A school period spent in the school library, either for a lesson on how to use libraries or for general private study. (In the US, this latter use may be called STUDY HALL, but does not usually take place in the library.)

library resources centre   A RESOURCES CENTRE that is attached (administratively if not physically) to the library in an institution. It stores, and gives staff and students access to, a wide range of materials and equipment (not just books and periodicals) but does not necessarily have facilities for producing such resources itself.

library science   Formerly known as 'librarianship' – studies connected with the organisation and use of print and non-print materials. Related to the field of INFORMATION SCIENCE.

life chances   An individual's likelihood of obtaining for himself the good things of life as defined by the CULTURE in which he lives. This varies with his INTELLIGENCE, SOCIAL CLASS, EDUCATION, and so on.

life class   Art class in which students draw, paint or sculpt from a live human model.

life experience credits   (US) Some colleges and universities are willing to give CREDITS to MATURE STUDENTS in recognition of valuable learning they have acquired not through formal study but through experience in work or other activity. The effect is to reduce the length of time such students need spend in obtaining a DEGREE.

life history   An approach to the psychological ASSESSMENT of an individual not through tests but through studying the whole course of his life to date. The approach was so named by Henry Murray in his *Explorations in Personality* (1938).

lifelong education   Same as CONTINUING EDUCATION, RECURRENT EDUCATION, etc.

life sciences   Branches of science concerned with the structure and activities of plants and animals, eg biology, physiology, bio-chemistry. (Contrast with PHYSICAL SCIENCES.)

life space   GESTALT psychology term for a person's position among the people, ideas and things that control his behaviour.

lifestyle   The attitudes, beliefs, habits and behaviour characteristic of a person or a group.

light box   A box with a flat glass surface, through which light can shine from a powerful lamp, allowing the user to view SLIDES or sheets of photographic film or to make tracings of illustrations on to any kind of paper.

light-pen   A photo-electric device with which a student interacting with a computer, perhaps while engaged in COMPUTER-ASSISTED LEARNING, can produce lines or other marks on the screen of a VISUAL DISPLAY UNIT as if using a pen.

Likert-type item   An ITEM in a test of interests or ATTITUDES in which a person is invited to indicate the extent to which he agrees or disagrees with each of a number of given statements, usually on a five-point scale, in which one extreme may represent 'strongly agree', the other extreme 'strongly disagree', and the central point a neutral stance.

linear programme   A form of PROGRAMMED LEARNING developed by SKINNER in which the student works through a sequence of FRAMES – units of information each consisting of a sentence or two requiring the student to respond in some way, usually by providing a word or figure to fill a blank left in one of the sentences. The material is so designed that the student makes very few errors as he learns. May be presented in book form or in a TEACHING MACHINE. Contrast with BRANCHING PROGRAMME.

linear programming   **1** The writing of PROGRAMMED LEARNING material in the linear style (LINEAR PROGRAMMES). **2** A mathematical technique much used in economics to simulate real-life situations (eg a production process) and decide the best allocation of resources or sequence of operations.

linear relationship   A statistical term indicating that the VALUES of two VARIABLES are strongly related, varying proportionately with one another. So pairs of values, one from each variable, would fall quite close to a straight line if plotted as points on a SCATTER DIAGRAM.

lines   An IMPOSITION (a form of school punishment) in which the offending pupil is required to write out some such relevant sentence as 'I must get my homework in on time' perhaps 50 or 100 times. (That is '50 or 100 lines'.)

linguistic analysis   An approach to the clarification of philosophical issues and disagreements (eg in education) through examining the language used by participants and revealing the underlying concepts.

linguistic code   See LANGUAGE CODE.

linked course   A course run jointly by two institutions. For example, a UK SECONDARY SCHOOL may design courses for senior

159

pupils in collaboration with a COLLEGE OF FURTHER EDUCATION, and part of the course will be held in each institution.

lip reading   The ability developed by deaf people to understand the speech of a person by watching the movements of his lips and face muscles.

List D school   A Scottish residential establishment providing education for children who are compulsorily in the care of the local AUTHORITY. Equivalent to a COMMUNITY HOME in England and Wales.

List 99   The confidential 'black list' kept by the DEPARTMENT OF EDUCATION AND SCIENCE recording the names of teachers who have been dismissed from their post in circumstances that make them unsuitable for employment in schools and colleges.

literacy   A person's ability to read and write as well as is expected from people in his group or CULTURE. A person considered literate by members of one group might be considered illiterate by those of another.

Literae Humaniores   (Lit Hum) An undergraduate course in CLASSICS at Oxford University. Also known as GREATS.

literary institute   One of two London EVENING INSTITUTES, offering NON-VOCATIONAL ADULT EDUCATION in ARTS subjects.

literature   **1** Published writings (plays, prose, and poetry) considered by literary critics to be of quality. **2** The systematic study of such writings, involving principles of literary history and literary criticism. See also THE LITERATURE below.

literature, the   The body of published writings (books, journal articles, etc) on a particular subject, with which experts in that subject are expected to be familiar.

literature search   Term used in research and LIBRARY/INFORMATION SCIENCE for the process of tracking down and evaluating books, articles, research reports, etc, (see THE LITERATURE) that might have a bearing on a particular research topic.

literature survey   A review of 'THE LITERATURE' on a subject, describing and commenting on the results of research so far, usually carried out by a scholar prior to commencing his own investigations.

Little Commonwealth   See LANE, HOMER.

little red schoolhouse   (US) A nostalgic reference to the small, cosy and usually one-room ELEMENTARY SCHOOLS of the rural US in the 19th century, with their CURRICULUM firmly rooted in the coherent CULTURE of the local community.

local authority   See AUTHORITY **1**.

local education authority (LEA)   Local government body responsible for the provision of education (in schools, colleges and polytechnics, but not universities) in a geographical area of the UK. England and Wales have 105 such LEAs (metropolitan district or county councils together with ILEA and the 20 Outer London boroughs), Scotland (where they are termed education authorities) has 12 and Northern Ireland has five. The LEAs operate with considerable autonomy (through their EDUCATION COMMITTEE, EDUCATION OFFICERS, ADVISERS, etc) but are always open to pressure from central government. The nearest US equivalent would be a LOCAL SCHOOL BOARD or BOARD OF EDUCATION.

local history   The historical study of a limited geographical area such as a village, town or county.

Locke, John   (1632–1704) A UK philosopher famous for his *Essay Concerning Human Understanding*. He also wrote *Some Thoughts Concerning Education* in which he urged the development of rationality, virtue, and such knowledge and skills as might be useful to a gentleman. He advised treating the child as a rational being and teaching, where possible, through a play approach.

lock step   The situation wherein each pupil in a class is forced to work at the same pace as every other pupil (and may be hampered thereby).

loco parentis   See IN LOCO PARENTIS.

locus classicus   (Latin, 'classical place'.) Any authoritative and much-quoted passage from THE LITERATURE of a subject.

log book   A diary of daily happenings (eg punishments and injuries) that every UK school is expected to keep. Such diaries date back to 1871 and many are fascinating historical documents.

logical operations   Another name for FORMAL OPERATIONS, the final stage of intellectual development as described by PIAGET.

logic blocks   Books of different colours, sizes and shapes. Used in INFANT SCHOOLS to help children acquire concepts by classifying and sorting things into sets according to their common qualities, eg making a set of red square blocks and then separating it into sets of big, red, square blocks and little, red, square blocks.

logical positivism/empiricism   A school of philosophy arguing that statements or propositions have meaning only if they are verifiable through empirical experience (and perhaps that the meaning lies in the manner by which they would be verified).

lollipop lady/man Person responsible for guarding children from traffic while crossing busy roads on the way to and from school. (So called because of the shape of the warning signal she/he carries.)

London allowance Extra salary paid to teachers (and many others) to help cover the extra cost of living in or travelling to the capital city.

longitudinal study/approach/enquiry, etc A research approach in which data is collected about the development of, and/or influences upon, an individual or group of individuals over a period of time. This period may span several years or even the individual's whole childhood or lifetime. (Contrast with CROSS-SECTIONAL STUDY.)

long-term memory The store of permanent memories, with enormous capacity. Contrasts with SHORT-TERM MEMORY (or IMMEDIATE MEMORY SPAN).

long vacation Term used, especially in universities, for the summer vacation, which separates one ACADEMIC YEAR from the next.

look-and-say A method of teaching reading in which the pupil is encouraged to recognise the shape of a whole word rather than to see it as separate letters and syllables whose sounds he must then blend to get the word. Contrasts with PHONIC METHOD.

Lord Kitchener National Memorial Fund A UK educational foundation dating from 1916 and awarding SCHOLARSHIPS to people who have been, or are, in the armed services.

lower class Usually means WORKING CLASS.

lower classman (US) A FRESHMAN or SOPHOMORE student.

lower school 1 Pupils in the first couple of years of a COMPREHENSIVE SCHOOL. **2** A school for pupils under a certain age who are expected to go on to a separate but related school when they reach that age.

lower-secondary school (US) School offering GRADES 7 to 10 and usually sending its pupils on to an associated UPPER SECONDARY SCHOOL.

lower sixth (form) Students in the first year of SIXTH-FORM studies. Roughly equivalent to GRADE 11 in the US.

loyalty oath (US) Oath of allegiance required by some states and BOARDS OF EDUCATION as a pre-requisite to employment as a teacher.

LVR   See LEARNER VERIFICATION AND REVISION.

lycée   A French state SECONDARY SCHOOL.

M

MA   Abbreviation for either MASTER OF ARTS or MENTAL AGE.

machine-paced learning   Where the rate at which a student is presented with LEARNING MATERIAL is determined by a machine (eg a radio or film-projector).

Macmillan, Margaret (1860–1931) and **Rachel** (1859–1917) Scottish sisters who were pioneers in demanding regular MEDICAL INSPECTION and PHYSICAL EDUCATION for children in school. Margaret pressed the need for NURSERY EDUCATION for all children and founded a TRAINING COLLEGE for nursery school teachers, naming it in memory of her sister. See her book, *The Nursery School* (1914).

MACOS   Acronym for 'Man: A Course of Study' which is a prime example of 1960s-style US CURRICULUM DEVELOPMENT. It is a complex INTEGRATED STUDIES course for schools on the nature of mankind as a species and the forces that shape our humanity. It involves a range of MEDIA and PACKAGED TEACHING materials and all teachers using it must have special training. It was developed by a large and distinguished team of educators, including Jerome BRUNER, and has been extensively used on both sides of the Atlantic.

Madras system   The version of the MONITORIAL SYSTEM (whereby older pupils teach younger ones) developed by ANDREW BELL while a missionary in India.

magic lantern   An early type of SLIDE PROJECTOR, used to project pictures on to a large screen for group viewing.

magna cum laude   US Latin tag sometimes added when a DEGREE or other academic qualification is awarded 'with great praise'. (Better than CUM LAUDE but not as good as SUMMA CUM LAUDE.)

magnetic board   A vertical sheet of steel on which the teacher may display to a class items that have small magnets attached to them so that they stay where they are placed. May be surfaced so as to serve also as a CHALK BOARD or FELT BOARD.

magnet school (US) A school with special facilities or offering special courses that attract pupils from a wider geographical area than other schools in the district, eg in order to improve the school's social or racial balance.

Maharishi Similar to GURU, in being a respectful name given to a Hindu teacher of religious and spiritual awareness.

maieutic An adjective derived from the Greek word for midwifery and pertaining to the SOCRATIC METHOD of eliciting or developing knowledge in a student through a series of questions and answers.

mainstreaming A policy of educating children with handicaps or special learning needs in normal classes along with children who have no such handicaps or needs.

maintained colleges Term used in England and Wales for institutions of FURTHER/HIGHER EDUCATION maintained out of public funds by a LOCAL EDUCATION AUTHORITY. Includes COLLEGES OF EDUCATION, COLLEGES/INSTITUTES OF HIGHER EDUCATION, COLLEGES OF FURTHER EDUCATION, TECHNICAL COLLEGES, and POLYTECHNICS. Universities are *not* in the MAINTAINED SECTOR and there are also some specialist colleges that receive funds direct from the DEPARTMENT OF EDUCATION AND SCIENCE and some (like SECRETARIAL and CORRESPONDENCE COLLEGES) that operate on a commercial basis.

maintained schools Term used in England and Wales for schools maintained out of public funds by a LOCAL EDUCATION AUTHORITY. Includes COUNTY SCHOOLS, VOLUNTARY AIDED, VOLUNTARY CONTROLLED and SPECIAL AGREEMENT SCHOOLS. Similar to US and Scottish PUBLIC SCHOOLS. About 95% of children in England and Wales of the appropriate age-range attend maintained SECONDARY SCHOOLS and the percentage attending maintained PRIMARY SCHOOLS is even greater.

maintained sector Term used in England and Wales to refer to all educational provision financed out of public funds by the LOCAL EDUCATION AUTHORITIES – that is, the MAINTAINED SCHOOLS/COLLEGES and their supporting services. The term excludes all INDEPENDENT SCHOOLS/COLLEGES and, usually, the universities (and some colleges) which, while receiving public funds, do so direct from central government rather than from a local education authority.

maintenance grants Allowance paid by LOCAL EDUCATION AUTHORITIES to UK students to help cover living (as opposed to tuition) expenses. May sometimes also be paid, if their parents have little income, to students wishing to stay on at school after the STATUTORY LEAVING AGE.

maintenance team   Term sometimes used in CURRICULUM DEVELOPMENT (eg in the OPEN UNIVERSITY) for the group of people responsible for the teaching and improvement of a course once it has been developed. Its tasks may include EVALUATION, updating, producing new ASSESSMENT and EXAMINATION material year after year, and re-designing parts of the course that prove ineffective.

major   (US) A student's main subject-area in college or university. Hence, he may major in, say history or economics, and would, accordingly, be described as a history-major or economics-major.

major-minor system   (US) System used in HIGH SCHOOL, and college and university, requiring students to obtain a specified number of CREDITS in MAJOR and MINOR subjects in order to graduate.

major premise   (or PREMISS)   Term used in logic for one of two statements from which a certain conclusion inevitably follows. (Technically, it is the statement containing the predicate of the conclusion.) See SYLLOGISM for an example.

make-up class/work   (US) A class (or ASSIGNMENTS) arranged for students who need to catch up (eg during a summer vacation) on work in which they have fallen behind their peers.

maladjusted child   One who is regarded as being unable to cope satisfactorily with social relationships and, especially, with the demands made by parents, teachers and other adults in everyday activities.

Malinowski, Bronislaw   (1884–1942)   Polish anthropologist based in England and the US, whose research was chiefly on the sexual behaviour of the peoples of New Guinea and Melanesia. Like that of MARGARET MEAD, his work reminds EDUCATIONALISTS of the value of CROSS-CULTURAL studies in the understanding of educational and child-rearing practices.

management education/training   Courses and other LEARNING EXPERIENCES designed to widen the outlook and improve the expertise of managers (or intending managers) by introducing them to such basic DISCIPLINES as economics, sociology, psychology and law; to such special topics as industrial relations, production methods, finance, and personnel; and to newer INTERDISCIPLINARY approaches such as systems analysis and op-

165

erational research. Management education has been very productive of new teaching approaches such as: CASE-STUDIES, CRITICAL INCIDENT TECHNIQUE, IN-TRAY EXERCISES and T-GROUPS.

managers   The term used, prior to the EDUCATION ACT 1980, for what are now called the GOVERNORS of a PRIMARY SCHOOL in England and Wales.

mandatory (or MANDATED) GRANT   A grant that must be made by a LOCAL EDUCATION AUTHORITY according to central government regulations, eg a student's MAINTENANCE GRANT. Contrasts with a DISCRETIONARY GRANT.

manipulation   **1** Handling equipment or materials in a co-ordinated or skilful manner. **2** Influencing the activities of other people towards goals that are not of their choosing and of which they are probably unaware and might not even approve.

manipulation test   A test of MANUAL DEXTERITY.

Mannheim, Karl (1893–1947)   Hungarian sociologist who came to England in 1933 and was Professor of Education in the University of London at the time of his death. He wrote particularly about the structure of society and about the SOCIOLOGY OF KNOWLEDGE. See his *Essays on the Sociology of Knowledge* (1952).

Mann, Horace (1796–1859)   Secretary of Massachusetts State Board of Education who campaigned for educational reform and development in such matters as: improved TEACHING METHODS, more humane discipline, better designed school buildings and equipment, critical study of CURRICULUM content, better pay and conditions for teachers and, especially, the creation of state NORMAL SCHOOLS to provide teacher-training. His reputation and influence extended beyond his state to all parts of the US and even to Europe.

Manpower Development and Training Acts 1962, 1963, 1965   (US) Federal legislation providing funds for VOCATIONAL and other training and re-training schemes for young people and, especially, the unemployed.

Manpower Services Commission (MSC)   UK body established in 1972 to coordinate employment and VOCATIONAL TRAINING services on behalf of the SECRETARY OF STATE FOR EMPLOYMENT.

manual   A HANDBOOK of instructions or information, perhaps intended to accompany a course or a piece of equipment.

manual dexterity   A person's ability to handle equipment or materials with precision and speed.

manual training   (US) Early term for school activities such as woodwork, metalwork and MECHANICAL or TECHNICAL DRAWING which, in time, became organised as INDUSTRIAL ARTS.

manuscript 1 A document or book written by hand. 2 The draft of a book or article submitted by an author for publication (even though it will have been typed).

marginalia Notes in the margins of a book or manuscript.

marginal man A term used in sociology for a person seen as being on the fringe of a group or CULTURE, perhaps unsure of his own status and not fully accepted by the other members of that group as having interests entirely consistent with their own.

market research The collection and analysis of data relating to the possible demand for a particular product (eg a new TEXTBOOK or even a college course), usually undertaken prior to deciding whether (or when and how) to produce it.

marking The writing of letter GRADES or numerical scores or percentages (and perhaps comments) on a student's work. A common outcome of the process of ASSESSMENT.

marking scale/scheme A method adopted to increase the probability that different assessors award the same MARKS to a given piece of student work, by ensuring (as in ANALYTICAL MARKING) that all will be looking for the same qualities and rewarding them similarly.

marks Numbers or letter GRADES used by the teacher to express his ASSESSMENT of the quality of a piece of work produced by a student.

Marshall scholarships US government awards to US graduates enabling them to undertake two years of POST-GRADUATE study at UK universities.

martial arts A collective name for the combat sports, deriving from the Far East, which have become popular with some young people in western countries in recent years, eg karate, kendo, ju-jitsu, judo, aikido, etc.

Marx, Karl (1818–1883) German historian and philosopher, and founder of modern communism, who lived and wrote in England from 1849. He held that human knowledge, actions and institutions are the product of economic relationships and believed the class struggle would lead to the overthrow of capitalism and to the establishment of a classless society. See his *Communist Manifesto* (1848, with Engels) and *Capital* (1867).

Maslow, Abraham (1908–1976) US psychologist, known particularly for his work on MOTIVATION and his HIERARCHY OF

NEEDS. In later years, became one of the FATHER-FIGURES of HUMANISTIC PSYCHOLOGY. See his *Motivation and Personality* (1954) and *Towards a Psychology of Being* (1962).

Mason, Charlotte (1842–1923) A UK EDUCATOR who questioned the quality of HOME EDUCATION, which many parents provided for their children (often with the help of a GOVERNESS) in the absence of acceptable schools. She founded the PARENTS NATIONAL EDUCATIONAL UNION (PNEU) to provide materials for home teaching and a college in which teachers were trained according to her principles, eg promoting INTER-DISCIPLINARY activity and discouraging competition between children. For details see her book *An Essay Towards the Philosophy of Education* (1925).

mass communication The sending of a standard message to a large number of people. (Contrasts with individualised communication in which the message is sent to a particular person, taking account of his idiosyncratic needs or interests.)

massed practice Learning a new skill by a continuous period of practice unbroken by other activities. Contrasts with DISTRIBUTED or SPACED PRACTICE.

mass education The education of large numbers of children, and particularly the commitment to educating the mass (or majority) of a country's children at public expense, which grew up in the industrialised nations during the 19th century.

mass media The means of communicating a standard message to large numbers of people, perhaps simultaneously. The first mass medium was the printed book, but mass media now include newspapers and magazines, film, radio and television, advertising, and recorded music. Sometimes seen as potential opponents of education in the moulding of cultural tastes and standards.

master of method Early term for the lecturers in TEACHER-TRAINING COLLEGES who were concerned with instructing students in how to teach a subject in school. The distinction between *what* and *how* to teach is now rarely made in TEACHER EDUCATION.

master performer Term used in the analysis of professional or craft SKILLS to denote a person who is regarded as an exemplary exponent of those skills. In many areas (eg economics or teaching), several different kinds of master performer may be identified.

master's degree (eg Master of Arts or Master of Science) In England and Wales, a HIGHER DEGREE from a university, which may be achieved by taking courses and examinations and/or by conducting research and presenting a DISSERTATION or a THESIS. At Oxford and Cambridge, the MA is granted, without further study, but after a suitable lapse of time and payment of a fee, to all students who have gained their FIRST DEGREE. In the Scottish universities, MA is a first degree.

master teacher (US) An experienced and particularly proficient school teacher who is recognised as capable of giving guidance to STUDENT-TEACHERS and INTERNS.

mastery learning The slogan of a movement associated with US psychologist BLOOM, and standing on the assertion that mastery of any topic or field of human knowledge is theoretically possible for practically all learners, provided each is given the optimum teaching appropriate to his needs and is enabled to learn at his own best pace.

mastery test Test designed to check that pupils have achieved mastery (however that may be defined in the particular context) of the topic that has been studied. In some context (eg IPI, or the KELLER PLAN), students are not allowed to move on to new material until they have demonstrated mastery of what has gone before.

matched groups A feature of experimental design in which two groups are chosen so as to be similar on all relevant VARIABLES save the one that is to be manipulated in the experiment. For example, a new teaching method may be compared with the traditional method by trying each on a different group of boys, but ensuring first that the two groups are matched on, say, age, intelligence, and previous attainment by checking that the MEAN and STANDARD DEVIATION of age, IQ and latest exam score is the same within each group.

matched pairs A highly rigorous way of forming MATCHED GROUPS. For each member of one group, a member must be chosen for the other group who is similar on every relevant VARIABLE. (That is, the groups must match member by member, not simply 'on average' overall.)

matching 1 A form of ITEM in an OBJECTIVE TEST where a person has to choose from a set of pictures (or words) the one that matches a given picture (or word). 2 The process in experimental design whereby MATCHED GROUPS or MATCHED PAIRS are formed.

matching funds/grants Method of financial support in which one organisation promises to help finance a scheme by granting

169

an amount of money in proportion to the amount contributed by some other organisation.

maternal deprivation The absence of a warm, intimate relationship with a mother (or mother substitute) which, according to psychiatrist, JOHN BOWLBY, can have a pernicious effect on a child's PERSONALITY if suffered in the first few years of life.

math The usual US abbreviation of mathematics. Contrasts with UK MATHS.

mathemagenics Techniques of inserting questions into textual LEARNING MATERIALS in order to improve the student's comprehension. Derived from PROGRAMMED LEARNING and associated with the name of US psychologist, Rothkopf.

mathetics An approach to training through the systematic analysis of skills using REINFORCEMENT theory. Pioneered by US psychologist, Tom Gilbert, it made a considerable contribution to the methodology of PROGRAMMED LEARNING and EDUCATIONAL TECHNOLOGY during the 1960s. See Gilbert's *Mathetics: The Technology of Education* (Longman, 1970).

maths The UK abbreviation of mathematics. Contrasts with US MATH.

matrices See PROGRESSIVE MATRICES TEST.

matriculation Old name given to satisfying the entrance requirements for admission to university as a student working towards a degree. In the UK, this once depended on success in certain subjects in the Higher SCHOOL CERTIFICATE examination, which was superseded in 1951 by the GENERAL CERTIFICATE OF EDUCATION (ADVANCED LEVEL).

matron Nurse responsible for the health of pupils in a UK BOARDING SCHOOL.

maturation The psychological and physical changes in an individual that occur because of internal factors (rather than training and environmental factors) as he passes through childhood towards adulthood. Increased abilities in some areas may depend on maturation rather than on learning; and some kinds of learning will be impossible before certain stages of maturation have been reached. See also READINESS.

mature student A student who is older than those normally entering HIGHER EDUCATION, perhaps having had a job for some years since leaving school. Often, such a student may be admitted without the usual ENTRY QUALIFICATIONS. (In the UK, a mature student is one for whom a parental MEANS TEST is not applicable in determining his MAINTENANCE GRANT.)

Maudsley Personality Inventory   UK PERSONALITY test designed by H J EYSENCK and purporting to measure the dimensions of NEUROTICISM and EXTROVERSION-INTROVERSION.

Maurice, F D   (1805–72)   Church of England clergyman and Professor of English Literature and History at King's College, London. A social reformer who advocated a higher, LIBERAL EDUCATION in the HUMANITIES (rather than narrow technical training) for working men; he was instrumental in starting the first of the WORKING MEN'S COLLEGES and became its first principal in 1854. He was also active in developing educational opportunities for women.

maze   A network of pathways, some leading to dead-ends, others towards a goal, as used in tests of INTELLIGENCE and learning ability in which a person (or animal) is encouraged to find the shortest route towards the goal.

McClelland, David   (Born 1917) US psychologist well-known for his work on MOTIVATION and especially on achievement, motivation and the desire to succeed. See his *The Achieving Society* (1961).

McDougall, William   (1871–1938) UK philosopher and psychologist who was a strong opponent of BEHAVIOURISM and is best remembered for his emphasis on the purposive nature of human activity. See his *Outline of Psychology* (1923) and *Character and the Conduct of Life* (1927). See INSTINCT THEORIES.

McGuffey, W H   (1800–1873)   US educator responsible for 'McGuffey's Eclectic Readers' which sought to instil moral principles by way of interesting stories.

McLuhan, Marshall   (1911–1980)   Canadian professor of English and analyst of MASS MEDIA, best known for his book *The Medium is the Message* (1967). See also his *Understanding Media* (1964).

McNair Report 1944   The UK REPORT of a committee on the recruitment and training of teachers and YOUTH LEADERS. It made proposals for improving the status of both, particularly through training and, in the case of teachers, proposed the setting up of INSTITUTES or SCHOOLS OF EDUCATION each to coordinate teacher-training in a given geographical area.

Mead, Margaret   (1901–1978) US anthropologist best known to educators for her comparative studies of ADOLESCENCE. See her

Coming of Age in Samoa (1928), *Growing up in New Guinea* (1930) and *Childhood in Contemporary Cultures* (1955).

meals See SCHOOL MEALS.

means test An assessment of the income and expenses of the parents of a UK pupil or student to determine the extent to which certain of his educational expenses might be financed out of public funds, eg by a MAINTENANCE GRANT or by an ASSISTED PLACE at an INDEPENDENT SCHOOL.

mean, the (or ARITHMETIC MEAN). In statistics, a form of AVERAGE (indeed, what most people think of as '*the* average') obtained by adding up a set of VALUES and dividing by the number of values contained in that set.

mechanical drawing See TECHNICAL DRAWING.

Mechanics' Institute One of the 19th century UK institutions that provided part-time (usually evening) courses in the crafts and sciences. By 1851, there were some 700, mostly in London and the principal industrial cities. They were the forerunners of the TECHNICAL COLLEGES and the CIVIC UNIVERSITIES.

mechanistic psychology Term applied to any SCHOOL of psychology that views people as if they were machines and ignores SUBJECTIVE experience.

media The channels by means of which messages are communicated, eg, books, film, radio, television, etc.

median A form of AVERAGE in statistics. If a number of VALUES of a VARIABLE are arranged in order of size, the median is whatever value lies in the middle. For example, in the set of values: 3, 8, 23, 42, 387, the median value is 23.

medical inspection See SCHOOL HEALTH SERVICE.

medical school A university institution that trains medical doctors.

meditation Deriving from the devotional practice of many religions, meditation has been promoted throughout the developed countries since the 1960s in a non-religious form known as 'transcendental meditation'; the practitioner seeks relaxation and mental refreshment by spending several minutes a day in silent repetition of a mantra. Many benefits are claimed, including relief from stress and improvement in educational performance.

memory A person's individual record of his past mental and sensory experience. Some aspects of memory may be measured by the individual's facility in RECALL, RECOGNITION and RE-

LEARNING; and hypnosis may assist in recovery of material not normally available to the conscious mind. The scientific study of memory began in the 19th century with the German experimental psychologist, Ebbinghaus, and with the quite different psychoanalytical approach of FREUD.

memory span A term used by psychologists to indicate the amount of information (eg the number of unrelated digits) a person can remember immediately after, or some time after, having had them presented to him.

Mensa International society open to people who make high scores on INTELLIGENCE TESTS.

mens sana in corpore sano Latin (from Juvenal), 'a sound mind in a healthy body'. A hearty slogan once popular with PHYSICAL EDUCATION teachers in the UK and emanating from the games-playing ethos of the PUBLIC SCHOOLS.

mental age A figure derived by comparing a child's score on an INTELLIGENCE TEST with the average scores of children of various ages. Thus, a ten year-old whose IQ is equal to that of the average eight year-old is said to have a mental age of eight years.

mental arithmetic An obsolete term for calculations that can be carried out 'in one's head' (without paper and pencil) – to which schools once devoted much attention.

mental defective Outmoded term used for children thought to be too deficient in INTELLIGENCE to profit from normal teaching in school, or for adults thought incapable of normal employment.

mental handicap Any mental condition posited as the reason for a child's performance that is poorer than expected for his age. See BACKWARDNESS, RETARDATION, SLOW LEARNER, EDUCATIONALLY SUBNORMAL, SEVERELY SUBNORMAL. (UK children classified as subnormal are usually catered for in SPECIAL EDUCATION.) Extreme forms of mental handicap caused by physical defects are found in sufferers from HYDROCEPHALY and DOWN'S SYNDROME.

mental set See SET.

mentor A trusted and friendly adviser or guide, especially of someone new to a particular role.

meritocracy A term coined by the sociologist, Michael Young, to label a society in which the power and status people attain is determined not by the wealth or social class of their parents but by the merit they themselves demonstrate in ways esteemed by society (eg IQ + effort = merit!). See Young's *The Rise of the Meritocracy* (1958).

meshing   Sociological term for harmonious interactions between members of a social group who agree on their respective roles and purposes.

methodology   **1** The investigative practices and techniques (together with the accompanying ways of formulating problems and criteria for judging interpretations of evidence) that are peculiar to a particular DISCIPLINE or craft or profession. **2** In schools, the term may refer to TEACHING METHODS, eg, the methodology of science teachers differs from that of history teachers.

metric system   A system of weights and measures, based on multiples of ten, that was first given legal recognition in France early in the Revolution. Most countries have changed to metric systems (especially of currency). Scientists use a particular metric system known as the SYSTÈME INTERNATIONAL D'UNITÈS.

Michaelmas term   Academic term between the summer vacation and Christmas at Oxford, Cambridge and some other UK universities and educational institutions.

microcomputer   A small, low-cost computer that can be based upon a single MICROPROCESSOR ('chip').

microfiche/form   A sheet of film, perhaps a quarter of the area of a page of this book, on which can be recorded a reduced image of many pages of text. The text can be viewed with special optical equipment that enlarges the pages to normal size again. Storage space is thus saved.

microprocessor   The silicon 'chip' – a tiny equivalent of the central processing unit (or 'brain') of a computer, capable of being mass-produced and thus reducing both the size and cost of computing systems.

microprojector   A precision instrument capable of projecting highly-magnified images from microscope slides or microscopic living specimens onto a screen.

microteaching   A technique used in TEACHER TRAINING for analysing and developing specific teaching skills. The student-teacher teaches a small group of pupils for up to 20 minutes, concentrating on a particular aspect of teaching, then analyses the 'mini-lesson' immediately afterwards with the help of the tutor and/or colleagues and a VIDEO-TAPE recording. Then he may teach the same 'mini-lesson' again, trying to make use of the FEEDBACK he has received.

middle class The term was, at least in origin, one of RANKING – used to identify that group of people thought by its users to be in some significant respect 'better' than the WORKING CLASS but not so good as the UPPER CLASS or nobility. The middle class consists largely of professional, managerial and 'white collar' workers, together with people from other occupational backgrounds who share similar VALUES and LIFESTYLES. Middle class values (like the willingness to work hard or study now for the sake of rewards delayed to some future date) are probably part of the HIDDEN CURRICULUM of SCHOOLING.

middle school 1 The term was first used in the early and middle 19th century when profit-making schools for middle-class children began to be established, resulting in the PUBLIC SCHOOLS no longer being an UPPER CLASS preserve. 2 Since the 1960s the term has been used for MAINTAINED SCHOOLS that, in many areas, aim to ease the transition of pupils between PRIMARY/FIRST SCHOOL and SECONDARY SCHOOL by taking them between the ages of 9–13 years (or 8–12 or 10–14 in some areas) and preparing them for the different kind of CURRICULUM and TEACHING METHODS they will meet in their secondary education. 3 Some COMPREHENSIVE SCHOOLS use the term for a particular age-range among their pupils. 4 The term is also used in some US school systems for schools for pupils between the ages of 10 and 14, thus catering for those who would normally be the older children in ELEMENTARY SCHOOL and the younger children in HIGH SCHOOL.

midterms (US) Tests or EXAMINATIONS, used during a term in HIGH SCHOOL, college or university to assess or encourage students' progress and perhaps to count towards their final course GRADES.

military academy or **school** (US) A private HIGH SCHOOL in which students wear military uniforms, and learn military skills in addition to the normal elements of a HIGH SCHOOL CURRICULUM.

milk-round The annual recruiting campaign during which representatives of large UK companies visit the CAMPUSES of universities and polytechnics with a view to finding suitable students who might join them after graduating.

Mill Hill Vocabulary Scale A test designed to measure a person's recall of information and ability in verbal communication as an aspect of INTELLIGENCE.

Mill, John Stuart (1806–1873) UK philosopher and economist. A child prodigy, he was given rigorous intellectual training by his father, resulting in a nervous breakdown in his late teens.

Henceforth, Mill advocated the education of a child's emotions and sensibilities (through art and poetry) which had been neglected in his case. He also believed that university education should be LIBERAL rather than VOCATIONAL. He was an active social reformer and strongly supported the view that women were intellectually equal to men. His best known book is *Essay on Liberty* (1859).

mimeograph The trade name for a REPROGRAPHICS machine that can produce multiple copies of text or line drawings from a stencil revolving on an inked drum; but the term is often applied to similar processes, whatever machine is used.

mimesis See MIMICRY.

mimicry Imitating the speech or other actions of another person. Among adults this is often done for satirical purposes but with children it can be part of the learning process in which, as it were, they consciously or unconsciously 'try on' aspects of another person's personality either to understand it better or to use it in modifying their own.

Minister of Education The old title of the UK Government cabinet member responsible for promoting the education of people in England and Wales between 1944 and 1964. Hitherto, there had been a BOARD OF EDUCATION headed by a PRESIDENT. In 1964 the Ministries of Education and Science were amalgamated as the DEPARTMENT OF EDUCATION AND SCIENCE. The ministerial title then changed to SECRETARY OF STATE FOR EDUCATION AND SCIENCE. (For Scotland and Northern Ireland there are separate departments and responsibility rests primarily with the Secretaries of State for Scotland and for Northern Ireland.)

Ministry of Education See MINISTER OF EDUCATION and DEPARTMENT OF EDUCATION AND SCIENCE.

Minnesota Multiphasic Personality Inventory (MMPI) A widely used test of PERSONALITY attempting to measure several different DIMENSIONS such as depression, paranoia, schizophrenia and masculinity.

Minnesota Test of Creative Thinking A series of creativity tests for children involving them in imaginative writing, suggesting unusual uses or improvements for common objects, and generating questions (and answers) about pictures, etc.

minor 1 A person under the age of majority, at present 18 years in the UK. **2** (US) A set of subsidiary subjects in a student's degree programme requiring fewer CREDITS to be obtained than in his MAJOR.

minority group   Any group of people within a society or CULTURE who are identifiable (by themselves or others) as having a common ethnic, racial, religious or ideological identity that makes them different from the majority, though not necessarily under threat from them.

minority time/subjects   Term used in discussion of UK SIXTH FORM studies and referring to time spent on SUBJECTS other than the main ones in which the student is to be examined – time which many believe essential to avoid narrow over-SPECIALISATION.

minor premise (or premiss)   Term used in logic for one of two statements from which a certain conclusion inevitably follows. (Technically, it is the statement containing the subject of the conclusion.) See SYLLOGISM for an example.

mirror writing   Handwriting in which words and individual letters are written the wrong way round, becoming legible when viewed in a mirror. Young children, or even adults when tired, drugged, or under stress, reverse letters or figures occasionally, but the only people thought to do it at all regularly are among those with other LEARNING DIFFICULTIES, especially DYSLEXIA. Interestingly enough, the notebooks of Leonardo da Vinci are all in mirror writing.

mission school   A school operated by a religious group as part of its missionary activities in a developing country.

Mittler, Peter   (Born 1930) UK psychologist and an authority on AUTISM and on the learning processes of people with MENTAL HANDICAPS. See his *Assessment for Learning in the Mentally Handicapped* (1973).

mixed ability group/class   A group of pupils covering a wide range of ability. Notionally, the children in the class might represent the total range of ability within their year-group in the school, and thus avoid the social divisiveness of some classes being thought superior and others inferior. This approach to grouping contrasts with STREAMING or SETTING and even BANDING which all reduce the range of ability contained in any one class. The US equivalent of a mixed ability class is an HETEROGENEOUS GROUP. See also MIXED ABILITY TEACHING.

mixed ability teaching   The teaching of pupils in MIXED ABILITY GROUPS. This is the almost universal practice in UK primary schools but is less common in secondary schools. It calls for the

177

use of a variety of teaching approaches which the teacher must pursue by dealing differently with different individuals and sub-groups. Teachers of 'sequential' subjects like mathematics and languages are particularly likely to claim that the technical difficulties of so doing outweigh any social advantages.

mixed school A school for children of both sexes.

mixing A term used in television production and sound recording for the combining of two or more different signals (eg from different cameras or microphones) to form a single image or sound.

mks units A METRIC SYSTEM of measurement based on the metre, kilogramme and second and on which THE SYSTÈME INTERNATIONAL D'UNITÉS (SI UNITS) is built.

MMPI See MINNESOTA MULTIPHASIC PERSONALITY INVENTORY.

mnemonic Any arbitrary but effective device to help a student recall facts that might otherwise be difficult to recall. For example, the statement 'Richard Of York Gained Battles In Vain' helps one remember in order the initial letters of the colours of the rainbow.

mobile classroom Classroom accommodation, perhaps in a large van, that can be moved from site to site according to where it is most needed at any given time.

mobile library A relatively small selection of books driven in a van to a succession of regular stopping points, for the benefit of readers (especially those in rural areas) who would find it difficult to visit the main library.

mobility, social The movement of people from one social group to another, usually through changes in occupation. Education is widely considered to be the chief means of 'upward' social mobility – into a group enjoying greater SOCIO-ECONOMIC STATUS.

mock examination A trial EXAMINATION arranged by an educational institution for those of its students who are due to take a PUBLIC EXAMINATION soon. The purposes and aims include acclimatising the students to examination conditions, testing out the administrative arrangements and, perhaps, deciding whether some of the students are not yet up to the standard required by the public examination.

mock-up Used especially in INDUSTRIAL TRAINING, a piece of apparatus similar but not identical to some device that a trainee is learning to operate. It is designed to give him the necessary practice safely and efficiently. Compare with SIMULATOR.

mode **1** A form of AVERAGE in statistics, the mode is the most frequently-observed value of a VARIABLE (eg in the UK, 8 might be the modal size in men's shoes). **2** The term may also refer to the kind of stimulus presented to a student (eg speech, pictures, real objects, etc). **3** See also BRUNER'S MODES.

mode 1–3 There are three different approaches to examinations in UK SECONDARY SCHOOLS. In Mode 1, the most usual, a PUBLIC EXAMINATIONS board prescribes a SYLLABUS which is followed by a number of schools and the board sets the examination papers which are marked by its own examiners (though some INTERNAL ASSESSMENT may be involved also). With Mode 3, especially used with the CERTIFICATE OF SECONDARY EDUCATION, the teachers in a school or group of schools develop their own syllabus and examination papers and do the marking themselves, subject to MODERATION by the examinations board which then issues appropriate certificates to successful candidates. Mode 2 is a little-used compromise between the features of Modes 1 and 3.

model **1** A replica of a real object, usually reduced or increased in size (eg a model of the solar system or a model of the heart). **2** When trying to understand or explain some complex social process or situation we may consider simplified ways of picturing it – perhaps using a diagram, or mathematics, or a verbal summary or analogy. (Models of type **1** or **2** may bring out the important features and help us come to grips with the reality; though there is always the danger that they might give rise to a distorted or impoverished impression.) **3** The term is also used of a person from whom a student might learn; see ROLE MODEL and SKILL MODEL.

model school Same as DEMONSTRATION SCHOOL or LABORATORY SCHOOL.

moderation The process whereby an EXTERNAL EXAMINER ascertains that the ASSESSMENT standards of a group of INTERNAL EXAMINERS are consistent from candidate to candidate and comparable with those of such examiners in similar institutions elsewhere.

moderations The first public examinations during a degree course at Oxford University, in which students are placed in one of three categories of honours. Sometimes shortened to 'Mods'.

Modern Greats Undergraduate degree course in politics, philosophy and economics (PPE) at Oxford University.

modern languages Any language still being spoken (as opposed to classical languages like Latin and Ancient Greek) but referring especially to those languages commonly taught in the school CURRICULUM, eg French, German, Spanish, Italian and Russian.

modern mathematics The slogan of a movement in education whose followers have, since the 1960s, been seeking to modify CURRICULUM (and teaching methods) in mathematics with a view to putting more emphasis on the understanding of mathematical concepts and structures and less on mere arithmetical computation and the memorising of theorems and formulae. New curriculum content includes sets, matrices, vectors and statistics, and most examination syllabuses now include such topics. Whether there has been any comparable increase in pupils' mathematical confidence or understanding is less easy to ascertain.

modern school (Or **secondary modern school**). Term used after the EDUCATION ACT 1944 for the SECONDARY SCHOOLS in England and Wales attended by those children (some 80% of their age-group) considered not sufficiently academic to benefit from secondary GRAMMAR or TECHNICAL SCHOOLS. Such schools rarely enjoyed public esteem or a distinctive sense of purpose and, during the 1960s and 1970s, most were transformed into COMPREHENSIVE SCHOOLS. (Between 1965 and 1979 their number fell from 3,727 to 547.) In Scotland, the JUNIOR SECONDARY SCHOOLS were broadly equivalent.

modern studies (or **side**) **1** Term used in UK PUBLIC SCHOOLS to distinguish subjects like history, geography, literature, modern languages and perhaps science (though this may form a separate subject division) from CLASSICAL STUDIES. **2** The term modern studies may also be used in some schools for a distinct INTER-DISCIPLINARY COURSE incorporating elements of politics, economics, geography, history, etc, related to current world issues.

modular course/programme A course or degree programme built around the study of a number of CURRICULUM units (or MODULES) with students free to choose different combinations and/or sequences of modules. The ASSESSMENT scheme is normally based on testing students' work after each module rather than at the end of the course (or programme).

module A unit of study within a MAJOR COURSE. It may involve CLASSWORK or SELF-INSTRUCTIONAL MATERIALS, or some combination of the two, and usually has in-built provision for student ASSESSMENT.

monastic school One of the mediaeval schools attached to monasteries that offered general education and religious instruction to young men, especially those preparing to enter a monastic order.

mongolism A term that offends many people but is commonly used to refer to DOWN'S SYNDROME.

monitor 1 A pupil made responsible by the teacher for carrying out certain routine duties for his class (eg cleaning chalkboards, distributing books, etc). 2 In the 19th century MONITORIAL SYSTEM, monitors were senior pupils with responsibilities for teaching younger ones. 3 In the US, a monitor is someone (perhaps a teacher) who acts as INVIGILATOR (or PROCTOR) in an examination.

monitorial school One of the 19th century schools established by two religious bodies (the NATIONAL SOCIETY and the BRITISH AND FOREIGN SCHOOL SOCIETY) to operate on the MONITORIAL SYSTEM of using senior pupils as assistant teachers.

monitorial system A method whereby one teacher could cope with large numbers of pupils by teaching his lesson to some clever senior pupils (the monitors) and having them teach it in turn to groups of younger or less clever pupils. Such 'mass production' methods enjoyed a considerable vogue in the 19th century particularly in the forms promulgated by ANDREW BELL and JOSEPH LANCASTER (though the basic ideas of involving children as teachers was centuries old).

monitoring Observing the work of students or teachers or assessors with a view to reporting on their performance or influencing the standards or methods being employed.

monotechnic Name sometimes used of an institution of HIGHER EDUCATION that specialises in one subject area, eg a COLLEGE OF EDUCATION (for the education and training of teachers).

Montessori, Maria (1870–1952). The first woman to qualify as a medical doctor in Italy who became an internationally recognised pioneer of PROGRESSIVE infant education. She devised school environments and apparatus that emphasised sensory experience and physical activity (eg the CLIMBING FRAME), with learning materials graded in complexity to suit the child's developing intelligence and skills. Her influence has been immense. See her *The Secret of Childhood* (1936).

moral development The growth of a child's ability to act on moral principles rather than out of expedience, self-interest, habit, fear of punishment, etc.

moral education Teaching intended to aid in a child's MORAL DEVELOPMENT.

moral tutor Member of the teaching staff of a UK school or college who has counselling or advisory responsibilities for certain students whom he may or may not teach. Sometimes called a PERSONAL TUTOR.

Morant, Sir Robert (1836–1920) A highly influential UK civil servant who was Secretary of the BOARD OF EDUCATION from 1902 to 1911, and whose ideas did much to shape the growth of ELEMENTARY SECONDARY and TECHNICAL EDUCATION in and around that period.

Moray House Tests A set of tests measuring various aspects of INTELLIGENCE and ATTAINMENT. Once widely-used in ELEVEN-PLUS selection. Named after Moray House College in Edinburgh where they were originally devised. See also THOMPSON, Sir Godfrey.

Mores The customs and ways of behaviour (and the underlying thoughts and beliefs) that are socially acceptable among the people in a group or CULTURE.

mortar board A black tasselled cap with a flat square top covered in cloth and worn as part of ACADEMIC DRESS. (Named after the board on which building workers carry their mortar.)

mother-figure A woman who is regarded by another person as if she were that person's mother, or who acts towards that person as a mother might.

mother tongue **1** The first LANGUAGE a person learns. **2** The language from which another language has been derived.

motion picture US equivalent of 'a film', in the sense of a series of still pictures on 8mm or 16mm film which give the illusion of movement when viewed at speed using an appropriate projector.

motivation Psychological term for the arousal and maintenance of behaviour directed towards goals. The goals may be intrinsic (the behaviour itself being satisfying) or extrinsic (the behaviour resulting in subsequent rewards or avoidance of subsequent punishment.) Motivation to engage in a specific task may arise spontaneously from within the individual or may be fostered by a teacher who knows the individual's interests. Psychologists such as MASLOW and MCCLELLAND have written extensively on motivation.

motor ability/activity etc Ability, activity, etc, involving physical movements of the body's muscles (eg from raising an eye-brow to swimming across a lake).

movement education/studies   A concern within the CURRICU-LUM (especially in PRIMARY SCHOOL) with developing BODY AWARENESS and co-ordinated, rhythmical movement in children. Usually associated with dance, drama and music, but may in-corporate elements of what would usually be seen as PHYSICAL EDUCATION or even (organised) GAMES. See DANCE IN EDUCATION.

moving average   In statistics, a technique for smoothing out the fluctuations in a series of figures collected at regular intervals over a period of time, with a view to identifying a trend and making forecasts for the future.

MRST   Acronym for 'Member of the Royal Society of Teachers'. Appended to the names of teachers who registered with the TEACHERS' REGISTRATION COUNCIL which existed between 1907 and 1949.

MS   **1** Abbreviation for MANUSCRIPT. **2** Abbreviation (chiefly US) for MASTER'S DEGREE in Science. **3** Title for a woman that (like the male Mr) gives no information about the marital status of the person to whom it attaches.

MSC   See MANPOWER SERVICES COMMISSION.

Mulcaster, Richard   (1530–1611)   A UK educator (first head-master of the Merchant Taylors' School) whose ideas were well ahead of those of his contemporaries. He urged the need for teachers to be trained and for all children to be educated; he stressed the importance of teaching physical education, music, mathematics and the native language; and he advocated that girls be given as rigorous an intellectual education as boys.

multidisciplinary approach/course/method, etc   Involving content and methodology from several DISCIPLINES (though not necessarily integrated as one might expect in an INTERDISCIPLINARY APPROACH).

multilateral school   An early type of UK COMPREHENSIVE SCHOOL that took in children of all levels of ability or aptitude but divided them into separate GRAMMAR, TECHNICAL, and SEC-ONDARY MODERN groups under the same roof.

multi-media materials/approaches/courses/packages   The integrated use of a variety of educational MEDIA within a teaching situation in order to take advantage of the special contributions each can make to the student's learning.

183

Multiphasic Personality Inventory See MINNESOTA MULTIPHASIC PERSONALITY INVENTORY.

multiple-choice question (or **item**)   A type of question common in OBJECTIVE TESTS in which the student is asked to choose from among a number of possible answers. If the test concerns, say, personality he may be asked simply to choose the answer that most closely agrees with his own opinion on the issue involved. With more academic tests, he is asked to choose the correct (best) answer. Normally only one is correct. The other answers should be plausible enough to prevent the correct answer being obvious.

multiple-choice test   A test consisting of MULTIPLE-CHOICE QUESTIONS.

multiple discrimination   A type of learning in which the learner has to distinguish between a number of similar but different items or events (and respond differently to them); for example, learning to identify by name the various coniferous trees.

multiple-facet question   Test ITEM in which the student is given some information and is then asked to answer several questions relating to it.

multiple marking   An approach to EXAMINATION MARKING in which each candidate's SCRIPT is assessed by more than one examiner, in the hope of avoiding SUBJECTIVE bias and of thus being fairer.

multiple regression analysis   Statistical technique used in establishing the relationship between a number of VARIABLES with a view to predicting or estimating the VALUES of one variable associated with given values of the other variables.

multi-sensory aids/materials, etc   Educational materials that involve the learner in using more than one sense, eg both sight and touch.

multiversity   (US) A university consisting of numerous colleges and institutions, perhaps geographically separated and enjoying a considerable degree of autonomy, eg the University of California. (In the UK, the University of London could be considered an example).

Munn and Dunning proposals   Proposals put to the SECRETARY OF STATE FOR SCOTLAND to introduce an ASSESSMENT system for all pupils of all levels of ability at the age of 16-plus, replacing the O-grade of the SCOTTISH CERTIFICATE OF EDUCATION; and for the introduction of a CORE CURRICULUM of English, mathematics and science. See MUNN REPORT and DUNNING REPORT,

Munn Report 1977   The REPORT of an enquiry into 'The Structure of the Curriculum in the Third and Fourth Years of the Scottish Secondary School'. See MUNN AND DUNNING PROPOSALS, and DUNNING REPORT.

museum school services   UK museums offer help to schools and colleges by loaning materials and arranging talks.

mutual system   A less common name for the MONITORIAL SYSTEM.

mystagogue   A teacher who instructs people preparing for INITIATION into the mysteries of certain Middle Eastern religious cults.

mystification   Term used in the SOCIOLOGY OF KNOWLEDGE to denote someone's attempt to obscure or make mysterious some aspect of experience (eg by describing it in esoteric JARGON or by surrounding it with ritual) in order to gain privileged status or exert power over others.

N

nAch   See NEED (FOR) ACHIEVEMENT.

Napier, John   (1550–1617) Scottish mathematician who invented logarithms and some early computing devices.

Napoleonic education   The kind of national education system founded in France by Napoleon Bonaparte in the first few years of the 19th Century – ie ELITIST and firmly controlled by central government.

National Central Library   Part of the lending division of the BRITISH LIBRARY, making books and other documents available through public and academic libraries throughout the UK.

National Certificates and Diplomas   See ORDINARY NATIONAL CERTIFICATE (and DIPLOMA) and HIGHER NATIONAL CERTIFICATE (and DIPLOMA).

National Child Development Study   a LONGITUDINAL study in which psychologists, teachers and health specialists are monitoring the progress through life of a sample of 16,000 UK children all born in the same week in 1958. For the latest report, see

Britain's Sixteen Year Olds edited by Ken Fogelman (National Children's Bureau, London, 1976).

National Defence Education Acts, 1958 and 1964   (US) Provided large scale funds for the improvement of teaching in science, mathematics, languages, and CIVICS as well as for VOCATIONAL COUNSELLING in schools and for loans to students in HIGHER EDUCATION. The original concern was with education as contributory to national defence, but the Acts helped improve education more widely.

National Development Project in Computer Assisted Learning (**NDPCAL**)   A four-year RESEARCH AND DEVELOPMENT project (1973–7) sponsored by the UK COUNCIL FOR EDUCATIONAL TECHNOLOGY.

National Education Association (**NEA**) (US) Supposedly the largest PROFESSIONAL BODY and TRADE UNION in the world, catering for teachers and administrators from all levels of education.

National Extension College (**NEC**) A non-profit-making UK CORRESPONDENCE COLLEGE founded in 1963 by the ADVISORY CENTRE FOR EDUCATION (ACE). It has some 10,000 adult students, mostly preparing for GCE examinations, for the OPEN UNIVERSITY, or for the EXTERNAL DEGREES of London University. Its courses combine printed correspondence materials, broadcasting, and occasional face-to-face teaching by part-time tutors. It also provides TEACHING MATERIALS for use in a large number of colleges of FURTHER or HIGHER EDUCATION some of which are used in FLEXI-STUDY courses.

National Foundation for Educational Research (NFER) A UK body funded by central government and LOCAL EDUCATION AUTHORITIES in England and Wales to undertake a wide range of educational research activities and issue numerous associated publications, including the journal *Educational Research*.

National Lending Library for Science and Technology Part of the lending division of the BRITISH LIBRARY, making books and documents on science and technology available through public and academic libraries throughout the UK.

National Listening Library A UK charity founded in 1972 to provide a postal lending service of tape-recorded 'TALKING BOOKS' for people who are blind or otherwise too handicapped to read conventional books.

National Schools ELEMENTARY SCHOOLS operated by the

Church of England's 'NATIONAL SOCIETY for Promoting the Education of the Poor in the Principles of the Established Church in England and Wales', founded in 1811. By the middle of the 19th Century, there were more than 17,000 such schools containing close on a million pupils.

National Society A pioneer of UK elementary education founded in 1811 as the 'National Society for Promoting the Education of the Poor in the Principles of the Established Church throughout England and Wales.' It took over the CHARITY SCHOOLS sponsored since the early 18th Century by the SOCIETY FOR PROMOTING CHRISTIAN KNOWLEDGE (SPCK) and, by the 1850s, operated more than 17,000 schools, following the MONITORIAL SYSTEM advocated by ANDREW BELL. Unlike the schools of the rival, non-conformist BRITISH AND FOREIGN SCHOOL SOCIETY, NATIONAL SCHOOLS gave instruction in the liturgy and catechism of the Church of England (though some schools allowed dissenters' children to be withdrawn from such lessons).

National Union of School Students (**NUSS**) A UK organisation that arose in the early 1970s, out of the demands for more PUPIL POWER (especially among older SECONDARY SCHOOL students who, in some areas, gained places on GOVERNING BODIES of schools. Had some 8,000 members in 1980 compared with about 20,000 when at its peak. Affiliated to NATIONAL UNION OF STUDENTS.

National Union of Students (NUS) UK organisation founded in 1922 and representing some 800,000 student-members in HIGHER EDUCATION. Its leaders negotiate with the DEPARTMENT OF EDUCATION AND SCIENCE for increases in MAINTENANCE GRANTS and it acts as a PRESSURE GROUP on all kinds of educational and political issues, generally taking a somewhat left-wing stance.

National Union of Teachers (NUT) The largest UK PROFESSIONAL BODY and TRADE UNION for teachers, with well over a quarter of a million members. It is affiliated to the TUC, is militant in its campaigns for improving teachers' status and, holding the majority of seats on the BURNHAM COMMITTEE, is the union with most influence over salaries.

nativism The belief that most knowledge and skill is INNATE in the individual at birth and can emerge only through MATURATION.

naturalistic observation A research method whereby the observer watches a situation that has arisen naturally (rather than one he has set up deliberately as an experiment) and tries to have as little personal effect on it as possible. (In that second respect at least, it contrasts with PARTICIPANT OBSERVATION.)

natural wastage The reduction of a work force (or STUDENT BODY) by allowing members to leave without replacing them.

nature-nurture controversy The long-running (and probably irresolvable) controversy as to whether various aspects of people's BEHAVIOUR and INTELLIGENCE are chiefly inherited and INNATE or are chiefly due to LEARNING and other interactions with the ENVIRONMENT after birth. (Also known as HEREDITY-ENVIRONMENT controversy.)

nature table Display area in PRIMARY SCHOOL on which plants, small animals, rock specimens etc, may be exhibited.

nature trail A country walk, planned to follow a route along which certain particular plants and animals or natural features of terrain can be observed. See also TOWN TRAIL.

nature walk US equivalent of NATURE TRAIL.

NDPCAL See NATIONAL DEVELOPMENT PROJECT IN COMPUTER ASSISTED LEARNING.

NEA See NATIONAL EDUCATION ASSOCIATION.

Neale Analysis of Reading Ability A UK test of READING ABILITY (accuracy, comprehension and speed) in children between 6 and 12 years. Helpful in diagnosis for REMEDIAL TEACHING.

NEC See NATIONAL EXTENSION COLLEGE.

Need for achievement (nAch) A concept of US psychologist, Henry Murray, referring to people's need to do well at whatever they involve themselves in.

Need (for) Achievement Test A test developed by the US psychologist, McCLELLAND, in which people are asked to write short stories about pictures they are shown. The stories are then scored according to features indicating the person's need for achievement, eg to obtain praise and respect, wealth, power, etc.

needs 1 Term used in theories of MOTIVATION to refer to the basic wants or desires that motivate people to behave in certain ways, either to attain a positive result or avoid a negative one. See also HIERARCHY OF NEEDS. 2 The term is also used of needs that may not be motivating because the person concerned is unaware of them. A wise teacher or counsellor, however, may be able to identify some such needs for a person and help bring them to his attention.

needs analysis/assessment The study of some person's or group's NEEDS, perhaps with a view to providing teaching designed to satisfy them.

needs, special See SPECIAL NEEDS.

negative correlation (or RELATIONSHIP) A statistical relation-ship between two VARIABLES such that high VALUES on one var-iable tend to be associated with low values on the other.

negative reinforcement Psychological term for any STIMULUS (or outcome) increasing the probability that a person (or animal) will act in such a way as to remove or avoid it. Loosely speaking, a PUNISHMENT. See REINFORCEMENT.

negative transfer Sometimes a student learns new knowledge or skills less easily than others because of INTERFERENCE from knowledge or skills he possesses already. See also INHIBITION and TRANSFER.

neglectee Another name for an ISOLATE as used in SOCIOMETRY.

negotiation 1 A term used by some sociologists in arguing that we form our knowledge and understanding of social reality out of the 'give and take' of offering meanings and interpretations to one another and reinterpreting them in terms of the responses we receive. 2 The process by which teachers' associations (or unions) and the employing authorities decide on the salaries and conditions of service of teachers.

Negro college/university (US) One of the institutions of HIGHER EDUCATION founded, particularly in the 19th century, for the benefit of negro students, eg Lincoln, Howard, and Shaw universities. Nowadays referred to as a black college/university.

neighbourhood school Term used to characterise a school drawing its pupils from the surrounding area (and possibly iden-tifying itself very closely with local community interests) rather than attracting pupils from near and far on some other kind of specialist appeal.

Neill, A S (1884–1973) Scottish EDUCATOR and pioneer of PRO-GRESSIVE EDUCATION who taught in Germany and Austria before returning to England to set up his famous school, SUMMERHILL, in Suffolk. His teaching was much influenced by the concepts of PSYCHOANALYSIS, and the influence of HOMER LANE could be seen in his practice of expecting his pupils to make their own rules. He wrote many books about the school: see *That Dreadful School* (1937) and *Summerhill: A Compilation* (1962).

neonate A new-born child in the first two or three weeks of life – a time of intense learning activity (as well as rapid development and great vulnerability).

neurosis A relatively mild form of mental disorder (eg anxiety states, depression, phobias, hysteria). The sufferer is aware that he is disturbed and he stands a good chance of recovery. (Contrasts with PSYCHOSIS.)

network analysis Generic term for such techniques as PROGRAMME EVALUATION AND REVIEW TECHNIQUE (PERT) and CRITICAL PATH ANALYSIS (CPA) which are methods of planning and monitoring a complex project by analysing it into its component parts and representing their inter-relationships over time by means of a FLOW CHART.

network diagram A VISUAL AID, representing a system of ideas or processes, using various symbols and inter-connecting arrows to show how the different components relate to one another. (See also ALGORITHM and NETWORK ANALYSIS.)

neuroticism v. stability A PERSONALITY DIMENSION described by the UK psychologist EYSENCK and relating to the degree to which a person is likely to be emotionally over-responsive and to break down under stress.

Newcastle Report 1861 The first thorough enquiry into the state of public education in England. The REPORT noted that almost half the eligible children were not receiving any form of education and no more than a quarter received an adequate one – even though it considered 10 or 11 the age at which the education of most children should end. Among the Report's many recommendations was that the financial support of schools should depend on the attainments of their pupils as tested by external examiners. This was implemented in the REVISED CODE of 1862 and, for individual teachers, led to PAYMENT BY RESULTS.

New Education Fellowship An international organisation formed by Beatrice Ensor at a conference in Calais in 1921 to further the common interests of groups and schools pursuing liberal CHILD-CENTRED education in America and Europe. It launched a journal, *The New Era*, which is still published. The organisation changed its name to WORLD EDUCATION FELLOWSHIP in 1966. See also NEW SCHOOLS MOVEMENT.

New Lanark A village in Lanarkshire, Scotland, founded by David Dale and Richard Arkwright as a centre of cotton manufacturing. David Dale set up schools for working children (from 1783) and was followed (in 1800) by his son-in-law, ROBERT OWEN, who extended the educational provision to include adult mill-workers, established the first INFANT SCHOOLS in Britain, identified the value of PLAY in education, and made the name of New Lanark famous in its time.

Newman, Cardinal John Henry (1801–1890) An English theologian who, after being an Anglican bishop and a leader of the Oxford Movement, was received into the Roman Catholic Church in 1845 and became Rector of Dublin's new Catholic university in 1854. Before becoming a cardinal in 1879 he wrote a widely-quoted book of lectures, *The Idea of a University* (1873), in which he explored his views of the nature of intellectual culture and the unity of knowledge and argued that the proper role of a university is to train mind and spirit rather than merely to impart information.

new mathematics Same as MODERN MATHEMATICS.

'news' A lesson or session, usually in a PRIMARY SCHOOL, where the teacher regularly gets children to discuss items of local current interest, and especially to tell the class about interesting things that they have recently done, perhaps with friends or families. The US equivalent is often called 'SHOW AND TELL'.

New Schools Movement A reforming movement (generally espousing such ideas as democratic socialism, ethical idealism, non-dogmatic religion, internationalism, and a liberal CHILD-CENTRED approach in education) that began in the UK with the founding of Abbotsholme School in 1889 and led to the founding of Bedales and of King Alfred school, Hampstead, as well as other schools in England and France. The same spirit was continued by the New Ideal Group formed in 1914 (one of whose members sponsored the educational experiments of HOMER LANE); and in 1921 the NEW EDUCATION FELLOWSHIP was launched at an international conference to further the common interests of such groups in America and Europe and still exists today as the WORLD EDUCATION FELLOWSHIP.

new sixth Term used in SECONDARY SCHOOLS in England and Wales to indicate that students staying on beyond the age of 16 (and entering the SIXTH FORM) are often different from those of earlier times – especially in that they are not necessarily aiming to prepare for HIGHER EDUCATION and may intend to leave after one year, perhaps having taken examinations for the CERTIFICATE OF EXTENDED EDUCATION (CEE).

Newsom Report 1963 a UK REPORT from the CENTRAL ADVISORY COUNCIL entitled 'Half our Future', concerning the education of less able pupils in SECONDARY SCHOOLS in England and Wales. Made many recommendations including: bonus payments to teachers working in difficult areas; a new outward-looking CURRICULUM; positive SEXUAL EDUCATION; reduced emphasis on

PUBLIC examinations; improved buildings; new TEACHING METH-ODS and equipment; and, most significantly, the immediate rais-ing of the SCHOOL-LEAVING AGE (from 15 to 16). Response to the report was slow and patchy, but the school leaving age was raised in 1972.

Newsom Report 1968   The first of two UK REPORTS by the Pub-lic Schools Commission into how the PUBLIC SCHOOLS might be in-tegrated with the state system of MAINTAINED SCHOOLS. Its chief recommendation (which was not well received) was that 38,000 children per year should be admitted to BOARDING (INDEPENDENT) SCHOOLS on the grounds of special need, with their fees being paid by LOCAL EDUCATION AUTHORITIES or by the Government.

NFER   See NATIONAL FOUNDATION FOR EDUCATIONAL RESEARCH.

night school   The provision of facilities (whether in school or college) for employed people to continue their education in the evenings. The term has more or less died out in favour of EVENING CLASSES.

NIIP tests   Series of UK APTITUDE TESTS (clerical, numerical, mechanical, etc) produced by the National Institute of Industrial Psychology.

nine year school   (US) A rare type of school combining the ELEMENTARY SCHOOL and JUNIOR HIGH SCHOOL GRADES.

nominal scale   See SCALES OF MEASUREMENT.

nomogram   A graph from which one can read off the VALUE of one VARIABLE (eg score on a mathematics test) that would cor-respond with a given value on another variable (eg score on a biology test). Used in SCALING marks.

nomothetic approach   An approach to the study of PERSONALITY and human BEHAVIOUR that considers large numbers of people with a view to deriving laws and hypotheses about human beings in general. Contrasts with IDIOGRAPHIC APPROACH.

non-book materials   Library term for learning materials other than books, eg sound tapes and historical documents. Also called NON-PRINT MATERIALS.

nonconformist academy   As DISSENTING ACADEMY.

non-denominational schools   All those schools (the majority nowadays in the UK and US) that have no special religious affiliation.

N-level   See ADVANCED LEVELS.

non-directive therapy   An approach to PSYCHOTHERAPY, pi-oneered by CARL ROGERS, in which the therapist's role is to provide the right emotional atmosphere for the patient to be free to work out his own solutions to his problems. The therapist may help the patient to clarify his thoughts and feelings but gives no direction and offers no solutions. Gave rise to NON-DIRECTIVE TEACHING.

non-directive teaching   An approach to teaching in which the teacher aims to help the student identify his own goals and find his own best way towards them, without imposing a structure on him. In TUTORIAL groups, the discussion is supposed to be student-initiated with the teacher interposing only to seek clarifications of student-contributions or to comment on the nature or implications of what is being said, but without offering judgments or attempting to lead. Developed by CARL ROGERS out of his experience with NON-DIRECTIVE THERAPY. See his *Freedom to Learn* (1969).

non-formal education   (US) Education taking place outside of schools, colleges and universities and aiming to develop knowledge, skills and attitudes that are not normally given prominence in formal educational institutions. (Unfortunately, the term sometimes gets used for what might better be called INFORMAL EDUCATION or for any education involving an INFORMAL APPROACH.)

non-graded schools/education   (US) System in which children are not divided among grades according to age but among classes formed by VERTICAL GROUPING (UK term).

non-maintained school   See INDEPENDENT SCHOOL.

non-parametric statistics/technique/tests   Statistical techniques (eg Chi-square and Mann-Whitney U test) for making INFERENCES about POPULATIONS on the basis of samples, without the usual assumptions that have to be made about the shape of the underlying DISTRIBUTION.

non-print materials (media)   A library term for LEARNING MATERIALS (MEDIA) that are not printed, eg AUDIO-and VIDEO TAPES. Also called NON-BOOK MATERIALS.

non-provided schools   Term used subsequent to the EDUCATION ACT 1902 for the DENOMINATIONAL SCHOOLS that had been VOLUNTARY and, while still not 'provided' by the newly-established LOCAL EDUCATION AUTHORITIES, were now eligible for some financial support from them (as well as considerable CURRICULUM control).

non-public school   (US) Any school that is financed privately (rather than out of public funds) and may well charge fees.

193

Non-readers' Intelligence Test   A UK test that can be presented orally to groups of children who cannot read.

non-resident student   One who is not resident in accommodation forming part of the college or university's campus.

non-respondent   Person who fails to complete a QUESTIONNAIRE or otherwise respond to a request for information in a statistical SURVEY. Too large a proportion of non-respondents may invalidate the survey.

non-selective school/institution   One that admits pupils without regard to their ability or attainment – like COMPREHENSIVE SCHOOLS but unlike GRAMMAR SCHOOLS in the UK.

non-streaming   See MIXED-ABILITY TEACHING.

non-traditional education   (US) See NON-FORMAL EDUCATION.

nonsense syllables   Meaningless combinations of letters (eg GUR, DIS, PEL) made up for use in research on MEMORY.

non-verbal communication   The communication of meaning through mime, gesture, posture, facial contortions, etc, rather than with words. (Non-verbal aspects of speech may also be included, i.e. accent, speed, pauses, tone, etc.)

non-verbal intelligence   The ability to reason without using words (eg by using patterns and shapes and numbers instead). Presumably measurable by non-verbal tests such as PROGRESSIVE MATRICES and the DRAW-A-MAN TEST.

norm   **1** With PSYCHOLOGICAL TESTS, a norm is a standard value on some measured DIMENSION, usually stated as the AVERAGE performance among people on whom the test has been tried. An individual's score on the test can then be compared with the norm. **2** In sociology, a norm is defined as a rule or standard of behaviour that a group of people appear to expect of one another.

normal school/college   A form of TEACHER TRAINING institution that developed particularly in the US during the 19th century (though the name betrays its French origin: école normale), in order to meet the growing demand for PRIMARY SCHOOL teachers.

normal curve/distribution   A bell-shaped DISTRIBUTION that frequently occurs when a graph is drawn showing how many people obtain each possible VALUE (or score) on some measured VARIABLE such as height. Thus very few people are extremely short or tall and the curve rises to a hump mid-way between those two extremes, showing that most people are around the medium height. Many human attributes are distributed in this fashion.

normative behaviour   See NORM **2**.

normative system   An inter-related set of social NORMS accepted by members of a social group.

normative test   A test that has been administered to a large group of people representative of the POPULATION to which the test is supposed to apply, and the mean score and variability calculated so that the scores of people subsequently taking the test can be compared.

norm-referenced testing   Where a student's test performance is compared with the performance of other students, and his GRADE is dependent on the average performance and variability of performance among those others. Contrast with CRITERION-REFERENCED and SELF-REFERENCED TESTING. See also 'GRADING ON THE CURVE'.

Norwood Report 1943   UK REPORT of the Secondary Schools Examinations Council that recommended drastic alterations in the SCHOOL CERTIFICATE and HIGHER SCHOOL CERTIFICATE examinations (giving rise eventually to the GCE and, later, the CSE).

Nuffield Foundation   A UK trust set up to advance education (and health, social well-being, and the care of the aged). It awards grants and fellowships and co-operates with numerous universities, government bodies, research councils etc, and has been energetic in sponsoring CURRICULUM DEVELOPMENT (eg in science, mathematics and languages).

null hypothesis   The statistically approved method of framing an HYPOTHESIS in scientific work. Thus, if we are testing a new teaching method against an old one, we should start out with the null hypothesis that there will be no real difference (ie none that could not be explained by chance variations) between the results of the two methods. Only if the difference is very large can we then reject this hypothesis and say that we will expect a difference to occur again in future comparisons between the two methods (given similar circumstances).

number on roll   The 'number on roll' in a UK MAINTAINED SCHOOL is the number of children officially registered as being pupils of that school.

number skills   The ability to understand the properties of numbers and use them.

number work   PRIMARY SCHOOL term for the early stages of learning mathematics.

numeracy Proficiency in NUMBER SKILLS, a term coined in the CROWTHER REPORT as a parallel with LITERACY. See also ORACY and GRAPHICACY.

Nunn, Sir Percy (1870–1944) Professor of Education in the University of London and Principle of the London DAY TRAINING COLLEGE whose book *Education: its Data and First Principles* (1920), asserting 'individuality' to be 'the supreme educational end:' was very influential between the wars.

nursery assistant/nurse A trained person employed to give assistance to teachers in UK NURSERY SCHOOLS or CLASSES (and perhaps in other classes in INFANT SCHOOLS).

nursery class A class within a PRIMARY SCHOOL for children below the age when compulsory education begins.

nursery education From PLATO onwards, through educators like COMENIUS, ROUSSEAU, PESTALOZZI, FROEBEL, OWEN, MONTESSORI, the MACMILLAN sisters, DEWEY and SUSAN ISAACS, the incalculable value of rich experience in the early (nursery) years has been urged. The PLOWDEN REPORT made much of this need. Unfortunately, it is the area of education that usually suffers most in times of economic stringency.

nursery school A school for children between the age of three years (sometimes two) and five when· they begin in PRIMARY SCHOOL or (in the US) KINDERGARTEN.

nurture unit/group See SPECIAL UNITS.

NUS See NATIONAL UNION OF STUDENTS.

NUSS See NATIONAL UNION OF SCHOOL STUDENTS.

NUT See NATIONAL UNION OF TEACHERS.

O

objective approach/method An approach to evidence using explicit rules of procedure that, theoretically, should result in all possible observers agreeing on what they had seen and what it meant. (Contrasts with SUBJECTIVE APPROACH which allows for personal judgments and differences of opinion.)

objectives An important term in CURRICULUM DEVELOPMENT and EDUCATIONAL TECHNOLOGY. Sometimes it refers in a general way to any learning goal or desired outcome of education; sometimes it refers more narrowly to explicitly-worded statements specifying the BEHAVIOUR that learners should be able to exhibit in some measurable form – see BEHAVIOURAL OBJECTIVES.

objective test A test designed in such a way that all qualified examiners should agree on what score has been earned by a particular candidate. It usually involves MULTIPLE-CHOICE QUESTIONS of one form or another, together with so explicit a MARKING SCHEME that marks may be allotted by someone unfamiliar with the subject-matter or even by a machine (as with COMPUTER-MARKED ASSIGNMENTS). Such tests are of value, if well-constructed, but do not allow ASSESSMENT of certain important student abilities for which SUBJECTIVE (eg ESSAY) tests are essential.

object lesson 1 An educational innovation of the 19th century wherein the classroom teacher would illustrate his lesson by showing the children an actual specimen of the object (eg a fish) he was lecturing them about. 2 An exemplary demonstration of how to do something, eg calming a noisy class.

object teaching Teaching method based on OBJECT LESSONS (sense 1).

observation 1 The study of human BEHAVIOUR at first-hand by watching people at work or play. See NATURALISTIC OBSERVATION and PARTICIPANT OBSERVATION. 2 Term used in statistics to indicate a single recorded VALUE of some VARIABLE, eg if we measured the heights of 30 children we would have a set of 30 separate observations.

obsession The continual recurrence of a persistent idea or impulse. In extreme cases it is part of a mental illness in which the sufferer feels compelled to perform certain irrational actions, eg perpetual hand-washing.

occasional closures (holidays) The ten days every year that may be nominated (sometimes by the GOVERNORS) as extra holidays for a UK MAINTAINED SCHOOL (ie *in addition to* the holidays fixed by the LOCAL EDUCATION AUTHORITY for all the schools in the area).

occupational guidance Advising people on occupations that might suit them, perhaps using APTITUDE TESTS. Related to CAREERS GUIDANCE and PLACEMENT GUIDANCE (US).

occupational programme (US) A programme of studies in JUNIOR COLLEGE that prepares the student for entry to a career

197

(probably at technician or clerical level) rather than for entry to a degree course programme in a STATE COLLEGE or UNIVERSITY.

occupational psychology   The psychology of human behaviour in work situations. It studies such factors as selection procedures, training, stress, job satisfaction, etc.

occupational therapy   The therapeutic use of HANDICRAFTS and creative hobbies in the mental or physical rehabilitation of people who are mentally or physically handicapped or ill.

oceanography   An INTER-DISCIPLINARY study concerned with the physics, chemistry, geology, biology, meteorology etc, of the world's seas and oceans.

off-air recording   The recording of radio and television programmes when they are broadcast (off-air), with the intention of playing them back to students at some later time.

off-campus   Referring to facilities and activities that a college or university might offer in some place other than its own buildings and grounds, eg EXTRA-MURAL classes.

office arts/practice   (US) A VOCATIONAL subject in the CURRICULUM, including topics such as secretarial skills, typing, filing, etc.

Office of Education   (US) Former branch of the DEPARTMENT OF HEALTH, EDUCATION AND WELFARE providing federal financial assistance, and other educational services, to local and state authorities and conducting research. See DEPARTMENT OF EDUCATION.

off-quota staff/teachers   Part-time teachers and others who might be employed by a UK school (or LOCAL EDUCATION AUTHORITY) in addition to those allowed under the prevailing QUOTA fixed by the authority. The QUOTA SYSTEM was abolished in 1975.

off-the-job-training   Training provided at some place other than the trainee's place of work. Perhaps in order to make use of special facilities or to avoid distractions.

ogive   In statistics, a distribution showing the total numbers of OBSERVATIONS that are greater or less than each VALUE of a VARIABLE.

O grade   Ordinary grade in the SCOTTISH CERTIFICATE OF EDUCATION.

old boy network   The informal network of contacts between former students of certain prestigious UK PUBLIC SCHOOLS and universities, widely assumed to be influential in creating power and career opportunities for its members. (The term is also extended to cover closely-knit groups from other backgrounds and of either sex.)

old boys (or **girls**) UK term for ex-pupils of a school. Equivalent to US ALUMNI (or alumnae).

O-levels See ORDINARY LEVELS.

Ombudsman (US) Person elected by a school or, more likely, by a college or university, to serve as advocate for students who have grievances. Similar to Scottish RECTOR.

Omnibus Personality Inventory A US PERSONALITY TEST for college students, covering many aspects relating to temperament and adjustment.

omnibus test Any psychological test that measures a number of different skills or mental abilities but produces only one overall score for the test as a whole.

ONC See ORDINARY NATIONAL CERTIFICATE.

OND See ORDINARY NATIONAL DIPLOMA.

one parent family A family from which the mother or (more likely) father is permanently absent, possibly resulting in economic, emotional and educational difficulties for the children.

one-trial learning Psychological term for LEARNING that can be accomplished without practice and repetition.

one-way screen A sheet of glass specially treated so that people on one side can look through it without being seen by people on the other. More commonly known as a one-way mirror or glass. Used by US psychologist, GESELL, for observing and filming the activities of children without disturbing them.

on-roll See NUMBER ON ROLL.

on-site training See ON-THE-JOB TRAINING.

'on the curve' See 'GRADING ON THE CURVE'.

on-the-job training Training provided at the trainee's normal place of work and perhaps arranged in such a way that he can learn the necessary knowledge and skills while carrying out the job itself.

opaque projector See EPISCOPE.

open access (or **open admission, open enrolment, open door policy**) The policy of admitting students to an educational institution (especially a university) regardless of whether they have the normal ENTRY QUALIFICATIONS. Access is becoming increasingly open in many universities in the developed countries, partly in response to MINORITY GROUPS' complaints of previous educational deprivation and partly because of the declining numbers of traditionally qualified applicants.

open admission   See OPEN ACCESS.

open air class/school   Found particularly when pulmonary tuberculosis was still common, and dedicated to pupils spending as much time as possible in the fresh air, with a view to improving their health.

open book examination/test   An examination where candidates are allowed to consult TEXTBOOKS and their own NOTEBOOKS while answering questions.

open circuit/channel   The broadcasting of television or radio signals to the general public. Contrasts with CLOSED CIRCUIT.

open classroom   Large teaching area (especially in a PRIMARY SCHOOL) that may be used by several classes at a time, perhaps with areas devoted to several different activities among which children can move. Sometimes there are devices such as folding doors to shut off areas for small group work. See also OPEN PLAN SCHOOLS.

open day   Day when an educational institution invites the public (especially parents, in the case of a school) to visit it and see and discuss the work it is doing.

open door policy   See OPEN ACCESS.

open education   The slogan of educators who wish to see open-ness (ie fewer restrictions) in selecting students, in CURRICULUM CONTENT and TEACHING METHODS, and in creating more DEMOCRATIC relationships between teachers and taught. See OPEN LEARNING SYSTEMS.

open-ended item/question/test   Used of ITEMS (etc) where the aim is to encourage a variety of different responses rather than a single correct answer.

open enrolment   See OPEN ACCESS.

open examinations   **1** Examinations that are open to anyone who wishes to be a candidate. **2** Examinations that relax some of the traditional constraints, eg by allowing unlimited time, publishing questions in advance, permitting students to consult their books and one another, and so on.

open learning (systems)   All arrangements intended to overcome restrictions on students' access to knowledge and education. See OPEN ACCESS and OPEN EDUCATION.

open plan schools   This term refers to many UK PRIMARY SCHOOLS and to some SECONDARY SCHOOLS built (in the 1960s and 70s especially) without traditional enclosed classrooms. Instead they have a number of large open areas (see OPEN CLASSROOM) in which more than one class can work. This architectural style supposedly facilitates such educational practices as TEAM TEACHING, VERTICAL GROUPING, INTEGRATED DAY and, in general, a more PUPIL-CENTRED approach to teaching with particular emphasis on individual work and small-group activity. It is certainly cheaper than traditional building, but many teachers complain of noise and distraction.

open scholarship   A SCHOLARSHIP at a university or other institution that can be competed for by anyone. (Contrasts with a CLOSED SCHOLARSHIP.)

open-shelf library   The usual kind of library, in which readers have access to the book-shelves and can browse among the books to make their selection. Contrasts with a CATALOGUE LIBRARY, where only the librarians have access to the shelves and would-be readers must make their selection from the catalogue.

Open Tech   A collaborative scheme currently proposed (1981) by UK Government to apply OPEN UNIVERSITY methods of DISTANCE TEACHING to TECHNICAL and VOCATIONAL EDUCATION.

Open University   A UK university established in 1969 to provide degree courses by correspondence for students of 21 years and over, regardless of whether they have the ENTRANCE QUALIFICATIONS normally required by universities. The university now (1981) has some 75 thousand students, the majority of whom have full-time jobs. They study at home about 12-15 hours a week for about 30 weeks of the year. Most of their work is with printed SELF-INSTRUCTIONAL MATERIALS and textbooks, though these are supplemented by some television and radio (broadcast specially by the BBC), and some face-to-face tuition is also available. Certain courses entail a week at SUMMER SCHOOL. Students can gain a credit for each year's work, six credits being needed for a degree and eight for an honours degree. Courses are available in arts, social sciences, educational studies, mathematics, science, and technology. Each year, approximately one in every 16 students graduating from UK institutions is from the Open University. Similar institutions offering HIGHER EDUCATION by DISTANCE TEACHING have been set up in several other countries including Pakistan, Venezuela, and West Germany.

Operant   Term used by US psychologist, SKINNER, to describe a unit of BEHAVIOUR like raising an arm, walking in a circle, saying one's name, etc.

operant conditioning The process whereby some unit of BEHAVIOUR already in the learner's reportoire is given REINFORCE-MENT so that the behaviour can be made more frequent and perhaps linked with other similarly-reinforced OPERANTS in order to develop a new pattern of behaviour.

operation Term used by PIAGET for any ability or skill that a person can carry out in his mind as well as in fact and can generalise to a variety of situations. The learning of such abilities constitutes intellectual development in a child. See also CONCRETE OPERATIONS and FORMAL OPERATIONS.

operational definition A definition phrased in terms implying the operations of measurement or OBJECTIVE observation, eg 'tiredness' might be defined in terms of 'number of hours without sleep' rather than by descriptive phrases like 'drowsy looking'; and 'creativity' might be defined as 'score obtained on a certain creativity-test'.

operationalise To translate a concept or HYPOTHESIS into terms that allow it to be investigated through the operations of measurement and/or OBJECTIVE observation.

opinionaire (US) QUESTIONNAIRE designed to elicit opinions rather than factual information.

opportunity class A class for pupils (particularly in PRIMARY SCHOOLS) who have fallen behind in their learning and either need time out from their normal class in order to catch up or to stay permanently with a group moving more slowly. May also be called a REMEDIAL CLASS and is similar to US MAKE-UP CLASS.

opportunity school (US) An institution offering VOCATIONAL training, mainly to adults and usually in the evenings.

option One of a number of alternatives (eg alternative courses or alternative questions in a test or examination) from which a student is free to choose.

Oracle The TELETEXT service provided by the ITV in the UK to owners of suitably-adapted television receivers and offering them a choice from hundreds of 'pages' of printed information (ranging from news and sport to food prices, recipes and the weather) that can be displayed on their TV screens.

oracy The ability to communicate fluently in speech. (Compare LITERACY and NUMERACY). Sometimes suggested as an essential addition to the basic skills referred to as the THREE Rs – reading, (w)riting, (a)rithmetic.

oral examination/test A *viva voce* – a form of ASSESSMENT in which candidates are tested (usually individually) in face-to-face discussion with the examiner, possibly on the basis of previous written work.

ordinal scale See SCALES OF MEASUREMENT.

ordinary degree A PASS DEGREE – one not classified into HONOURS.

Ordinary grade (**SCE**) See SCOTTISH CERTIFICATE OF EDUCATION.

Ordinary level (**GCE**) See GENERAL CERTIFICATE OF EDUCATION.

Ordinary National Certificate (**ONC**) A UK technical qualification, roughly equivalent in standard to ADVANCED LEVEL GCE, and usually awarded after a two-year part-time course in a TECHNICAL or FURTHER EDUCATION COLLEGE. Like most courses aimed at technicians, the ONC is now being assimilated with the courses of the TECHNICIAN EDUCATION COUNCIL or BUSINESS EDUCATION COUNCIL.

Ordinary National Diploma (**OND**) Similar qualification to ORDINARY NATIONAL CERTIFICATE but awarded after a two-year full-time course.

Orff, Carl (Born 1895) A German composer whose ideas have been influential in musical education in schools. His approach is based on creative music-making, with strong emphasis on rhythm, and the use of specially-made simple instruments, the pentatonic scale, and the TONIC SOLFA.

organisational analysis/theory The study of the function and structure of organisations (business firms, schools, churches, etc), and the BEHAVIOUR of groups of people within them. Has considerable relevance to EDUCATIONAL INNOVATION and other aspects of life in educational institutions.

organised games See GAMES.

organiser Same as ADVISER. But see also ADVANCE ORGANISER.

organ scholar Student holding a SCHOLARSHIP on the understanding that, in addition to following the same CURRICULUM as other students, he serves as organist in the college chapel.

orientation Sociological term referring to the nature of a person's reasons for undertaking a particular task, eg out of orientation to achievement or orientation to wealth.

orientation course   Same as INDUCTION COURSE.

orienteering   A sport that combines cross-country running and map-reading. Contestants race on foot over a cross-country course, locating check-points with the aid of map and compass.

origami   The HANDICRAFT of paper-folding (originating in Japan).

Osgood, Charles E   (Born 1916) US psychologist and authority on communication, best-known for his widely-used technique of ATTITUDE measurement – the SEMANTIC DIFFERENTIAL. See his *The Measurement of Meaning* (1957).

other-directed   Term used by US sociologist, Riesman, for the kind of CULTURE in which people are motivated by the responses they expect and get from other people rather than by any strong inner principles. Contrasts with INNER-DIRECTED.

Oswego method   The version of OBJECT TEACHING introduced by Edward SHELDON at Oswego Normal School (New York State) in the 1850s. The method attracted considerable attention, and its influence spread widely. But it was also heavily criticised (largely because it could so easily be aimless and stultifying) and was dying out by 1872.

outcome   Term used in CURRICULUM DEVELOPMENT and EDUCATIONAL TECHNOLOGY for the expected or hoped-for results of a course or LEARNING EXPERIENCE or EDUCATIONAL INNOVATION (eg the OBJECTIVES) and also for the actual results (which may be more or less than, or quite different from, what was expected).

out-county student/pupil   A UK pupil in a school, or student in a FURTHER EDUCATION college, whose home is outside the area of the LOCAL EDUCATION AUTHORITY responsible for that school or college.

outdoor education centre   Facilities for enjoying outdoor sports (eg canoeing, riding, hill-walking, etc) and FIELD STUDIES, often operated by a LOCAL EDUCATION AUTHORITY.

out-group   All people other than those a person considers to be in his IN-GROUP. That is, 'them' as opposed to 'us'.

out-of district student   (US) Student attending school in a SCHOOL DISTRICT other than the one in which he lives. Similar to UK EXTRA-DISTRICT or OUT-COUNTY STUDENTS.

out-of-school-activities   EXTRA-CURRICULAR ACTIVITIES that may be pursued elsewhere than on the school's premises (or on the school premises but outside the normal timetable).

out-of-school education   Same as NON-FORMAL EDUCATION.

out-of-state student   (US) Student attending an educational institution outside of his own state and perhaps paying higher fees on that account.

outreach program   (US) An attempt by a college or university to improve relations with the surrounding community.

outreach workers/staff   People employed by, for example, the YOUTH SERVICE (UK) to make contacts with and attract people who might not otherwise have enjoyed a certain service.

Outward Bound Trust   A UK trust providing short-term residential courses for teenagers, in which the emphasis is on developing stamina, self-discipline, teamwork and a spirit of adventure, by engaging in such activities as sailing and mountaineering.

over-achiever   Student who is doing better than he is considered really capable of. The implication of the term is that his current success may not be sustained, or only at some unacceptable personal cost.

overhead projector   A device that can project an enlarged image of whatever the user cares to write or draw on a transparent plastic sheet about 25 cm square, while he is still facing his audience. Can be used without darkening the room.

overlearning   Learning that has been achieved by practice continued beyond what would be needed for short-term retention of the KNOWLEDGE or SKILL learned. It is supposed to be of benefit when there is a need to recall the knowledge or recover the skill after a period of disuse.

overt response   A RESPONSE that a student makes in some physical and observable way (eg by speaking, writing, using a tool, etc), rather than simply by thinking or feeling.

Owen, Robert   (1771–1858) Socialist mill-owner and philanthropist who, firmly believing that better social and working conditions might make people 'intelligent, rational and good', set about improving working conditions in his mills at NEW LANARK and provided education both for his workers and for their children. The fame of New Lanark ensured that Owen became a pioneer of infant education and the educational value of PLAY in the UK. See his *A New View of Society* (1813) and *Autobiography* (1857).

Oxbridge A term invented by the novelist, Thackeray, to lump together the universities of Oxford and Cambridge. It is now used to suggest the traditions, values, styles, attributes, and educational characteristics common to those most prestigious UK universities. Similar connotation to IVY LEAGUE in the US.

Oxford Movement A movement within the Anglican Church, initiated by tractarians like NEWMAN at Oxford in the 1830s, that opposed liberalising tendencies and sought to reinstate the Catholic heritage.

Oxon Latin abbreviation representing Oxford University.

P

p<1% Such symbols as p< 1% (or 0.01) or p<5% (or 0.05) are likely to be seen in educational research reports. They indicate that a certain reported result (eg an improvement in student learning) has a probability (p) less than one in a hundred (or less than five in a hundred) of having occurred by chance. See also SIGNIFICANCE.

pacing The rate at which a student is presented with LEARNING MATERIAL (eg in a lecture or when watching a television programme) or (self-pacing) the rate at which he chooses to learn (eg with a TEXTBOOK or SELF-INSTRUCTIONAL MATERIAL).

package A MULTI-MEDIA collection of materials on a certain topic for individual or group learning, together with suggestions as to how they might be used. May be one of several such MODULES in a PACKAGED COURSE.

packaged course One that is based on pre-recorded materials (books, tapes, films, etc) in the form of a series of related PACKAGES. Does not necessarily imply SELF-INSTRUCTION, for teachers and students can work together in the classroom with such materials.

packaged teaching Teaching that has been thought out in advance of learners coming to it, and recorded in the form of PACKAGES for the use of learners working either on their own or with the help of teachers who will help them interpret it.

paddle (US) See PADDLING.

paddling (US) Type of CORPORAL PUNISHMENT, often performed with a flat wooden bat. Rarely used in schools.

paediatrics   Branch of medicine concerned with the health and diseases of children.

paedagogy   Less common spelling of PEDGAGOGY.

paired comparisons   A research method whereby every item (or person) in a large group is compared, in turn, with just one other item in that group. The items can then be ranked in order of preference.

pantograph   A device consisting of pivoted arms and levers by means of which one can trace over a drawing or map etc, at the same time producing a copy to any required scale.

paper   An essay, scholarly article or research report, or a learned address given to a conference or SYMPOSIUM.

paper-and-pencil test   Any test or examination that involves the candidate in making marks on paper (even if with a pen) as opposed to those that require him to engage in another activity (like conversing with an examiner or playing a musical instrument).

paper qualifications   Recognition of a person's attainments or experience attested to in a document, especially a certificate of examination performance or, perhaps, REFERENCES or TESTIMONIALS.

paradigm   A term used in the SOCIOLOGY OF KNOWLEDGE to indicate the set of related PERSPECTIVES that a person brings to the performance of a task, the solution of a problem, or, more generally, to engaging in the concerns of his profession. It includes all the concepts, assumptions, VALUES, methodologies and criteria for proof and truth that the person (and like-minded colleagues) operates with. Different SCHOOLS OF THOUGHT within a DISCIPLINE might be said to be operating within different paradigms.

paragraphia   The habitual tendency to insert or omit words unintentionally while writing; possibly associated with some mental disorder.

paramedical   Relating to facilities, personnel, etc, supporting the work of the medical profession.

parameter   A figure that would help describe a POPULATION, eg the average weight, or the variability in weight, of all Scottish ten-year-olds. Such figures are usually impossible to obtain and so are estimated from a SAMPLE. The word is also used loosely (in the plural) to mean something like limiting factors or boundaries (perhaps out of confusion with 'perimeters').

parametric statistics/techniques/tests   Statistical techniques in

207

which certain generalisations are made from SAMPLES on the assumption that the PARENT POPULATION has a certain shape. Contrasts with NON-PARAMETRIC STATISTICS.

paranoia Form of mental disorder (slight or incapacitating) in which a person has delusions (and maybe hallucinations), especially involving fear and anxiety and a sense of being threatened or persecuted by things or people.

paraplegia Paralysis of the lower body and legs, usually as a result of disease or spinal injury.

paraprofessional (US) A person who has been trained to act as an assistant to someone who is fully qualified in a profession, eg as an AIDE or AUXILIARY may assist a classroom teacher.

parental choice In allocating children to UK MAINTAINED SCHOOLS, the LOCAL EDUCATION AUTHORITIES should respect parents' desires to have their children go to one school rather than others – as was intended by the EDUCATION ACT OF 1944 and has been provided for even more strongly in the EDUCATION ACT OF 1980.

parent and child centers (US) Local centres for low-income families with children under three years. The centre is concerned with the pre-school health and education of the children and with educating mothers in child-care and household management.

parent association Organisation consisting of the parents at a particular school from which, for one reason or another, the teachers are excluded. See PARENT-TEACHER ASSOCIATION.

parent co-operative nursery school (US) Non-profit NURSERY SCHOOL financed and managed by parents who may also act as AIDES.

parenthood education Preparing SECONDARY SCHOOL students for the role of being parents by having them work with children, learn about child development and family relationships, and so on.

parent population Could mean the population of parents (of children at a particular school) but is more likely to be used in a statistical context, referring to the POPULATION from which a particular SAMPLE is drawn.

Parent's National Educational Union (**PNEU**) A society formed by CHARLOTTE MASON in 1888 and providing TEACHING MATERIALS for children, from the age of three onwards, especially those temporarily overseas, who are learning at home with parental help.

parents' night/weekend Time when a school invites parents to see special displays or pupil activity, to discuss the school's work or education more generally, and perhaps to talk with individual teachers about their children's progress.

parent-teacher association (PTA) Organisation of parents and teachers at a particular school, who may undertake any of a range of social and fund-raising activities, and, it is hoped, facilitate mutual understanding at the same time.

parity of esteem A widely quoted piece of wishful thinking from a 1947 publication of the UK MINISTRY OF EDUCATION to the effect that the new SECONDARY MODERN SCHOOLS should expect to secure equality of status with the SECONDARY GRAMMAR SCHOOLS. Given the backgrounds and career opportunities of both teachers and pupils within those schools, it is not surprising that the parity was never attained.

Parker, Francis (1837–1902) US EDUCATOR and, as a follower of FROEBEL, a pioneer of PROGRESSIVE EDUCATION in the US. Advocated the value of FIELD WORK in geography and natural history teaching, and promoted INFORMAL METHODS in schools. Helped set up the QUINCY PLAN.

parochial school (US) Denominational, fee-paying school unsupported by public funds. At least 14% of US pupils attend such schools, mainly Roman Catholic.

partial correlation Statistical technique for analysing the relationship between two VARIABLES, taking account of the fact that they are both influenced by some other variable.

partially sighted/seeing Similar to VISUALLY HANDICAPPED or VISUALLY IMPAIRED and relating to children and adults who cannot see properly (although they are not blind).

participant observation A research technique for studying the BEHAVIOUR of small groups 'from the inside', as a participating member. Thus the observer is free to make suggestions that have an effect on what is being studied, but does have to take account of whether such groups might act quite differently if they did not have him as a member. (Contrast with NATURALISTIC observation.)

participation-rate Term used in planning for FURTHER and HIGHER EDUCATION indicating the proportion of students in a given age-range (or other category) who seek more education (or some other benefit).

part method   An approach to LEARNING (eg of a poem or of a procedure) in which the task is broken down into a set of parts, each of which is taught and practised separately. Then the parts are brought together and practised as a whole.

part-work (or **publication**)   A UK publishing term for a series of magazines issued at weekly or monthly intervals but designed to be collected or bound together as a complete course or encyclopedia.

pass degree   A UK degree awarded to students who have just failed to reach honours standard or who perhaps have taken a separate course aimed at below honours level. Might also be called an ORDINARY or UNCLASSIFIED DEGREE.

pass-fail course/option   (US) A college or university course in which ASSESSMENT leads to students being graded simply 'pass' or 'fail' instead of A, B, C, etc.

pass-no credit course/option   (US) A college or university course in which ASSESSMENT leads to students either obtaining a 'pass' or having nothing at all recorded against their name. Supposedly protects students from fear of recorded failure.

passive learning   The kind of learning expected of a student who is 'taught at' – being given no opportunity to make any ACTIVE RESPONSE or contribute his own experience or understanding to what is being discussed. Part of a FORMAL APPROACH. Sometimes used pejoratively of any 'learning by listening', even though that can be a mentally active process.

passive counselling   Follows same principles as NON-DIRECTIVE THERAPY. (It is, of course, the counsellor who is being passive, encouraging the client to work out his own solutions.)

passive vocabulary   The words one can recognise and understand when used by others in their speech and writing. Contrasts with the (smaller) ACTIVE VOCABULARY one uses oneself.

pass mark   The mark it is decided all candidates should achieve in order to be deemed to have passed a test or EXAMINATION. It may be decided in advance of the marking, thus allowing of the possibility that all candidates might pass or all fail; or it might be decided after the marks have been awarded in order to allow only a pre-determined PROPORTION of the candidates to pass.

pass rate   The percentage of candidates achieving the PASS MARK on a test or EXAMINATION.

pastoral care/tutor   To do with the non-educational welfare and social relationships of pupils. Some schools have special staff with pastoral responsibility, in others it is part of every teacher's responsibility. (See MORAL TUTOR).

pathetic fallacy   Speaking or writing of nature (or an inanimate force or object) as if it possessed human feelings (eg 'the weather took pity on us').

Pattison, Mark   (1813–1884) An Oxford DON and stern critic of the low standards of the PASS DEGREE in his day. He saw research as the basis for effective university teaching: 'The instructor does not lay down principles, he initiates into methods; he is himself an investigator, and he is inviting the pupil to accompany him on his road'. His ideas for university reform are developed in *Suggestions on Academical Organisation* (1868).

Pavlov, Ivan   (1849–1936) Russian physiologist whose work on the CONDITIONED REFLEX in dogs contributed considerably to the study of human mental disorder and paved the way to BEHAVIOURISM and theories of learning that emphasise CONDITIONING. See his *Selected Works* (1955).

'payment by results'   Part of the REVISED CODE OF 1862 whereby HER MAJESTY'S INSPECTORS examined the work of pupils in schools and the pay of teachers often depended, at least to some extent, on their pupils' results. The system was gradually ameliorated over the remaining years of the century. (See NEWCASTLE REPORT, 1861.)

Payne, Joseph   (1808–1876) First professor of education in England (at the College of Preceptors in London). He came from a poor family, and began earning his living as a teacher and journalist. His college post was offered him in 1873 as a result of his campaigning for the improvement of educational METHOD. He was a strong advocate of TEACHER-TRAINING and the education of women.

Payne, William H   (1836–1907)   First US professor of education, (specifically, of the 'art and science of teaching'), a post created at the University of Michigan in 1897 to provide pre-service and in-service instruction and guidance for high school teachers, principals, and SUPERINTENDENTS OF SCHOOLS. Payne had himself been a superintendent of schools and his *Chapters on Social Supervision* (1875) was influential in its sensible, systematic approach to the professionalisation of education.

PE   See PHYSICAL EDUCATION.

pedagogics 1 Same as PEDAGOGY.

pedagogue 1 A teacher. (From the Greek word meaning the slave who looks after his master's son.) **2** A PEDANT.

pedagogy The principles, methodology, and profession of teaching and instruction.

pedant The word was once used simply to indicate a schoolmaster. Nowadays it usually denotes someone who is tediously concerned to display or impart more knowledge than the audience wishes to hear, or to insist on the observance of a host of petty details or rules.

pediatrics US spelling of PAEDIATRICS.

peer assessment The ASSESSMENT of a student's work by other students in his group, his peers.

peers People who are equal in status, eg class-mates, children of the same age, students who are at a similar level of academic attainment.

peer teaching Wherein pupils or students take some responsibility for teaching one another.

pegboard test One of many different tests of manual dexterity – or the co-ordination of mind and fingers – in which a person has to fit pegs into holes in a board within various time-limits.

Pelham scale Until 1976 this was the salary scale for UK COLLEGE OF EDUCATION staff as negotiated by the Pelham Committee. (Such staff are now catered for by one of the BURNHAM committees.)

pencil-and-paper test See PAPER-AND-PENCIL TEST.

per capita grant/allowance From Latin, 'according to heads'. A total sum of money arrived at by allowing a fixed sum for each pupil or student. See CAPITATION ALLOWANCE.

percentile A statistical term indicating the point in a set of recorded VALUES that exceeds in size a certain given percentage of those values. Thus, among a set of recorded heights, the 45th percentile is the point below which 45% of the heights will fall.

percentile rank The position of an individual recorded VALUE in a DISTRIBUTION, expressed as a PERCENTILE. Thus, the height of a person who is taller than 60% of the people measured will have the percentile rank of 60.

perceived self A person's image of what he or she is. Contrasts with IDEAL SELF.

perception   The process by which a person (or animal) obtains and interprets information from the environment, using any of the SENSES (sight, hearing, touch, etc).

Percy Report 1945   A UK REPORT on higher TECHNICAL EDUCATION which found serious shortcomings in the training of TECHNOLOGISTS and whose recommendations led (ten years later) to the establishment of COLLEGES OF ADVANCED TECHNOLOGY.

perfect correlation   A CORRELATION between two VARIABLES such that, as VALUES of one variable increase, each will be associated with a proportionately bigger value (perfect positive) or a proportionately smaller value (perfect negative) of the other variable. On a SCATTER DIAGRAM, the plotted points would lie along a straight line.

performance contracting   (US) Scheme whereby a commercial organisation undertakes to provide instructional services to a SCHOOL DISTRICT on the understanding that its fee will be determined by its degree of success – as measured by the subsequent performance of students on CRITERION TESTS.

performance test   **1** A test where the candidate is actually required to do something rather than merely talk or write about it. **2** A test (eg a selection test) that requires the candidate to perform as he would in the job being applied for. **3** A test of present ability or attainment rather than of potential.

period   The basic unit of time around which TIMETABLES are arranged (in SECONDARY SCHOOLS, especially). Each period (usually of 30–45 minutes) will be devoted to a different SUBJECT or activity. The word SESSION may also be used.

peripatetic teacher   A teacher who travels round from school to school, either to fill short-term vacancies (as a SUPPLY TEACHER) or to provide specialist teaching (eg of a musical instrument) for which no single school has a full-time need. If he is a HOME TUTOR he will be visiting pupils' homes. Similar to US CIRCUIT or ITINERANT TEACHER.

permanent education   See CONTINUING EDUCATION, an ideal to which the Council of Europe pledges itself.

permissive   Used of teaching or of classroom situations that might alternatively be described as LAISSEZ-FAIRE or NON-DIRECTIVE.

perseverance   The degree to which a person continues to make an effort at some task in the face of tiredness, boredom, or other difficulties.

213

perseveration 1 The tendency for an image, or idea, or feeling, once formed, to disappear rather slowly, or to recur, despite the originating STIMULUS having been removed. 2 The inability to switch from one's previous method of working after starting on a new task.

personal chair A CHAIR (or professorship) that is awarded to an individual academic in recognition of his personal distinction in research and/or teaching. (It is a professorship that belongs to the person, not to the post he happens to be holding.)

personal construct theory Theory of US psychologist, KELLY, that an individual's PERSONALITY can be defined in terms of the idiosyncratic system of bi-polar constructs (eg sympathetic-hostile, exciting-boring, strong-weak) which he normally uses in responding to other people and forming his PERCEPTION of the world around him. Can be explored with individuals by using the REPERTORY GRID technique.

personal development A term used very loosely in education, usually to identify an AIM other than, or at least wider than, ACADEMIC attainment. That is, it is hoped or intended that the pupil will become not only more knowledgeable or skilful but also more wise, more confident, more self-reliant, more generous, etc – in short become richer in his own PERSONALITY and more capable in social relationships.

Personalised System of Instruction (**PSI**) Another name for KELLER PLAN.

personality For the individual: all the aspects of BEHAVIOUR, thought and feeling that make the person unique. For psychologists: a major area of THEORY and research.

personality dimension See DIMENSION.

personality test Any of a number of tests purporting to appraise or measure a person's PERSONALITY.

personality trait A person's characteristic location on any DIMENSION that seems particularly pertinent in describing his personality and is presumed to be an enduring aspect of that personality. Thus, gregariousness and generosity may be seen as characteristic traits in one person, solitariness and mean-ness in another, and so on.

personal tutor See MORAL TUTOR.

perspective A term used in sociology for a person's approach or orientation to a problem, emphasising the fact that any approach implies some underlying assumptions or THEORY or PARADIGM.

PERT   See PROGRAMME EVALUATION REVIEW TECHNIQUE.

Pestalozzi, Johann Heinrich   (1746–1827) Swiss educator influenced by ROUSSEAU and the experience of teaching orphan children and whose own ideas influenced HERBART and FROEBEL. Believed that education must be concerned with the development of the individual mind and spirit, and must be based on an attempt to understand how children actually do develop, with school life resembling that in a family. Emphasised that learning must begin in concrete experience before leading on to verbal knowledge and that children need to investigate the familiar and simple before studying more distant or complex ideas. His main work is *How Gertrude Teaches Her Children* (1801).

Peters R S   (Born 1919) UK philosopher of education. Leading proponent of the analysis of educational concepts and value-judgments. Known particularly for his conception of education as 'initiation into worthwhile activities'. See his *Logic of Education* (1970) and *Philosophy of Education* (1973).

PGCE   See POSTGRADUATE CERTIFICATE OF EDUCATION.

phenomenology   An approach within psychology, sociology and philosophy that originated in the writings of Husserl and is centred on the detailed understanding of an individual's experience from his own point of view.

philosophy of education   The branch of philosophy concerned, on the one hand, with the building of systems of ideas concerning knowledge, understanding and the purpose of education as a social institution and, on the other hand, with clarifying the meaning of educational concepts. The former emphasis (seen in the works of, eg PLATO, KANT and DEWEY) has in recent years been less in favour than the latter (as seen in the work of, eg, PETERS).

phobia   A neurotic fear of, or aversion to, a particular object or situation, eg of snakes or of open spaces.

phonic method   An approach to the teaching of reading through teaching the sounds of letters or groups of letters, thus enabling children to attempt to read new words by blending the component sounds. Contrasts with LOOK-AND-SAY.

physical education (PE)   Activity within the school CURRICULUM, intended to aid the pupils' physical development (with some

215

associated overtones of 'a healthy mind in a healthy body') through organised GAMES, gymnastics, exercises, etc.

physical sciences   Those sciences concerned with non-living matter, energy and the physical properties of the universe, eg physics, chemistry, geology, astronomy.

physical training   (**PT**) Out-of-date term for PHYSICAL EDUCATION (PE).

PI   See PROGRAMMED INSTRUCTION.

Piagetian stages   The psychologist, PIAGET, suggests that children mature through four stages of intellectual development between birth and adolescence – the SENSORY-MOTOR STAGE, PRE-OPERATIONAL STAGE, CONCRETE OPERATIONS and FORMAL OPERATIONS – as each child becomes increasingly objective about his environment and increasingly capable of abstract, logical thought and language.   .

Piaget, Jean   (1896–1980) Swiss psychologist and observer of children in their intellectual and moral development. He has had enormous influence on the ideas and practices of PRIMARY SCHOOL teachers, particularly through his observations on how children need continuous interaction with the environment in order to learn and how they go through a succession of intellectual stages (see PIAGETIAN STAGES) that make it useless to teach a child certain skills or understandings before he has reached the appropriate stage. See *The Growth of Logical Thinking* (1958).

pictogram   Statistical diagram in which quantities of a certain item are represented by an equivalent number of pictorial symbols. Thus, the number of schools in each of several countries may be compared on a pictogram in which, alongside the name of each country, there will be one school-symbol for, say, every 1,000 schools.

pictograph   **1** Sometimes used to mean PICTOGRAM. **2** Also, a pictorial symbol representing a word or group of words, eg a Chinese 'character'.

picture phone   Telephone system allowing users to see as well as hear each other. Possible application in DISTANCE EDUCATION.

pie chart (or **diagram**)   Statistical diagram allowing visual appraisal of the relative contribution made to some total quantity by a number of contributory categories. It consists of a circle divided into segments (one for each category), with the angle at the centre of the circle increasing in proportion to the percentage contribution of that category to the overall total.

pilot study   A preliminary study undertaken prior to some major project. May be intended as a FEASIBILITY STUDY. Or may be used to practise the proposed methods, or try out alternatives, while there is still an opportunity to make modifications.

Pitman, Sir Isaac   (1813–1897) English inventor of a system of SHORTHAND based on symbols representing spoken sounds. Supporter of SPELLING REFORM and grandfather of SIR JAMES PITMAN.

Pitman, Sir James   (Born 1901) Inventor of the INITIAL TEACHING ALPHABET.

PL   See PROGRAMMED LEARNING.

place   As in 'student place', the opportunity for a student to join an educational institution. Thus, a college that can accept 100 students is said to have 100 places.

placebo effect   In medicine, a placebo is a medically inactive substance (eg a sugar pill or coloured water) usually given to a patient who insists on medication when the doctor considers it unnecessary. Nevertheless, even patients suffering observable symptoms do, if given a placebo, sometimes make a better recovery than those given nothing at all: this is the placebo effect. The term is sometimes used in educational research as an alternative to the similar HAWTHORNE EFFECT. See also PYGMALION EFFECT.

place notation/value   The rules by which, in arithmetic, the value of a given digit differs according to its position among other digits. Thus, in '435', the digit 3 represents a number ten times as big as the 3 in '23' but only one tenth the size of that represented by the 3 in '6381'.

placement guidance   (US) Similar to CAREERS GUIDANCE in UK.

plagiarism   To pass off another person's work as one's own. Teachers often complain of students plagiarising, eg by simply copying from obscure texts without mentioning the source, by vigorous paraphrasing, or by appropriating the explanatory schemes of others. To be fair, however, students are often given little guidance as to where the legitimate use of other sources ends and plagiarism begins.

PLAN   (US) Stands for 'Program for Learning in Accordance with Needs'. COMPUTER-MANAGED, INDIVIDUALISED LEARNING scheme developed in 1967 by the American Institutes for Research and Westinghouse Learning Corporation, and launched in fourteen SCHOOL DISTRICTS. On the basis of considerable test data about ATTAINMENT, LEARNING STYLE, interests, estimated potential, etc, of the individual child (in ELEMENTARY SCHOOL), the teacher and pupil agree a programme of studies for the year. This consists of a selection of MODULES in all areas of the curriculum. Each module directs the pupil to certain commercially-available LEARNING MATERIALS, giving him guidance on how to use them and tests to determine whether he should proceed to the next module or to remedial material. Similar to, but more elaborate than, IPI.

Plato (about 427–347 BC) Greek philosopher whose influence on philosophy, especially from the RENAISSANCE on, has been profound and continuing. His educational thinking was linked both with his THEORY of knowledge (particularly his distinction between human perceptions and the universal ideas or forms which they reflect) and with his political and social beliefs (particularly concerning the attainment of a harmonious city-state through the selection and rigorous TRAINING of an intellectual elite who would be capable of apprehending the true nature of goodness and be able, wisely, to control all aspects of civic life). See his books *The Republic* and *Laws*.

PLATO 'Programmed Learning and Teaching Operation'. A widely used COMPUTER ASSISTED/MANAGED LEARNING system developed originally at the University of Illinois.

plateau See LEARNING PLATEAU.

play Play is worth mentioning in a dictionary of education because it has long been recognised as a serious business. Through activities that adults have often dismissed (despite the evident involvement and concentration of the child) as trivial or time-wasting, the child is often exploring the environment of things, and people, and processes. Such exploratory activity contributes significantly to the child's intellectual, moral and social development, and guided play is especially important in PRE-SCHOOL and PRIMARY EDUCATION.

playback Re-running an AUDIO-TAPE or VIDEO-TAPE so that the recorded sound and/or pictures can be heard and/or seen.

play centre Premises and facilities provided for very young children (especially those not yet attending school), perhaps at the expense of a LOCAL EDUCATION AUTHORITY in the UK, or by parental subscription, and enabling children to play together creatively with their peers and a variety of materials and equipment. (See also ADVENTURE PLAYGROUND.)

playground Area outside a school's buildings that is used for informal games and recreational activities.

playgroup Usually organised by parents wishing to enable their children to have experience of social PLAY before beginning school. Children usually attend for half a day, several times a week. Regarded by many (in the UK) as a stop-gap until such time as the authorities provide universal NURSERY EDUCATION.

playing hooky See TRUANT.

play leader Person with responsibility for stimulating and supervising children's PLAY, perhaps in an ADVENTURE PLAYGROUND or PLAY CENTRE.

play pen A small enclosure, with a floor and barred sides, and usually portable, in which a very young infant can be left to play in safety.

play school See PLAY GROUP.

play therapy The use of games and specially-designed materials in the treatment of mentally or physically ailing or handicapped children.

play-time See BREAK.

play way Any approach to teaching knowledge or skills in which the teacher seeks to engage the pupils' MOTIVATION through learning activities akin to what children might regard as PLAY.

pledge (US) **1** A solemn oath of loyalty to a FRATERNITY or SORORITY in a college or university. **2** A person who is accepted provisionally by a fraternity or sorority.

plenary (session) Sessions at which the members of a class or SYMPOSIUM or conference, are gathered together for discussion, before or after breaking up into smaller groups working independently.

ploughing Failing a course or examination. Like US FLUNKING.

Plowden Report 1967 A UK REPORT based on extensive research into PRIMARY EDUCATION and the transition to SECONDARY EDUCATION in England and Wales. Among its many recommendations were: closer home-school relationships (to recognise the important role played by parental attitudes to their children's education); extra resources for socially deprived areas (EDUCATIONAL PRIORITY AREAS); the expansion of NURSERY EDUCATION; the use of schools for community purposes; the establishment of more MIDDLE SCHOOLS; the ending of CORPORAL PUNISHMENT in PRIMARY SCHOOLS and of STREAMING in JUNIOR SCHOOLS; and the wider acceptance of 'LEARNER-CENTRED' teaching methods. Not all the recommendations were accepted but the Report was of considerable influence in PRIMARY EDUCATION not only in the UK but also (indirectly) in the US.

PLR See PUBLIC LENDING RIGHT.

pluralism The existence, within a society, of groups having different CULTURES, religions, ethnic origins, IDEOLOGIES, etc, resulting in diverse social and political goals that may conflict but without any one necessarily or justifiably over-riding all others.

PNEU See PARENTS' NATIONAL EDUCATIONAL UNION.

pocket money A small amount of spending money given to UK children each week by their parents. Equivalent to US 'allowance'.

poll degree A PASS DEGREE at Cambridge University.

polemic(s) The practice of dispute or argumentation over ideological issues, especially in that manner (common in education and particularly among politicians) where the emphasis is on hammering home one's own point of view or on demolishing that of an opponent.

polyglot Having command of, or displaying, many languages.

polymath A person who has a good knowledge of many subjects and is well-regarded academically. Might even be acclaimed as 'something of a RENAISSANCE MAN'.

polytechnic The term has been used in the UK, since the last years of the 19th century, to refer to POST-SECONDARY institutions providing courses in a number of DISCIPLINES, especially those based in science. Since 1966, however, the term has applied especially to the 30 new institutions of HIGHER EDUCATION (established largely by merging existing colleges) in England and Wales. The polytechnics offer courses at degree level and below (the qualifications usually being validated by the COUNCIL FOR NATIONAL ACADEMIC AWARDS), with more emphasis than most universities on science and technology, but also covering the humanities, art and design, business studies and management, social sciences, and education. A polytechnic's finance and general policy is controlled by the LOCAL EDUCATION AUTHORITY but its day-to-day running is the concern of a body of GOVERNORS and its ACADEMIC BOARD. At present, the polytechnics have a total of some 200,000 full-time and part-time students.

pool 1 A general fund to which all UK LOCAL EDUCATION AUTHORITIES subscribe and from which they draw in financing certain advanced courses in FURTHER/HIGHER EDUCATION, and in providing MAINTENANCE GRANTS for students and for teachers on full-time IN-SERVICE TRAINING courses. **2** A local education authority will also have its own pool of resources that have not been allocated to schools as CAPITATION ALLOWANCE and on which schools may be able to draw in case of special needs; similarly it may have a pool of teachers who have not been assigned to specific schools.

pool of ability The idea that there is a fixed limit to the number of people with the ability to benefit from a given type of educational provision. May be used by those arguing that not all such people have yet been discovered and catered for; or by those who claim that they have all been catered for, so to increase the number of students would be to lower the quality. Yet others argue that the size of the pool depends on social and educational interventions in the early years of children's lives and the responsiveness of teaching methods to individuals' needs and LEARNING STYLES subsequently.

pool post The appointment of a newly-qualified teacher to a UK LOCAL EDUCATION AUTHORITY's 'pool' of teachers, thus guaranteeing him a post in one of its schools even if not in the one he originally applied for.

population In statistics, the entire set of entities or events that are relevant to the subject of enquiry, eg the heights of all twelve year old girls, the PASS-RATES in all degree examinations, the reading speeds of all adult males. Usually the characteristics of the population have to be inferred from a SAMPLE.

portfolio Collection of items from a student's COURSE WORK (especially paintings, drawings, etc, in the case of an art student) such as might be presented for ASSESSMENT.

positive correlation In statistics, a relationship between two VARIABLES such that larger VALUES of one tend to be associated with larger values of the other, and smaller with smaller.

positive discrimination A policy of giving preferential treatment to people, groups or areas believed to be in particular need, in order to bring their standards of health, education, etc, closer to those enjoyed by some more advantaged group. (For example, by putting extra funds, staff and equipment into schools in an EDUCATIONAL PRIORITY AREA.)

positive reinforcement The presentation of a STIMULUS that acts to reinforce (increase the probable re-occurrence of) some associated RESPONSE. Loosely speaking, a reward.

positive transfer Said to happen when a person finds it easier to learn certain new knowledge or skill because of something similar he learned previously. For example, someone who has previously played rounders may learn to play baseball more easily than someone who has not.

positivism A philosophical viewpoint, associated with Auguste Comte, which asserts the existence of a world of positive facts and phenomena, and rules governing them, that can be objectively ascertained through sensory PERCEPTION, as constituting our only source of KNOWLEDGE. Human intentions and interpretations (see PHENOMENOLOGY) are irrelevant to this view of knowledge.

postal tuition Teaching by means of a CORRESPONDENCE COURSE.

post-compulsory education Education sought or received beyond the minimum statutory SCHOOL-LEAVING AGE.

post-doctoral Referring to students or staff who have already taken DOCTORATES or to courses for such people, or to their advanced studies and research.

post-experience courses/training, etc Courses for people who have already had work experience, though not necessarily in the field covered by the course. Could be a REFRESHER COURSE or a RE-TREAD COURSE (US) or it could amount to RE-TRAINING. IN-SERVICE TRAINING is one form it might take.

postgraduate Referring to a person who has already obtained a FIRST DEGREE or to the further studies or courses undertaken by such a person, eg towards a POSTGRADUATE DEGREE. In the US, the word 'GRADUATE' is used.

Postgraduate Certificate of Education (**PGCE**) A UK certificate taken by graduates (usually straight after they have completed a first degree) that qualifies them to teach. It normally involves a one-year course of educational studies and TEACHING PRACTICE.

postgraduate degree See HIGHER DEGREE.

postgraduate student One who has already obtained a FIRST DEGREE and is studying for a HIGHER DEGREE. Equivalent to US GRADUATE student.

Postlethwait audio-tutorial system (US) See AUDIO-TUTORIAL.

postgraduate university (US) See GRADUATE SCHOOL.

post-school education Education sought or received after leaving school.

post-secondary education The education a person might receive after leaving secondary school. Includes TERTIARY EDUCATION and CONTINUING EDUCATION.

post test   Test given to students after they have been involved in a COURSE or LEARNING EXPERIENCE of any kind. May be used simply to ascertain their present knowledge and skills or, by comparing their results with those obtained earlier on a PRE-TEST, to ascertain how much they have learned since then.

potential   An ability that is assumed to be latent in a particular person though not yet realised.

power test   Any test in which the emphasis is on ascertaining the level of difficulty the student can cope with rather than on how fast he can work. Thus, the ITEMS may be arranged in increasing order of difficulty and the student stops when he can go no further (rather than for lack of time). Contrast with a SPEED TEST.

PPE   The Oxford University FIRST DEGREE course of MODERN GREATS (politics, philosophy and economics).

practicals   Learning sessions involving physical activities often in a workshop or laboratory.

practice effect   In general, an improvement in ability due to repetition. The term is sometimes used more specifically of an improvement in test score, without a corresponding improvement in the ability supposedly being tested, due to the fact that the candidate has had previous practice with the test questions.

practice school   1 See DEMONSTRATION SCHOOL, LABORATORY SCHOOL, or MODEL SCHOOL. 2 A school that takes STUDENT-TEACHERS for TEACHING PRACTICE.

practicum   (US) 1 A practical handbook or MANUAL. 2 A 'how-to-do-it' course on some aspect of education.

pragmatism   A philosophical viewpoint asserting that the validity of knowledge, meaning, and value is to be judged in terms of practical consequences. The viewpoint is of US origin (late 19th century) and JOHN DEWEY was its best known educational exponent.

praxis   The practical aspects of a profession or DISCIPLINE, as opposed to the theory.

preceptor   Defunct term for teacher or tutor, preserved in the name of the UK College of Preceptors, a London teacher-training organisation that dates from the mid-19th century and still awards its own diplomas.

pre-clinical course A course in basic anatomy, physiology and other subjects, taken by a medical student before beginning on the (clinical) courses that bring him into contact with patients.

pre-coded question A MULTIPLE-CHOICE QUESTION (eg in a QUESTIONNAIRE or COMPUTER-MARKED ASSIGNMENT) to which respondents' answers can be processed automatically, even by a machine.

predictive validity The VALIDITY of a test as judged by the CORRELATION between success on the test and success in some supposedly related activity. Thus, the predictive validity of college entrance examinations might be said to depend on whether the higher scores are those of students who subsequently graduate with the highest grades.

prefect A traditional role in UK SECONDARY SCHOOLS for senior pupils who are appointed or elected to exercise some authority and disciplinary responsibility among their fellows.

prelims **1** The first set of examinations taken towards a BACHELOR'S DEGREE in some universities. **2** The pages of a book prior to the main matter, ie title page, contents list, etc. **3** Term used in Scotland for MOCK EXAMINATIONS prior to O GRADE and H GRADE in the SCOTTISH CERTIFICATE OF EDUCATION, the results of which are used for guidance in cases of appeal or absence from the EXTERNAL EXAMINATIONS.

pre-medical course Course in basic sciences (biology, physics, chemistry) taken by students prior to beginning the study of medicine.

premise Term used in logic for one of two related statements leading to an inevitable conclusion. (See SYLLOGISM for an example.)

pre-operational stage The second stage in a child's intellectual development as postulated by PIAGET, lasting between the ages of about two and seven years. It is characterised by the development of LANGUAGE accompanied by an egocentric and (to the adult mind) illogical view of relationships between things and events in the environment. (See SYNCRETIC REASONING.)

prep Short for 'preparation', meaning HOMEWORK or private study done in school (especially in BOARDING SCHOOL), in preparation for a lesson on some subsequent day.

preparatory school (or **prep school**) **1** In the UK, an INDEPENDENT (fee-paying) school (often a BOARDING SCHOOL) preparing pupils (mostly boys) to take the COMMON ENTRANCE EX-

AMINATION for admission to PUBLIC SCHOOLS after the age of 13 years. **2** In the US, a fee-paying HIGH SCHOOL preparing students for entry to colleges and universities (particularly to prestigious ones). Similar to UK PUBLIC SCHOOL.

pre-prep school (or **department**) Separate fee-paying school (or section of a PREPARATORY SCHOOL) for children between the ages of about five and eight years, prior to their entry to preparatory school.

pre-primary education Any organised EDUCATION prior to PRIMARY EDUCATION, eg NURSERY education. See PRE-SCHOOL EDUCATION.

prep school See PREPARATORY SCHOOL.

pre-requisite abilities/knowledge/skills etc See ENTRY BEHAVIOUR.

pre-school child Child who is not yet old enough to begin attending school.

pre-school education EDUCATION for children to prepare them for school life and learning. The emphasis is on providing a richly stimulating ENVIRONMENT and opportunities for social and language development.

pre-school playgroup See PLAYGROUP.

prescriptive Term used for an approach to management, or therapy, or educational intervention where the emphasis is on telling people what they should be doing rather than on, say, helping them decide their own options.

presenter **1** Television term for any person who appears on screen at the beginning of a programme (and often at intervals subsequently) to introduce it or help it along. **2** (US) A speaker or lecturer.

presentation (US) A speech or lecture, particularly one involving AUDIO-VISUAL materials.

pre-service training Term used in TEACHER-EDUCATION for professional training (obtained at college or university) prior to employment as a teacher. Contrasts with IN-SERVICE TRAINING.

president (US) Chief executive of a college or university. Equivalent to UK PRINCIPAL, DIRECTOR or VICE-CHANCELLOR.

President of the Board of Education Head of the UK BOARD OF EDUCATION which in 1944 was upgraded to MINISTRY OF EDUCATION.

press Term used by US psychologist, Henry Murray, in his theory of PERSONALITY, to indicate the external determinants of a person's BEHAVIOUR – those that come from the ENVIRONMENT. (Contrasts with NEEDS – the determinants that come from within the person.)

pressure groups People with shared beliefs and values who come together to use various communications MEDIA in persuading other people to adopt the views or practices advocated by the group, eg to abolish CORPORAL PUNISHMENT, to provide more NURSERY EDUCATION, and so on.

Prestel The version of VIEWDATA made available by the Post Office in the UK.

pre-test Test given to a student before embarking on a COURSE or LEARNING EXPERIENCE. Its purpose may be to check that he has the appropriate ENTRY BEHAVIOUR or, by comparing his pre-test results with those on a subsequent POST-TEST, to determine how much he has learned.

prima facie (Latin, 'first face', or at first sight.) Referring to evidence that seems to suggest, or even establish, the truth of a certain proposition, unless it can be contradicted by further evidence.

primary education EDUCATION provided prior to SECONDARY EDUCATION and catering for children in the age-range of about 5–11 years. In the UK it is conducted in PRIMARY SCHOOLS (INFANT and JUNIOR or, in some areas, FIRST and MIDDLE) and (for the children of fee-paying parents) in PREPARATORY and PRE-PREP SCHOOLS; in the US in ELEMENTARY or GRADE SCHOOLS, usually catering for GRADES 1 – 3 (ages 6 – 8).

primary grades (US) Grades 1–3 in an ELEMENTARY or GRADE SCHOOL.

primary group Sociological term for the group of people with whom a person has the most intimate and/or enduring relations, eg a family. (Contrasts with SECONDARY GROUP.)

primary mental abilities View of the nature of INTELLIGENCE proposed by THURSTONE as an alternative to the idea of 'general intelligence (G FACTOR) plus special abilities'. It postulates primary mental abilities such as verbal comprehension, word fluency and number ability, not necessarily showing a POSITIVE CORRELATION with one another.

primary relationships Those between members of a PRIMARY GROUP.

primary schools 1 (UK) The term usually refers to MAINTAINED

SCHOOLS catering for children from the age of five (the statutory starting age for education) until they go to SECONDARY SCHOOL at the age of 11 or 12; or, in some areas, before they go to MIDDLE SCHOOLS at the age of nine. (Middle schools that pupils enter at the age of eight, however, are deemed primary.) About half of all primary schools in England and Wales combine both INFANT and JUNIOR SCHOOLS (or departments) on one CAMPUS and with one overall HEADTEACHER; the others cater for infants only or juniors only. In areas that operate middle schools, the schools that children attend between the ages of five and either eight or nine are often called FIRST SCHOOLS. **2** (US) Schools or classes catering for graded 1–3 (ages 6–8).

primary source (of information) In historical or other investigations, primary sources might be objects or documents created by the people, or during the time, in question. Contrasts with SECONDARY SOURCES, which are documents about those earlier sources and are therefore assumed to be less reliable.

primus inter pares (Latin, 'First among equals'.) A person who is given, or takes, precedence over other people who are nominally his peers, eg as leader of a discussion group.

principal In the UK, this title normally denotes the chief executive of an institution in FURTHER or HIGHER EDUCATION; in the US it refers to the HEAD TEACHER (chief administrator) of an ELEMENTARY or HIGH SCHOOL.

principal lecturer Senior academic post in UK colleges and POLYTECHNICS.

principal teacher Head of a subject department in a Scottish secondary school.

private college (US) College financed from private rather than state funds.

private education EDUCATION other than that provided out of public funds and financed privately, particularly by the fees collected from those who participate in it.

private school An INDEPENDENT or NON-STATE SCHOOL: one that is financed out of private funds (eg the fees paid on behalf of pupils) rather than out of public funds. Confusingly, in England and Wales, the most famous private schools are the so-called PUBLIC SCHOOLS.

private study Reading, writing and other study activities carried out by pupils in school time without the immediate direction, and without the physical presence, of a teacher. Likely to occupy more of the time of SIXTH-FORMERS than of younger pupils.

private university   (US) A university financed primarily out of private funds rather than state funds (though it may benefit from federal government funds for research contracts). Contrasts with STATE UNIVERSITY. (The UK's only comparable institution is the Independent University at Buckingham.)

probabilistic   Referring to a claim to be able to make reasonable predictions about what will happen to a group as a whole, while admitting that one cannot forecast what will happen to individual members of that group. For example, previous experience may suggest that ten per cent of new students will drop out before the end of their first year, though no-one could predict a named individual who will do so.

probability   A statement of the chances of a particular thing happening or failing to happen. Probability is expressed along a scale ranging from 0 (no chance at all) to 1 (certainty). Thus a probability of 0.05 means that the chances are 5 in 100 that the thing in question will happen (or 95 in 100 that it will not).

probation   **1** Test period in a post during which one proves one's suitability for permanent appointment. **2** A court-imposed period of supervision by a PROBATION OFFICER as an alternative to custodial punishment for offenders over 17. **3** (US) HIGH SCHOOLS, and especially COLLEGES, may place on probation certain students who are failing to produce satisfactory COURSE WORK.

probationary teacher   A teacher still in his PROBATIONARY PERIOD.

probationary period   In the UK, newly-qualified teachers must serve one year on probation before their appointment may be confirmed, provided the LOCAL EDUCATION AUTHORITY is by then satisfied as to their competence. (People allowed to teach SHORT-AGE SUBJECTS *without* having qualified may be asked to spend two or more years as probationers.) In the US, teachers taking up a new appointment may be on probatiion for three to five years before becoming eligible for TENURE.

probationers   Term used of teachers in their PROBATIONARY PERIOD.

probation officers   Officials employed by the UK courts to offer advice, assistance, and friendly supervision to offenders placed on PROBATION (and to carry out other SOCIAL WORK, especially with prisoners and ex-prisoners).

problematic   To regard a situation or process (eg an educational system) as 'problematic' is to assume that it may be susceptible to fundamental criticism; that is, it (or statements about it) must not be taken for granted.

problem-centred courses/curricula   Courses designed with a view to having students develop the desired KNOWLEDGE and SKILLS while in the process of defining and tackling relevant problems; rather than, say, by learning 'the basics' of the SUBJECT before (or perhaps instead of) applying them to problems.

proceedings   The published account of the discussions of a committee or of the PAPERS read, together with the subsequent discussion, at a SYMPOSIUM, or conference, or meeting of a LEARNED SOCIETY.

process education   EDUCATION in which the emphasis is on the learning of intellectual processes or SKILLS (eg hypothesising, observing, analysing, problem-solving, interpreting, etc) rather than subject-content.

pro-chancellor   Deputy to the CHANCELLOR of a university.

proctor   **1** At some UK universities, especially Oxford and Cambridge, a member of the academic staff exercising a special disciplinary role for a period of time. **2** Especially in the US, an INVIGILATOR at an EXAMINATION. **3** A student providing some tuition or ASSESSMENT help to less advanced students, under the guidance of the teacher, eg in the KELLER PLAN.

profession   Any occupation that is regarded as prestigious, generally on the grounds that its members are not only well-paid but also: need lengthy ACADEMIC training founded on some systematic body of knowledge; exercise considerable freedom of decision in their day-to-day work; recognise ethical standards in their activities; serve society; continue to learn and develop the profession while practising it; and so on.

professional association/body/organisation, etc   One whose aim is to enhance the status and authority of its members as a learned and responsible PROFESSION. Often, as in the case of teachers' organisations, it also acts as a TRADE UNION in negotiating salaries and conditions of work.

professional class   Broadly equivalent to MIDDLE CLASS.

professional degree   A DEGREE awarded in a professional subject such as law, medicine, accountancy, teaching, etc.

professional sanctions   Actions taken by teachers involved in dispute over pay and conditions, usually by withdrawing some services that are normally given voluntarily, without actually going on strike.

professional school (US) Usually a GRADUATE SCHOOL in a university, and offering training in such PROFESSIONS as law, medicine and business administration.

professional tutor UK school teacher given the role of MENTOR to PROBATIONARY TEACHERS joining the school. (As recommended in the JAMES REPORT, 1972.)

professor 1 In the UK, the title is awarded only to the top-ranking academic staff in universities (and some POLYTECHNICS). 2 In the US, practically all academic staff in college and university have the title, although a distinction is made between ASSISTANT, ASSOCIATE and FULL PROFESSORS. Only the latter are comparable in status with UK professors.

professor emeritus See EMERITUS PROFESSOR.

professorial fellow The holder of a FELLOWSHIP carrying the status, if not the title, of PROFESSOR.

professoriate The professors, as a group.

professorship The post held by a professor. Also known as a CHAIR.

profile As a result of ASSESSMENT, a person's overall academic attainment or personality may be summed up with a simple overall grade or descriptive label. Alternatively, a 'profile' may be presented, showing the person's scores on a number of separate VARIABLES or DIMENSIONS. This may give a more informative picture of how that person differs from others who might have had the same overall grade or label. Some UK schools and other educational institutions are experimenting with profiles as an alternative or supplement to conventional examination grades. See RECORD OF PERSONAL ACHIEVEMENT and SCOTTISH PUPIL PROFILE.

prognosis Prediction as to the future achievement of a person, based on what is presently known about him.

program The usual US spelling of PROGRAMME.

programme 1 Generally, a planned sequence of study or research. 2 More specifically, a sequence of PROGRAMMED LEARNING.

Program for Learning in Accordance with Needs (US) See PLAN.

programmed instruction   Same as PROGRAMMED LEARNING (but perhaps the preferred term in INDUSTRIAL TRAINING).

programmed learning   SELF-INSTRUCTIONAL MATERIALS that take the student at his own pace, one step at a time, through a carefully structured sequence of TEACHING POINTS towards specific BEHAVIOURAL OBJECTIVES, with the student making an ACTIVE RESPONSE and obtaining KNOWLEDGE OF RESULTS at each step. The materials or PROGRAMMES (programs in the US) may be in LINEAR, BRANCHING, or MATHETICS form or in a variety of mixtures, and may be presented in a PROGRAMMED TEXT or in a TEACHING MACHINE, perhaps as COMPUTER-ASSISTED INSTRUCTION. The heyday of programmed learning was in the 1960s, when it was particularly associated with the ideas of US psychologist, SKINNER. While the term is no longer much used in education, and learning materials rarely appear obviously programmed, many of the original features of programmed learning have been incorporated into educational practice to some degree: much of the self-instructional material used in DISTANCE EDUCATION (including that of the OPEN UNIVERSITY) reveals its debt to programmed learning; and the emphasis on testing and revising material with students until it can be relied on to teach well gave rise to much of the current concern with DEVELOPMENTAL TESTING, EVALUATION, and (in the US) LVR, and has made an important contribution to the development of EDUCATIONAL TECHNOLOGY.

programmed text   A book that presents SELF-INSTRUCTIONAL MATERIAL involving the reader in PROGRAMMED LEARNING.

programme evaluation and review technique   Like CRITICAL PATH METHOD, a form of NETWORK ANALYSIS for use in planning and monitoring complex projects.

progressive education   A movement towards more flexible, democratic and LEARNER-CENTRED APPROACHES to education that began in the late 19th century as a reaction against the formal CURRICULUM, methods, and human relations then prevailing in schools. It began with the setting up of new PRIVATE SCHOOLS (often co-educational BOARDING SCHOOLS) in the UK and US. But many of its emphases (eg on creativity, self-expression, minimal punishment, informality of pupil-teacher relationships, pupil-participation in school government, activities based on the emerging needs of individual pupils, etc) are now reflected in the practices of MAINTAINED SCHOOLS (especially in PRIMARY EDUCATION).

231

progressive matrices test   A NON-VERBAL, MULTIPLE-choice test of INTELLIGENCE requiring a person to complete a series of designs which become progressively more difficult.

progressive school   Strictly speaking, one of the few PRIVATE SCHOOLS (eg A S NEILL's SUMMERHILL) that are committed to PROGRESSIVE EDUCATION. But, more loosely, any school that is relatively PERMISSIVE in curriculum, teaching methods, pupil-teacher relationships, pupil-participation in school-government, etc.

project   A learning task with some or all of the following features: it arises in the interests of the learners; demands original investigation or experiment; is more concerned with developing ATTITUDES and intellectual SKILLS than with specific KNOWLEDGE; can be tackled by an individual learner or by groups; cuts across SUBJECT-barriers in an INTER-DISCIPLINARY way; uses the teacher as FACILITATOR, guide and counsellor rather than as conveyer of information; may result in a report or in the demonstration and discussion of what has been produced or discovered. Projects are much used in PRIMARY SCHOOLS and in POST-GRADUATE education, but less so in the intervening years.

project approach/method/work   An approach to teaching that centres around the regular use of PROJECTS.

project assessment   The ASSESSMENT of students' qualities and capabilities as revealed in their work on a PROJECT which may be believed to give a more valid picture than EXAMINATION results.

projection   Term used in PSYCHOANALYSIS for the DEFENCE MECHANISM of ascribing to other people one's own unacceptable fears, and desires, and weaknesses.

projective test/technique   Any test (especially a PERSONALITY TEST) that requires the person to respond to an ambiguous stimulus (eg an inkblot); in so doing, he supposedly projects his own feelings, attitudes, needs, etc, so that they can be observed and assessed. Examples of such tests are the THEMATIC APPERCEPTION TEST and the RORSCHACH INKBLOT TEST.

projector   A device for projecting a pictorial image (still or moving) on to a large screen, with or without sound, for the benefit of a group of viewers (eg EPIDIASCOPE, FILM-PROJECTOR, OVERHEAD PROJECTOR, etc).

prom   (US) A formal ball held at the end of the ACADEMIC YEAR in schools and colleges.

prompt An alternative term for CUE used in PROGRAMMED LEARN-
ING. See FORMAL PROMPT and THEMATIC PROMPT.

proprietary school A PRIVATE school operated for profit by a
board of directors or governors.

prospectus Booklet published by a UK educational institution
describing its courses and facilities for the benefit of prospective
students. See CALENDAR also. The US equivalent might be called
CATALOG or BULLETIN.

Protestant ethic A sociological theory linking the rise of capitalism with the rise of Protestantism by way of the latter's emphasis on seeking salvation (and earthly esteem) through
individual responsibility, hard work, delayed gratification, discipline (and the accumulation of possessions). Seen as underlying
MIDDLE-CLASS attitudes and much of what goes on in education.
(Also referred to as the WORK ETHIC.)

protocols 1 (US) Printed, audio, or video-recordings of conversations or classroom discussions that can be reviewed and
analysed by educational researchers or student-teachers in training. 2 Filled-in QUESTIONNAIRES or TEST answer-sheets.

pro-vice chancellor A deputy to the VICE-CHANCELLOR of a
university.

provided schools The UK COUNTY SCHOOLS, fully-maintained
by the then newly-established LOCAL EDUCATION AUTHORITIES
subsequent to the EDUCATION ACT OF 1902 (and prior to the
EDUCATION ACT 1944).

provincial university 1 Term that includes any university in
England and Wales other than Oxford, Cambridge and London,
but not usually the Scottish universities. 2 In Canada, a university directly financed by a provincial government.

provost 1 (UK) The head of some schools and colleges (particularly OXBRIDGE). 2 The chief academic officer of some institutions of higher education, usually universities.

PSI PERSONALISED SYSTEM OF INSTRUCTION. See KELLER PLAN.

psychiatrist A medical doctor who has specialised in the diagnosis and treatment of mental disorders.

psychoanalysis Systems of understanding, preventing, and
treating mental disorders, based upon the theories of SIGMUND
FREUD and his followers.

psychobabble A derogatory term coined during the late 1970s
to refer to the JARGON used by people in the HUMAN POTENTIAL

MOVEMENT and associated cults that arose over the previous decade, especially in the US.

psychodrama   The use of drama as a means of GROUP-THERAPY for people who are mentally disturbed, eg by having them act out situations from their lives and discuss the results.

psycholinguistics   The study of language from a psychological viewpoint; especially concerned with children's acquisition of language, the mental processes underlying adult language usage, and language disorders.

psychological inventory   See INVENTORY.

psychological set   See SET.

psychological test   Any test devised by psychologists to appraise or measure aspects of people's COGNITIVE, AFFECTIVE or PSYCHOMOTOR functioning. Especially tests of APTITUDE, INTELLIGENCE, PERSONALITY, etc.

psychology   The scientific study of the workings of the human mind, insofar as they can be ascertained from human speech and other BEHAVIOUR.

psychometrician   A psychologist who specialises in PSYCHOMETRICS.

psychometrics (or **psychometry**)   The branch of psychology concerned with the design of psychological tests, and the application of statistical methods to the resulting data in pursuit of the OBJECTIVE measurement of human variability.

psychomotor abilities/skills   Those that require coordination between mind and muscle. (That is, all movements other than REFLEX ACTIONS.) For example, tying shoelaces, using a pen or typewriter, driving a car, and so on.

psychopath   A mentally-disturbed person who is likely to behave anti-socially, even violently, without feelings of guilt or sympathy for others.

psychopathology   The study of mental disorder (without any necessary interest in its treatment).

psychopharmacology   The study of drugs that affect mental behaviour, including LEARNING abilities and MEMORY.

psychosexual   Relating to the mental and emotional aspects of sexual behaviour.

psychosurgery   Any surgical operation on the brain with a view to alleviating mental disorder, eg frontal lobotomy.

psychosis Severe mental disorder characterised by distorted PERCEPTION, defective memory, and impaired language use. By contrast with NEUROSIS, the sufferer may not recognise he is ill. Schizophrenia and manic depression are well known psychoses.

psychosomatic Relating to ailments that take physical form (eg ulcers, migraine) but which may be caused or aggravated by mental stress.

psychotechnics (US) The use of psychological knowledge and methods to modify or control human behaviour.

psychotherapy The treatment of mental disorders by verbal discussion with patients rather than by physical methods, eg PSYCHOANALYSIS and NON-DIRECTIVE THERAPY.

psychotic Person suffering from a PSYCHOSIS.

pyschoticism A DIMENSION OF PERSONALITY described and tested by the psychologist, EYSENCK.

PT See PHYSICAL TRAINING.

PTA See PARENT-TEACHER ASSOCIATION.

PTR See PUPIL-TEACHER-RATIO.

puberty The beginning of ADOLESENCE (about age 10–14) when a person becomes capable of reproduction.

pubescent Approaching, or having arrived at, PUBERTY.

public broadcasting system (US) Non-commercial broadcasting, chiefly of educational, cultural, and public service programmes.

public education That financed out of public funds (rates and taxes).

public elementary school (US) ELEMENTARY OR GRADE SCHOOL financed out of public funds. About 85% of all elementary schools are so financed.

public examination An examination that is open to any candidates, not just those from a particular institution.

public lending right The right of authors to benefit financially when their books are borrowed from public libraries.

publicly maintained schools Schools that are maintained out of public funds, eg by LOCAL EDUCATION AUTHORITIES in UK, and by LOCAL SCHOOL BOARDS in US.

public orator College or university official elected to make formal speeches on certain public occasions.

public schools **1** (US and Scotland) PUBLICLY-MAINTAINED

SCHOOLS. **2** (England and Wales) Independent fee-paying SCHOOLS, especially the 200 or so HEAD MASTERS' CONFERENCE SCHOOLS which are mainly single-sex BOARDING SCHOOLS catering for some two per cent of the relevant age-group (and securing some 20% of university PLACES); they were called 'public' to distinguish them not from PRIVATE SCHOOLS (which they clearly are) but from 'local' schools not open to children from other areas. **3** In Scotland, all public schools are of type **1** while type **2** schools are termed INDEPENDENT.

Public Schools Commission UK body appointed to report on how best to integrate the PUBLIC SCHOOLS with the STATE EDUCATION SYSTEM. Its REPORTS of 1968 and 1970 (see NEWSOM REPORT 1968) said that public schools are divisive in society and recommended a scheme of ASSISTED PLACES (half their places should become available to children of low-income families) for pupils in need of BOARDING education, the timing and details to be worked out by a Boarding School Corporation. The recommendations were resisted.

public sector See PUBLIC EDUCATION.

public university One financed out of public funds (rates or taxes). Contrasts with PRIVATE UNIVERSITIES (which are common in the US).

Pueblo Plan See SEARCH.

pump-priming funds A small quantity of money put into a project in hope of stimulating other people to put even more into it. Similar to SEED-FUNDING.

punishment A penalty imposed upon an individual (or group) with a view to discouraging certain BEHAVIOUR and/or encouraging alternative behaviour. May range (in education) from BODY LANGUAGE, through verbal rebuke, DETENTION, LINES and other impositions, to CORPORAL PUNISHMENT/SUSPENSION and even EXPULSION.

pupil In the UK, this term tends to be applied to all school-children from 5 – 18 years, and even, on occasions, to university students. In the US only the very youngest are 'pupils' but gain the honorific title of 'students' while still in ELEMENTARY SCHOOL.

pupil-centred approach/education/teaching See LEARNER-CENTRED APPROACH.

pupil council See STUDENT GOVERNMENT.

pupillage The one-year period in which a newly qualified UK barrister is attached as pupil ('in chambers') to an experienced barrister before being allowed to practise.

pupil power Slogan of a movement claiming that PUPILS should have more say in the CURRICULUM and government of their schools. See NATIONAL UNION OF SCHOOL STUDENTS.

pupil-teacher 19th-century term for a young person training to be a school teacher, mostly by serving a five year APPRENTICESHIP after leaving ELEMENTARY SCHOOL at the age of about 13, with the most successful going on to spend three years at TEACHER-TRAINING college and emerging as certificated teachers.

pupil-teacher ratio (PTR) The ratio between the number of pupils and the number of teachers in a school. This is fixed annually by each LOCAL EDUCATION AUTHORITY for all the schools in its area, with SECONDARY SCHOOLS enjoying a more favourable PTR (that is fewer pupils per teacher) than do PRIMARY SCHOOLS. The national average (which has been improving over recent years) is about 16:1 for secondary schools and 22:1 for primary schools (in 1980), but there is wide variation.

pure research Research that aims chiefly to add to the store of human knowledge rather than to improve the particular situation being studied. Contrasts with ACTION RESEARCH or RESEARCH AND DEVELOPMENT.

Pygmalion effect The idea that teachers' expectations as to a pupil's POTENTIAL (even if misguided) may act like a SELF-FULFILLING PROPHECY, somehow pushing the child on or holding him back, so that he comes to act more in accordance with the expectations (whether high or low) than he would otherwise have done. The name was taken from Greek mythology by US educational researchers, Rosenthal and Jacobson, who wrote of the effect in their book *Pygmalion in the Classroom* (1968).

Q

Q-level See ADVANCED LEVEL.

quad (or QUADRANGLE) Rectangular open space surrounded by the buildings of a school or college.

quadrivium The four SUBJECTS forming the basis of the mediaeval CURRICULUM in LIBERAL ARTS: arithmetic, geometry, astronomy and music. See also TRIVIUM.

Quaker education See Friends' schools.

qualifications The educational attainments and/or life-experiences that are thought to make a person suitable for some particular role. For one role, a physics degree may be seen as an essential qualification; for another, the experience of having reared three children in a one-parent family may be deemed to qualify a person. Usually, people think only of 'paper qualifications', particularly examination certificates. Similar to credentials.

qualified teacher All teachers in UK maintained schools must satisfy the Department of Education and Science that they are qualified. To qualify they must have satisfied the assessment criteria of a three- or four-year course at a college of education or polytechnic or, in the case of graduates, of a one-year post-graduate course of teacher-training; and all must satisfactorily complete a one-year probationary period in school. (See shortage subjects for exceptions to this.) The qualifying criteria in Scotland are somewhat more stringent than in England and Wales. (See General Teaching Council for Scotland.) In further and higher education in the UK (and elsewhere), teachers are not normally required to be trained; subject-matter expertise is generally regarded as the only essential qualification.

qualitative data Research term for information that takes the form not of numbers (quantitative data) but of words, pictures, etc, that might come from interviewing people, observing and reporting on their interactions, sketching and photographing them and their environment, reading their essays and log-books, and so on. An essential ingredient of illuminative evaluation.

quality rating scale Method of assessment used especially in the US in the early years of this century, and particularly with material that is difficult to assess objectively (eg essays). Essentially, assessors are given a number of sample essays that have already been marked by experienced examiners and represent a range of quality. To assess a student's essay they then decide which of the samples it most closely resembles in quality and give it the same mark.

quango Acronym for a 'quasi-autonomous non-governmental organisation' of which there are many in UK education, eg the Council for Educational Technology, the Schools Council and the University Grants Committee.

quantitative data Research term for information that arises from counting and measuring, and takes the form of numbers and quantities to which STATISTICAL METHODS may be applied.

quarter system (US) System used by some educational institutions whereby the ACADEMIC YEAR is divided into four terms.

quartiles Statistical term for the 25th, 50th and 75th PERCENTILES in a FREQUENCY DISTRIBUTION, dividing it into four equally-sized groups of OBSERVATIONS.

quartile deviation A statistical measure of VARIABILITY in a FREQUENCY DISTRIBUTION. It is half the distance between the 25th and 75th PERCENTILES (or 1st and 3rd QUARTILES).

Queen's scholarships Scholarships introduced in 1846 by Sir James KAY-SHUTTLEWORTH. Successful PUPIL-TEACHERS competed for them by examination at the end of their apprenticeship. The scholarship entitled holders to a three-year course at a TRAINING COLLEGE from which they would emerge as fully qualified teachers.

question bank See ITEM BANK.

questionnaire Printed form containing structured questions that are either PRE-CODED or leave space for an answer to be written. Often used in SURVEYS, questionnaires are more economical than INTERVIEWS but may give less useful information. They need to be designed very carefully and tested in a PILOT STUDY.

questions Important to teachers both as a means of finding out what students have learned or can do (ASSESSMENT) and as part of a teaching technique (eg SOCRATIC DIALOGUE) designed to lead students towards answers already anticipated by the teacher or to encourage them to examine their personal experience with a view to producing insights of their own. Important also in that education should be equipping students not merely to answer other people's questions but to formulate their own questions and to obtain answers (from teachers or from elsewhere).

Quincy methods An influential new approach to PRIMARY EDUCATION pioneered in Quincy, Massachussetss, in the 1880s by Colonel FRANCIS PARKER (Superintendent of Schools). It involved: the use of concrete experience; an effort to combine SUBJECTS; and an attempt to provide a broad general EDUCATION, going far beyond the THREE Rs.

quinquennium A period of five years. The grants to UK universities made by the UNIVERSITY GRANTS COMMITTEE to cover recurrent expenditure were, until 1972, quinquennial. Since then, inflation has led to grants covering only one year at a time.

quintain   A mediaeval device used by knights when learning how to use a lance in tilting at a target. It is sometimes quoted as an early 'TEACHING MACHINE' in that it was constructed so as to give FEEDBACK – by knocking the knight off his horse if he rode by without managing to strike the target!

Quintilian (Marcus Fabius Quintilianus)   (About 35–100 AD) A Spanish-born rhetorician who taught in Rome and, in retirement, wrote *Institutio Oratoria* dealing in part with his ideas of a LIBERAL EDUCATION and giving much practical advice on teaching through rewards and encouragement in PRIMARY EDUCATION.

quota scheme   A scheme originated by the UK DEPARTMENT OF EDUCATION AND SCIENCE in time of teacher-shortage and meant to share teachers out fairly across the UK by means of quotas stipulating the maximum number each LOCAL EDUCATION AUTHORITY could employ. Abandoned in 1975.

quotient   An expression of how someone's score on a test of some VARIABLE (eg spelling ability, or intelligence) compares with the AVERAGE score for a specified age-group: thus 'spelling quotient' or 'INTELLIGENCE QUOTIENT'. Usually calculated so that 100 becomes the average score.

Q-sort   Technique in PERSONALITY TESTING in which a person sorts out a number of descriptive statements into those he believes are true of him and those that he believes are not.

R

r   In statistics, the symbol representing a widely-used COEFFICIENT OF CORRELATION.

RAC   See REGIONAL ADVISORY COUNCILS.

racialism (racism)   Belief that some races are inherently superior to others. Often blatant in out-moded school TEXTBOOKS (eg in the treatment of American Indians or the people of Britain's THIRD-WORLD ex-colonies) but evident also, occasionally, in quite recent schoolbooks or children's stories that introduce people of certain races only in trivial or demeaning roles that readers are unlikely to identify with. Likewise, some are written as if with the assumption that the reader must be of a particular (white) race. See also SEXISM.

RADA   The 'Royal Academy of Dramatic Arts' – the UK's best-known institution for the teaching of practical theatre arts.

radiovision   Form of educational broadcasting in which students using certain radio programmes in school or college are provided with visual materials (eg FILMSTRIP, SLIDES, or illustrated booklets) containing pictures or diagrams to which the broadcast will be referring. The broadcast form of AUDIOVISION.

rag   An annual event in many UK university towns, usually lasting a week, in which, with the avowed object of raising money for charity, students organise a number of events and festivities (perhaps enjoying rather more licence than usual), often culminating in a fancy-dress procession with decorated vehicles.

ragged schools   A form of free ELEMENTARY SCHOOL for poor children, sponsored by philanthropists in the early years of the 19th century, and operating both in the US and the UK. (The UK had some 600 by the time they were superseded as a result of the EDUCATION ACT 1870.)

ragging   Rowdy practical joking and other relatively mild harassment among students that may (if older students are ragging younger ones) degenerate into BULLYING. Similar to US HAZING.

Raikes, Robert   (1735–1811) UK publisher and pioneer of the SUNDAY SCHOOL movement who opened his first Sunday school in 1780 and employed teachers using the MONITORIAL SYSTEM for the teaching of reading.

Rampton Committee   A UK COMMITTEE OF ENQUIRY at present (1981) looking into the education of children from ethnic MINORITY GROUPS, and due to publish a REPORT shortly.

R and D (R & D)   See RESEARCH AND DEVELOPMENT.

random learning   See INCIDENTAL LEARNING.

random sample   A SAMPLE whose members are chosen in such a way that every member of the POPULATION has an equal chance of being in the sample. (It is hoped that the sample will thereby be representative.)

range   Statistical term for the difference in size between two extreme OBSERVATIONS in a FREQUENCY DISTRIBUTION - a rough and ready measure of VARIABILITY among a set of measurements.

rank   The position of a person or thing in an ordered sequence that has resulted from RANKING.

241

ranking   The process of arranging a number of people or things in order according to whether they are judged to possess more or less of some quality or VARIABLE (eg height, beauty, intelligence, honesty, etc). In the UK, the highest rank goes to the person or thing with the most of the quality and is numbered 1, the second highest is 2, and so on. In the US however, rank numbers are usually assigned in the reverse fashion, with 1 being the lowest.

rapid eye movements (REM)   A phenomenon known to occur in adults while they are asleep and dreaming and used by researchers in monitoring mental activity.

rapid reading   Largely thanks to the INFORMATION-EXPLOSION and ever-swelling examination syllabuses, there has been much interest in recent years in teaching adults how to read faster. However, many of the claims regarding increased speed are somewhat dubious, partly because the kind of comprehension checked for is often rather trivial, and partly because people seem not to maintain their increased speed. What may be more important than speed is the ability to decide which material one needs to read very carefully (maybe more than once) and which can be skimmed.

rate support grant   In the UK, only about 40% of expenditure on public education comes out of rates (local taxes). The remainder is obtained as a result of annual negotiations between the local authorities and the Government's Department of the Environment (not the DES) which makes a grant to support the spending from rates on all local services (including hospitals, housing, roads, etc, as well as education).

rating   **1** See RANKING. **2** A method of ASSESSMENT in which either a piece of student work is compared with each of several specimens representing different standards (see QUALITY RATING SCALE) or several aspects of someone's performance (eg a student-teacher's) are each graded on a scale of, say, 1–5. **3** With broadcast radio and television, a figure indicating the size of audience for a particular programme.

rational curriculum planning   An approach to CURRICULUM DEVELOPMENT that was given its initial impetus by the US educator, TYLER, in the 1940s and has since become closely associated with EDUCATIONAL TECHNOLOGY. It is characterised by its emphasis on choosing teaching content and methods on the basis of pre-determined OBJECTIVES and then evaluating and improving the teaching system until the objectives are achieved. It is still influential, particularly as an analytical model, but practical curriculum development is often better pursued through what is sometimes called ILLUMINATIVE CURRICULUM PLANNING.

rationalisation 1 A term used by SIGMUND FREUD for a DEFENCE MECHANISM in which a person unconsciously produces a plausible and socially-acceptable 'reason' for some past action, thus concealing the real but less acceptable reason. 2 The term is also used by educational (and other) administrators to describe organisational changes that involve reducing staff and resources; but they are justified in this use only if the quality of the services offered is not thereby reduced also.

ratio scale See SCALES OF MEASUREMENT.

Raven's progressive matrices See PROGRESSIVE MATRICES TEST.

raw data Data collected in a statistical survey or other investigation but not yet processed by any kind of mathematical operation.

raw score A score on a test (eg of INTELLIGENCE or ACHIEVEMENT) that has not yet been statistically processed to make it comparable with other scores.

R & D See RESEARCH AND DEVELOPMENT.

reaction See RESPONSE.

reaction formation A DEFENCE MECHANISM whereby a person adopts some (acceptable) BEHAVIOUR as a reaction against some impulse that is not acceptable. Often the behaviour is opposite in kind to that of the forbidden impulse, eg extreme prudishness as a defence against sexual impulses.

reaction time The interval between a STIMULUS and a person's RESPONSE.

read, to (UK) To 'read' a subject is to study it at DEGREE level. Usually refers to the main subject studied, like MAJORING in the US.

readability 1 Ease with which print or handwriting can be deciphered. Same as legibility, and depends on physical factors – size of letters, spacing, colour of ink and paper, etc. 2 The ease and interest with which material can be read and understood. Depends on style and such features as length of words and sentences, familiarity of language, the author's tone, the balance between abstractions and concrete examples, and so on.

reader 1 (UK) Next highest academic rank to PROFESSOR. Equivalent rank in the US is somewhere between ASSOCIATE and FULL PROFESSOR. 2 Someone who advises a publisher on the qualities of a MANUSCRIPT offered for publication. **3** Book designed to help children learn to read. **4** A collection of READINGS, usually with editorial introduction and linking comments. **5** An optical device that enables one to view the 'pages' of a MICROFICHE.

readiness   The notion that a person needs to be in a state of preparedness (ie not just ready and willing, but also mentally and physically able), before he can learn new knowledge or skills. The PRE-REQUISITE ABILITIES may depend not simply on prior learning but also on degree of MATURATION. The term is used particularly in connection with the early stages in the teaching of READING.

reading   Reading implies not merely the ability to recognise and say aloud the words printed on a page, but also the ability to comprehend them and say what they mean. As the first of the THREE Rs, reading has been the key subject in the CURRICULUM for young children for centuries, and continues to be an area of considerable research activity and controversy. (See RAPID READING.)

reading age   A child's proficiency in reading compared with the average for children of his age. Thus, a six-year old child who can read at the level of the average eight-year old is said to have a reading age of eight years. May be expressed as a 'reading QUOTIENT'.

reading list   A list of books and other materials that students may be asked to read during a course (especially in college and university courses).

reading programme   See READING SCHEME.

reading readiness   See READINESS.

reading recorder   Device for recording the manner in which a person reads a page of text: eg the number of times his eyes pause at a point (FIXATIONS); where they pause and for how long; whether they return to pause again at an earlier point; and so on.

readings   Research papers, learned articles, newspaper reports, chapters from books, and extracts from other longer works, all with a bearing on a particular subject and collected together as a LEARNING RESOURCE for a course in that subject; perhaps published in book form as a 'READER'.

reading scheme/programme   A series of books, graded in difficulty, for children learning to read.

reading skills   The COMPONENT or ENABLING skills involved in learning, or being able, to read, eg distinguishing between letter shapes, moving the eyes in the appropriate direction along a line, associating sounds with symbols, etc.

reading week   In college or university courses, a period (perhaps just before an examination or some other ASSESSMENT event) when no classes or tutorials are held, leaving students free to catch up on their reading and prepare for what lies ahead.

ready reckoner   A book of tables of numbers, used instead of performing calculations of, for example, interest rates, discounts, etc.

realia   A term from EDUCATIONAL TECHNOLOGY for real objects and real events (and even real people, if they are observed rather than interacted with), when considered together as a type of LEARNING RESOURCE.

REBs   See REGIONAL EXAMINING BODIES.

rebus   A kind of punning puzzle or 'coded' message often found in Victorian children's books, in which words or syllables are represented by pictures of objects with similar-sounding names: thus the word 'pie' might be represented by putting the letter 'p' before a picture of an eye.

recall   A person's ability to recall information is one aspect of his MEMORY and offers one way of measuring it.

recapitulation theory   A now defunct theory of US psychologist, Hall (1844–1924), that growing children pass through the same stages as the human race has passed through during its development; and that this should somehow be reflected in the CURRICULUM.

received pronunciation   The accent of standard English as expected of middle-class people in the South-east of England, especially 'BBC English' still to be heard among TV newsreaders and Radio 3 announcers.

reception centres   Short-stay homes run by some UK local authorities for children whose family life has been disturbed.

reception class   Class for youngest children in INFANTS SCHOOL who are starting school for the first time and who therefore need help in making the transition from home to school life.

reception learning   Term used by US psychologist, Ausubel, (not in criticism) to refer to the kind of learning required when the subject-matter to be mastered is presented to the learner in its final, complete form. This implies EXPOSITORY TEACHING and contrasts with DISCOVERY LEARNING.

245

recess (US) **1** Interlude between lessons, like UK BREAK or PLAYTIME, in which pupils can relax and perhaps play games outside the school buildings. **2** A VACATION.

recidivism A person's habitual relapse into crime or delinquency, despite having been punished.

reciprocated pair Two people who choose one another in a SOCIOMETRIC SURVEY.

reciprocity **1** Identified by BRUNER as an important source of INTRINSIC MOTIVATION — the feeling that one's own role is complementary to those of other people within a group cooperating towards some common goal. **2** In HIGHER EDUCATION, the mutual recognition by any pair of institutions that their CREDITS or QUALIFICATIONS are comparable, thus allowing easier transfer of students between the two. **3** See also RECIPROCATED PAIR.

recitation **1** Once a common way of 'doing' poetry in schools. Children memorise lengthy poems and speak them aloud in public. **2** (US) The oral presentation of any kind of prepared materials by students in class. **3** (US) A lesson devoted to (2) above.

recitation hall (US) A LECTURE THEATRE or assembly hall.

'recognised efficient' The status given a UK INDEPENDENT SCHOOL/COLLEGE that has been inspected by HER MAJESTY'S INSPECTORATE, on behalf of the DEPARTMENT OF EDUCATION AND SCIENCE or the SCOTTISH EDUCATION DEPARTMENT, as having acceptable educational (and residential) standards.

recognition A person's ability to recognise ideas encountered previously is one aspect of his MEMORY and offers one way of measuring it.

recognition span Term used in reading research for the number of letters an individual normally 'takes in' each time his eyes pause in moving along a line of print. People with larger recognition spans make fewer pauses, and so read more quickly.

record card A card (or set of documents) that serves as a confidential CUMULATIVE RECORD of a pupil's academic progress, conduct, attendance, family circumstances, etc, over a period of years. Unlike a REPORT it is not sent to parents, and a UK school may well deny them access to it if they do become aware of its existence. In the US, however, the BUCKLEY AMENDMENT guarantees parents access to their children's records. See SCHOOL RECORDS.

record of personal achievement (**RPA**) A form of PROFILE in which teachers describe the qualities and achievements of a pupil leaving school (especially one who has taken no PUBLIC EXAMINATIONS). The intention is to encourage the pupil and to help him in obtaining employment. The scheme was pioneered in schools in Swindon, England.

rector **1** Chief executive of a college or university, particularly in Europe. **2** HEADMASTER of some Scottish schools. **3** A representative elected for a fixed period by students in Scottish universities to speak on their behalf and protect their interests. The rector may attend or chair the university COURT and frequently is an outside celebrity. Similar to US OMBUDSMAN. **4** A clergyman responsible for a congregation.

recurrent education Basically the same as CONTINUING EDUCATION, but its advocates are generally more committed to a radical restructuring of the educational system.

red-brick university UK term for PROVINCIAL UNIVERSITIES, (or CIVIC UNIVERSITIES), especially those of 19th century origin.

redistricting (US) The process of amalgamating SCHOOL DISTRICTS to form larger and, it is hoped, more efficient units. The number of school districts is now less than 20% of what it was just after World War II.

reductionism Any attempt to explain some complex phenomenon in terms of some more simple phenomena: eg to say that all human behaviour can be explained in terms of STIMULUS and RESPONSE. (The word is often used disparagingly, to suggest that a particular attempt is futile or trivialises and distorts the truth.)

re-education Term used particularly by people wishing to take systematic steps towards changing the ideological affiliations of another group of people (eg after a political coup or revolution).

reel-to-reel Term used of the kind of TAPE-RECORDER where the magnetic tape unwinds completely off one reel or spool and onto another quite separate one during the course of recording or PLAYBACK. (Contrasts with CARTRIDGE/CASSETTE RECORDERS where the tape is enclosed within a sealed box container.)

re-examinee A student taking an examination again, probably having failed it previously.

refectory Communal dining hall in an educational institution.

referee **1** Umpire or judge who ensures that the rules of a game or sport are complied with. **2** Someone to whom the editors of a LEARNED JOURNAL will refer for an opinion as to the quality of a PAPER submitted for publication. **3** Someone willing to offer a confidential opinion as to the character and capabilities of a person known to him, usually with respect to that person's suitability for a particular job.

refer, to 1 To fail a student on an examination, but allow him to take it again. 2 See REFERRAL.

reference 1 A printed note in a book or PAPER, referring the reader to another source (or to another section of the same book or paper). 2 The section or source referred to in 1 above. 3 A confidential statement as to someone's character and capabilities in respect of a job application, as written by a REFEREE.

reference books Encyclopaedias, atlases, dictionaries, and books that cover many subjects, are more general than most books on a specific subject, and are therefore consulted more than most.

reference group The group of people with whom a person shares values and aspirations and with whose behaviour he compares his own.

reference library A library (or section within a library) consisting of REFERENCE BOOKS, and perhaps other materials, that may be consulted on the premises but not borrowed.

referent The thing, person, event, experience, or abstraction referred to by a particular word or phrase.

referral The process of enabling someone to consult with a person better able to help him than himself. For example, a teacher might refer a disturbed child to an educational psychologist employed by the same LOCAL EDUCATION AUTHORITY.

reflective v impulsive See IMPULSIVE V REFLECTIVE.

reflex action/response An involuntary action made as an automatic unlearned RESPONSE to a STIMULUS, eg blinking when an object suddenly approaches the eye, or jerking the lower leg when one's knee is tapped.

reflexive behaviour Same as REFLEX ACTIONS.

reform A term used quite commonly in the 19th century to describe deliberate changes made in educational systems and CURRICULA. Like the present-day term INNOVATION, but with stronger moral overtones.

reformatory Generic title for institutions specialising in the corrective training and REHABILITATION of young criminal offenders. Like BORSTALS (UK) and REFORM SCHOOLS (US).

reform school (US) State-run REFORMATORY similar to UK BORSTAL.

refresher course A course designed to up-date a person's knowledge and skills within the field in which he is working. A form of IN-SERVICE TRAINING.

regents (US) Governors of a STATE COLLEGE or UNIVERSITY. In some states they are elected by the citizens, in others they are appointed by the state governor.

Regional Advisory Councils Nine bodies with responsibility for co-ordinating FURTHER, and non-university HIGHER EDUCATION in different areas of England. They are set up by the LOCAL EDUCATION AUTHORITIES; the membership of each represents the authority, the colleges, and industry and commerce. (In Wales, this responsibility is exercised by the WELSH JOINT EDUCATION COMMITTEE.)

Regional Educational Laboratory (US) One of the many non-profit institutions set up under the ELEMENTARY AND SECONDARY EDUCATION ACT 1965 to promote research-based CURRICULUM DEVELOPMENT activity in schools, as a bridge between theory and improved practice.

regional examining boards The 14 UK examining boards that administer the CERTIFICATE OF SECONDARY EDUCATION (CSE) examinations in England and Wales.

regional examining bodies/unions Six independent regional councils, institutions or unions, each administering examinations for students in colleges of FURTHER EDUCATION in its area of England or Wales.

regional management centres UK centres for POST-EXPERIENCE MANAGEMENT EDUCATION, founded in 1971, and mainly based in POLYTECHNICS.

regional school (US) School serving a wider region than the usual SCHOOL DISTRICT (perhaps because it offers some special facility).

register **1** The number of children officially registered as being members of a school (ON ROLL) or of a particular class. **2** The book in which their names are listed and their daily attendances and absences noted.

registered child minder See CHILD MINDER.

registrar Senior administrator in a UK college or university responsible only to the SECRETARY (if there is one), or directly to the chief executive officer, for student enrolments, records, examination arrangements, etc. Not normally a teacher though he may be called Academic Registrar.

registration fee   Fee charged for enrolment in a course or institution and not repayable if an applicant subsequently withdraws.

regius professor   One whose CHAIR (at one of the older UK universities) is in the gift of the King or Queen.

regression   **1** In PSYCHOANALYTIC terms, a person's return to the behaviour of an earlier stage of his emotional development or to some previously discarded way of coping with a given situation. **2** In statistics, the term relates to techniques of analysing relationships between two or more VARIABLES with a view to predicting (or estimating) VALUES of one from values of the other(s).

regulations   (UK) The statutory instructions that the SECRETARY OF STATE FOR EDUCATION AND SCIENCE can legally enforce upon the LOCAL EDUCATION AUTHORITIES under the terms of the EDUCATION ACT 1944. These concern administrative and organisational issues rather than matters of CURRICULUM.

rehabilitation   Helping someone recover from a period of mental or physical handicap (or disgrace) and again become capable of independent life in society and/or of holding a job.

reification   What one might call 'thingification'. The process or result of treating an idea or abstraction (eg INTELLIGENCE, MOTIVATION) as if it had real or concrete existence rather than as a construction; an interpretation of events, that might not appear the same to other people.

reinforcement   The occurrence of a STIMULUS or event (eg a word of praise or a cash payment) that increases the probability of a certain RESPONSE or BEHAVIOUR occurring again in similar circumstances. See REINFORCEMENT SCHEDULE and REINFORCER.

reinforcement schedule   A plan for reinforcing whatever RESPONSES are to be encouraged. On a *fixed interval* schedule, REINFORCEMENT is given at constant time intervals. With a *variable interval* schedule, the time gap between reinforcements varies in length. Similarly a *fixed ratio* schedule delivers each reinforcement after a fixed number of responses while a *variable ratio* schedule reinforces after varying numbers of responses. Variable schedules give what is called INTERMITTENT REINFORCEMENT (which is the kind that captivates anglers and devotees of the fruit-machine).

reinforcer   Any STIMULUS or event that provides REINFORCEMENT. REINFORCERS may be positive ('rewards') or negative ('punishments').

rejectee A person who is chosen by no-one in a SOCIOMETRIC SURVEY.

re-learning Another aspect of, and means of measuring, MEMORY. (Like RECALL and RECOGNITION.) The degree to which a person who appears to have forgotten something can learn it again more easily than he learned it in the first place is a measure of the degree to which he did partially remember it.

released time (US) Time when pupils may be withdrawn from classes in PUBLICLY-MAINTAINED SCHOOLS in order to take part in RELIGIOUS INSTRUCTION (since religion is banned from the regular CURRICULUM).

reliability The extent to which a given question, or test, or examination will result in a given set of students obtaining the same scores on different occasions, or if marked by different assessors, or by the same assessors on different occasions. Broadly speaking, MULTIPLE-CHOICE QUESTIONS are more reliable than ESSAY questions.

religious education (RE) The term may be used of any teaching involving religion, from straightforward INDOCTRINATION to the non-partisan, comparative study of the religions of the world, the psychology and sociology of various belief systems, religious history, the nature of moral behaviour, and so on. Religious education is the only subject that must appear in the CURRICULUM of UK MAINTAINED SCHOOLS (since the EDUCATION ACT 1944); while in such schools in the US it seems to be the only subject that is legally banned!

religious instruction (RI) Religious education of a form that is unashamedly closer to INDOCTRINATION than to the open-minded, non-committed study of religious experience.

religious knowledge (RK) Defunct CURRICULUM term for what is more likely to be called RELIGIOUS EDUCATION (RE).

remake The process and result of improving a course (especially one that is based on SELF-INSTRUCTIONAL MATERIALS) by altering parts that are ineffective or out-dated, but without scrapping and replacing the course.

remand centre/home A UK establishment to which young people, accused or convicted of criminal offences, may be sent while awaiting trial or sentence. Now known as COMMUNITY HOMES.

remedial class A class, usually containing fewer pupils than a usual class, for children who need extra and special help on

251

account of specific or general learning difficulties. See also SPECIAL UNIT.

remedial education/teaching Education designed for children whose educational progress is thought to be less than might be expected, and who might benefit from more intensive teaching by staff trained and experienced in helping children overcome specific or general LEARNING DIFFICULTIES. Such teaching is likely to involve DIAGNOSTIC TESTING, considerable individual tuition and working in very small groups. In the UK, many schools have a REMEDIAL TEACHER on the staff (especially in COMPREHENSIVE SCHOOLS), organising their own remedial groups and classes. Much remedial education, however, takes place in CHILD GUIDANCE CLINICS or other special centres, and certain children with particular problems are taught in SPECIAL SCHOOLS. See also SPECIAL UNITS.

remedial frame A FRAME in a BRANCHING PROGRAMME that gives extra help to a student who has answered a MULTIPLE-CHOICE QUESTION incorrectly. (Also called a WRONG-ANSWER FRAME.)

REM See RAPID EYE MOVEMENT.

remedial loop Used in a BRANCHING PROGRAMME when a single REMEDIAL FRAME is insufficient to help a student overcome an error and he is taken through a sequence of remedial material before being returned to answer the original question again.

remedial post That of a REMEDIAL TEACHER.

remedial teacher One specialising in REMEDIAL EDUCATION.

remove In some UK PUBLIC SCHOOLS, a special class for pupils of about 14 years who need different treatment from their contemporaries (perhaps because they are slower learners).

Renaissance 1 The period of European history often seen as bringing the 'Middle Ages' to a close and initiating the 'modern world'. 2 the spirit and CULTURE of this period, generally recognised as spreading out from 14th century Italy, and including: intensified interest in classical antiquity; scientific and geographical discovery; the assertion of secular over religious concerns; the awakening sense of individualism and personal human potential; and the liberalising power of education.

'Renaissance man' A term applied, sometimes with a mild hint of mockery or of disbelief, to a person of our own times who professes an unusually broad range of intellectual interests. Similar to, but more emotive than, POLYMATH.

repertory grid A technique developed by US psychologist,

KELLY, and based on his PERSONAL CONSTRUCT theory. It is used to discover the terms in which a person views the social world; for example, by asking him to decide which two people out of three known to him are more alike and why. The 'why' reveals one of the person's CONSTRUCTS (eg, generosity, honesty) and the process is repeated with other sets of three names until all such constructs are elicited.

replication The repetition of an experiment or research study, perhaps because the original methods or results are suspect or inconclusive. It may or may not produce the same results.

report Regular written report made by teachers to the parents of pupils, commenting on academic performance, conduct, attitudes, etc. Some schools have experimented with encouraging pupils and parents to write their own appraisals into the report also. See also REPORTS ON EDUCATION.

report card Canadian term for GRADE CARD.

reports on education Many 'reports' are mentioned in this dictionary, eg, NEWSOM REPORT, PLOWDEN REPORT, WARNOCK REPORT, etc. Such a report contains the deliberations and recommendations of a group of specially convened experts, or of an existing committee (under the chairmanship of the person whose name is usually given to the report), commissioned by the UK government to collect evidence and give its considered advice on some educational issue or area in which changes of policy or provision may seem called for. The reports are published by Her Majesty's Stationary Office (HMSO).

representational thinking The ability to model in the mind (that is, to manipulate in imagination) objects and actions that are not presently available to the senses.

representative sample A SAMPLE drawn from a POPULATION in such a way that it should (or does) contain members of various categories and classifications in the same proportions as they appear in the population. (For example, a sample drawn from the UK population could not be representative if only ten per cent of its members were females).

repression A FREUDIAN DEFENCE MECHANISM by means of which one excludes from the conscious mind those thoughts and emotions and desires that might threaten one or cause anxiety.

reproduction, social Sociologists sometimes use the biological metaphor to describe the social processes (eg education) by

253

which a CULTURE ensures its values and practices are inherited by each new generation.

reprography   The technology of copying, reprinting, and producing multiple copies of printed materials.

required course   A course that all students following a particular programme of studies are required to take. Contrasts with an OPTIONAL COURSE.

requirements   1 As ENTRY QUALIFICATIONS. 2 Whatever activities or STANDARDS are expected of a student during a course. 3 (US) The type and total number of CREDITS required for a degree – usually about 120 for a FIRST DEGREE.

research and development (R & D)   An approach to research that concentrates on issues that arise out of immediate practical concerns and aims to produce results that can be used at once in working towards some practical goal. This approach is often used by educational researchers concerned with CURRICULUM DEVELOPMENT. It may also be called ACTION RESEARCH and contrasts with PURE RESEARCH, where the emphasis is on adding to the store of human knowledge rather than on improving the situation being studied.

research assistant(ship)   A paid post in an institution of HIGHER EDUCATION for a POST-GRADUATE student who helps senior colleagues with their academic research work, while perhaps studying, or carrying out private research, in his own spare time.

research course   A course in HIGHER EDUCATION, usually towards a HIGHER DEGREE, that is centred on a RESEARCH PROJECT or other personal investigation. Contrasts with TAUGHT COURSE.

research fellow   Someone employed in an institution of HIGHER EDUCATION, usually for a limited period, and holding a FELLOWSHIP concerned with researching a particular topic (usually one chosen by whoever provided the necessary funds).

research grant   An amount of money made available to an institution, or to particular members of its staff, to finance research into a particular topic.

research librarian   A librarian whose duty and specialisation is to help teachers to obtain (and possibly to organise and interpret) the printed and other source material they need for their research.

research seminar   A seminar given by a researcher on the subject of his investigations and intended for fellow-specialists rather than for students. The term might be used to distinguish it from a TEACHING SEMINAR.

research student A POSTGRADUATE STUDENT (GRADUATE STUDENT in the US) who is working on a research project with a view to obtaining a HIGHER DEGREE. The topic is often of his own choosing but in some DISCIPLINES it is common for such students to assist with a research project initiated and managed by senior academic staff. In such cases, the research student operates much like a RESEARCH ASSISTANT (but without pay).

research supervisor Senior member of the academic staff in an institution of HIGHER EDUCATION, one of whose tasks is to guide and comment on the work of RESEARCH STUDENTS studying for HIGHER DEGREES. He may do this as an INTERNAL supervisor (for students in his own institution), and/or as EXTERNAL supervisor (for students from elsewhere).

reserved teacher A RELIGIOUS EDUCATION teacher appointed to a UK VOLUNTARY (eg SPECIAL AGREEMENT) SCHOOL by its GOVERNORS (rather than by the LOCAL EDUCATION AUTHORITY).

residence See HALL OF RESIDENCE (UK) or, in the US, DORMITORY or residence house.

residence house See DORMITORY (US).

residential institution Institution providing accommodation for most if not all of its members, eg a BOARDING SCHOOL.

resource bank Collection of RESOURCE MATERIALS, indexed and catalogued to facilitate access.

resource-based learning/education A mode of learning in which students work very much on their own (or in small groups) using LEARNING RESOURCES – especially TEXTBOOKS, PROGRAMMES, HOME EXPERIMENT KITS and other SELF-INSTRUCTIONAL MATERIALS – that have been specially selected or developed to enable students to learn all that is required in a particular course, with little or no need for group sessions with a teacher. See DISTANCE EDUCATION, FLEXISTUDY, IPI, KELLER PLAN and PLAN.

resource based teaching 1 An approach to teaching in which the emphasis is on RESOURCE-BASED LEARNING (that is, with the students using specially developed resources largely on their own). 2 An approach to teaching in which the teacher makes abundant use of learning resources in EXPOSITORY TEACHING.

resource materials Non-human LEARNING RESOURCES: that is, LEARNING MATERIALS such as books, worksheets, tapes, films, models, specimens, etc.

resources 1 The money, materials and people necessary for the pursuit of some goal. 2 See LEARNING RESOURCES.

resources centre/unit Facility within an educational institution for the storage and use of LEARNING RESOURCES. (Perhaps attached to the library and including books.) May have a comprehensive cataloguing system, enabling staff to locate suitable materials, and may provide facilities (and technical advice) to enable staff to produce their own materials. Often associated with an EDUCATIONAL DEVELOPMENT or EDUCATIONAL TECHNOLOGY unit.

resource person (US) Specialist teacher who moves from class to class teaching his special subject (and perhaps available to advise colleagues on how to teach it).

resources unit See RESOURCES CENTRE.

respondee/respondent Person who is responding on a PSYCHOLOGICAL TEST, or one who has filled in and returned a QUESTIONNAIRE.

response The reaction of some organism (eg a student or a teacher) to some STIMULUS or situation. The response may be conscious or unconscious; it may be intentional or REFLEXIVE; it may be mental only or it may have physical manifestations; it may consist of glandular or muscular changes, or of thoughts, speech, or PSYCHOMOTOR activity.

response-chaining The linking together of several RESPONSES in a CHAIN or sequence leading to a goal, eg the dancing of a waltz figure, or the starting of a car.

response set See SET.

response shaping A method of developing a desired RESPONSE in a learner (human or otherwise) by rewarding closer and closer approximations to it.

restricted code Term used by BERNSTEIN, referring to one of his two LANGUAGE CODES. The restricted code consists of short, simple utterances, often ambiguous and ungrammatical; they would probably be incomprehensible if reported to someone unaware of the context. This code does not allow for the precise expression of a person's individuality and emotions (which would be attempted by NON-VERBAL COMMUNICATION) or for complex COGNITIVE LEARNING. Bernstein argues that WORKING-CLASS children suffer from having this code only, while MIDDLE-CLASS children learn an ELABORATED CODE also.

resumé (US) See CURRICULUM VITAE.

256

retardation 1 The condition of an UNDER-ACHIEVER – a child whose attainment of knowledge and skills, in general or in a particular area, is less than would be expected of him, based on other evidence as to his POTENTIAL (eg INTELLIGENCE TEST results). 2 Confusingly, however, the term is sometimes used simply to refer to a SLOW LEARNER – without any indication that he might be expected to be doing better.

retarded child/reader One whose attainments seem to suggest RETARDATION – perhaps an UNDER-ACHIEVER, perhaps a SLOW LEARNER.

retardedness See RETARDATION.

retention The ability to recognise or recall knowledge or to demonstrate skills that were learned at some earlier time. Without occasional PRACTICE, the level of retention declines over time.

retraining Training that is designed to equip a person with new knowledge and skills, usually so as to enable him to do a new job.

retread programme (US) REFRESHER COURSE or RETRAINING.

retroactive inhibition Interference with the RETENTION of one piece of learning brought about by a subsequent piece of learning, eg learning the Spanish phrase for 'please' may hinder recall of the previously learned equivalent in Italian.

reversal Reading or writing letters or digits in an incorrect order, eg, reading or writing 1918 instead of 1981. Common symptom in DYSLEXIA.

reverse discrimination Policies or actions meant to protect MINORITY GROUPS (eg immigrants) that thereby act to the disadvantage of the majority group. May be a result of POSITIVE DISCRIMINATION.

review See REVISION.

Revised Code, 1862 Change in UK Government regulations (based on NEWCASTLE REPORT, 1861), the most controversial feature of which was that grants to schools were henceforth to depend on the attendance of children and their performance in the basic skills of reading, writing and arithmetic, which led in turn to teachers getting 'PAYMENT BY RESULTS'. Overall, the effects on teachers' morale and the quality of teaching were not beneficial.

revision Looking back over material learned earlier, with a view to refreshing the memory or seeking a deeper understanding, or linking the material with ideas learned more recently – perhaps in preparation for an examination or prior to starting on a new project. The more usual term in the US would be REVIEW.

reward Whatever it is that an individual receives from engaging in an activity (eg learning) that encourages him to continue doing so. In this sense, 'freedom from PUNISHMENT' can be a reward. See INTRINSIC and EXTRINSIC MOTIVATION, and REINFORCEMENT.

Rhodes Scholarships Founded by Cecil Rhodes, the 19th century explorer, and, since 1904, awarded annually on merit to 72 US and Commonwealth GRADUATES to enable them to study for two and sometimes three years at Oxford University.

RI See RELIGIOUS INSTRUCTION.

rigidity An inability to change one's mental SET in order to try different approaches to a taxing problem or situation.

'rising fives' UK law requires INFANT SCHOOLS to provide PLACES for children as from the beginning of the term after their fifth birthday. Some schools, however, are able and willing to start children earlier – in the term in which they will become five. These children are the 'rising fives'.

rites de passage French term referring to formal rituals or ceremonies that occur to mark the passage of an individual from one stage of life to another, eg a school-leaving ceremony, or a wedding, or an 'INITIATION ceremony' by new work-mates.

RK See RELIGIOUS KNOWLEDGE.

Robbins Report 1963 Highly influential UK REPORT on the provision of HIGHER EDUCATION. Recommended a big expansion, to make PLACES available for all students who might benefit (especially encouraging more women and WORKING-CLASS students). It also recommended up-grading the TEACHER-TRAINING COLLEGES (re-naming them COLLEGES OF EDUCATION, and advocating a four-year course leading to a B Ed degree); and up-grading the COLLEGES OF ADVANCED TECHNOLOGY to the status of TECHNOLOGICAL UNIVERSITIES able to award both FIRST and HIGHER DEGREES.

rod and frame test A test designed to measure FIELD-DEPENDENCE V INDEPENDENCE by getting a person to try aligning a rod with the vertical, inside a square frame that can be tilted away from the vertical.

Rogers, Carl (Born 1902) US psychologist and pioneer of NON-DIRECTIVE THERAPY and NON-DIRECTIVE TEACHING (especially in HIGHER EDUCATION). An influential opponent of the BEHAV-

IOURIST approaches associated with SKINNER and an advocate of democratic, LEARNER-CENTERED approaches, with SELF-ACTUALISATION as an important aim. See especially his *Client-Centred Therapy* (1951), *On Becoming a Person* (1961), and *Freedom to Learn* (1969).

role   The social BEHAVIOUR expected of, and usually exhibited by, people occupying certain positions in society (eg mother, wife, teacher, friend, etc). Each person has to learn a succession of roles during his social development and, at any age, will have to be able to act in several different roles.

role conflict   **1** Conflict within one person who is being called upon to fulfil two or more competing ROLES, eg friend v critic. **2** Conflict between two people explicable in terms of their having competing roles.

role differentiation   The process whereby members of a group come to accept different and (perhaps complementary) ROLES, eg, manager, encourager, drudge, jester, scapegoat, etc.

role model   Someone a person looks to as an example while learning or adopting a ROLE.

role perception   What a person sees his ROLE (or that of another person) to be.

role playing   The deliberate acting out of a ROLE (possibly a role that one would not normally occupy), as part of GROUP THERAPY or of a learning session directed towards understanding that role or the situations with which its occupants have to cope.

role separation   The extent to which one can be sure which of one's various ROLES one is operating in at a given time. For example, separating the roles of mother and teacher would become more difficult for a woman-teacher if her own child joined her class.

role set   The set or network of ROLES occupied by the members of a coherent social group, eg the relationships between the roles of members of a family, or of a school's teaching staff, pupils, governors, parents, etc.

roll   (US) See REGISTER (UK).

Rorschach ink blot test   A PROJECTIVE TEST, consisting of ten cards on which are symmetrical ink-blots. A person is given the cards in sequence and asked to say what he sees in each. His responses are then interpreted as revealing various aspects of his PERSONALITY.

ROSLA   UK acronym used around 1972 for Raising of the

School Leaving Age. The statutory minimum leaving age was raised from 15 to 16 in 1972–73 (as recommended by the NEWSOM REPORT 1963). Pupils kept on at school by this change were called ROSLA pupils, courses prepared specially for them were called ROSLA courses, and so on.

roster   Or rota. List of people's names and the duties of each.

rota   As ROSTER.

rote learning   Learning facts mechanically ('by rote'), with much practice and repetition, but without any attempt at understanding.

rote memory   Memory for the kind of material that can be acquired by ROTE LEARNING.

Rothwell-Miller Interest Blank   An INVENTORY developed in Australia and revised in UK to ascertain the tastes and interests of individual young people and adults as a basis for VOCATIONAL GUIDANCE.

Rousseau, Jean Jaques   (1712–1778) French philosopher whose educational and social theories were mostly based on a belief that men are naturally good but become warped by the corruptions of society. In two books, *The New Héloise* (1761) and *Emile* (1762) he suggested a form of education to preserve children from corruption: the teacher should rely on the child's natural appetite for learning; treat him as a child rather than as a miniature adult; and allow him to learn through his senses from the environment rather than from books. Much of this emphasis on the individual autonomy of the pupil was romantic and impractical, but it paved the way for the LEARNER-CENTRED and PROGRESSIVE EDUCATION approaches that were to follow.

RPA   See RECORD OF PERSONAL ACHIEVEMENT.

rul-eg   The abbreviation for 'rule followed by examples' – a teaching approach advocated by some practitioners of PROGRAMMED LEARNING. It suggested that the student should first be presented with a verbalisation of the rule or principle he is expected to learn and then be given examples. (A DEDUCTIVE approach.) Contrast with EG-RUL.

rules of management   Equivalent of ARTICLES OF GOVERNMENT for MANAGERS of some UK PRIMARY SCHOOLS prior to EDUCATION ACT 1980.

rushing   (US) The recruitment of new members by FRATERNITIES and SORORITIES at the beginning of the academic year in a college or university.

Russell, Bertrand (1872–1970) UK philosopher who, from 1927–1932, ran a PROGRESSIVE private school in Sussex. He was opposed to the influence of church and state on education and wished to foster children's individuality (especially in courage, vitality, sensitivity to other people, and intellectual curiosity). This he believed was achievable, through approaches derived from BEHAVIOURIST and FREUDian psychology. His chief educational writings are *On Education* (1926) and *Education and the Social Order* (1932).

Russell Report 1973 A UK REPORT that recommended major expansion in the provision of ADULT EDUCATION.

rusticate, to To banish a student from a university for a certain period (sending him to the country, as it were), as a punishment for some breach of the rules.

S

sabbatical (or **sabbatical year**) A period of leave allowed to academic staff in some institutions of HIGHER EDUCATION, enabling them to take as much as a year away from normal duties (perhaps once in every seven years of service), on full or part salary, so that they can pursue research or other further study experience.

saccade In reading, the sweeping movement of one's eyes along a line of print, between one FIXATION and the next.

safeguarding clause Clause in a contract of employment guaranteeing the holder of a post (eg a teacher) that he will not lose financially if his organisation (eg a school or college) is re-organised in such a way that the post is abolished or accorded a lower salary grade.

safety patrol (US) Group of pupils with some responsibility for guiding fellow-pupils in safe behaviour within and around school (especially with regard to road traffic).

salutatorian (US) A school or college student who, at graduation, gains the second highest academic honours (beaten only by the VALEDICTORIAN) and who delivers the welcoming speech (the salutatory or salutation) at the graduation ceremony.

sample Statistical term for a group selected from some larger group (the POPULATION) with a view to using what is discovered about that sample to make inferences about the population as a whole. (For example, the average height of all the children in a school may be estimated from a sample consisting of five children from each class.) The reliability of the estimates or inferences depends on how far the sample is REPRESENTATIVE (and RANDOM).

sample statistics Statistical term for numbers that describe aspects of a SAMPLE. For example, the MEAN, MEDIAN and MODE are sample statistics (or just statistics) that indicate a typical or representative value; while the statistics of RANGE or STANDARD DEVIATION describe the VARIABILITY of values in the sample. Statistics, drawn from a sample, are used to estimate the PARAMETERS of a POPULATION.

sampling Any statistical method of drawing a SAMPLE from some larger POPULATION with a view to making generalisations about the population based on what is seen in the sample. For example, one method of sampling gives a simple RANDOM SAMPLE, while another produces a STRATIFIED RANDOM SAMPLE.

sampling distribution The FREQUENCY DISTRIBUTION that could be expected if a particular STATISTIC (eg MEAN, STANDARD DEVIATION, CORRELATION COEFFICIENT) were calculated for an infinite number of samples of a given size from the same POPULATION.

Sampson, George (1882–1950) UK EDUCATIONIST and one time schools inspector, Sampson was an advocate of new approaches to the teaching of English: see his *English for the English* (1926). He is famous for his dictum: 'Every teacher is a teacher of English'.

san or **sanatorium** Centre with medical and nursing facilities in a UK BOARDING SCHOOL.

sanctuary See SPECIAL UNITS.

Sanderson, Frederick William (1857–1922) English EDUCATIONIST who, after a period at Dulwich College, became headmaster of Oundle School, where he set up laboratories and workshops to embody his belief that boys who were bored with classics would respond to 'real work', reflecting the world beyond school. He emphasised co-operation rather than individual achievement and said that 'education must be fitted to the boy, not the boy to education'.

sandwich course A UK course, usually at undergraduate level, in which periods of full-time study in COLLEGE, POLYTECHNIC or UNIVERSITY alternate with periods of supervised experience and training in an appropriate industrial firm, in commerce, or in a professional situation. The period of full-time study must exceed eighteen weeks per year or such a course would be called a BLOCK RELEASE COURSE. A distinction is made between 'thin' and 'thick' sandwich courses, the latter involving a whole year off campus. The nearest US equivalent is a COOPERATIVE COURSE (or program) or, sometimes, a WORK STUDY COURSE.

SAT (US) See SCHOLASTIC APTITUDE TEST.

satori A Japanese word from Zen Buddhism meaning a flash of sudden, ineffable, intuitive enlightenment. Akin to what Westerners might call the 'Ah-ha! experience'.

scale posts In England and Wales, school teachers below the level of SENIOR TEACHER are paid according to one of four overlapping salary scales. Scale posts are those earning more than the basic Scale 1. Teachers become eligible for them by taking on extra responsibilities (eg being head of a department); but the number a school can offer is limited by the number and ages of its pupils.

scales of measurement In statistics, there are four scales on which items can be differentiated and/or measured. The most basic is the *nominal* scale where the item is merely put in one category or another (eg blue eyes, brown, green etc). With the *ordinal* scale, items can be put in categories, each representing more or less of some quality than the others do (eg beautiful, plain, ugly). With an *interval* scale, each item has a number attached to it indicating the amount of some quality that it possesses (eg degrees of heat or score on an INTELLIGENCE TEST). Finally, a *ratio* scale not only attaches a number to such items but also implies that zero means the item possesses none of the quality in question (eg height, income, weight, etc) and that if one item has a value, say, twice as big as another it also has twice as much of the quality. (This would not be true of temperature for example.) As one goes from nominal towards ratio scales, more and more precise statistical operations become possible.

scaling Statistical term for the adjustment of scores obtained by students on a test or examination so that they can be compared with the scores obtained on some other test. Strictly speaking, if scores from different tests are to be added to arrive at an overall RANKING for the students, all scores should at first be scaled or the results may be unfair. This can be done, roughly, using a NOMOGRAM or, more rigorously, by adjusting all the scores to a common MEAN and STANDARD DEVIATION, so as to produce STANDARDISED SCORES.

263

scatter diagram A statistical diagram used in studies of COR-RELATION and REGRESSION. Pairs of VALUES from two VARIABLES can each be represented by a point plotted on co-ordinates and the strength of the relationship between the two variables judged by the extent to which the points scatter away from an imaginary straight line running through them.

scattergram Same as SCATTER DIAGRAM.

SCE See SCOTTISH CERTIFICATE OF EDUCATION.

SCEEB SCOTTISH CERTIFICATE OF EDUCATION EXAMINATION BOARD.

scenario **1** In SIMULATION GAMES, the background information regarding the imaginary game and its participants. **2** In TECH-NOLOGICAL FORECASTING, a description of some possible future environment or sequence of events, eg a scenario for World War III.

schedule **1** A form on which questions are answered, eg a QUES-TIONNAIRE, or an INTERVIEW schedule. **2** US word for TIMETABLE. **3** A list of items appended to a document. **4** See REINFORCEMENT SCHEDULE.

schema (or plural: **schemata**) Term used by PIAGET and other psychologists to refer to the conceptual structures we use to interpret the information presented to our SENSES by the external world or to think out or MODEL aspects of the real world in our minds. When we encounter a new object or situation we match it against our existing schemata and treat it accordingly. If the results are inappropriate we change the schemata or develop additional ones. More sophisticated and differentiated schemata are developed as a child encounters more and more new experiences and as his cognitive powers develop. See ACCOMMODATION and ASSIMILATION.

scheme A planned sequence of learning activity, as in a READING SCHEME.

schizophrenia A diagnostic term for a combination of certain psychotic symptoms such as withdrawal from reality, distortion of thought, speech and emotion, fear of persecution, delusions, and extreme lethargy.

schola cantorum CHOIR SCHOOL.

scholarship **1** Academic knowledge and skill of high quality. **2** A financial award made to a promising student to help finance further studies, eg QUEEN'S SCHOLARSHIPS and STATE SCHOLARSHIPS.

scholarship committee (US) COLLEGE or UNIVERSITY committee responsible for monitoring ACADEMIC STANDARDS.

scholarship examination Examination in which many candidates compete for the available SCHOLARSHIPS.

Scholarship papers Examination in GCE at a higher level and covering a wider syllabus than ADVANCED LEVEL; introduced in 1951 to facilitate competition for SCHOLARSHIPS and help in selection for HIGHER EDUCATION. Replaced in 1963 by S LEVEL (Special) papers.

scholastic agencies UK commercial organisations offering advice to parents on choice of PRIVATE SCHOOLS, colleges and tutors (in return for fees from the schools, colleges or tutors).

Scholastic Aptitude Test (SAT) (US) Predictive tests supplied by the COLLEGE ENTRANCE EXAMINATION BOARD and used by HIGH SCHOOLS in the penultimate year of a student's course to advise on applications to college or university, and (as part of the so-called 'COLLEGE BOARDS') by the colleges and universities themselves in selecting students.

scholasticism The system of mediaeval philosophy, theology and teaching (attempting to reconcile the writings of ARISTOTLE with classical theology) that dominated the universities prior to the RENAISSANCE. Its exponents were known as SCHOOLMEN.

Schonell, Sir Fred (1900–1968) Australian educational psychologist known especially for his work on the testing and teaching of backward children. See his *Backwardness in the Basic Subjects* (1942), *The Psychology and Teaching of Reading* (1945) and *Diagnostic and Attainment Testing* (1949). Many of his reading and arithmetic tests are still in use.

school 1 An institution providing EDUCATION for young people up to the age of about 19 years. 2 A department or group of departments within a university, eg London School of Economics; particularly an institution devoted to POSTGRADUATE studies, eg Harvard Law School or Manchester Business School. 3 A particular group of students in higher education, eg the honours mathematics school. 4 In the US, attending any college or university may be referred to as 'going to school'. 5 A group of thinkers subscribing to a particular set of ideas, doctrines or methods might regard themselves as a 'school of thought'. 6 Colloquially, any prolonged situation that enforces learning may be referred to as school, eg 'school of life', 'school of hard knocks', etc.

school allowance See CAPITATION ALLOWANCE.

school base An idea, current in the UK after the Second World War, of basing several different kinds of school on the same site, to enable shared sporting and catering facilities, and closer social academic links.

school-based examinations Examinations set and marked within a school for its own pupils – INTERNAL EXAMINATIONS. Contrast with EXTERNAL (or PUBLIC) EXAMINATIONS, set by an outside body for any school's pupils to take.

school board 1 (US) The local authority or committee of management responsible for the schools in a SCHOOL DISTRICT. May be called a BOARD OF EDUCATION and has a role similar to that of a UK LOCAL EDUCATION AUTHORITY. 2 (UK) Former type of body made responsible for local schools by the new LOCAL EDUCATION AUTHORITIES created in England and Wales by the EDUCATION ACT OF 1902.

school bond (US) See SCHOOL DEBENTURE.

School Certificate Former UK school leaving examination introduced in 1917 and lasting until it was replaced by the GENERAL CERTIFICATE OF EDUCATION (GCE) in 1951. The School Certificate had two levels: the first conferred MATRICULATION and the second became known as the HIGHER SCHOOL CERTIFICATE. The system differed from the GCE principally in that the student obtained the certificate only if he passed in several subjects (rather than getting a separate certificate for each subject passed).

school council 1 A committee of elected pupils (and perhaps staff) in a SECONDARY SCHOOL who meet to discuss school policy and practices. Although usually without authority, it may sometimes be able to exert influence on the running of the school. 2 In Scotland, a committee set up by an EDUCATION AUTHORITY to oversee a group of schools – similar to GOVERNING BODY of a MAINTAINED SCHOOL in England and Wales.

school debentures (US) Loans raised from parents and others to finance capital expenditure by schools in some parts of Canada and the US. Also called SCHOOL BONDS.

school district (US) The geographical area whose educational provision is organised by a local SCHOOL BOARD. The US has about 18,000 such districts.

school experience Opportunities for STUDENT-TEACHERS to visit schools to observe teachers teaching or children at work or to study school organisation, or undertake other non-teaching activities. The term usually excludes TEACHING PRACTICE.

school fund An amount of money raised by a school from such sources as school dances and fêtes and parental contributions, and used for projects that normal funds (CAPITATION ALLOWANCE) will not cover, eg running a mini-bus.

school governors See GOVERNING BODY.

school health service The school health service in England and Wales is provided, as part of the National Health Service, by the area health authorities working in co-operation with the LOCAL EDUCATION AUTHORITIES. Pupils are usually medically examined on starting at school and at other times if thought desirable; dental examinations are carried out more regularly. If treatment is necessary, it may be carried out by the family doctor or dentist, or at a school clinic, a community health centre or a hospital.

schooling A person's education, or the process by which it is obtained, especially if it involves schools or other formal educational institutions.

school-keeper See CARETAKER.

school leaver Pupil about to leave school or one who has recently left.

school leaving age Earliest age at which a pupil is legally entitled to withdraw from full-time education. In the UK, the REVISED CODE OF 1862 set it, in effect, at 12 years but subsequent Acts have raised it through 13 years (1880), 14 (1918), 15 (1947), to the present 16 years which it reached in 1972. (See ROSLA.) Sixteen years is also the minimum leaving age in the US and most European countries.

school leaving certificate In the UK there is no standard form of certificate that all pupils show to potential employers or institutions of POST-SECONDARY education as a record of their school careers. Instead we have GCE (A LEVEL and O LEVEL) certificates and CSE certificates from a variety of examining bodies, (and SCE in Scotland), together with other certificates such as those awarded by the Royal Society of Arts and the College of Preceptors. Any of these may be backed up by (or, in the case of lower ability pupils, substituted for) REFERENCES and TESTIMONIALS of varying detail, veracity and usefulness. See also RECORD OF PERSONAL ACHIEVEMENT and SCOTTISH PUPIL PROFILE.

schoolman A teacher in one of the schools or universities of the Middle Ages who was well versed in SCHOLASTICISM.

school meals   The EDUCATION ACT 1980 relaxes the former statutory obligation of LOCAL EDUCATION AUTHORITIES in England and Wales to provide meals and milk for pupils attending MAINTAINED SCHOOLS. It is now left to their discretion what they provide and how much they charge – except for pupils from certain low-income families who must be provided for free of charge.

school of education   The section within a UK university that provides TEACHER EDUCATION.

school of the air   Institutions providing broadcast lessons for children unable to attend school. Found particularly in Australia, where they supplement the CORRESPONDENCE EDUCATION of children in the outback and enable them to talk with teachers and one another on two-way radio.

school of thought   Term used of a commonly-held set of beliefs, concepts, methodologies, etc, or of the people (as a group) who hold them. Thus, a psychoanalyst might belong to the FREUDian school of thought, or to the ADLERian school, the JUNGian school and so on.

school party   Collective term for a group of UK pupils and teachers visiting some location away from their school.

school phobia   Intense, often irrational, fear of school, often based in anxiety about separation from parents, and often with PSYCHOSOMATIC SYMPTOMS.

school practice   See TEACHING PRACTICE.

school psychological services   UK local authorities employ educational psychologists who work from CHILD GUIDANCE CLINICS (usually with help from psychiatrists and social workers) to deal with children referred to them by teachers or parents because of handicaps, learning difficulties or disruptive behaviour. After diagnosis, they may provide remedial activity for the child at the clinic and/or suggest ways in which his teacher might help him in school or recommend him for SPECIAL EDUCATION.

school records   Supposedly confidential records kept on each pupil, stored in the school files, and passed on to any subsequent school the pupil attends. They contain judgments about the child's progress in school, together perhaps with information about family or social background that might have a bearing on his progress and personality, etc. Such records may be referred to by teachers seeking information about children they are teaching for the first time or when writing REFERENCES or TESTIMONIALS for a potential employer. Many UK parents are annoyed that they have no right to see these secret records, and so cannot verify that the information they contain is accurate. (In the US, the BUCKLEY AMENDMENT guarantees parents access.)

school refusal/refuser Term sometimes used of a pupil whose SCHOOL PHOBIA or other antipathy to school is so strong that he refuses to attend.

school report Regular written report made by schools (usually SECONDARY SCHOOLS) to parents, on the educational progress and general conduct of their children. Similar to US REPORT CARD.

Schools At Oxford University, the final honours degree examinations or the university building (examination schools) in which examinations are held.

Schools Broadcasting Council for the United Kingdom Body that advises the BBC with regard to television and radio programmes specially produced for use in schools. Membership includes representatives from teachers' organisations, the LOCAL EDUCATION AUTHORITIES, and the DEPARTMENT OF EDUCATION AND SCIENCE, the SCOTTISH EDUCATION DEPARTMENT and the DEPARTMENT OF EDUCATION OF NORTHERN IRELAND.

Schools Council, The An independent UK body established in 1964 by the SECRETARY OF STATE FOR EDUCATION AND SCIENCE to initiate and monitor CURRICULUM DEVELOPMENT projects in PRIMARY and SECONDARY schools in England and Wales and to advise on forms of PUBLIC EXAMINATION. The Council is funded partly by central government and partly by LOCAL EDUCATION AUTHORITIES. Teacher representatives out-number all others on most of its committees. It is a prolific publisher of research studies and working papers in the area of curriculum and examinations and, as the most active and influential UK body in curriculum development, of actual teaching materials.

schools fellowship See SCHOOLTEACHER FELLOWSHIP.

schools of industry A form of free education for the very poor that was recommended by the English philosopher, John Locke, and which came into being in the second half of the 18th century. Children were taught to spin, knit, mend shoes, tend gardens and so on; and the product of their labours was sold to meet the school expenses. Religious instruction, and sometimes reading, was also provided for, together with the usual emphasis on accepting a humble status in society.

school superintendent   (US) See SUPERINTENDENT OF SCHOOLS.

school-supervised teaching practice   TEACHING PRACTICE where a STUDENT-TEACHER's classroom experience is monitored and assessed by staff of the school rather than by tutors from the student's institution of teacher-education.

school tax   (US) Tax levied specifically for the support of schools.

school teacher fellowship   A FELLOWSHIP held in a college, polytechnic or university by a practising teacher on SECONDMENT from normal duties, and giving him an opportunity to study and pursue research.

school visit   **1** Visit to a school made by student-teachers for SCHOOL EXPERIENCE other than TEACHING PRACTICE. **2** Visit made by a SCHOOL PARTY to somewhere out of school.

school-within-a-school   (US.) An attempt to foster closer communities within a large school by breaking it down into a number of self-contained and partly autonomous smaller units on the same campus and sharing some common facilities (eg for sports and school meals).

school without walls   (US) An innovative approach to urban HIGH SCHOOL education that began in the 1960s with the Parkway Project in Philadelphia. Such schools operate with few classrooms and class teachers; they use the city as their campus and its business and government offices, museums, factories, stores and people as their learning resources. The approach is highly informal, and English and mathematics are usually the only compulsory subjects.

school year   As ACADEMIC YEAR.

science-based discipline   One of the DISCIPLINES like physics, chemistry, and engineering in which the emphasis is on controlled experiment, QUANTITATIVE METHODS and concern with maximum objectivity. Contrasts with ARTS-BASED DISCIPLINES, where the emphasis is on literary studies and creative reflection on experience, leading to qualitative, subjective interpretations. The so-called SOCIAL SCIENCES (eg economics, sociology, psychology, geography) often claim to be science-based nowadays but are not usually regarded as such by physicists, chemists, and the like.

scientific method   Of course, multitudes of methods are used by scientists. However, the term most commonly refers to a problem-solving approach in which a person identifies a problem (eg some unexplained irregularity among observed events or some possible relationship), develops an HYPOTHESIS that might solve or explain it, and proceeds to carry out observations or perform tests designed so as to allow him either to accept that hypothesis or to reject it in favour of an alternative that more closely accounts for the observations he has made.

score A student's numerical mark or result on a test or examination.

SCOTBEC SCOTTISH BUSINESS EDUCATION COUNCIL.

SCOTEC SCOTTISH TECHNICAL EDUCATION COUNCIL.

Scottish Business Education Council (SCOTBEC) The Scottish counterpart of BUSINESS EDUCATION COUNCIL.

Scottish Certificate of Education (SCE) The Scottish equivalent of GCE, with one examining board catering for eligible pupils and students throughout Scotland. The O GRADE is taken at the end of the fourth year in SECONDARY SCHOOL (age 16-plus) and the H GRADE one or two years later (particularly by pupils seeking entry to HIGHER EDUCATION). Since 1968, a CERTIFICATE OF SIXTH YEAR STUDIES has been available, in Scotland only, for pupils after H grade. There is no equivalent of the CSE for less academic pupils at 16-plus. The DUNNING REPORT 1977 recommended a new examination system to cater for all Scottish pupils at 16-plus.

Scottish Certificate of Education Examining Board Responsible for the examinations for the SCOTTISH CERTIFICATE OF EDUCATION, and for the CERTIFICATE OF SIXTH YEAR STUDIES, in SECONDARY SCHOOLS and institutions of FURTHER EDUCATION throughout Scotland.

Scottish Council for Research in Education (SCRE) Scottish equivalent of the NATIONAL FOUNDATION FOR EDUCATIONAL RESEARCH.

Scottish Education Department UK Government department through which the SECRETARY OF STATE FOR SCOTLAND controls education in Scotland (apart from that in universities which come under the UK UNIVERSITY GRANTS COMMISSION). The Scottish education system is not only separately controlled but is also different in several respects from that of England and Wales.

Scottish Leaving Certificate The name used between 1951 and 1961 for what is now the SCOTTISH CERTIFICATE OF EDUCATION. (The name was changed to mark the fact that the examinations

271

were now open to students from FURTHER EDUCATION institutions, and others, as well as to school-leavers.)

Scottish pupil profile   A form of PROFILE in which teachers describe the achievements and qualities, such as conscientiousness, perseverance and confidence, of a pupil leaving school. The scheme has been experimented with recently in the hope that it may help the school-leaver find employment and may be useful in the absence of a PUBLIC EXAMINATION like the CSE in which the majority of children might obtain EXTERNAL ASSESSMENT.

Scottish Teachers' Salaries Committee   The body responsible for negotiating the salaries of full-time teachers employed by LOCAL EDUCATION AUTHORITIES in Scotland. Equivalent to BURNHAM COMMITTEE(s) in England and Wales.

Scottish Technical Education Council (SCOTEC)   The Scottish counterpart of TECHNICIAN EDUCATION COUNCIL.

scout   At Oxford University, a college servant.

SCR   See SENIOR COMMON ROOM.

Scottish Union of Students (SUS)   Founded in 1888 for the benefit of university students, but admitting college students from 1945, the SUS fulfils a similar role to that of the NUS in England and Wales.

scrambled book   A PROGRAMMED TEXT in BRANCHING form, requiring the reader to turn backwards and forwards through the pages according to which of the answers he chooses in response to each of a number of occasional MULTIPLE-CHOICE QUESTIONS.

SCRE   See SCOTTISH COUNCIL FOR RESEARCH IN EDUCATION.

screening   Any process for identifying or selecting people (eg on the basis of background, experience, abilities, learning difficulties, etc) in order perhaps to provide special educational facilities or job opportunities.

script   **1** Handwriting, as distinct from print. **2** The answer paper written by a student in an EXAMINATION. **3** A document containing words to be spoken and technical directions to be followed in producing audio- or AUDIO-VISUAL MATERIALS.

SDS   (US) See STUDENTS FOR A DEMOCRATIC SOCIETY.

search committee   A group of people given the responsibility of searching out suitable candidates for a senior appointment.

Search, Preston W   (1853–1932) A US pioneer of INDIVIDUAL-ISED INSTRUCTION who advocated that, except in areas like music and physical education, each pupil should be enabled to work by himself at his own rate. He first experimented with his 'individual-study plan' in the teaching of book-keeping in 1877 but developed it further as the 'Pueblo Plan' at Pueblo in Colorado which, in turn, helped generate the WINNETKA PLAN and the DALTON PLAN. Search's general (PROGRESSIVE) educational ideas are expressed in his *An Ideal School* (1901).

seat of learning Facetious (or somewhat pompous) reference to an educational institution.

secondary education Full-time EDUCATION provided in SECONDARY SCHOOLS, usually for pupils between the ages of 11 or 12 and 18-plus years.

secondary modern school See MODERN SCHOOL.

secondary re-organisation (UK) The process of re-organising SECONDARY GRAMMAR, MODERN or TECHNICAL SCHOOLS into COMPREHENSIVES that has been in motion (at varying speeds) since the DEPARTMENT OF EDUCATION AND SCIENCE issued CIRCULAR 10/65 in 1965 (and before then in some areas). More than 90% of all MAINTAINED SCHOOLS in England and Wales are now (1981) comprehensive.

secondary school Any school whose pupils are aged between 11 and 19 years. In the UK, such schools mostly draw their pupils from PRIMARY SCHOOLS or, in some areas, from MIDDLE SCHOOLS; though INDEPENDENT (fee-paying) secondary schools may draw theirs from PREPARATORY SCHOOLS. (In Scotland, secondary school pupils begin at 12-plus.)

secondary school leaving certificate (US) Same as HIGH SCHOOL DEGREE (DIPLOMA).

secondary sources In research, secondary sources are those that purport to give information about a PRIMARY SOURCE. Thus, a drawing or prose account of a particular school building would be a secondary source while the building itself would be a primary source. Generally speaking, secondary sources must be regarded as fallible.

second-chance education That provided by any institution offering, say, MATURE STUDENTS an opportunity to study (and gain qualifications) that they were unable to enjoy at an earlier (more usual) age because of, eg, economic or social pressures. The OPEN UNIVERSITY is often cited as an example, but much ADULT EDUCATION is of this kind.

second degree See HIGHER DEGREE.

second master/mistress Term sometimes used of the DEPUTY

HEADTEACHER in UK INDEPENDENT SCHOOLS or, confusingly, for the teacher third in status (after the head and deputy, but paid on the deputy head salary scale) in large MAINTAINED SECONDARY SCHOOLS.

secondment Taking up a temporary post or assignment away from one's normal work-place, and possibly with another employer, with a view to returning to that place subsequently.

second-order discipline (or **study**) A DISCIPLINE that depends for its subject matter on the prior existence of some other discipline, eg sociology of education, or history of science.

secretarial college Commercially-operated institution offering courses in shorthand, typing, and other secretarial and office skills.

secretariat Term often used in international organisations like UNESCO or COUNCIL OF EUROPE for the group of administrators (together with supporting secretarial and clerical staff) who service the various policy-making groups and implement their decisions.

secretary A title that can be used by a wide range of people: from the man or woman who types and files and answers the telephone for someone, to the chief administrator of a university or a senior government minister (and, confusingly, one or more of the senior civil servants who administer his department).

Secretary of State for Scotland UK Government minister responsible for Scottish affairs, including the control of education in Scotland (except for the universities) through the SCOTTISH EDUCATION DEPARTMENT. His powers and responsibilities, and those of his Minister of State, are similar to those of the SECRETARY OF STATE FOR EDUCATION AND SCIENCE in England, but wider than those of the SECRETARY OF STATE FOR WALES.

Secretary of State for Wales UK Government minister responsible for PRIMARY and SECONDARY EDUCATION in Wales through the WELSH OFFICE in Cardiff.

Secretary of Education (US) Cabinet-level head of the DEPARTMENT OF EDUCATION which discharges federal responsibilities in US education.

Secretary of State for Education and Science Senior UK Government minister responsible for education in England and (post-secondary only) in Wales through the operations of the DEPARTMENT OF EDUCATION AND SCIENCE. (He is also responsible, aided by a Minister of State and two Parliamentary Under-Secretaries of State, for science and libraries.)

'Section 12' Notice A public notice, served under Section 12 of the UK EDUCATION ACT 1980, to the effect that a LOCAL EDU-CATION AUTHORITY intends to cease maintaining a particular school, or to enlarge it or amalgamate it with another, or to change its character. Two months are allowed for the public to register protests. Similar provisions were made in the EDUCATION ACT 1944 (in section 13).

secular trend Statistical term (used in analysis of TIME SERIES data) referring to an upward or downward movement in the periodically measured VALUES of some VARIABLE (eg the number of entrants to higher education) that has persisted over a considerable period of time. (Contrasts with seasonal and other short-term variations.)

SED SCOTTISH EDUCATION DEPARTMENT.

seed funding Funds provided to initiate a project in the expectation that subsequent funding will be generated by the project or come from some other source. Similar to PUMP-PRIMING.

seen examination EXAMINATION for which students are allowed to see the questions (and so begin to consider possible answers) some days before the date of the examination.

segregated school Any school that is not open to all children of the relevant age-range segregates to some extent (by setting some children apart from others), but the term is usually used only of schools that exclude pupils on the grounds of race or religion. SINGLE-SEX schools may also be so called.

selection procedures Most institutions of POST-SECONDARY education have means of choosing which applicants to accept and reject. They may set their own EXAMINATIONS or rely on public examinations like GCE or SCE and may or may not interview applicants. (The OPEN UNIVERSITY is unusual in being open to all on a 'first come, first served' basis). In PRIMARY and SECONDARY EDUCATION, however, except in those areas where GRAMMAR SCHOOLS still survive, UK MAINTAINED SCHOOLS do not select pupils on the basis of ability or aptitude; but certain VOLUNTARY SCHOOLS may give preference to pupils of particular religious denominations. INDEPENDENT SCHOOLS usually operate selection procedures, involving tests (eg 'COMMON ENTRANCE') and interviews.

selective perception Psychological term for the process by which a person pays attention to only a limited number of the many STIMULI or messages that may be presented to him at any one time. (Often this involves disregarding messages that are threatening, unwelcome, or do not fit in with his pre-conceived ideas.)

selective school   Any school that admits only pupils it believes to have high academic ability, eg the UK GRAMMAR and INDEPENDENT SCHOOLS. Entrance to grammar schools required an acceptable score in the ELEVEN-PLUS TESTS and independent schools may require an acceptable performance on the COMMON ENTRANCE EXAMINATION.

self actualisation   The ultimate stage in the HIERARCHY OF NEEDS postulated by MASLOW – the need to become everything that one feels capable of becoming in order to be at peace with oneself.

self-assessment questions   Questions that enable a student to test his own learning. May be given to students on a course or may appear at intervals in a TEXTBOOK or SELF-INSTRUCTIONAL MATERIALS.

self-concept   How a person sees himself (eg competent, amusing, homely, etc). This may differ from other people's views of him though it will have been influenced by them.

self-discipline   Logically, this can only mean a person's controlling his own behaviour (as opposed to being either uncontrolled or else subject to external control). In practice, people often use it only if the behaviour so controlled is such as they would approve of.

self-esteem   How a person judges and values himself. People who have little self-esteem are likely to be depressed and apathetic, while those who have a great deal may be bumptious and unsympathetic to others.

self-expression   The expression and extension of one's personality, often held to be one of the aims of art education, educational DRAMA, CREATIVE WRITING, etc.

self-fulfilling prophecy   Defined by US sociologist, Robert Merton, as a false belief, the expression of which starts off a chain of events that makes the initial belief come true. For example, if a teacher believes his pupils are delinquent and constantly acts towards them as if they were, they may well become considerably more delinquent than they ever were or would have been. (See PYGMALION EFFECT.)

self-help group   A group of people banding together to provide for themselves some service for which they might normally have looked to an outside specialist. For example a group of students might get together to help each other in the absence of a tutor.

self-image See SELF-CONCEPT.

self-instruction Process whereby students teach themselves using PROGRAMMED LEARNING or other SELF-INSTRUCTIONAL MATERIALS or RESOURCE-BASED LEARNING, working towards fairly explicit objectives, without direct help from a teacher.

self-instructional course A course that is based on the use of SELF-INSTRUCTIONAL MATERIALS. (If face-to-face teaching or discussion with other students is also available, this will account for a small fraction of the total study time and may be regarded as non-essential to success in the course.)

self-instructional device Any machine used to present a student with SELF-INSTRUCTIONAL MATERIALS, eg a TEACHING MACHINE.

self-instructional materials Teaching materials structured in such a way (eg written exposition interspersed with SELF-ASSESSMENT QUESTIONS) that the student can be expected to acquire from them certain fairly predictable understandings and/or skills, without direct help from a teacher, eg PROGRAMMED TEXTS. See also SELF-STUDY MATERIALS.

self-instructional package A set of integrated SELF-INSTRUCTIONAL MATERIALS (books, tapes, films, specimens etc) perhaps forming a course, or a MODULE within a course, from which the student can learn without direct help from a teacher.

self-instructional text A book embodying the principles of self-instruction, eg a PROGRAMMED TEXT.

self-paced Referring to materials, learning, courses etc where the student is free to learn at his own pace. That is, the speed of presentation of learning materials is not decided by a teacher, a machine, or other students in a group, eg as in INDEPENDENT LEARNING.

self-presentation The way in which a person consciously or unconsciously presents other people with a view of himself that he would like them to adopt as theirs.

self-social distance rating The extent to which a person accepts or rejects the group in a SOCIOMETRIC SURVEY.

self-study materials Learning materials designed for use by students, without help from a teacher. The term could include SELF-INSTRUCTIONAL MATERIALS, but might also be used of materials whose authors were not so concerned to guide students towards particular pre-specified LEARNING OUTCOMES, eg textbooks and television programmes.

self-teaching materials The term might be used either of SELF-INSTRUCTIONAL MATERIALS or of SELF-STUDY MATERIALS as defined above.

self-teaching package See SELF-INSTRUCTIONAL PACKAGE.

semantic cue See THEMATIC PROMPT.

semantic differential A technique of ATTITUDE measurement developed by US psychologist, OSGOOD. A person is asked to rate any given concepts (eg loyalty, myself, work) on several seven-point scales whose extremes are marked by any bi-polar adjectives such as good-bad, fast-slow, boring-exciting, etc.

semantics The study of meaning in words and symbols.

semester (US) Half of the ACADEMIC YEAR (the normal duration of a course) lasting between 15 and 18 weeks.

semi-interquartile range or **quartile deviation** A statistical measure of VARIABILITY; it is half the distance between the 25th and 75th PERCENTILES (that is, the first and third quartiles in a FREQUENCY DISTRIBUTION). It is often used in association with the MEDIAN.

seminar (From Latin 'SEMEN', seed.) **1** A small group-discussion session, usually based on an essay or paper that has been presented orally to the group. **2** The group of students who meet regularly with a tutor for such discussions. **3** A short course consisting of a number of seminar sessions, allowing considerable student-participation.

seminary **1** Theological institution providing training for would-be priests (especially of the Roman Catholic Church). **2** Term once used of some private secondary schools for girls.

semiology Alternative term for SEMIOTICS.

semiotics The study of signs and symbols, especially the relationship between written and spoken signs (words, phrases, utterances) and whatever it is they stand for in the physical world or in the world of abstract ideas.

senate The academic governing body in many colleges and universities, usually composed of senior members of the academic staff, and usually subordinate to a COUNCIL or BOARD OF REGENTS (US) on matters of corporate policy and finances.

send down See SENT DOWN.

senior (US) A student in his SENIOR (final) YEAR.

senior college (US) That division of a college whose students span the last two years (junior and senior) of a FOUR-YEAR COLLEGE course, some perhaps having transferred there from the first two years in a JUNIOR COLLEGE.

senior combination room See SENIOR COMMON ROOM.

senior common room (**SCR**) Also called senior combination room. The room(s) used for relaxation and informal gatherings by academic staff of an educational institution or, by extension, the staff-members themselves.

senior high school (US) A HIGH SCHOOL for pupils in GRADES 9 or 10 to 12. (That is, from the age of 15 or 16 to 18.) (JUNIOR HIGH SCHOOL caters for grades 7, 8 and perhaps 9.)

senior lecturer A UK academic rank that, in most colleges of further and higher education, is higher than LECTURER but not so high as PRINCIPAL LECTURER. In universities, senior lecturers enjoy slightly lower status (but not salary) than READERS, and less, of course, than PROFESSORS. But they are roughly equivalent to ASSOCIATE PROFESSORS in the US.

senior master/mistress Term used pretty much as SECOND MASTER/MISTRESS.

senior secondary school Type of SELECTIVE Scottish SECONDARY SCHOOL providing courses to SCE O GRADE and above. Most, if not all, pupils are selected at 12-plus. Equivalent to GRAMMAR SCHOOLS in England and Wales.

senior teacher A salary grade in UK schools between those of assistant teacher and the DEPUTY HEAD salary scale. Up to four senior teacher posts are permissible in the largest SECONDARY SCHOOLS.

senior year (US) The final year at HIGH SCHOOL, college or university. (See FRESHMAN, SOPHOMORE, and JUNIOR.)

sense modalities The SENSES.

senses, the **1** The so-called 'five senses' through which humans perceive the external world – sight, hearing, smell, taste and touch – plus the KINAESTHETIC PERCEPTION of movement, weight, resistance, muscle tension and bodily position, which is usually regarded as a sixth sense. **2** The term may also be applied quite differently, eg in 'artistic sense', 'moral sense', etc, indicating that a person demonstrates a certain set of attitudes and behaviours. 'Sensibility' might be the more appropriate term.

sense modality Any one of the SENSES.

sensitivity training A form of group training in social skills in which the emphasis is on understanding the personal interactions within the group so that individuals can learn to see how others see them and predict the consequences of their own behaviour in the group.

sensori (or **sensory**) **motor stage** Postulated by PIAGET as the first stage in a child's COGNITIVE DEVELOPMENT, it covers roughly the first two years of life and is concerned with the child developing SCHEMATA that will coordinate his sensory perceptions with his actions. It culminates with the child becoming capable of imagining the consequences of his actions before acting, indicating a developing awareness of cause-and-effect relationships.

sensory Of or relating to the SENSES, eg 'sensory input' – external events or situations of which a person becomes aware through sight, smell, touch etc.

sensory deprivation A technique developed in psychological studies of PERCEPTION (and used to disturbing effect in BRAIN-WASHING and interrogation) where a person is prevented for a sustained period from receiving any stimulation through the SENSES.

sensory receptors The nerves that receive the STIMULI to be interpreted by the SENSES.

sent down A student 'sent down' from a university is expelled – usually for academic failure or grave disciplinary offences.

sentence completion A technique used in some QUESTIONNAIRES or PSYCHOLOGICAL TESTS whereby a person is invited to complete sentences in his own words (eg, 'The most unsatisfactory thing about this dictionary is . . . . . .'). Such open-ended questions have the advantages of PROJECTIVE TECHNIQUES.

sentence method An approach to the teaching of reading in which children are required to respond in the first instance to whole sentences, rather than to the separate words (LOOK AND SAY METHOD) or to the separate sounds within a word (PHONIC METHOD).

serialist approach/method/strategy A LEARNING STYLE or strategy for problem-solving in which the person tends to tackle a problem or topic of study in small sections at a time and only later joins the sections together to make a complete picture. (Contrasts with HOLIST APPROACH.)

280

serials LITERATURE published at regular intervals, eg journals and YEARBOOKS.

Sesame Street (US) A series of daily hour-length television programmes for pre-school children (especially those presumed to be DISADVANTAGED), using all the techniques of commercial television (film, puppets, sketches, games, cartoons, etc) to teach basic NUMBER and LITERACY skills and help prepare children for life in school.

set 1 More fully, MENTAL SET, PSYCHOLOGICAL SET or RESPONSE SET. A person's disposition to respond in a certain way to a particular problem or type of problem. It may be temporary or relatively permanent, susceptible to modification or relatively fixed. If it is both inappropriate to the problem and relatively fixed, the person will not obtain very satisfactory results. 2 See SETTING.

set books REQUIRED READING for a course.

setting Putting pupils from one CLASS with pupils from other classes so as to make up a number of groups (SETS) for certain subjects (especially mathematics or languages). Each set will cater for pupils of a different level of ability in that subject. Thus, a particular pupil may be in the top set for mathematics and the bottom set for French. It is like STREAMING but within a class.

'Seven Sisters' (US) Prestigious female equivalent of the Ivy LEAGUE colleges; namely Barnard, Bryn Mawr, Mount Holyoke, Radcliffe, Smith, Vassar and Wellesley. (Some of these colleges have now gone, or are going, CO-EDUCATIONAL.)

severely handicapped Term often used of children with disabilities severe enough to prevent their being educated in normal classes.

severely subnormal (SSN) Referring to people of very low intellectual ability who will be educated in SPECIAL SCHOOLS (formerly JUNIOR TRAINING CENTRES.)

sex education Education concerned to develop children's understanding not simply of the mechanics of sex (anatomy, physiology, birth-control, child-bearing, etc) but also of the human and moral issues involved in sexual relationships.

sexism Treating one sex (usually the female) as if its members were inherently inferior to one's own. This is seen in much sexual discrimination (eg in employment) within society. It is also seen in many school books in which girls and women are ignored or patronised or depicted as being involved in trivial and unexciting activities. This may encourage undesirable SEX-TYPING. Sexism is akin to RACISM.

sex-typing The process by which children take on (or that by which they are *made* to take on) the distinctive attitudes and behaviours expected of males and females (eg boys playing 'rough games' and girls playing with dolls).

Sheldon, Edward Austin (1823–1897) US educator who first operated a RAGGED SCHOOL and then organised the PUBLIC SCHOOLS and state NORMAL SCHOOLS in OSWEGO, New York, where he pioneered the influential but controversial method of OBJECT-TEACHING.

Shop (US) Vocationally-oriented technical subject in school CURRICULUM, eg metalwork, printing, electronics. (That is, a 'workshop' subject.)

shortage subjects SUBJECTS in the school CURRICULUM for which it is difficult to find sufficient numbers of qualified teachers, eg mathematics and science are usually 'shortage subjects', especially in girls' schools.

shorthand Any system for making a written record of a spoken message that is faster than writing down the literal equivalents of the spoken words. It uses abbreviations and special signs instead.

short list From among a number of candidates (eg for a job), the few most likely-looking are chosen and 'short-listed'; they are then probably invited to attend an INTERVIEW at which the most outstanding candidate may be chosen.

short term memory See IMMEDIATE MEMORY SPAN.

'show and tell' See 'NEWS'.

sibling A person's brother or sister.

sight method Can be used of the LOOK AND SAY or SENTENCE METHOD in teaching reading.

sight vocabulary The words a person can recognise and read without having to 'build' them using PHONIC skills.

significance In statistics, the results of an experiment or survey are called significant if they are unlikely to have happened by chance. Usually the odds have to be at least 20 to 1 and preferably 100 to 1 against pure chance for significance to be claimed. Researchers apply standard 'significance tests' to determine the SIGNIFICANCE LEVEL. But notice that 'significant' (in the statistical sense) does not mean 'big' and certainly not 'important'.

significance levels In statistics, the odds against a certain result having occurred by chance alone. Two levels of SIGNIFICANCE are commonly used: the 5% (or 0.05) level – where the odds are 20 to 1 against the result being due to pure chance; and the more stringent 1% (or 0.01) level – where the odds are 100 to 1 against.

significant See SIGNIFICANCE.

significant others People by whom one is influenced (consciously or unconsciously), especially in the formation of one's SELF-CONCEPT. Parents, teachers and friends are likely to be significant others to a child in school.

signing Communicating by means of a SIGN LANGUAGE.

sign language Any agreed system for communicating by means of manual signs and gestures, eg as used by deaf people.

simulation A specially arranged representation (or MODEL) of some real-life environment or situation (perhaps physical, perhaps involving interactions between people) that allows the learner to obtain safe and controlled experience in dealing with problems that might occur only infrequently, haphazardly, or dangerously in the real situation. See GAME and SIMULATOR.

simulation game See GAME.

simulator A device constructed to give safe and effective practice in handling a machine or piece of equipment in a way that would be impossible, dangerous or costly with the equipment itself. For example, aircraft pilots learn emergency and other procedures using a flight-simulator without leaving the ground.

'sin-bin' See SPECIAL UNITS.

single concept film Usually an 8mm film dealing with a single concept that can be illustrated, usually without sound commentary, in four minutes or less, and presented in a CASSETTE as a continuous loop that begins again from the beginning as soon as it reaches the end.

single honours degree Honours DEGREE resulting from intensive study of a single subject.

sinistrality Preference for using the left hand (or foot, eye, ear, etc) rather than the right. Special case of LATERALITY. Contrasts with DEXTRALITY.

sit (an examination) To 'take' or 'go in for' an examination.

sit-in A form of protest in which buildings are occupied by a group of people (eg students) who wish to draw attention to their cause by bringing the normal activities of the building to a stop (or, alternatively, continuing such activities when the authorities would wish them to cease).

'sitting next to Nelly' Somewhat derisory training term for the 'method' by which new employees are left to pick up the knowledge and skills needed in their job by watching it performed by someone more experienced. It can be effective, of course, if 'Nelly' knows how to explain her actions and cares enough to do so.

situated Term used by sociologists to remind themselves that, no matter how narrowly they focus on a particular social activity for analysis, that activity remains influenced by outside forces from the wider sphere in which it is situated. Therefore, they refer, eg, to 'situated activities'.

situational ethics The view that a moral judgment may have validity in one particular context (eg 20th century England) without necessarily being valid in another context (eg 19th century Japan).

S I units See INTERNATIONAL SYSTEM.

sixth form The most senior class in a UK SECONDARY SCHOOL, whose students are aged 16 or more (equivalent to US GRADES 11 and 12). They may be following one, two or three year courses, usually in far fewer subjects than in previous classes. Some will be re-taking GCE O LEVEL examinations; some will be taking the CERTIFICATE OF EXTENDED EDUCATION; some will taking the ADVANCED LEVEL GCE (especially those intending to go on to HIGHER EDUCATION). In Scotland, sixth form students will be taking the CERTIFICATE OF SIXTH YEAR STUDIES.

sixth form college UK junior college that takes students of 16-plus from several COMPREHENSIVE SCHOOLS in a particular LOCAL EDUCATION AUTHORITY and so is able to offer a wider range of staff, facilities and courses than any one of those schools could do individually if it ran its own SIXTH FORM.

sixth former A student in a SIXTH FORM.

sizar An UNDERGRADUATE at Cambridge University or Trinity College, Dublin, who receives financial assistance from his college. At one time this was in return for certain college duties which are now done by college servants. The poet, Milton, was a sizar at Christ's College, Cambridge.

skew In statistics, a FREQUENCY DISTRIBUTION is said to be skewed if more OBSERVATIONS have been recorded towards one end of its range of VALUES rather than the other. This makes the graph of the distribution unsymmetrical, and pulls the MEAN away from the MEDIAN.

skill A physical, mental or social ability that is learned through practice, repetition and reflection; and in which it is probably always possible for the individual to improve.

skill acquisition curve See LEARNING CURVE.

skill centres Centres for INDUSTRIAL TRAINING in the UK, formerly known as Government Training Centres, and operating under the TRAINING SERVICES DIVISION to provide government-supported training and re-training schemes, especially for people who are unemployed.

skill-model Any person (not necessarily a trained teacher) who possesses a certain KNOWLEDGE or SKILL (eg anything from vegetable-growing to vehicle repair) and is able and willing to demonstrate it to would-be learners (who might themselves model other skills). Such people might be part of a LEARNING NETWORK.

skills-analysis Identification of the physical and mental and social components of a particular kind of skilled performance, probably with a view to providing training for would-be practitioners of those skills.

Skinner, B F (Born 1904) US experimental psychologist, best known to teachers through his work on OPERANT CONDITIONING (especially of rats and pigeons), his BEHAVIOURIST theory of learning, and his advocacy of PROGRAMMED INSTRUCTION and TEACHING MACHINES. See his *Technology of Teaching* (1969) and *About Behaviour* (1974). He has also made controversial excursions into the area of SOCIAL ENGINEERING; see *Walden Two* (1948) and *Beyond Freedom and Dignity* (1970).

Skinner box An experimental environment created by Professor B F SKINNER in which it was possible to give controlled REINFORCEMENT to animals in studying OPERANT CONDITIONING.

Skinnerian programme See LINEAR PROGRAMME.

skip (a grade) (US) A form of ACCELERATED STUDIES whereby a student gets promoted two GRADES above his present one, eg skipping directly from grade 7 to grade 9, leaving out grade 8.

skip (branching) programme A style of PROGRAMMED LEARNING in which a student making an acceptable response to questions on certain FRAMES is allowed to by-pass a number of subsequent frames.

slate A writing tablet much used by children in 19th century schools. It consisted of a sheet of dark grey, smooth-surfaced layered rock. It could be written on with chalk and easily wiped clean for re-use.

sleep-learning The possibility that people might be able to do a considerable amount of ROTE-LEARNING (with the help of AUDIO-TAPES) while asleep has been researched for at least 15 years; but so far without any very convincing results.

S level See S PAPER.

slide A FRAME of film-strip pressed between glass plates a few centimetres square and used to project a picture or diagram for group viewing.

slide projector A device used for projecting a picture using SLIDES.

slide-sequence A specially arranged sequence of SLIDES, probably accompanying a lecture or spoken commentary. If the commentary is recorded on AUDIO-TAPE, the slides may be synchronised with the tape to form a SLIDE-TAPE/TAPE-SLIDE SEQUENCE.

slide-tape sequence See TAPE-SLIDE SEQUENCE.

slow learner A term often used rather loosely of any child whose attainments have always fallen noticeably behind those of other children of the same age, without any implication as to what might be thought to be the cause (eg deprived background, BRAIN DAMAGE, slow MATURATION, lack of MOTIVATION, etc) or whether the child might be enabled to speed up or catch up. Sometimes, however, the term is used to indicate children who are not only expected to remain slow learners but also to be unable ever to learn as much as others. Some people would even restrict the term to pupils who are EDUCATIONALLY SUBNORMAL.

small group discussion (or **teaching**) Form of teaching possible in HIGHER EDUCATION (and SIXTH FORMS) where the student to staff ratio is relatively low, and allowing for intensive interaction among a small group of participants.

social class One of a few RANKED groups of people, each group enjoying differing prestige in society. A person may be seen to belong to one class or another according to such criteria as: occupation, education, wealth, income, family history, LIFE-STYLE and VALUES, etc. See MIDDLE-CLASS, UPPER-CLASS, WORKING-CLASS.

social climate The ethos or prevailing spirit in the social relationships among people in a society or group. For example, the social climate may be authoritarian and repressive or democratic and supportive.

social distance The degree of intimacy one person is willing to allow between himself and another.

social engineering The MANIPULATION of individuals so as to achieve the kind of society favoured by whoever recommends it.

socialisation The process and result of learning the ROLES and BEHAVIOURS expected of one in society (or in PROFESSIONAL and other SUB-CULTURES within it), so that one can become accepted by and interact successfully with other members. It looms large in all education and in professional training, but it is also effected informally in interactions with members of any new social group to which we seek entry.

social learning The learning that results from SOCIALISATION.

social mobility See MOBILITY, SOCIAL.

social orientation The disposition shown by an 'OTHER-DIRECTED' person – one who seems to desire the company and approval of other people and behaves so as to involve himself with them.

social psychology The psychology of the interactions of individuals in groups. Involves such concepts as: ATTITUDES, prejudice, GROUP DYNAMICS, SOCIALISATION, etc.

social sanctions Constraints or punishments with which members of society discipline those of their number who transgress the social NORMS, eg by ridiculing or cold-shouldering them. More subtle and less-defined than formal, legal sanctions.

social role See ROLE.

Social Science Research Council (SSRC) UK body established in 1965 and responsible to the DEPARTMENT OF EDUCATION AND SCIENCE to carry out research in the SOCIAL SCIENCES (including education). It funds research projects and also provides MAINTENANCE GRANTS for POST-GRADUATE research students.

social sciences DISCIPLINES such as economics, sociology, psychology, politics and geography, which study social relationships and institutions. Opinions differ as to how far the term 'sciences' (rather than, say 'studies') is justified as a description of the way such disciplines normally operate.

social self Those aspects of an individual's PERSONALITY that he consciously or unconsciously presents to others in social relationships.

social skills Skills that help a person in making and maintaining relationships with others, eg the ability to communicate his ideas and feelings and to identify the ideas and feelings of others.

social survey   The collecting of information about a social group using SURVEY TECHNIQUES.

social studies   Generally a term used for a school CURRICULUM subject that studies issues in social life (eg inflation, immigration, abortion, vandalism) using some of the concepts and methods of the SOCIAL SCIENCES.

social work   A wide range of activities – some funded by central or local government and some by voluntary agencies – designed to alleviate the difficulties encountered by certain people in society (especially the poor and aged) and to improve the welfare of children.

social worker   A professional person trained to engage in SOCIAL WORK.

Society for Promoting Christian Knowledge (SPCK)   Founded in 1698 to carry out missionary education in the UK and abroad. It sponsored and co-ordinated the CHARITY SCHOOLS that grew up from the beginning of the 18th century (some 2,000 by 1740) and was the main source of school books in the 19th century. It is still a major publisher of religious works translated into many languages and is active in religious education abroad.

Society for the Diffusion of Useful Knowledge   UK organisation established in 1825, inspired by HENRY BROUGHAM, with the object of popularising science and general knowledge by publishing cheap instructional books.

Society of Friends   The official name of the Quakers. See FRIENDS' SCHOOLS.

socio-economic status   A person's status or position within society (or any smaller social group) as determined by SOCIAL CLASS and wealth or income.

sociogram   A diagram that can be drawn as a result of a SOCIOMETRIC SURVEY and showing the social relationships (in terms of expressed affinities and antipathies) among a group of people, eg the pupils in a class. It may indicate which members are most popular, which are ISOLATES, which form cliques, which express preferences that are not reciprocated, and so on.

socio-linguistic codes   Same as BERNSTEIN'S LANGUAGE CODES but with the prefix 'socio' putting stress on the manner in which his two codes reflect and facilitate different social relationships.

With an ELABORATED CODE, speakers are aware of individual differences and have less formalised ROLES. With a RESTRICTED CODE, speakers have communally-defined roles and are less aware of individual differences.

socio-linguistics The study of LANGUAGE in terms of the social relationships it reflects and facilitates.

sociology The study of organisation and relationships within human social groups.

sociology of education SOCIOLOGY applied to educational organisation and relationships.

sociology of knowledge Application of theories and methods from sociology to the understanding of knowledge (its definition, origins, development, and uses) as a product of social relationships. Initiated by MANHEIM's *Essays on the Sociology of Knowledge* (1952), but in recent years dominated by MARXist approaches.

sociomatrix A table used in SOCIOMETRY for indicating, eg, which pupils in a class choose, and are chosen by, certain other pupils in their group. Can be converted into a SOCIOGRAM.

sociometric rating A measure of the relationship between an individual and other members of the group, established by a SOCIOMETRIC SURVEY.

sociometric survey A SURVEY (eg by QUESTIONNAIRE) to identify the relationships (as defined by SOCIOMETRY) among a group of people.

sociometry A technique for measuring social relationships by establishing the affinities (or preferences) and antipathies (or rejections) that people express for one another within a group of colleagues or acquaintances. For instance, each person may be asked which of the other members he would like, dislike or feel indifferent to as a companion in some activities. The results may then be represented in the form of a SOCIOMATRIX or a SOCIOGRAM. The technique was developed by social psychologist, J L Moreno, and has been extensively used in education.

Socrates (470 BC – 399 BC) A Greek philosopher whose beliefs are known only through the writings of PLATO and Xenophon, and who is credited with what is known as SOCRATIC DIALOGUE.

Socratic diaologue (or **method**) A TEACHING METHOD that was used by SOCRATES' teacher, Zeno, and which PLATO reports Socrates having used extensively. It consists of the teacher asking a student a succession of LEADING QUESTIONS about the matter under discussion and aiming to have the student work towards the same understanding as the teacher, chiefly by considering whether he agrees or disagrees with the teacher's statements.

soft money Term used in CURRICULUM DEVELOPMENT and other projects for funds that have come from outside bodies (eg PUMP-PRIMING funds, or SEED MONEY) and that will eventually have to be replaced by HARD MONEY from the budget of the institution in which the project is based.

soft option Any course or subject that is considered, by people expert in more prestigious subjects, to make few demands on students' abilities.

software Originally a term used in the computer world for the programs that are needed in addition to the equipment (the HARDWARE). However, it has been extended to refer also to the tapes, films, etc that are needed with AUDIO-VISUAL AIDS.

somaesthetic Relating to overall body awareness, particularly involving the TACTILE and KINAESTHETIC senses.

somatic Relating to the human body rather than mind.

sophistry A subtle line of argument intended to mislead: it sounds plausible but is actually invalid and leads to untrue conclusions or conclusions that have not been supported by the PREMISES.

sophomore (US) A student in his SOPHOMORE YEAR.

sophomore year (US) The second year of a college or university course. (After the FRESHMAN year but before the JUNIOR or SENIOR YEARS.)

sorority (US) The female students' equivalent of a men's FRATERNITY in college or university.

Southgate group reading tests Reading tests that can be administered to a whole class at once, developed by UK psychologist, Vera Southgate. They involve WORD SELECTION and SENTENCE COMPLETION and cover a range of reading ages between 5 years 9 months and 9 years 7 months.

spaced practice See DISTRIBUTED PRACTICE.

S paper S (special level) examination papers may be taken by some specially-able students at the same time, and in the same subjects, as their ADVANCED LEVELS in GCE. The S papers are more searching and meant to provide institutions of HIGHER EDUCATION with additional information about the quality of applicants (though advanced levels dominate the SELECTION PROCEDURES). Special papers were introduced in 1963 to replace SCHOLARSHIP PAPERS.

spastic A child or adult whose limb muscles remain in a state of spasm or convulsion due to brain damage before or during birth. The form and the extent of the disability varies from one person to another and although children with spasticity usually need to be educated in SPECIAL SCHOOLS, they span the normal range of intelligence.

spatial (reasoning) ability The ability to perceive the relationships between objects occupying space; an ability measured in many INTELLIGENCE TESTS.

SPCK See SOCIETY FOR PROMOTING CHRISTIAN KNOWLEDGE.

Spearman, Charles (1863–1945) English psychologist, best known for his pioneering work on FACTOR ANALYSIS and for his TWO-FACTOR THEORY of INTELLIGENCE. See his *The Abilities of Man* (1927).

special agreement school A type of UK VOLUNTARY SCHOOL (for secondary pupils). A LOCAL EDUCATION AUTHORITY (LEA) was empowered (by special agreement) to pay up to 75% of the building costs, and it now shares the running costs as with an AIDED SCHOOL. The voluntary body appoints the majority of the GOVERNORS; the LEA appoints the remainder, and all of the teachers other than those dealing with RELIGIOUS EDUCATION.

special charter school district (US) A SCHOOL DISTRICT operating on a state charter giving it different (usually greater) powers than those of most school districts.

special degree Similar to a SINGLE HONOURS DEGREE – one taken after intensive study of a single subject.

special education Education meant to meet the needs of children who cannot be educated in ordinary classes; usually those who are mentally or physically handicapped, or who are experiencing unusual learning difficulties and/or are presenting emotional or behaviour problems. Must be provided by LOCAL EDUCATION AUTHORITIES under the terms of the EDUCATION ACT 1944. The main options are these: withdrawing children from ordinary classes to give them individual help; organising special full-time or part-time classes within ordinary schools (see SPECIAL UNITS); sending them to SPECIAL SCHOOLS (which may be day or BOARDING SCHOOLS); or arranging for their tuition in hospitals with special facilities. The prevailing viewpoint in special education (reiterated by the WARNOCK REPORT 1978) is that children should never be placed in special schools unless it really is impossible to meet their needs in ordinary schools.

specialist   (US) Often used of a person who, in the UK, might be called an ADVISER or INSPECTOR.

specialisation   The concentration of studies within a single subject or a narrow range. SECONDARY SCHOOL pupils in England and Wales begin to specialise (eg in ARTS-BASED or in SCIENCE-BASED subjects) much earlier than pupils in other countries (even those in Scotland) and in the SIXTH-FORM years may be studying only two or three closely-related subjects. (See ADVANCED LEVELS for some of the alternative examination patterns that have recently been suggested with a view to avoiding the narrowness of over-specialisation.)

Special level   See SPECIAL PAPER.

special needs   In 1978 the WARNOCK REPORT recommended that the provision of SPECIAL EDUCATION should be based not on defined categories of mental or physical handicap but on the apparent special educational needs of individual children. Thus, special education treatment was to be extended to include children having particular learning difficulties and/or displaying behavioural problems (whether also 'handicapped' or not). The report estimated that one in five children will have such special needs at one time or another; and that one in six will be in need at any one time.

Special place   Under the terms of the EDUCATION ACT OF 1902, UK GRAMMER SCHOOLS were to reserve 25% of their places free for the local children who were most successful in competitive examinations. By 1930, half the places had to be free; and under the EDUCATION ACT 1944 all places had to be free, and available to children who passed the ELEVEN-PLUS examination.

special school   School for children who need special educational help because of some mental or physical handicap or emotional disturbance. There are more than 1600 such schools MAINTAINED by the LOCAL EDUCATION AUTHORITIES in the UK (about one quarter of them being BOARDING SCHOOLS), together with another 110 non-maintained special schools. They are more generously staffed than ordinary schools and aim to provide physiotherapy, speech therapy and a variety of special treatments. See also SPECIAL EDUCATION, SPECIAL NEEDS, SPECIAL UNITS, and WARNOCK REPORT 1978.

special units   Various kinds of units providing part-time or full-time help (usually in very small classes) for pupils with SPECIAL NEEDS whose difficulties are not severe enough that they need be taken away from ordinary schools altogether and sent to

SPECIAL SCHOOLS. Such units may be known by such names as: nurture unit, sanctuary, withdrawal unit, and, sad to say, where the pupils have been disruptive, 'sin bins'.

speech day/prize day Annual occasion in some UK schools featuring a ceremony at which speeches are made by visiting dignitaries (perhaps OLD BOYS/GIRLS) and prizes are given for academic, sporting and other achievements. Similar to US COMMENCEMENT or GRADUATION.

speech reading See LIP READING.

speech therapy Helping individuals overcome defects and disorders of speech.

speech training Teaching pupils to speak clearly and perhaps to use an approved form of pronunciation. Sometimes appears in the CURRICULUM (especially in PREPARATORY SCHOOLS) as ELOCUTION – the learning of voice production, delivery and use of gesture for effective public speaking and recitation.

speed reading See RAPID READING.

speed test The type of test where the interest is in how many ITEMS a student can answer in the limited time available. (Contrasts with a POWER TEST where it will not be lack of time but the difficulty of some of the questions that halts the student.)

Speedwriting The tradename of a form of SHORTHAND in which groups of letters (rather than special squiggles) are used to represent sounds or short common words.

Spencer, Herbert (1820–1903) Prolific English writer on philosophy, biology, sociology, psychology and numerous social topics including education. He vigorously advocated giving science pride of place in the CURRICULUM (at the expense of the CLASSICS). See his *Education: Intellectual, Moral and Physical* (1861).

Spens Report 1938 A UK report on SECONDARY EDUCATION especially concerning those children who were to leave school at the age of 15. The report rejected the idea of COMPREHENSIVE SCHOOLS, advocated the TRIPARTITE SYSTEM (GRAMMAR, TECHNICAL and MODERN secondary schools), and recommended raising the school-leaving age to 16.

spiral curriculum/learning An approach associated with BRUNER and consisting of a series of learning experiences arranged in such a way that the student works through all the main concepts of a subject at an elementary level before spiralling upwards to tackle the same concepts again and again, but at successively more rigorous and sophisticated levels. Sometimes called the CONCENTRIC METHOD.

Spock, Benjamin   (Born 1903) US physician and paediatrician whose theories of child-care (influenced by PSYCHOANALYSIS) have, in turn, influenced the upbringing of generations of children in the US and UK since the publication of his *The Common Sense Book of Baby and Child Care* in 1946.

split half reliability   A measure of the RELIABILITY of a test obtained from the CORRELATION between students' scores on the odd-numbered ITEMS and their scores on the even-numbered items.

split-site campus   Where two or more educational institutions have been amalgamated under a common name, the new institution will have its CAMPUS split between two or more different sites.

SQ3R   Acronym for 'Survey-Question-Read-Recall-Review', often recommended in 'how to study' books as an effective approach to reading for information and understanding.

spree day   (US) Annual day for students to 'let off steam' at college or university. Similar to UK 'RAG' but without any necessary benefit to charities.

Spring term   The term following the Christmas vacation in educational institutions north of the equator. (Some call it 'Lent term').

Sputnik I   The first man-made satellite to orbit the earth, It was launched in 1957 and, since it was Russian, many US politicians and educators bewailed it as evidence that the US was falling behind in the 'space-race' (or in technology generally). As a result, education (as well as space research) benefited from increased funding, and CURRICULUM DEVELOPMENT projects, especially in mathematics and the sciences, proliferated as never before.

S-R   Stands for STIMULUS-RESPONSE and may refer to connections between the two, to theories of learning or cognitive development expressed in terms of stimulus and response, and so on.

SSN   See SEVERELY SUBNORMAL.

staff college   Training and further-education establishment for senior officers in the police or military services.

staff development   Any planned and/or reflected-upon experience (whether or not deliberately conceived of as IN-SERVICE TRAINING) that provides a member of staff (eg a teacher) with new knowledge, skills or attitudes, enabling him to do an existing job more effectively/efficiently or to prepare for a new one. Staff development is much talked of in institutions of HIGHER EDUCATION around the world, but is rarely a high-priority activity.

staff-student ratio   The ratio between the number of teachers and the number of students in an educational establishment. It is the reverse of PUPIL-TEACHER RATIO (or STUDENT-TEACHER RATIO). Generally speaking, the bigger the ratio, the smaller can be the size of classes.

staff turnover   The rate at which teachers leave an educational institution (because of promotion, retirement, ill-health, etc) and are replaced by new ones. High staff turnover may sometimes indicate an unsatisfactory SOCIAL CLIMATE.

stage school   School for children whose parents wish them to prepare for a career in entertainment (especially dancing, singing and acting) while at the same time pursuing a basic school CURRICULUM.

standard book number   See INTERNATIONAL STANDARD BOOK NUMBER.

standard deviation   In statistics, the most used measure of the VARIABILITY among the VALUES of a FREQUENCY DISTRIBUTION. Any given value can be said to be so many 'standard deviations' from the MEAN of the distribution.

standard error   The estimated STANDARD DEVIATION of a SAMPLING DISTRIBUTION, indicating, for example, the VARIABILITY that might be expected among the MEANS or CORRELATION COEFFICIENTS of an infinite number of SAMPLES of a certain size drawn from the same POPULATION. It therefore suggests how near to the population mean (or correlation coefficient, etc) is the figure that is obtained from just one actual sample.

standardised scores (marks)   Scores in a test or examination that have been adjusted (by reference to a given MEAN and STANDARD DEVIATION) so that they can be compared with scores from a different test. See Z-SCORES.

standardised test   A test that has been thoroughly tried out and modified to ensure its VALIDITY and RELIABILITY and for which NORMS have been established (allowing an individual's performance to be compared with that of other people), together with standard procedures for the test's administration.

standards   1 See ACADEMIC STANDARDS. 2 System of school organisation (and assessment) introduced in the UK by the RE-

VISED CODE OF 1862. Children entered Standard I at the age of six years and progressed through one standard per year (being tested at the end of each year on the knowledge and skills laid down as appropriate to each standard) until their final year of ELEMENTARY SCHOOLING in Standard VI. The learning required of children in Standards V and VI increased gradually over the years, allowing for assessment of subjects like history, geography and elementary science as well as the THREE R's; in 1882 a Standard VII was introduced.

standard works   Books that are generally recognised by experts in a particular subject as being reliable and authoritative sources of information on that subject – the kind of books they would refer to regularly and recommend to students.

Stanford-Binet test   The first individually applied INTELLIGENCE TEST to be widely used in the US (in 1916) and, in many subsequent revisions, on both sides of the Atlantic, especially in CHILD GUIDANCE. The test contains both verbal and non-verbal items.

star   A person who is chosen by many others in a SOCIOMETRIC SURVEY.

state board of education   (US) Group of people with responsibility for publicly-funded education within a state.

state board of examinations (or **examiners**) (US) A type of organisation with responsibilities for such activities as: testing in schools; entrance examinations for HIGH SCHOOLS and COLLEGES; examining people who perhaps need to be committed to institutions; and (if also a 'state licensing board') examining applicants requesting certificates to practise a profession, eg teaching.

state board of trustees (or **REGENTS**)   (US) Group of people responsible for managing a STATE UNIVERSITY.

state college   (US) Similar to STATE UNIVERSITY, offering four-year degree courses, but probably little or no POST-GRADUATE DEGREE work.

state of the art review   A survey of the LITERATURE and the latest thinking in any subject-matter area (not necessarily in one of the arts).

State scholarships   Beginning in the 1920s, what was then the BOARD OF EDUCATION in the UK offered scholarships to help successful students from GRANT-AIDED GRAMMAR SCHOOLS to go on to HIGHER EDUCATION. Starting with about 200 such scholarships a year, some 4000 per year were being awarded by 1961 when the scheme was abolished in favour of students obtaining support solely from LOCAL EDUCATION AUTHORITIES.

state schools Strictly speaking, there are no state (-run) schools in the UK. People using the term are most probably referring to the MAINTAINED SCHOOLS, supported out of public funds by the LOCAL EDUCATION AUTHORITIES.

state sector/system (of education) Strictly speaking, there is no state (-run) education in the UK. Rather, responsibility is divided between central government, LOCAL EDUCATION AUTHORITIES and the teaching profession: in the words of the DEPARTMENT OF EDUCATION AND SCIENCE: 'a national system locally administered'. However, people do use the term 'state system' to refer to the system of educational institutions maintained out of public funds raised by rates and taxes.

state textbook commission (US) A group of people responsible for selecting the textbooks to be used in the schools of the state.

state university (US) Any university financed by a state as part of its public educational provision. Contrasts with PRIVATE UNIVERSITIES.

statistically significant See SIGNIFICANCE.

statistical methods Methods of collecting and analysing quantitative data about a limited number of cases (eg a SAMPLE) and using it to make sensible and reliable inferences and decisions about a wider number of cases – ie, the POPULATION.

statistical significance See SIGNIFICANCE.

statistics 1 STATISTICAL METHODS, as used in collecting and analysing quantitative data. 2 Collections of data resulting from above. 3 Certain specially-calculated figures (eg the MEAN and STANDARD DEVIATION) that somehow characterise such a set of data and which can be used in making inferences about the POPULATION from which they came. 4 The CURRICULUM SUBJECT concerned with the theory and practice of 1–3 above.

statutory leaving age Age at which a young person is free to finish his education. See SCHOOL LEAVING AGE.

staying on Term sometimes used of UK students electing to remain at school beyond the STATUTORY LEAVING AGE. About nine per cent of pupils in MAINTAINED SCHOOLS in England and Wales choose to stay on until the age of 18.

Steiner, Rudolf (1861–1925) Austrian philosopher who developed a mystical belief system called anthroposophy and an educational theory to go with it. The Steiner approach to education (or WALDORF METHOD as it is sometimes called, after his early Waldorf School in Stuttgart) is now followed by a number of educational institutions in the UK and Europe and in the US. The Steiner method is based on CO-EDUCATIONAL, MIXED-ABILITY teaching with as much attention paid to the development of feeling and a sense of values as to intellectual development. Specialisation is delayed as long as possible and each child receives a broad education in the arts and sciences (often approached, at least in the earlier years, through fairy tales and myth, art work and EURHYTHMICS). In the later years, children are prepared for PUBLIC EXAMINATIONS and entry to HIGHER EDUCATION.

stem   The part of a MULTIPLE-CHOICE QUESTION that precedes the alternative answers. For example in '2^3: is equal to: (a) 6; (b) 8; (c) 9; (d) 23, the stem is '2^3 is equal to:'.

step-size   A PROGRAMMED LEARNING term referring to the amount (or sometimes the CONCEPTUAL DENSITY) of new learning material that the student is given between opportunities for him to make an ACTIVE RESPONSE and receive KNOWLEDGE OF RESULTS. Generally speaking, step-size is small in LINEAR PROGRAMMES, and large in BRANCHING PROGRAMMES.

stereoscope   A visual aid by means of which a student can view two slightly different photographs of a scene or object photographed in such a way that, when viewed simultaneously through two separate eye pieces, they unite to give a three-dimensional illusion of depth and relief. Useful, for example, in the study of architecture, physical geography, crystallography, etc.

stereotype   An attitude to, or belief about, people or things of a certain category that is probably over-simplified and incorrect but, nevertheless, leads all of us who share that stereotype to expect, for example, all Scandinavians to be blonde-haired and blue-eyed, boys to be more aggressive than girls, all aspects of a certain pupil's work to be good (or bad) and so on. Some stereotypes are resistant to contrary experience (eg see HALO EFFECT).

stereotyped   Referring to habitual attitudes or behaviours that are repeated many times with little or no variation, eg by a particular person in certain kinds of situation or by all members of a certain defined group, like all adult males, or all teachers.

Stern apparatus   Structural materials developed by US educationist, Catherine Stern, to help young children develop an understanding of number and arithmetical operations through fitting wooden blocks, representing various numbers, into boards and cases specially designed to reveal the properties of the numbers and operations thus performed.

stichometry
A method
of setting out
a prose text
in lines that are broken
according to the sense units
so as to indicate
the phrasal rhythms.
(Sometimes seen in reading books for young children.)

stimuli   Plural of STIMULUS.

stimulus   Any object or event that impinges upon the SENSES and causes an organism (eg a human) to react with a RESPONSE (mental or physical). The stimulus may be inside or outside the body and some users of the term would include mental stimuli (eg thoughts).

stimulus discrimination   Distinguishing between (that is, making different responses to) two similar but different STIMULI, such as two different musical notes. The bigger the difference, the easier the discrimination will be.

stimulus generalisation   Reacting to a new STIMULUS with a RESPONSE that one has learned to make to some different but similar stimulus, eg one may believe two musical notes to be the same even though they differ by a quarter tone. The smaller the difference, the more likely will be the generalisation.

stimulus response (SR) theory   Theory of learning proposed by US psychologist, E L THORNDIKE, that views learning as explicable in terms of the formation and strengthening of bonds between STIMULI and RESPONSES.

storefront schools   (US) Informal schools developed in run-down urban areas in the 1960s and aiming chiefly to provide ALTERNATIVE EDUCATION for students alienated by normal schools and, sometimes, for adults. They were often located in former store premises and, while some received public funding, others were financed by political groups or by charities with a commitment to helping organise the poor.

Stott, D H   (Born 1909) UK psychologist who has taught for many years in Ontario, Canada, and is an authority on learning difficulties and the MALADJUSTED CHILD. See his *Studies of Trouble-*

some Children (1966). He also designed the *Stott Programmed Reading Kit* (1962) to teach children PHONIC skills through a series of individual and group games that are largely self-correcting.

strabismus   A weakness of the muscles of the eyeballs such that a person is unable to direct both eyes at the same object and therefore has a 'squint'. Severe cases may necessitate an operation.

strap   A leather strap used in some schools for CORPORAL PUNISHMENT. In Scotland it is referred to as a belt or a tawse.

strategies   Term used by BRUNER and others for the differing techniques or styles that different people use in thinking, learning and remembering.

stratified sample   A sample chosen in such a way that the proportions in the SAMPLE reflect those in the POPULATION. Thus, if a population of 1200 students in a college are thought of as having three strata - 1st year, 2nd year and 3rd year students – and there are 400 in each, a stratified sample of 300 students could have 100 students drawn at RANDOM from each of the three strata.

straw man   A device that may be used by someone to win an argument even though the facts may be against him. What he does is describe his opponent's viewpoint in a distorted form, exaggerating it or weakening it so that (like a man made of straw) it is easy for him to destroy. Uncritical listeners or readers (and even the person himself) may not realise that the opponent's real viewpoint is still unchallenged.

streaming   Equivalent to US TRACKING. A form of school organisation in which the children making up a particular YEAR-GROUP are divided into ranked CLASSES according to some estimate of their differences in general ability. Many teachers, especially of mathematics and languages, claim that a class is easier to teach if its members are fairly similar in ability (whether, high, medium or low) but others believe streaming is pernicious in encouraging social divisiveness and in confirming low aspirations among the children in lower streams. (That is, streaming may act as a SELF-FULFILLING PROPHECY.) When children from within a class join with others from different classes, according to ability, for certain subjects only, the system is known as SETTING. Streaming contrasts with MIXED-ABILITY teaching. See also BANDING.

stream of consciousness   Term originated by psychologist, William JAMES, for the continuous flow of thoughts, images and feelings that form the content of a person's consciousness. Elaborated as a literary technique by such writers as James Joyce to reveal the mental processes of their fictional characters in lengthy passages of soliloquy.

street academics (US) A form of STOREFRONT SCHOOL, often funded by private industrial and commercial firms and staffed by STREET WORKERS and college students.

street worker (US) SOCIAL WORKER in urban areas, particularly concerned to help poor families and DROPOUTS from HIGH SCHOOL.

Strong-Campbell Interest Inventory An INVENTORY of interests and preferences designed to help in OCCUPATIONAL GUIDANCE. Produces a comprehensive PROFILE with the scoring based on comparison with responses made by workers in a great variety of occupations.

structural apparatus (materials) Apparatus, used especially in mathematics teaching, to help children understand concepts and relationships through manipulating physical objects. See COLOUR FACTOR, CUISENAIRE, DIENES, STERN, etc.

structural communication A form of PROGRAMMED LEARNING in which the student reacts to each of a series of lengthy passages of text by choosing a set of responses from several alternatives presented to him and getting individual FEEDBACK according to which particular set of responses he chooses.

structural functionalism A school of sociology, particularly strong in the US, that assumes shared values among people from different groups and levels within society, and asserts that stability and equilibrium are thus to be expected as the norm in society.

structuralism A form of social and literary analysis developed out of the work of the Swiss linguist, de Saussure, and the French social anthropologist, Levi-Strauss. Essentially its interest is in delineating the patterns and structures of meaning that surround the use of language and non-verbal behaviour and symbols within particular social groups, and that tell the analyst much about the way participants structure their experience and how this differs from that of other social groups.

structured interview An INTERVIEW in which the interviewer plans the course of discussion in advance by deciding the sequence of topics to be covered or even the content and wording of the questions he will ask. (These plans may be somewhat frustrated if the interviewee has also decided to structure the interview!)

structured teaching   A term that might be applied, with varying degrees of justification, to any teaching that shows some evidence of planning and is not totally impromptu and *ad hoc*.

student   See PUPIL.

student adviser   (US) Member of staff of school or college who advises students on their educational progress and choice of courses.

student body   The collective term for the students enrolled at an educational institution.

student-centred curriculum   A CURRICULUM, or programme of courses, planned so as to relate to the supposed interests, backgrounds, and LEARNING STYLES of students. See LEARNER-CENTRED APPROACH.

student-centred approach/teaching/education   See LEARNER-CENTRED APPROACH.

student contact hours   See CONTACT TIME.

student council   A group of student representatives making some contribution to policy-making in a school.

student full-time equivalents   See FULL-TIME EQUIVALENTS.

student government   Participation by pupils or students in the policy-making of their educational institutions, eg through membership of a SCHOOL COUNCIL or GOVERNING BODY.

student loans   Loans that may be available to students instead of grants to enable them to pursue studies at college or university and due to be repaid in the first years of subsequent employment. The idea was frowned upon as too heavy a burden on students by the NORWOOD REPORT 1943 but is revived from time to time as a suggested alternative to MAINTENANCE GRANTS.

student mortality   See STUDENT WASTAGE.

student power   Demand for, or achievement of, participation by students in the making of decisions about the curriculum or organisation and policy of an educational institution.

student proctor   A student providing some tuition or ASSESSMENT help to less advanced students, under the guidance of the teacher, eg in the KELLER PLAN.

Students for a Democratic Society (SDS)   (US) A radical student organisation that sprang up during the early 1960s with a vision of the universities as agencies for social change.

students' union   1 The association of students in a particular college, polytechnic or university. **2** The building or rooms available for students' leisure-time activities.

student teacher A student who is learning to teach, ie going through a TEACHER-TRAINING course.

student-teacher ratio Like PUPIL-TEACHER RATIO and reverse of STAFF-STUDENT RATIO.

student teaching (US) Practical teaching experience in school as part of course work for a degree in education.

student trainee A trainee from industry or commerce engaged in FURTHER EDUCATION, eg on BLOCK RELEASE.

student wastage Rate at which students DROP OUT from a college or university course. Also called STUDENT MORTALITY.

study guide Written advice to students on how to approach the study of a particular course or MODULE within it.

study hall (US) Session on the school TIMETABLE when students are expected to engage in PRIVATE STUDY in the school library or in a specially-furnished room which may be known as the 'study hall'.

study methods/skills/techniques Methods used by students in studying: reading; listening critically to lectures; participating in discussions; note-making; writing essays; memorising formulae; revising for examinations; etc. Many educational institutions now give special training in appropriate techniques of study and help their students explore and develop methods appropriate to their own study purposes.

styles of learning See LEARNING STYLE.

styles of teaching See TEACHING STYLE.

subconscious The part of the mind that is outside of a person's normal consciousness but can be brought there by recall of past experience.

sub-culture Sociological term for a CULTURE that exists within the framework of some larger culture, eg we may talk of a WORKING-CLASS sub-culture or of a teenage sub-culture. Members of a sub-culture normally adhere to many of the VALUES and NORMS of the wider culture but probably differ from them in some special respects. When there are several sub-cultures, one usually becomes dominant and imposes its values and norms as the standard for the whole society.

sub-discipline An area of human knowledge and enquiry that clearly lies within some larger more widely-embracing DISCIPLINE but nevertheless has a coherence of its own – its own LEARNED JOURNALS or professional associations or its own space in the curriculum. Thus, physical geography, climatology, economic geography and human geography can all be seen as sub-disciplines within the discipline of geography.

sub-degree course　A course leading to a qualification of lower status than a degree, eg a certificate or diploma course.

subject　**1** An organised body of knowledge, usually an established DISCIPLINE with its own acknowledged place in the educational CURRICULUM, eg geography, physics, mathematics etc. **2** In psychology, the term is also used of a person whose responses are being studied in some kind of research situation.

subject catalogue　A library catalogue in which the books are classified in sequence according to subject.

subject-centred　Relating to an approach to teaching in which the emphasis is on transmitting some content or subject-matter defined by an authority external to the teaching situation, rather than on responding to the individual interests of the student or on negotiating a mutually-agreeable SYLLABUS between teacher and student.

subjective　This adjective is used of the kind of analysis, method, description or judgment in which people are likely to differ because their values, opinions, attitudes, preferences, biases, perceptions, etc are different (and there are no explicit rules to attain consensus). Contrast with OBJECTIVE.

subjective assessment/test　ASSESSMENT in which different but equally qualified assessors could be expected to respond differently in judging the quality and characteristics of a student's work, and so award it differing MARKS or GRADES. Contrasts with OBJECTIVE TESTS.

subject-matter　The content of concepts and principles and METHODOLOGY in a SUBJECT or academic DISCIPLINE.

sublimation　A FREUDian concept involving the gratification of some primitive impulse by channelling it into some more socially acceptable activity. Thus sexual DRIVES may supposedly be sublimated in artistic creativity.

subliminal perception　PERCEPTION of, or unconscious RESPONSE to, a STIMULUS, without awareness of its occurrence.

sub-professionals　As PARAPROFESSIONALS.

subsidiary subject　A subject studied by a student at a lower level or for a shorter period of time than his major or special subject. Similar to US MINOR.

subscription library A lending library run as a profit-making enterprise.

substantive (US) Sometimes used, especially in HIGHER EDUCATION, of an academic DISCIPLINE like, say, geography or economics that has an established subject-matter, to distinguish it from a CURRICULUM activity such as COMPOSITION that is essentially a METHODOLOGY.

subvention A financial grant, aid or subsidy such as might be made by government to an educational institution.

successive approximations Term used in psychology for the teaching technique of providing REINFORCEMENT for each of a series of student BEHAVIOURS or performances that take him progressively nearer (getting more and more polished or perfect, step by step) to some desired ideal performance.

suggestibility A person's readiness to accept the suggestions of another person and act accordingly – either as an aspect of his normal PERSONALITY or under hypnosis.

summa cum laude (US) A Latin tag sometimes added when a DEGREE or other academic QUALIFICATION is awarded 'with the utmost praise'. It is the highest of three such designations for academic performance above average. See also CUM LAUDE and MAGNA CUM LAUDE.

summative assessment ASSESSMENT of a student that is designed to report on his overall or final achievement at the end of some period of learning, eg at the end of SECONDARY EDUCATION. Contrasts with FORMATIVE ASSESSMENT where the emphasis is on using whatever information is gained to help the student improve during his education.

summative evaluation EVALUATION that sums up the effects and effectiveness of some educational project or teaching activity once it is concluded. Contrasts with FORMATIVE EVALUATION which is meant to gather information to help improve the project or activity while it is in progress.

summer camps (US) Educational, social and sporting gatherings attended by many school children in the summer vacation. College and university students often help run them in the role of CAMP COUNSELLORS.

Summerhill UK PROGRESSIVE BOARDING SCHOOL in Suffolk founded in 1921 by A S NEILL. The boys and girls have almost

305

total freedom except where their health, safety or the freedom of others might be at risk. (Attendance at lessons is not compulsory, for instance.) The school is governed democratically after the manner of HOMER LANE's Little Commonwealth, with each student and member of staff having a vote on issues of policy. See Neill's books *That Dreadful School* (1937) and *Summerhill: A Compilation* (1962).

summer institute (or **session**) (US) Courses run during the summer vacation: perhaps special courses of IN-SERVICE TRAINING for teachers; perhaps repeats of courses offered during earlier SEMESTERS, for students who were unable to take them then or who failed; perhaps entirely new courses offered by VISITING PROFESSORS.

summer school Any courses given during the summer vacation, usually in an institution of HIGHER EDUCATION either for its own students or, more likely, for people normally in full-time employment, eg teachers or, in the UK, the students of the OPEN UNIVERSITY. See SUMMER INSTITUTE. In the US, summer schools are often established for students who have failed courses.

summer term 1 The term prior to the summer vacation in educational institutions in the northern hemisphere. 2 (US) Sometimes used to mean SUMMER SESSION.

summer vacation See LONG VACATION.

Sunday schools These schools originated in the UK in the 18th century thanks to pioneers like ROBERT RAIKES. Their rules stated: 'Be diligent in teaching the children to read well .... Neither writing nor arithmetic is to be taught on Sundays'. Reading the Bible and religious tracts and attending church or chapel were the chief activities. The movement was immensely popular and it is estimated that by 1833 one and a half million children were attending Sunday schools in Great Britain. Their great significance lay in fostering the idea of a free ELEMENTARY EDUCATION for all children, and in giving our educational system a religious flavour that lingers still. Present-day Sunday schools are organised by individual churches and usually confine themselves to religious instruction.

Sunrise Semester (US) Since 1963, New York University's College of Arts & Sciences has organised four courses around a series of early morning television programmes, helping thousands of part-time students to obtain college CREDITS.

superintendent (US) 1 The SUPERINTENDENT OF SCHOOLS (equivalent to UK CHIEF EDUCATION OFFICER or DIRECTOR OF

EDUCATION). **2** A school caretaker (janitor), in which case he is called a building superintendent.

superstructure A MARXIST term referring individually or collectively to social agencies, institutions (eg schools) that are autonomous yet remain dependent upon the base of economic relationships.

supervisor **1** Teacher in HIGHER EDUCATION who advises and monitors the work of a RESEARCH STUDENT. **2** A college tutor, or a teacher from within a PRACTICE SCHOOL who is supervising the work of a STUDENT-TEACHER on TEACHING PRACTICE. **3** (US) A school inspector.

supplementary courses (for teachers) After World War II, UK teachers who had already qualified in a two-year teacher-training course could take a specialised 'third year' course, usually at teacher-training college, in certain 'SHORTAGE SUBJECTS' such as mathematics and science, handicrafts and physical education. Such courses tended to disappear in the 1960s after the introduction of a three-year INITIAL TRAINING.

supply teacher A UK teacher who is employed by a LOCAL EDUCATION AUTHORITY, usually on a daily basis, to fill temporary vacancies in schools where, for example, a teacher is absent or has not yet been able to take up an appointment. Similar to US SUBSTITUTE (or RELIEF) TEACHER.

surface level processing Term used in discussion of STUDY SKILLS for the kind of reading done by a student who is engaging with the material at a shallow level, picking out isolated facts and learning them by ROTE rather than penetrating beneath the surface of the text to identify the underlying meaning and relate it to his own ideas and experience. Contrasts with DEEP LEVEL PROCESSING.

survey course (US) A course designed to give a broad panoramic view of some area of culture, eg 'THE RENAISSANCE' or '19th Century literature'.

survey techniques Research methods whereby data is collected from a SAMPLE of people, (usually by such devices as QUESTIONNAIRES and STRUCTURED INTERVIEWS) with a view to making assumptions and/or decisions about some wider POPULATION.

SUS See SCOTTISH UNION OF STUDENTS.

suspension A form of PUNISHMENT in which a pupil or student is told to stay away from school, college or university. Pupils in UK schools can be suspended for a limited period only; the

GOVERNORS need to give their approval; and the parents can appeal. See also EXCLUSION and EXPULSION.

Suzuki method   A method of teaching very young children (from three years) to play musical instruments 'by ear', starting by imitating records and only learning to read musical notation after achieving considerable instrumental proficiency. The method was developed in Japan by Shinichi Suzuki (born 1897), whose string orchestras of very young children were renowned, and who has had a following in musical education in Europe and North America since the mid 1960s.

Swann Report 1966   UK REPORT pointing out that the best-qualified science and engineering graduates tended to remain in the universities rather than entering industry or schools. The report recommended new forms of post-graduate training with practical links between the universities and industry, and new ways in which highly qualified scientists and engineers could be encouraged into educational roles.

Swansea Evaluation Profile   A UK ASSESSMENT procedure for early identification of children likely to have difficulties (and the kind of difficulty) in their INFANT SCHOOLS. Developed as part of a research project in COMPENSATORY EDUCATION.

swot   Informal term for a pupil or student who is thought by his PEERS to devote too much time or interest to studying. (Hence also, the verb 'to swot' means to study 'excessively.')

sylbs and sylfs   A distinction in LEARNING STYLE, made by UK psychologist, Liam Hudson, between students who are 'syllabus-bound' (preferring to be told what to study) and those who are 'syllabus-free' (preferring plenty of choice in the matter).

syllabus   An outline of the topics to be covered in a course (or in a text). Does not usually stipulate the method (or order) of teaching or indicate the LEARNING OBJECTIVES. The term CURRICULUM is sometimes used instead.

syllogism   A term used in logic for a form of DEDUCTION in which two PREMISES or statements lead to an inevitable conclusion. Consider the following: 'All bachelors are single; Bob is a bachelor; therefore Bob is single'. Here, the first statement is called the MAJOR PREMISE, and the second statement is called the MINOR PREMISE. The two together lead us to the conclusion that Bob is single.

symbol   A symbol is any thing, person or event to which a generally agreed meaning has been arbitrarily assigned and which people have learned to accept as representing something other than itself. Thus, words, flags and human gestures are examples of symbols.

symbolic interactionism A form of social analysis which developed at the University of Chicago in the 1930s and enjoyed a resurgence in the 1970s. It provides a distinctive view of individuals, social interaction and social structure: people are seen as active agents in constructing social situations and meanings; social interaction is seen as the dynamic interweavings of the actions of individuals in pursuit of their own goals; and social structure is seen as dynamic and constantly changing. In METHODOLOGY, the symbolic interactionists incline towards NATURALISTIC OBSERVATION with theoretical analysis of situations preceded by non-theoretical 'exploration' or description of how the situation seems to the participants. See Herbert Blumer's *Symbolic Interactionism: Perspective and Method* (1969).

symbolic (mode of) representation See BRUNER'S MODES.

sympathetic circularity An aspect of a RESTRICTED CODE as described by BERNSTEIN, 'sympathetic circularity' is seen in such expressions as 'you know', 'right?', 'like', 'and that', which discourage the person to whom they are addressed from asking for more precise or elaborated statements of the subject being talked about.

symposium (Via Latin from the Greek for 'to drink together'.) **1** A gathering of people hearing and discussing a number of papers on a subject of common interest. **2** A collection of papers, usually forming a publication, that could have been but were not necessarily presented at a symposium in sense **1**. **3** In classical Greece, a drinking party with intellectual discussion.

syncretic reasoning Method of reasoning used by children in the PRE-OPERATIONAL stage: since the child has no organised system of operations for tackling a problem, he takes only one or two aspects of it into account in offering a solution. He may easily have a change of mind and give a different answer based on other aspects of the problem.

syndicate **1** Term used in HIGHER EDUCATION (and especially MANAGEMENT EDUCATION) for each of the groups into which a class may be split, each syndicate having the task of considering a particular topic or engaging in a particular exercise, and reporting back to the full class subsequently. **2** A group of students acting independently of their tutors, as a SELF HELP GROUP.

synectics A type of problem-solving technique, associated with

BRAINSTORMING, that depends on systematic methods of creative thinking, involving analogy, fantasy, the bringing together of ideas and data that are usually separate, and informal conversation among a small group of people with widely different backgrounds and expertise.

syndrome   A term of medical origin, indicating a group of signs or symptoms usually found together and presumed to relate to the same underlying cause.

systematic teaching   Like STRUCTURED TEACHING, this term might be applied, reasonably or otherwise, to any teaching that shows evidence of planning; especially, perhaps, if it has been planned with specific LEARNING OUTCOMES in view and the TEACHING METHODS and MEDIA are chosen and used accordingly.

système international d'unités   See INTERNATIONAL SYSTEM.

systems approach   An approach to the design of teaching and learning systems that was closely identified with EDUCATIONAL TECHNOLOGY in the late 1960s and early 1970s. It drew rather haphazardly upon the concepts and methodologies developed in the 'systems analysis' of business and military organisations and its main emphasis was on the need to decide the desired *outputs* of an educational system (eg OBJECTIVES), as a preliminary to choosing appropriate *inputs* (eg CURRICULUM content, TEACHING METHODS, MEDIA, etc).

T

taboo   One of the many individual restrictions on behaviour accepted by members of a social group as a sign of their acceptance of group NORMS. Thus, in Western society, in different groups, enquiring about another person's earnings, using certain swear-words, expecting to eat in certain restaurants when not wearing a tie (if a man) or when wearing trousers (if a woman) may all be regarded as taboo.

tabula rasa   (From Latin, 'scraped tablet'.) A belief, expressed in the writings of JOHN LOCKE, that the child's mind is like a clean slate upon which knowledge and understanding can be written.

tabulation   The arrangement of statistical data in rows and columns to facilitate comparison and analysis.

tachistoscope A device, used in research on PERCEPTION and MEMORY, that allows for visual images to be displayed for fractions of a second.

tactile diagrams Diagrams on which the lines are raised and/or textured so that a blind learner can 'read' them, with his fingers.

take (an examination) Submit oneself to ASSESSMENT as an examination candidate. (Also described as 'sitting' an examination.)

'take away' examination See SEEN EXAMINATION.

take-up rate The proportion of the people eligible for some advertised benefit (eg an opportunity to enter college) who actually take it up.

'talking book' A book read aloud on AUDIO-TAPE for the use of blind people.

talking heads Derogatory name given to the kind of television programme whose visual content consists almost entirely of people's faces, accompanied by their voices. Supposedly the most boring of formats but this depends, of course, on whose heads are featured and how well they can talk.

talking typewriter A device that teaches reading by enabling a pupil to hear the sound of letters and words as he types them.

tape library A catalogued collection of AUDIO- and/or VIDEO-TAPES.

tape loop A continuous AUDIO-TAPE containing a message that automatically repeats from the beginning as soon as it reaches the end.

tape-recorder Electrical device for the recording (and PLAY-BACK) of sound and/or moving pictures on magnetic tape.

tape-slide sequence A SLIDE SEQUENCE synchronised with an AUDIO TAPE commentary in such a way that the slides in the SLIDE PROJECTOR are changed automatically by signals from the tape.

target population 1 Same as a statistical POPULATION. 2 The group of students for whom a particular course or set of LEARNING MATERIALS is designed.

target sociogram A type of SOCIOGRAM drawn like a target, with concentric circles showing the most popular people at the centre and the least popular ones at the outer edge.

target student A member of the TARGET POPULATION in sense **2** above.

tariff questions (or **paper**) Such questions are used in an examination or test where the candidate can choose to answer a few difficult questions or a larger number of easier ones and is told the maximum mark available for each question.

task analysis The systematic analysis of the demands being made upon a person in performing a particular task, with a view to designing appropriate TRAINING for new people learning that task.

TAT See THEMATIC APPERCEPTION TEST.

taught course A term used particularly at POST-GRADUATE level to distinguish between 'taught courses' in which students receive normal teaching, and RESEARCH COURSES in which they learn by carrying out their own investigations.

tautology A statement that says less than it appears to say at first sight, because the same thing is being said twice in different words, eg 'Not only is he a bachelor; he's not even married'. Frequently, however, the tautologous nature of a statement may emerge only after close critical examination.

tawse A leather strap or belt used to administer CORPORAL PUNISHMENT (usually to the hand) to pupils in Scottish schools.

taxonomy A classification system in which each separate class of items is given a name and contains items that are more like one another than like items in other classes, eg the DEWEY DECIMAL SYSTEM. See also BLOOM'S TAXONOMY.

Taylor Report 1977 UK REPORT on 'the management and government of maintained primary and secondary schools in England and Wales'. It suggested considerable changes including: equal representation in school government for parents, teachers, representatives from the local community and representatives of the LOCAL EDUCATION AUTHORITY; pupil representation; election of members of GOVERNING BODIES; and power for those bodies to establish the school's OBJECTIVES, decide the CURRICULUM and rules of conduct, and to have access to professional guidance from INSPECTORS and ADVISERS. Its proposals are strongly reflected in the provisions of the EDUCATION ACT 1980.

teacher-aides See AIDES.

teacher centres See TEACHERS' CENTRES.

teacher-centred approach/method An approach to teaching in which the teacher teaches whatever content and by whatever methods he feels happiest with, making no attempt to adapt content or methods to individual differences (in needs or LEARN-

ING STYLE) among his pupils. Contrasts with LEARNER-CENTRED APPROACH.

teacher-coordinator (US) A teacher who teaches the technical subject matter and co-ordinates classroom work with ON-THE-JOB TRAINING in a CO-OPERATIVE COURSE.

teacher education This term is wider than TEACHER-TRAINING in that it includes not simply a teacher's VOCATIONAL TRAINING (whether INITIAL, PRE-SERVICE TRAINING or subsequent IN-SERVICE TRAINING) but also whatever general POST-SECONDARY EDUCATION he has that contributes to his growth as a person regardless of his future profession. Thus, teacher education courses include the study of one or more ACADEMIC DISCIPLINES as well as educational subjects and SUPERVISED TEACHING PRACTICE.

teacher fellowship See SCHOOL-TEACHER FELLOWSHIP.

teacher intern See INTERNSHIP.

teacher placement bureau (or **service**) (US) A teachers' employment agency.

teacher-pupil ratio See PUPIL-TEACHER RATIO.

teachers' agency (US) Teachers' employment agency.

teachers' aides See AIDES.

teachers' centres UK centres, financed by LOCAL EDUCATION AUTHORITIES, at which teachers can meet with one another and with ADVISERS to discuss educational issues, develop new TEACHING MATERIALS and engage in IN-SERVICE TRAINING.

teachers' college (US) A college, perhaps part of a university, specialising in TEACHER EDUCATION and/or TRAINING. Same as SCHOOL OF EDUCATION.

teachers' oath Same as LOYALTY OATH.

teacher's pet A pupil believed by his peers to be specially (and perhaps unduly) favoured by their teacher.

Teachers' Registration Council This UK body was set up in 1907 with a view to improving teachers' status and preventing those who were not registered from teaching. However, registration never became compulsory and the Council had little influence on training, qualifications, appointments and promotions compared with that of the Government's BOARD OF EDUCATION (and that of the LOCAL EDUCATION AUTHORITIES). By the 1930s, few new teachers were registering and the Council was closed down in 1949. But see GENERAL TEACHING COUNCIL FOR SCOTLAND.

teacher-student ratio See STAFF-STUDENT RATIO and PUPIL-TEACHER RATIO.

teacher training See TEACHER EDUCATION.

teacher-training college Term used in the UK for COLLEGES OF EDUCATION prior to the mid-1960s.

teacher turnover See STAFF TURNOVER.

teach-in An informal and probably rapidly-arranged conference on a subject of topical interest, usually held on college or university premises, often organised by the students rather than the staff, and involving contributions from a variety of people with differing viewpoints intended to lead to vigorous discussion.

teaching assistant (US) Normally a GRADUATE STUDENT assisting with instruction (eg as a STUDENT PROCTOR in a COLLEGE or UNIVERSITY.

teaching auxiliaries See AIDES.

teaching brother (or SISTER) A member of a religious group (Roman Catholic) who devotes himself (or herself) to teaching.

teaching company scheme Some UK universities and POLYTECHNICS have made arrangements with local firms whereby POST-GRADUATE students, eg in engineering or management, can work on practical problems within these 'teaching companies' (under active guidance from their tutors) to the benefit of student and company alike. (Similar idea to TEACHING HOSPITALS and PRACTICE SCHOOLS.)

teaching fellow The holder of a FELLOWSHIP that involves teaching. Contrasts with RESEARCH FELLOW.

teaching fellowship Post held by TEACHING FELLOW.

teaching hospital A hospital that is associated with a university MEDICAL SCHOOL, providing facilities for students' CLINICAL TRAINING.

teaching/learning unit A PACKAGE of TEACHING MATERIALS and LEARNING MATERIALS, with guidance to teacher and students on how they might be used.

teaching load Same as CONTACT TIME.

teaching machine A mechanical or electrical device for presenting a student with PROGRAMMED LEARNING material, usually in such a way that he must indicate his RESPONSE to each FRAME before being shown the next.

teaching materials This term can apply to any natural or man-made things the teacher might use in communicating with pupils – eg AUDIO-VISUAL AIDS, REALIA, STRUCTURAL APPARATUS, TEXT BOOKS, and so on.

teaching media   The means teachers use in communicating educational messages to (and receiving FEEDBACK from) students, eg face-to-face contact, books, audio-tapes, etc.

teaching methods   The many ways in which teachers can organise their classes, present ideas to their pupils, and use their TEACHING MEDIA so as to advance their pupils' learning. These vary from subject to subject, age-group to age-group, and teacher to teacher.

teaching points   The main ideas a teacher plans to present in a classroom lesson or in self-instructional material.

teaching practice   Part of the professional training of a STUDENT TEACHER in which he spends a period in a school teaching but with some guidance and supervision from college and/or school staff.

teaching seminar   A SEMINAR held with the intention of advancing the knowledge and understanding of the students involved. Contrasts with a RESEARCH SEMINAR.

teaching sister   See TEACHING BROTHER.

teaching style   Usually refers to the ways in which teachers differ in the kinds of relationship they establish with their pupils (eg formal or informal) and the kinds of SOCIAL CLIMATE they establish (eg AUTHORITARIAN or DEMOCRATIC).

teaching system   Same as LEARNING SYSTEM but seen from teachers' viewpoint rather than that of learners.

teaching techniques   See TEACHING METHODS.

team teaching   An arrangement whereby a group of teachers co-operate so that their classes have contact with more than one of those teachers during a given learning session or PERIOD. For example, the teacher with most knowledge of, or interest in, each particular topic in a course might introduce it to all the classes together and then join with his colleagues in pursuing follow-up work with individual pupils and small groups.

technical college   A FURTHER EDUCATION institution maintained by LOCAL EDUCATION AUTHORITIES and providing a mainly VOCATIONAL EDUCATION (chiefly technical and commercial subjects) for students over the age of 16.

technical drawing   A subject in the SECONDARY SCHOOL CUR-

RICULUM (now often part of a TECHNOLOGY course) in which the student learns to make accurate scale drawings of objects (eg machines or components) from which dimensions could be taken in order to manufacture those objects.

technical education   Largely VOCATIONAL EDUCATION in technical subjects (eg building, engineering, agriculture, etc) especially for people planning to pursue careers in skilled crafts or as TECHNICIANS or TECHNOLOGISTS.

technical high (or **secondary**) **school**   School with a strong emphasis on TECHNICAL EDUCATION. In the UK, technical schools have waxed and waned in popularity over the years since they were introduced after the EDUCATION ACT OF 1870. They were recommended by the SPENS and NORWOOD REPORTS and became part of the TRIPARTITE SYSTEM after the EDUCATION ACT OF 1944, but were phased out following CIRCULAR 10/65 in 1965.

technical institute   (US) A POST-SECONDARY institution offering two or three year courses of VOCATIONAL EDUCATION directed towards technical careers.

Technical Instruction Act 1899   UK legislation that empowered local authorities to levy a local rate to finance TECHNICAL EDUCATION, which led to the establishment of TECHNICAL COLLEGES.

technical school   See TECHNICAL HIGH SCHOOL.

technician   **1** In general, a person who applies more complex knowledge and skills than a craftsman (or woman) but within a more routine or standardised situation, and with less need for flair or originality, than a TECHNOLOGIST. **2** In educational institutions, 'technician' is the job-title of people whose role is to prepare and maintain equipment and materials in workshops and laboratories. (Though very often, especially in university research laboratories, senior technicians need to be TECHNOLOGISTS.)

Technician Education Council (**TEC**)   UK body established in 1973 by the SECRETARY OF STATE FOR EDUCATION AND SCIENCE to rationalise the education of TECHNICIANS in England and Wales. This it does (like the BUSINESS EDUCATION COUNCIL in the commercial field) by advising/approving suitable courses, establishing and assessing standards of performance and awarding certificates and diplomas to successful students. It has a Scottish counterpart: the SCOTTISH TECHNICAL EDUCATION COUNCIL (SCOTEC).

technological forecasting Attempts to predict changes in technology (tools and techniques, etc) and their likely implications for society in general and for particular organisations and their concerns.

technological university One with a strong bias towards research and teaching in the applied sciences and technologies. Such universities in the UK are based on what were the COLLEGES OF ADVANCED TECHNOLOGY (ie Aston, Bath, Bradford, Brunel, City, Heriot-Watt, Loughborough, Salford, Strathclyde and Surrey Universities). An outstanding US example is the Massachusetts Institute of Technology (MIT).

technologist A well qualified person who uses TECHNOLOGY to tackle practical problems. Such a person is generally distinguished from a TECHNICIAN in being expected to cope with a wider range of problems and to be creative in developing new and more powerful tools and techniques.

technology The creative application of scientific and other systematic knowledge to the solution of practical problems, eg in industry and commerce, agriculture, housing, health care, or education. Usually includes both tools and techniques.

TEFL Acronym for the professional activity of 'teaching English as a foreign language'. (ie to students in countries where the MOTHER-TONGUE is not English). Contrasts with TESL.

telecine Equipment for connecting a film projector to a television camera so as to show a film over a television system.

teleclass Form of DISTANCE TEACHING involving students and teacher in a telephone hook-up. See CONFERENCE CALL.

telecommunication The communication over distance of spoken or written words, coded sounds and pictures, by telephone, telegraph, cable, radio and television.

teleological fallacy, the Speaking or writing of natural processes as if objects could have intentions or purposes of their own, eg 'The heart beats faster during exercise in order that more blood can reach the muscles' rather, than, say, 'The faster heart beat during exercise enables more blood to reach the muscles'.

teleology The interpretation of events or human activities in terms of purpose, eg 'X happens in order to achieve Y'. (Historically associated with the search for evidence of design in nature.) Compare with AETIOLOGY.

Teletext The version of VIEWDATA using broadcast television signals in which Britain was the pioneer. The BBC version is called CEEFAX and ITV's is ORACLE. They are more limited than the Post Office's PRESTEL in that their capacity is about a thousand pages and users cannot interrogate the computer storing the information; on the other hand, the information can be updated more easily.

telewriter A TELECOMMUNICATIONS device enabling writing or line drawings produced in one place to be transmitted as signals and reproduced in some distant place. Can be used in DISTANCE TEACHING. See also CONFERENCE CALL.

telling Term sometimes used of formal, EXPOSITORY TEACHING, allowing only minimal student participation.

Telstar Either of two communications satellites launched by the US in 1962 and 1963 and used, among other things, for the transmission of television programmes and telephone messages.

temperament The AFFECTIVE or emotional aspects of an individual's PERSONALITY.

Tenth Amendment (to the US Constitution) An amendment of 1791 making PUBLIC EDUCATION the responsibility of individual states, subject to their separate institutions and laws, rather than an activity to be controlled by the federal government.

tenure The recognition that a person has the right to continue in a certain post or institution until retirement. This may be granted only after a satisfactory PROBATIONARY PERIOD.

tenured post One that gives the occupier TENURE.

term **1** In the UK, a division of the ACADEMIC YEAR, normally one third of it. **2** In the US, the academic year is divided into two halves, usually called SEMESTERS but sometimes terms. (In HIGH SCHOOLS, each semester is sometimes divided into two terms, ie the QUARTER SYSTEM.)

Terman, L M (1877–1956) US psychologist known chiefly for his work on the measurement of INTELLIGENCE. He introduced the term 'INTELLIGENCE QUOTIENT' (IQ) and, with Maude Merrill, developed the STANFORD-BINET TEST in 1916, which is described in their *Measuring Intelligence* (1937).

Terman concept mastery test An INTELLIGENCE TEST for adults, with questions drawn from many different fields of study and purporting to measure a person's ability to deal with abstract ideas.

term appointment A person's appointment to a post for a limited period of time.

terminal Computer name for a device that is located at some distance from the computer, yet allows a person using it to feed information or instructions to the computer and receive data from it in return. Thus a computer in, say Glasgow, could service terminals throughout England, Wales and Scotland.

terminal assessment ASSESSMENT of a student's work or abilities at the end of a course or period of study. Contrasts with CONTINUOUS ASSESSMENT.

terminal behaviour The qualities and abilities a student can, or should be able to, demonstrate in his BEHAVIOUR or performance at the end of a course or period of study.

terminal curriculum (US) A two-year course of VOCATIONAL EDUCATION provided by a JUNIOR COLLEGE.

terminal degree The highest, most-esteemed degree that can be obtained in a particular field, eg a PhD or even a HIGHER DOCTORATE.

terminal education Term sometimes used of those stages of a student's education that are meant to conclude it rather than prepare him for further study at a higher level.

terminal qualification 1 A QUALIFICATION awarded on conclusion of TERMINAL EDUCATION, ie not meant to help gain further educational opportunities. 2 As TERMINAL DEGREE.

term paper (US) An essay or research paper reporting on an investigation into some limited topic as part of the work a student completes in a single SUBJECT in the course of a TERM.

tertiary college A college providing courses in TERTIARY EDUCATION. In the UK, colleges so-named may offer some courses taught also in SECONDARY SCHOOLS, eg GCE courses, and are attracting students who might otherwise have been SIXTH FORM pupils.

tertiary education Formal education at a higher level than that offered in SECONDARY SCHOOL. Includes HIGHER EDUCATION and much of FURTHER EDUCATION. The term is widely used in Australasia.

tertion Third year student at the Scottish universities of Aberdeen and St Andrews.

TESL Acronym for the professional activity of 'teaching English as a second language', eg for the benefit of immigrants to an English-speaking country who have previously learned some other language. Contrasts with TEFL.

test Any means by which the absence or presence or amount or nature of some quality or ability in a student can be observed or inferred, and appraised or even measured. May include, eg, INTERVIEWS, PAPER-AND-PENCIL TESTS, SITUATIONAL TESTS, and so on.

test-battery See BATTERY.

testimonial A written opinion of the character and capabilities of a person, produced by someone who knows him well, which he may use when applying for jobs, study-opportunities, or other benefits. It differs from a REFERENCE in that its contents will be known to the person being described and is not being written with a particular job, (or college, etc) in mind.

test of significance See SIGNIFICANCE.

test paper **1** The question sheet of a test or examination. **2** The paper on which the student records his answers.

test protocols Completed QUESTIONNAIRES or TEST PAPERS.

test-sophistication Students with previous experience of taking certain kinds of tests (eg INTELLIGENCE TESTS and OBJECTIVE TESTS) have often been found to have an advantage over inexperienced students when they come to tackle new but similar tests. This test-taking skill, or test-sophistication, may arise from greater self-confidence as a result of knowing what is expected. It may also be due to a student having noticed techniques used by question writers that act as 'give-aways', increasing his ability to guess the correct answer even if he is ignorant of the subject-matter. This is sometimes called 'test-wiseness'.

test-wiseness See under TEST-SOPHISTICATION.

Teviot Scale Scottish equivalent to the BURNHAM SCALE.

text **1** The words in a printed, or typed or hand-written book or document. **2** The main body of words in a book or document, as opposed to its footnotes, illustrations etc. **3** The topic or subject of a discussion or lecture (especially of a sermon). **4** Short for TEXTBOOK.

textbook A book on which the main ideas of a course of study are based or on which it draws for examples, case studies, exercises, etc. Many books are adopted as textbooks whether or not their author meant them as such. Books written intentionally as textbooks are likely to make use of such devices as overviews, summaries, glossaries, objectives, worked examples, student exercises, etc. With some textbooks (especially in the US) there may be a supplementary teacher's MANUAL.

T-group training   A form of SENSITIVITY TRAINING.

thanatology   (US) The name given to a new SUBJECT in the POST-SECONDARY CURRICULUM – the study of death.

Thematic Apperception Test (TAT)   A PROJECTIVE TEST of PERSONALITY in which a person is shown a series of ambiguous pictures and asked to tell a story about each one.

thematic approach   A teaching approach in which classroom work is organised around a broad theme, eg 'progress', 'children's games in many lands', 'transport', etc.

thematic prompt   A PROGRAMMED LEARNING term for a clue or hint that helps the student give a correct RESPONSE by providing him with discussion or examples emphasising the theme or meaning of what is being taught. Contrasts with FORMAL PROMPT.

theme   1 (US) A student's essay or COMPOSITION. 2 A main idea or topic in a THEMATIC or TOPIC-BASED approach to teaching.

theological college   College providing VOCATIONAL TRAINING for priests or members of the clergy. See also SEMINARY.

theory   1 In science, a theory is a testable law or generalisation based on observation and describes some aspect of the world, explains it, and predicts what would happen if certain features of a situation were to be changed. 2 Educational theory, however, is more concerned to indicate desirable ends, to identify the means whereby those ends may be attained, and to recommend that those means be adopted towards the specified ends. Thus an educational theory needs to be judged by the acceptability of the assumptions it makes about what ends are most worthwhile as well as by those it makes about the relationship between those ends and the suggested means.

thesis   See DISSERTATION.

think-tank   A group of specialists engaged in study, research and discussion with a view to making long-term predictions, to questioning existing policies and procedures, and to anticipating future problems.

Third Age, University of the   An educational movement among HIGHER EDUCATION establishments in Europe and North America to provide CONTINUING EDUCATION specially designed for retired people (in their 'third age', after the ages of childhood and of working life). The movement (which began at the University of Toulouse in France) is also concerned to improve the training of professionals in the care of the elderly, to carry out appropriate research, and to enhance the position in society of elderly people.

third force psychology   See HUMANISTIC PSYCHOLOGY.

third-level education   See TERTIARY EDUCATION.

third session   See EXTENDED DAY.

Third World   Collective term for the countries of Africa, Asia, and Latin America when viewed as undeveloped economically and politically independent of the two major power blocks of East and West.

thirteen plus   Term attached to the idea of transferring pupils to SECONDARY SCHOOL especially when a SELECTIVE SCHOOL) at the age of 13-plus years. Contrasts with ELEVEN-PLUS.

Thompson, Sir Godfrey H (1881–1955)   British psychologist and mathematician who became Professor of Education at Edinburgh University and established Moray House College as the largest producer of INTELLIGENCE TESTS and other mental tests in Europe. (This activity is now carried on by the Godfrey Thompson Unit in Edinburgh University.) His books include *A Modern Philosophy of Education* (1929) and *The Factorial Analysis of Human Ability* (1939). See also MORAY HOUSE TESTS.

Thorndike E L (1874–1949)   US psychologist who studied with WILLIAM JAMES and whose theories of learning, based on experiments with animals, were highly influential in educational psychology during the first half of this century. See his *Psychology of Learning* (1914).

three-hour examination   The assessment method calling upon students to answer under controlled conditions three or four questions chosen from a larger number. Still seen by most institutions of HIGHER EDUCATION as perhaps the truest, and certainly the most traditionally respectable, way of testing what students have learned from a course. This view is challenged by proponents of CONTINUOUS ASSESSMENT, OPEN EXAMINATIONS, PROJECT ASSESSMENT, etc.

three year junior college   (US) Junior COLLEGE that provides, in addition to the FRESHMAN and SOPHOMORE years, the equivalent of a final year in HIGH SCHOOL or the JUNIOR YEAR of STATE COLLEGE.

three Rs   Informal term for what are often regarded as the 'basics' of education: reading, (w)riting and (a)rithmetic. See also FOUR Rs.

three year senior high school   (US) A high school covering

GRADES 10, 11, and 12; usually linked with a JUNIOR HIGH SCHOOL covering grades 7, 8 and 9.

threshold Level of intensity at which a STIMULUS (eg sound or light) becomes noticeable or, in certain contexts, painful.

threshold effect The theory stating that, above a certain minimum level of intelligence, there is no relationship between IQ and CREATIVITY.

threshold school (US) An INDUSTRIAL TRAINING institution providing training for new employees.

Thring, Edward (1821–87) Headmaster of the English PUBLIC SCHOOL, Uppingham, between 1853 and 1887, Thring was one of the most vigorous educational innovators of the century. He started from the assumption that 'every boy is good for something' and set about broadening the CURRICULUM. Compulsory subjects like English, mathematics and classics were studied in the mornings, but in the afternoons the boys were given a choice from a wide range of options including science, modern languages, carpentry and metalwork, art and music. He had a strong interest in TEACHING METHODS, which he explored in his books: *Education and School* (1864) and *Theory and Practice of Teaching* (1883). He was also a keen advocate of HIGHER EDUCATION for women.

Thurstone attitude scale A type of ATTITUDE TEST in which a person has to say whether he agrees or disagrees with a number of ITEMS, each of which has a value on a scale between 1 and 11, which mark the most extreme attitudes. The person's score is the MEDIAN scale value of the items with which he agrees.

Thurstone Interest Schedule Checklist prepared by THURSTONE to reveal the strength of a person's preferences among such fields or activities as: physical science, business, language use, arts and music etc.

Thurstone, L L (1887–1955) US psychologist and professor of psychology at Chicago University from 1927, best known in education for his work in PSYCHOMETRICS.

Thurstone Temperament schedule An INVENTORY developed by THURSTONE to measure seven aspects of TEMPERAMENT: vigour, impulsiveness, activity, dominance, stability, sociability and reflectiveness.

Tillich bricks STRUCTURAL APPARATUS used in the early years of this century to help young children learn mathematics.

timed test Test that must be completed within a given period of time. Compare with SPEED TEST.

time line A chart sometimes used in history teaching, whereby the dates of key events within a period are entered along a calibrated line with the intervals between them giving a visual image of the relative amount of time that elapsed between any two.

time sampling A research technique whereby the behaviour of a person or people being observed is recorded only at certain fixed intervals of time, eg every fifteen seconds or every minute.

time series Statistical data gathered by recording the VALUE of a certain changing VARIABLE (eg temperature) at regular intervals of time or by recording the maximum value that has been attained during each of a series of equal time intervals (eg weekly totals of children absent from school). A time series often forms a pattern that helps in forecasting values for future points or periods.

timetable A detailed chart showing, for each class and teacher or for an educational institution as a whole, which subjects will be studied at what times during the week. The US term is SCHEDULE.

TMA Tutor marked assignment.

TO See TRADITIONAL ORTHOGRAPHY.

toilet training Training a child to control bowels and bladder at an early stage of life.

token economy/system A learning environment (eg a class-room or a mental hospital) in which BEHAVIOUR acceptable to the person in charge obtains REINFORCEMENT in the form of tokens which have no intrinsic value but which the pupil or patient can collect and exchange later for something he does value, eg time free to play, or access to a favourite television programme.

tokenism The admittance to some sought-after situation (eg to university or to senior posts in management) of people from groups that are usually discriminated against (eg blacks or women) but in such small (and unrepresentative) numbers that the function of these 'token members' is clearly to help the people who control entry to avoid censure under the prevailing laws or agreements that prohibit discrimination.

Tolman E C (1886–1959) US psychologist, professor of psychology at the University of California, Berkeley, from 1918. His learning theory was BEHAVIOURIST in origin but was much modified by his idea of goal-directed behaviour guided by cognitive processes. (He developed the concept of COGNITIVE MAPS.) See his *Purposive Behaviour in Animals and Men* (1932).

Tonic solfa A method of learning to sing 'at sight' from written music, with the notes of the major scale being sung as the syllables: doh, ray, me, fah, soh, la, te. It was developed by JOHN CURWEN in the 1860s and was widely used in schools and amateur singing groups until the early years of this century.

topic approach/method An approach to teaching (especially in PRIMARY SCHOOLS), based on having children spend days or even weeks investigating a topic or theme, eg 'animals in winter' or 'mediaeval warfare'. Similar to THEMATIC APPROACH but, in primary school, the teacher may make a conscious attempt to bring in some work on number, drama, science, art, music, and so on, to whatever topic is being pursued, so as to ensure that no important aspect of the CURRICULUM gets neglected.

topping up Adding further qualifications to existing ones in order to reach a higher level of certification, eg in the OPEN UNIVERSITY six full CREDITS are needed for an ordinary degree but students can then go on to qualify for an HONOURS DEGREE by studying for two additional credits.

TOPS See TRAINING OPPORTUNITIES SCHEME.

Torrance, E P (born 1915) US professor of educational psychology best known for his studies of CREATIVITY and the GIFTED CHILD. See his *Guiding Creative Talent* (1962) and *Gifted Children in the Classroom* (1965).

Torrance Tests of Creative Thinking Verbal and pictorial tests, designed by E P TORRANCE, purporting to measure thinking of a kind that features in activities generally recognised as creative, eg elaborating upon a given idea or picture.

total institution An organisation of people that enables some to control closely the BEHAVIOUR and VALUES of others in the group, eg BOARDING SCHOOLS, prisons and monasteries.

total population See POPULATION.

TOTE Acronym for 'Test-Operate-Test-Exit', a model used by some psychologists to describe human BEHAVIOUR. The idea is that a person '*tests*' to see whether a given situation is satisfactory in terms of some desired GOAL (eg is the point of his pencil sharp enough?). If not, he '*operates*' (sharpens it) and '*tests*' again; and this sequence will repeat until the result is satisfactory. He will then be able to '*exit*' to some other activity that may again be described by TOTE.

township school   (US) HIGH SCHOOL serving a township that forms an administrative division of a county (especially in New England).

township school administration   (US) Local SCHOOL BOARD responsible for the schools in a township or similar area (especially in New England).

town trail (or **urban trail**)   The urban equivalent of a NATURE TRAIL, being a guided walk through areas of a town regarded as having educational interest in terms of architecture, town planning, INDUSTRIAL ARCHAEOLOGY, etc.

tracking   The US equivalent of STREAMING.

track record   By analogy with athletics, the cumulative record of how a person has performed in education or career over some considerable period of time. It might be used in predicting his future performance.

trade education   (US) VOCATIONAL TRAINING for industrial trades (or crafts) at the semi-skilled, skilled, or supervisory level.

trade (or **vocational high school**)   (US) A HIGH SCHOOL whose courses are oriented towards industrial craft skills.

trade centre   VOCATIONAL or TRADE SCHOOL. (Also can be an advisory service for importers and exporters.)

trade course   A course providing some kind of TRADE EDUCATION, perhaps enabling a person to qualify as a tradesman (or craftsman).

trade school   In the UK, trade schools of one sort or another date from at least Elizabethan times (when they supplemented APPRENTICESHIP) through to the 19th Century when they also supplemented the ELEMENTARY SCHOOLS (and were often attached to MECHANICS' INSTITUTES) sometimes providing narrow VOCATIONAL TRAINING preparing youngsters for a particular local trade (eg printing or tailoring), sometimes developing into TECHNICAL SCHOOLS offering a more general education. Nowadays, the term is used largely for training units within industrial and other organisations employing craftsmen.

trade test   Test of a craftsman's competence in his trade or craft.

trade union   An organisation representing people in a particular occupation (originally in a trade but nowadays in professions also), especially in negotiations with employers about pay and conditions of employment. In the case of teachers, their PROFESSIONAL ASSOCIATIONS usually act also as trade unions.

traditional orthography (**TO**) The traditional means of writing down the spoken sounds of the English language using an alphabet of twenty-six lower-case and twenty-six upper-case letter shapes together with accepted rules of spelling. (There have been other attempts to improve the written representation of sounds, especially the INITIAL TEACHING ALPHABET.)

trainability A person's ability to learn a particular task or job in a reasonable time, if given the normal training.

training The systematic development in a person of the KNOWLEDGE, ATTITUDES and SKILLS necessary for him to be able to perform adequately in a job or task whose demands can be reasonably well identified in advance and that requires a fairly standardised performance from whoever attempts it. Contrasts with EDUCATION, though education may include much training.

training audit The identification of training needs within an organisation.

training bay Area within a factory or other work-place, reserved for TRAINING activities.

training centre **1** Unit within an industrial or other organisation, staffed and equipped to carry out TRAINING. **2** Obsolete term for a UK educational centre for children classed as SEVERELY SUBNORMAL (SSN).

training college Same as TEACHER-TRAINING COLLEGE.

training hospital Same as TEACHING HOSPITAL.

training officer A specialist in TRAINING within an organisation who may: carry out TRAINING AUDITS; plan and supervise the work of instructors or trainers; and carry out training himself.

Training Opportunities Scheme (**TOPS**) UK facilities provided by TRAINING SERVICES DIVISION to encourage and carry out RE-TRAINING.

training manual A guide for instructors (and perhaps trainees) detailing the OBJECTIVES and STANDARDS to be attained and the methods to be used in TRAINING for a particular job or task. (Often produced by manufacturers of new and complex equipment whose operators will need RETRAINING.)

training package A PACKAGE of INTEGRATED TEACHING/LEARNING MATERIALS (perhaps MULTI-MEDIA) for use in TRAINING for a particular job or test.

training school   **1** A school giving VOCATIONAL TRAINING. **2** (US) See DEMONSTRATION SCHOOL.

Training Services Agency   See TRAINING SERVICES DIVISION.

Training Services Division (**TSD**)   A UK statutory body responsible to the MANPOWER SERVICES COMMISSION (under the EMPLOYMENT AND TRAINING ACT 1973), for the TRAINING OPPORTUNITIES SCHEME (TOPS), TRAINING WITHIN INDUSTRY (TWI), and the coordination of the INDUSTRIAL TRAINING BOARD. See also UNIFIED VOCATIONAL PREPARATION. (Was previously known as Training Services Agency.)

Training Within Industry (**TWI**)   Courses on the techniques of supervision for supervisors within industry, commerce and public service organisations, based on principles imported into the UK from the US in the 1940s. TWI courses are organised by the TRAINING SERVICES DIVISION (TSD) or the TWI-trainers within firms who were themselves trained by TSD (or, earlier, by the Department of Employment and Productivity).

trait   An enduring PERSONALITY characteristic (eg aggressiveness) that leads a person to respond in a particular manner to a wide range of situations.

transactional analysis   The study and interpretation of verbal and NON-VERBAL interactions between two or more people in a social situation (eg teacher and pupils) especially in terms of the meanings that participants attach to one another's behaviour.

transcendental meditation   See MEDITATION.

transcript   **1** Written record of what was said in a speech, discussion, or broadcast. See also PROTOCOL. **2** (US) Official document from a school, college or university showing the courses a student has taken and the GRADES achieved in each.

transfer   **1** The effects of previous learning on subsequent attempts to learn. See NEGATIVE and POSITIVE TRANSFER. **2** To move from one educational institution to another in order to continue a course of studies at the same level.

transfer credit   CREDIT granted to a TRANSFER STUDENT by the institution he is transferring to, in recognition of work done previously.

transfer curriculum   Two year course in LIBERAL ARTS in a JUNIOR COLLEGE enabling a student to TRANSFER to college or university for the final two years of a degree course.

transference   Term from PSYCHOANALYSIS indicating a person's tendency to re-direct the attitudes and emotions he feels towards one person (eg a parent) on to a substitute (eg the analyst) in the course of therapy.

transfer rate   In the UK, the proportion of children moved from one school to another (usually from SECONDARY MODERN to GRAMMAR SCHOOL) in the TRIPARTITE SYSTEM after it had become apparent that they were incorrectly placed by the ELEVEN PLUS SELECTION PROCEDURE.

transfer student   A student transferring from one educational institution to another at a similar level.

transformer   Term used by some communications specialists for a person with skills in teaching or communication who liaises with an expert in some subject-matter and translates the expert's knowledge into a form (eg a chart or a course) that allows it to be grasped by lay persons (eg students of the subject).

trauma   A powerful injury or shock, physical or mental, that may result in long-term mental disturbance.

travellers' class/school   Teaching provided for gipsy children (and perhaps for their parents).

travelling teacher   Same as ITINERANT or PERIPATETIC teacher.

treatment group   Same as EXPERIMENTAL GROUP.

trend   A general upward or downward movement of successive VALUES in a TIME SERIES, eg the increasing proportion of the relevant UK age-group staying at school beyond the STATUTORY LEAVING AGE.

trial-and-error   An approach to problem-solving or LEARNING in which a person makes a number of guesses, based on what little he knows of the matter in hand, until he happens to hit on the solution.

triangulation   A research technique for increasing the VALIDITY of one's results by using different (and independent) methods in collecting data on a problem, perhaps by using more than one researcher or even by collecting different kinds of data on the problem.

triangle   SOCIOMETRY term for a reciprocated social relationship among three people.

trimester   A three-month period, and the name given to each of the three divisions of the ACADEMIC YEAR in some US educational institutions.

trinity term   The term between Easter and the LONG VACATION at Oxford University and some other educational institutions.

trip Term used for educational visits and journeys made by pupils or students as part of their studies, eg a FIELD TRIP.

tripartite system The system established in England and Wales subsequent to the EDUCATION ACT 1944 (though the Act itself did not stipulate such a system) whereby children were allocated among three distinct types of SECONDARY SCHOOL: GRAMMAR, MODERN, and TECHNICAL. The system has been in accelerating decline since the issue of CIRCULAR 10/65 in 1965.

tripos The final honours examinations for the BA degree at Cambridge University. (Named after the three-legged stool used by the examiner in mediaeval times.)

trivium The three basic subjects of the mediaeval CURRICULUM of LIBERAL ARTS: grammar, rhetoric and logic. The other four subjects (arithmetic, geometry, astronomy and music) were known as the QUADRIVIUM.

truancy A pupil's deliberate absence from school without being able to offer any reason (eg medical) that would satisfy the authorities. Causes are manifold, eg boredom with lessons and fear of BULLYING. See also INTERNAL TRUANCY.

truant A pupil who is engaging in TRUANCY, especially if he does so persistently.

truant officer (US) Someone responsible for checking why students are absent from school. Like the former UK term ATTENDANCE OFFICER or the present EDUCATION WELFARE OFFICER (though the latter has a wider role).

true-false item An ITEM in an OBJECTIVE TEST that presents a person with a statement and asks him to say whether it is true or false.

true-false test A test consisting of a number of TRUE-FALSE ITEMS.

trustees **1** (US) The board of people appointed to manage an educational institution, especially PRIVATE SCHOOLS, COLLEGES and UNIVERSITIES, and with similar powers to a SCHOOL BOARD in deciding policy and overseeing the administration. **2** A group of people responsible for the running of a trust or foundation for the benefit of others.

TSA/TSD See TRAINING SERVICES DIVISION.

t-test In STATISTICS, a frequently used test of SIGNIFICANCE (eg of the difference between the MEANS of two SAMPLES.)

tuck shop   A shop on or near the campus of a UK school, where pupils buy food and drink.

tuition   **1** The teaching given students during a course. **2** (US) The fees paid by students for their course.

tuition academy   (US) See ACADEMY.

tuition fees   Fees paid for teaching (as opposed to those paid for food and accommodation).

tutor   **1** A teacher. **2** A teacher who works with pupils individually, perhaps out of school hours in return for a fee. **3** A college or university teacher, especially when teaching a single student or a very small group. **4** A teacher who has special responsibility for advising students, as their MORAL or PERSONAL tutor. **5** (US) In some colleges and universities, a teaching assistant of lower rank than INSTRUCTOR. **6** A SELF-INSTRUCTIONAL TEXT for people wanting to learn to play a musical instrument, eg a piano tutor.

tutor group   Group of students for whom a certain teacher has responsibility, probably as PERSONAL or MORAL TUTOR individually, but also perhaps as a teacher of the group.

tutorial   A meeting between a tutor and a single student (or sometimes a small group of students) in which intensive face-to-face teaching and discussion can take place, often based on material written by the student(s).

tutorial class   Term used in the WORKERS' EDUCATIONAL ASSOCIATION for a group of students following a three-year course.

tutorial fellowship   **1** Teaching post as a TUTOR and FELLOW at an OXBRIDGE college. **2** See TEACHING FELLOWSHIP.

tutorial-in-print   Term sometimes used of a SELF-INSTRUCTIONAL TEXT that attempts to simulate the dialogue between tutor and student by punctuating the text with frequent questions requiring a response from the reader and then going on to discuss possible answers.

tutorial system   An approach to teaching in HIGHER EDUCATION (especially identified with the OXBRIDGE colleges) centred on TUTORIALS (rather than on lectures).

tutor-marked assignment (**TMA**)   Term used by the OPEN UNIVERSITY and some other institutions to distinguish between students' assignments that are to be marked by a tutor (eg ESSAYS) and those that are to be marked by a computer or machine (eg OBJECTIVE TESTS). Contrasts with COMPUTER-MARKED ASSIGNMENTS (CMA).

tutor-organiser A common title in UK ADULT EDUCATION for someone who organises courses and acts as a tutor on some of them.

TWI See TRAINING WITHIN INDUSTRY.

twin studies Often referred to in NATURE-NURTURE CONTROVERSY when identical twins who happen to have been brought up separately are studied in an attempt to see how far their different upbringings (given their presumably common genetic inheritance) have influenced their INTELLIGENCE and ATTAINMENTS.

'two cultures' A catch-phrase introduced in 1959 by British novelist, C P Snow, indicating his belief that modern education is so specialised that one group of specialists is incapable of understanding the concerns of another; this being seen most clearly in the two polar CULTURES of the arts and the sciences.

two factor theory A theory of INTELLIGENCE put forward by SPEARMAN early in this century and postulating a general factor in mental ability together with various specific abilities.

two-tier system A form of COMPREHENSIVE SCHOOL organisation introduced in the UK by LEICESTERSHIRE LOCAL EDUCATION AUTHORITY, whereby pupils enter a junior comprehensive school at the age of 11-plus and then transfer to a senior comprehensive school at the age of 13 or 14.

two-year junior college (US) The conventional form of JUNIOR-COLLEGE. See also THREE-YEAR JUNIOR COLLEGE and FOUR-YEAR JUNIOR COLLEGE.

Tyler, Ralph, W (1902–) US psychology professor at Stanford Institute and an early advocate of RATIONAL CURRICULUM PLANNING based on OBJECTIVES. See his *Basic Principles of Curriculum and Instruction* (1949).

typology A classification scheme – ideally one in which there is a class for every possible item to be classified and no doubt as to which class it belongs in.

tyro A novice or beginner.

U

UCCA See UNIVERSITIES CENTRAL COUNCIL ON ADMISSIONS.

UGC See UNIVERSITY GRANTS COMMITTEE.

uncertificated teacher   One who does not have a CERTIFICATE indicating that he has successfully completed a course of professional TEACHER-TRAINING. See also QUALIFIED TEACHER.

unclassified degree   A UK degree for which the student has not been awarded honours. See PASS DEGREE.

unclubbable, an   Refers to a young person who seems unwilling to involve himself in youth clubs or other adult-initiated organisations for young people and may therefore be regarded as non-social (if not potentially anti-social).

unconditioned reflex   See REFLEX ACTION.

unconditioned response   See REFLEX ACTION. Contrasts with CONDITIONED RESPONSE. See also CONDITIONING.

unconscious   According to SIGMUND FREUD, a part of the mind in which are stored ideas, memories and feelings from past experience, that may, unknown to a person himself, influence his present behaviour.

underachiever   A pupil whose educational achievement is markedly less than might have been expected from estimates of his potential, eg as suggested by INTELLIGENCE TESTS.

underclassman   (US) Student in the first or second (FRESHMAN or SOPHOMORE) year of a HIGH SCHOOL, COLLEGE or UNIVERSITY course. Contrasts with UPPERCLASSMAN.

undergraduate   Student who is taking a course leading to a FIRST DEGREE, eg a BACHELOR'S DEGREE.

undergraduate collection (or **library**)   That part of a library (or a separate library) to which undergraduates have access. (Some institutions reserve some books and journal collections for graduates only.)

undergraduate college   (US) See UNDERGRADUATE SCHOOL.

undergraduate course   Course leading to the award of a FIRST DEGREE, eg a BACHELOR'S DEGREE.

undergraduate library   See UNDERGRADUATE COLLECTION.

undergraduate school   (US) Division within a COLLEGE or UNIVERSITY providing UNDERGRADUATE COURSES only. Contrasts with GRADUATE SCHOOL.

undergraduate special   (US) A COLLEGE or UNIVERSITY course organised and financed by the students rather than by the institution, but with the institution's approval of its content and conduct.

underground press Newspapers and magazines produced by people who feel their views are not given sufficient coverage or treated seriously enough by those who control the production and distribution of commercial newspapers and magazines. They are often radical and, by offering alternative visions of society, will usually offend some body of established opinion.

underground university See FLYING UNIVERSITY.

Underwood Report 1955 A UK REPORT making 97 recommendations concerning the medical, social and educational problems of MALADJUSTED CHILDREN: especially that there should be a large expansion in the facilities available, with a comprehensive CHILD GUIDANCE service (including a school psychological service, a school medical service, and child guidance clinics) available in every LOCAL EDUCATION AUTHORITY area.

UNESCO United Nations Educational, Scientific, and Cultural Organisation. Established in 1946 to promote 'international cultural and educational cooperation'. Among other aims, it seeks to extend the right to free education for all and to improve its quality through CURRICULUM DEVELOPMENT, research into new media and methods, and the training of teachers.

ungraded schools (US) Same as NON-GRADED SCHOOLS.

unidimensional measurement The attempt to construct tests (eg of PERSONALITY) that measure only one DIMENSION of personality and produce results that are not contaminated by unidentified additional aspects.

unidisciplinary approach/teaching An approach to teaching involving just one ACADEMIC DISCIPLINE. Contrasts with INTERDISCIPLINARY or MULTIDISCIPLINARY approaches.

uniform Many schools in the UK have traditionally expected pupils to wear special blazers, hats, badges, ties, etc, in school colours. Some of these requirements still survive, especially in the more prestigious schools.

unified (school) district (US) A SCHOOL DISTRICT providing a full range of ELEMENTARY and HIGH SCHOOL education.

unified studies Same as INTEGRATED STUDIES.

Unified Vocational Preparation (UVP) A five-year experimental programme of pilot schemes devoted to developing and testing forms of VOCATIONAL EDUCATION suitable for young people employed in jobs that give no opportunities for FURTHER EDUCATION or systematic training. The programme was launched in 1976 and is being run jointly by the TRAINING SERVICE DIVISION of the MANPOWER SERVICES COMMISSION, the DEPARTMENT OF EDUCATION AND SCIENCE and the WELSH OFFICE. Many FURTHER EDUCATION COLLEGES are involved.

unit **1** Department within an institution with staff and facilities to offer some particular service, eg, AUDIO-VISUAL AIDS unit. **2** MODULE within a course. **3** (US) In HIGH SCHOOL, one hour in class per day of a subject (for five days a week over the ACADEMIC YEAR) counts as one course unit of that subject.

United Nations Educational, Social, and Cultural Organisation See UNESCO.

Unit total UK scheme whereby the number of pupils of different ages in a SECONDARY SCHOOL helps determine such matters as the HEADTEACHER's salary and the number of teaching posts that can be offered on the higher salary scales. See SCALE POSTS.

universal education The ideal of extending improved educational opportunities to all, regardless of race, religion, colour, sex, age, ability, nationality, etc.

universe See POPULATION.

Universities Central Council on Admissions (UCCA) Central clearing-house set up by UK universities in 1961 to facilitate the annual admissions procedure by collecting all applications for PLACES, distributing them among the relevant universities, and relaying the universities' decisions back to the individual applicants.

university An institution of HIGHER EDUCATION in which both research and teaching are expected to be of the best. It will award its own DEGREES, both FIRST DEGREES and HIGHER DEGREES. Some institutions of university status (especially in the US) will be known as COLLEGES or INSTITUTES.

university colleges **1** The name formerly given to the UK CIVIC UNIVERSITIES which, when first set up, did not have the power to grant their own degrees and usually granted those of London University instead. The last such (Leicester) became autonomous in 1957. **2** In addition, Oxford, Cambridge Durham and London each has a college named University College, and it is also the name of the INDEPENDENT UNIVERSITY at Buckingham.

university extension movement A late 19th century UK movement, starting from Cambridge University but involving London, Oxford and a variety of provincial institutions, providing courses of lectures (with written work and examinations) for townspeople who were not officially students of the universities.

The movement contributed much to spreading the ideal of HIGHER EDUCATION and in two towns, Exeter and Reading, the classes led to the establishment of UNIVERSITY COLLEGES. (The present day equivalent is called EXTRA-MURAL TEACHING.)

university extension   See EXTENSION SERVICES and UNIVERSITY EXTENSION MOVEMENT.

University Grants Committee (UGC)   A UK body of some 20 people, mostly academics, who are chosen by the SECRETARY OF STATE FOR EDUCATION AND SCIENCE to act as a link, on financial matters, between the government and the universities. The Committee informs the government of the universities' (total) financial needs and receives a block grant which it then distributes among the individual universities according to its own criteria.

university high school   (US) A DEMONSTRATION SCHOOL linked to the TEACHER-EDUCATION unit of a university.

university of the air   A term that might be used of a college or university that broadcasts its teaching to the general public on radio and/or television. Sometimes used of the UK's OPEN UNIVERSITY in its early years.

university school   A demonstration school linked to the TEACHER-EDUCATION unit of a university.

university week   (US) A one-week programme of lectures, exhibitions, concerts, etc organised by a university as part of its EXTENSION SERVICES.

university without walls   The idea of a university whose students are not collected together on a campus but are pursuing their studies in diverse parts of a city or country. It is usually assumed also that the studies will be INDEPENDENT and PROJECT-BASED.

unobtrusive evaluation/testing/techniques   Techniques of EVALUATION that can be employed without people (eg students) realising that evaluation is taking place. Includes NATURALISTIC OBSERVATION and the use of archives (eg local statistics on drug convictions) and physical artefacts (eg students' EXERCISE BOOKS).

unselective school   See NON-SELECTIVE SCHOOL.

unstructured interview   An INTERVIEW for which no questions have been formulated in advance, thus allowing the discussion to develop freely from the interests of the participants. Contrasts with STRUCTURED INTERVIEW.

untenured post A temporary post whose holder does not enjoy TENURE.

updating courses/training Training designed to acquaint a person with the latest ideas, materials and methods in his field and help him gain the necessary new KNOWLEDGE, SKILLS and ATTITUDES.

upgrading courses/training TRAINING designed to give a person additional KNOWLEDGE, SKILLS or ATTITUDES, perhaps with a view to enabling him to carry out more demanding tasks.

upper class The class of people generally assumed to have highest social status in society, eg the aristocracy or the landed gentry. See also MIDDLE CLASS and WORKING CLASS.

upperclassman (US) Student in the third or fourth (JUNIOR or SENIOR) year of a course in HIGH SCHOOL or college or university. Contrasts with UNDERCLASSMAN.

upper division college (US) College offering only the second two years (JUNIOR and SENIOR) of a college course, like a SENIOR COLLEGE, together perhaps with GRADUATE courses.

upper school 1 The UK COMPREHENSIVE SCHOOL to which pupils go (usually at the age of about 14) in LOCAL EDUCATION AUTHORITIES that operate MIDDLE SCHOOLS. 2 Pupils of 15-plus in a UK COMPREHENSIVE SCHOOL taking the full 11 – 18-plus age-range. 3 In Canada, an extra grade 13 added to HIGH SCHOOL studies, perhaps to give a student ADVANCED STANDING on entering college.

upper secondary school (US) An educational institution offering grades 11 to 14, ie the top two grades in a regular HIGH SCHOOL plus the two years of JUNIOR COLLEGE. Usually draws its pupils from an associated LOWER SECONDARY SCHOOL.

upper sixth (form) Students in their second year of sixth form studies in a UK SECONDARY SCHOOL. Roughly equivalent to US grade 12.

Upward Bound Program (US) Federal government scheme introduced in 1965 to increase the number of students from poor families obtaining admission to college or university.

Urban Aid Programme A UK programme introduced in 1968 (following the PLOWDEN REPORT) and sponsored by five central government departments hoping to improve life in certain deprived social areas eg by providing more NURSERY EDUCATION in the EDUCATIONAL PRIORITY AREAS.

urban education The education of children in schools at the centre of cities and conurbations, suffering all the attendant problems of poverty, overcrowding, crime, lack of playing space, etc.

urban trail   See TOWN TRAIL.

US Commissioner of Education   The Chief Executive of the former US OFFICE OF EDUCATION. Replaced by a SECRETARY OF EDUCATION in 1979.

US customary system • System of weights and measures derived from the British IMPERIAL SYSTEM but differing from it in some respects (eg in liquid measure). In scientific work and technology it is being superseded by the INTERNATIONAL SYSTEM (or SI UNITS).

usher   **1** An offical performing such duties as showing people to their seats in a church or theatre, guiding people into order for a procession, acting as doorkeeper, and so on. **2** An obsolete term for a teacher or assistant to a teacher.

US Department of Health, Education and Welfare   See DEPARTMENT OF HEALTH, EDUCATION AND WELFARE (US).

'Uses of Objects' test   A test of creativity in which a person is asked to think of as many uses as possible for a series of everyday objects, eg a brick or paper-clip.

USOE   See OFFICE OF EDUCATION (US).

US Office of Education   See OFFICE OF EDUCATION (US).

utilitarianism   The beliefs of a group of UK philosophers (led by JEREMY BENTHAM and JOHN STUART MILL), summed up in the view that the value of anything was to be judged in terms of how far it produced happiness (or diminished unhappiness) in the greatest possible number of people. Utilitarianism inspired the CURRICULUM reforming of HERBERT SPENCER and T H HUXLEY in their advocacy of teaching science (rather than the CLASSICS).

utopianism   **1** The kind of speculation associated with social reformers who write stories or travel accounts set in imaginary societies that illustrate their ideal of the perfect society. Named after Sir Thomas More's *Utopia* (1516). The word is from the Greek for 'no place'. **2** Unrealistic ideals for the improvement of society.

UVP   See UNIFIED VOCATIONAL PREPARATION.

V

vacation Period between TERMS or SEMESTERS in an educational institution when staff and students are on holiday or pursuing private study or research.

vacation school Same idea as SUMMER SCHOOL, but could be held in Easter or even Christmas VACATION.

vacation work Jobs undertaken by students during vacations to earn money (rather than to gain experience relevant to their courses).

valedictorian (US) Student ranking highest among his PEERS on graduation and who delivers the valedictory (or farewell speech) at the graduation ceremony.

Valentine C W (1879–1967) British educational psychologist and Professor of Education at Birmingham University from 1919–46, particularly known for his work on the psychology of childhood. See his *The Psychology of Early Childhood* (1942) and *The Normal Child* (1956).

validation 1 The process whereby an educational institution may submit formal plans for new courses to the scrutiny and approval of an outside body. Thus, a UK COLLEGE OF EDUCATION or POLYTECHNIC may have its courses validated by a university or by the CNAA. 2 A PROGRAMMED LEARNING term meaning DEVELOPMENTAL TESTING.

validity The extent to which a TEST (or any ASSESSMENT technique) really touches upon the student qualities it is meant to assess. Thus a PAPER-AND-PENCIL TEST in which students are asked what they would do in a given situation may not be a valid test of what they would actually do in that situation, eg whether or not they would act honestly.

value judgment A person's subjective appraisal of the quality or worth of someone or something, based on his own VALUE SYSTEM or that of his PEERS.

values 1 The moral and aesthetic principles, beliefs and standards that give coherence and direction to a person's decisions and actions. Where such values are held by, or are imposed upon, the majority of people in a society, they may be known as social NORMS. 2 In statistics, the different quantitative or qualitative states in which an entity can be with respect to some VARIABLE; that is, different categories or measurement.

value system   The set of beliefs, principles and standards a person has in relation to a particular subject, eg COMPREHENSIVE SCHOOLS. It is a system insofar as the beliefs etc are related to one another (so that, knowing one, we could predict the others and, if one were to change, the others would need to do so also).

vanishing   See FADING.

variable   In statistics and research, some attribute or characteristic (eg height, intelligence, weight, sex, colour) in terms of which an entity (eg a person) can be assigned to one of several categories or measured as having one of many possible VALUES.

variance   In statistics: **1** same as VARIABILITY or DISPERSION. **2** A particular measure of variability, ie the square of the STANDARD DEVIATION. See also ANALYSIS OF VARIANCE.

VCR   Often used as an abbreviation for VIDEO CASSETTE RECORDER (or recording), though actually the trade name used by one particular manufacturer.

VDU   See VISUAL (or VIDEO) DISPLAY UNIT.

Veblen, Thorstein (1857–1929)   US economist and sociologist who analysed social institutions, criticising what he called the 'leisure class' as retarding the development of the technocratic society he favoured, in which efficiency and workmanship is valued. See his *The Theory of the Leisure Class* and *The Theory of Business Enterprise* (1904).

verbal ability (or **aptitude**) **tests**   Tests of a person's skill in understanding and using written and spoken language.

verbal intelligence test   Test of INTELLIGENCE that involves a person in understanding written or spoken language.

verbal reasoning test   Test of INTELLIGENCE concentrating on the ability to understand and use written and spoken language (rather than, say, numbers or spatial patterns).

verification principle   Or principle of verifiability. A doctrine from the philosophical movement of LOGICAL POSITIVISM. It states (in its mild form) that a proposition or statement is only meaningful in so far as we can see what evidence would enable us to accept it as true or reject it as false. In the strong form, the principle asserts that the meaning *is* the method of verification.

vernacular school   Mediaeval school providing instruction for poor children in their own language rather than in the Latin used by scholars and priests.

Vernon, P E (born 1905)   British psychologist, (who retired as professor of educational psychology at University of Calgary, Canada) and an authority on PERSONALITY and INTELLIGENCE and their measurement. His work led to considerable scepticism about the measurement of intelligence and speeded the demise of the ELEVEN-PLUS. His many books include *The Measurement of Abilities* (1940), *Personality Assessment* (1963) and *Intelligence and Cultural Environment* (1969).

Vernon Report 1972 The REPORT of a COMMITTEE OF ENQUIRY into the education of the VISUALLY HANDICAPPED. Made recommendations about medical services, advice to families, care of the pre-school child, activities in schools, and national policy and planning for the visually handicapped.

vertical grouping See FAMILY GROUPING.

veterans' education (US) Education provision for ex-servicemen from World War II and the Korean and Vietnam Wars, financed from federal funds.

vice-chancellor The chief executive of a UK university. Compares with PRESIDENT in US and with RECTOR in Europe.

vice-principal Deputy or assistant to the PRINCIPAL.

videocassette VIDEOTAPE stored, recorded upon and played back within a CASSETTE (rather than reel-to-reel), allowing easy use by unskilled operators (eg pupils).

videocassette recorder (VCR) A device enabling the recording on VIDEOCASSETTE of television programmes (moving pictures plus sound) together with subsequent PLAYBACK.

videodisc An alternative to VIDEOCASSETTE for recording, storing and PLAYBACK of moving pictures with sound.

video display unit See VISUAL DISPLAY UNIT.

videophone A telephone device allowing the participants to see as well as hear each other.

videotape Magnetic tape used to record and PLAYBACK sound and moving pictures, usually with the help of a VIDEOCASSETTE RECORDER.

videotape recorder (VTR) A REEL-TO-REEL alternative to a VIDEOCASSETTE RECORDER.

videotex The internationally accepted term for VIEWDATA systems like the British Post Office's PRESTEL.

Viewdata Information retrieval and processing systems, (known internationally also as VIDEOTEX) in which a telephone line is used to link a television viewer in home or office with thousands of 'pages' of information (eg news, weather reports, business information, advertisements, consumer advice, airline timetables, recipes, etc) contained in a computer. Unlike the simpler TELETEXT system, Viewdata allows users to interrogate the computer. The British version, operated by the Post Office, is called PRESTEL.

village colleges A UK scheme in COMMUNITY EDUCATION initiated in rural Cambridgeshire in the 1930s, with a number of colleges each serving a group of villages not only as a SECONDARY SCHOOL but also as a cultural and recreational centre for old and young alike out of school hours. The scheme was later adopted by several other largely-rural counties.

Vincent mechanical diagrams test A UK test of mechanical aptitude.

Vineland Social Maturity Scale A US instrument for assessing a child's social development (eg in self-help, communication, socialisation, etc) by observation of how the child behaves in certain situations and comparison with a large number of descriptions standardised for different age-levels.

Vire, to See VIREMENT.

virement In educational (and other) budgeting, the authorised transfer of funds from an area of the budget that is in surplus to balance another area that would otherwise show a deficit.

visitation An official visit for the purpose of inspecting or examining an institution or its students.

visiting fellow A college or university FELLOW appointed for a short period, perhaps a term or a year.

visiting professor A person holding a short-term or part-time PROFESSORSHIP, probably while on SECONDMENT or leave of absence from another academic (or government or industrial) institution.

visiting teacher Same as CIRCUIT or PERIPATETIC teacher.

visitor An honorary position within a university or polytechnic, usually held by a distinguished ACADEMIC who may advise the governing body and chief executive on academic issues and may act as 'ombudsman' for staff and students.

visual aids Pictures, models, maps, films etc, used as aids in teaching and learning. See also AUDIO-VISUAL AIDS.

visual (or **video**) **display unit** Computer term for the television-type screen on which the computer displays information from its memory (in print or line diagram) and confirms information or instructions that the operator is feeding to it through the associated keyboard or with a LIGHT PEN.

visual literacy The ability to understand and use visual symbols other than printed words and digits, ie maps, graphs, etc. Similar to GRAPHICACY.

visual-motor (or visuomotor) Relating to the coordination of the eyes and body muscles, eg in judging the distance and drop when jumping across a stream.

visually handicapped Similar to PARTIALLY SIGHTED and VISUALLY IMPAIRED, and referring to children or adults who cannot see properly, (although they are not blind).

visually impaired See VISUALLY HANDICAPPED.

viva Abbreviation of VIVA VOCE.

viva voce An ORAL examination. (From the Latin, 'with living voice'.)

vocabulary All the words a person uses with understanding in his own speech or writing (ACTIVE VOCABULARY) or the larger number of words he can understand in the speech or writing of others (PASSIVE VOCABULARY).

vocabulary test Usually a test of a person's PASSIVE VOCABULARY, sometimes as part of the assessment of INTELLIGENCE.

vocation 1 Once a 'calling' (eg by God or a sense of duty) to some special and probably self-abnegating form of service. (Apart from the priesthood, teaching and nursing were once spoken of primarily as vocations in this kind of sense.) 2 Nowadays, a vocation may be any chosen trade, profession, or way of earning one's living.

vocational counsellors Specialists who provide VOCATIONAL or OCCUPATIONAL GUIDANCE.

vocational education Educational activities designed to develop a person's capability for some prospective career or occupation. Perhaps distinguishable from vocational TRAINING in so far as the student is being prepared for a wider range of activities in which he can exercise more individuality or originality.

vocational guidance Same as OCCUPATIONAL GUIDANCE.

vocational (high) school (US) Same as TRADE HIGH SCHOOL. (The term is sometimes used by private institutions offering general education at college level combined with VOCATIONAL TRAINING.)

vocational-technical high school (US) HIGH SCHOOL offering VOCATIONAL and technical courses, some leading to POST-SECONDARY TECHNICAL EDUCATION.

vocational-technical college (US) POST-SECONDARY institution providing two-year courses in VOCATIONAL and TECHNICAL EDUCATION.

vocational test Any of several tests designed to make clear a person's occupational interests, preferences, aptitudes, etc, eg the STRONG-CAMPBELL INTEREST INVENTORY.

vocational training Training designed to teach the KNOWLEDGE, SKILLS and ATTITUDES required for proficiency in a certain job or task. See also VOCATIONAL EDUCATION.

vocational work experience (US) The industrial/commercial component of a COOPERATIVE COURSE.

voluntary aided schools See VOLUNTARY SCHOOLS.

voluntary colleges of education (UK) Usually CHURCH COLLEGES.

voluntary duties Duties that UK school teachers normally perform in addition to their teaching duties and without payment (eg supervising school meals), but which they sometimes refuse to carry out by way of protest over deteriorating salaries or conditions. See CONDITIONS OF SERVICE.

voluntary schools UK MAINTAINED SCHOOLS run by voluntary bodies (usually the Church of England or the Roman Catholic Church) who provide part or all of the building and/or repair costs but who also receive financial help from their LOCAL EDUCATION AUTHORITY (LEA) or from the DEPARTMENT OF EDUCATION AND SCIENCE and are subject to varying degrees of control from the LEA according to how much financial help they receive. There are three types: AIDED, CONTROLLED and SPECIAL AGREEMENT SCHOOLS. Voluntary schools account for about one third of all maintained PRIMARY SCHOOLS and about one fifth of all maintained SECONDARY SCHOOLS in England and Wales.

voucher system A system that has been experimented with in the US, and proposed elsewhere, in which parents are given vouchers by the local body responsible for education, which they can then 'spend' on behalf of their children at institutions of their choice. (The institutions then 'cash in' the vouchers with the issuing body.) This has been proposed as a way of ensuring parental choice, among private as well as MAINTAINED SCHOOLS, and of channeling extra resources to those schools that best satisfy parents' requirements. Such proposals leave many issues unclear, not least being how all parents are to make valid choices, and how the 'unpopular' schools are to be improved.

VTR   See VIDEOTAPE RECORDER.

Vygotsky, L S (1896–1934)   Russian psychologist influenced by PIAGET, and well known for his theories emphasising the multiplicity of ways in which individuals acquire LANGUAGE and concepts in early life. See his *Thought and Language* (1936).

Vygotsky blocks   Wooden blocks of various shapes, sizes and colours, designed to test a person's ability to sort things into categories using different criteria.

W

Waddell Report 1978   A UK REPORT recommending that a common system of PUBLIC EXAMINATIONS at 16+ (combining the GENERAL CERTIFICATE OF EDUCATION and the CERTIFICATE OF SECONDARY EDUCATION) was both feasible and desirable, and suggesting how it might be achieved by 1985.

WAIS   See WECHSLER ADULT INTELLIGENCE SCALE.

Waldorf method of education   Another name for Steiner Method, described under entry for RUDOLF STEINER.

Ward   A person, especially a MINOR or one legally incapable of handling his own affairs, who is placed under the control or protecton of a guardian or of a court.

warden   1 Member of teaching staff of college or university with special administrative or pastoral responsibilities. Used especially of the staff member responsible for a HALL OF RESIDENCE. (Like 'head resident' in US). 2 The HEAD TEACHER of some UK INDEPENDENT SCHOOLS. 3 The head of some UK COLLEGES. 4 A LOCAL EDUCATION AUTHORITY term for the person in charge of a COMMUNITY COLLEGE or of a TEACHERS' CENTRE.

Warnock Report 1978   The UK REPORT of a COMMITTEE OF ENQUIRY into the education of handicapped children and young people. The report proposed a framework of SPECIAL EDUCATION based on the special educational needs of individual children – regardless of whether they fell into some defined category of bodily or mental handicap. Thus, children with significant learning difficulties and/or presenting BEHAVIOUR problems would qualify as needing special educational treatment (though as far as possible in normal schools). In 1980, the Government issued a WHITE PAPER based on its acceptance of this recommendation.

washback A PROGRAMMED LEARNING term for the process of returning a student to re-read some earlier part of a PROGRAMME, probably because he has failed to score sufficiently well in a test at the end of a section.

wastage See STUDENT WASTAGE.

Watson, John B (1878–1958) US psychology professor at Johns Hopkins University, 1908–1920, and the founding father of BEHAVIOURISM. He experimented not only with animals but also (eg in researching the acquisition of emotions) with children. See his *Behaviourism* (1925) and *Psychological Care of Infant and Child* (1928).

WEA See WORKERS' EDUCATIONAL ASSOCIATION.

Weaver Report 1965 A UK REPORT on the government of COLLEGES OF EDUCATION. It recommended greater independence for colleges and led to the establishment of more broadly-based GOVERNING BODIES and of ACADEMIC BOARDS. It was soon followed, however, by the JAMES REPORT which led to considerable reorganisation in UK TEACHER EDUCATION.

Weber, Max (1864–1920) German sociologist and historian who held CHAIRS at the Universities of Freiburg, Heidelburg and Munich. He made contributions to the study of many aspects of the SOCIAL SCIENCES, especially through his generalisations based on the comparative study of different societies and CULTURES, and through his insistence on seeing social conditions in terms of the actions of individuals. Wrote many books but is best known for his *The Protestant Ethic and the Spirit of Capitalism* (1904).

Wechsler Adult Intelligence Scale (WAIS) A set of verbal and non-verbal INTELLIGENCE TESTS for adults, developed from the Wechsler-Bellevue Scale in the US.

Wechsler Intelligence Scale for Children (WISC or WISC-R) A set of verbal and non-verbal INTELLIGENCE TESTS (measuring verbal, numerical and spatial skills) for children aged 5–15 years, developed in the US.

Wechsler Memory Scale A US test of MEMORY, for use in the DIAGNOSTIC TESTING of adults with special learning or communication difficulties, eg APHASIA.

Wechsler Pre-school and Primary Scale of Intelligence

(**WPPSI**)   US INTELLIGENCE TEST for children between four and six and a half years, thus overlapping with the WECHSLER INTELLIGENCE SCALE FOR CHILDREN.

weighting   **1** The practice in ASSESSMENT of allowing, say, some questions in an EXAMINATION (or some SUBJECTS) to have disproportionate influence in deciding a student's total score. For example, out of five questions (or subjects) one may be weighted so as to account for 50% of the total available score. **2** An additional allowance payable to teachers in certain circumstances, especially when there is a need to compensate for higher living costs, eg a 'London Weighting'.

welfare officer   See EDUCATIONAL WELFARE OFFICER.

welfare school   (US) School for MALADJUSTED CHILDREN.

Welsh Department   Established in 1907 as the Welsh Department of the BOARD OF EDUCATION to ensure 'the better administration of primary, secondary and technical education in Wales and Monmouthshire'.

Welsh Office   The Welsh equivalent of the DEPARTMENT OF EDUCATION AND SCIENCE based in Cardiff with its own INSPECTORATE, and administering Welsh PRIMARY and SECONDARY EDUCATION under the SECRETARY OF STATE FOR WALES.

Welsh intermediate schools   MAINTAINED SECONDARY SCHOOLS set up as a national system by an Act of 1889, to form a link between the ELEMENTARY SCHOOLS and the Federal University of Wales. (England had to wait until 1902 for similar encouragement of maintained secondary schools.)

Welsh Joint Education Committeee (**WJEC**)   A body established in 1948 to advise on PRIMARY, SECONDARY and FURTHER EDUCATION in Wales. It coordinates policies and promotes Welsh ideas about EDUCATION by providing a forum for discussion among Welsh LOCAL EDUCATION AUTHORITIES and teachers and by its representation in, or consultation by, decision-making bodies. It also acts as the examining board for both GCE and CSE in Wales.

weltanschauung   (German, 'world view'.) A comprehensive personal perspective or system of ideas, embracing an unusually wide range of phenomena.

Wendy house   A model house (or room) that is large enough for children to enter, and equipped for them to 'play house'. Used in UK INFANT SCHOOLS and named after the house built for Wendy in J M Barrie's *Peter Pan* (1904).

wet area   That part of a PRIMARY SCHOOL classroom in which floors and furnishings are suited for work with water, paint, clay, etc.

whiteboard   A white plastic substitute for a blackboard or chalkboard on which one can write with large felt-tipped pens.

Whitehead A N (1861–1947)   British mathematician and philosopher, professor of applied mathematics at Imperial College, London University, 1914–1924, and of philosophy at Harvard University, 1924–1937. Author, with BERTRAND RUSSELL, of *Principia Mathematica* (1910–1913). He believed that learning should involve the active acquisition of general ideas (tested and applied and inter-related in real-life situations) rather than the storing of inert facts. He preferred quality and thoroughness in teaching, rather than wide coverage, and believed learning should proceed through three overlapping stages: romance, precision, and generalisation. See his *Aims of Education* (1929).

White Paper   A document issued by the UK government (and others) outlining its policy on a matter about which legislation is planned and thus allowing preliminary public discussion.

whole method   An approach to learning a task (eg the recitation of a poem) by practising the task as a whole several times until proficient. (Rather than learning one section at a time as in the PART METHOD.)

Wilderspin, Samuel (1792–1866)   An English pioneer of INFANT EDUCATION whose treatise, *On the Importance of Educating the Infant Children of the Poor* (1823), led to his having considerable influence both on the CURRICULUM and on the architecture of mid-19th century ELEMENTARY SCHOOLS. His ideas were similar to those of PESTALOZZI, and, apart from his over-emphasis on memorisation, very different from those prevailing in the contemporary DAME SCHOOLS. He stressed the need to work with a child on his own level, with kindness, patience and sympathy; and he advocated music, games and physical activity, believing the PLAYGROUND to be as important as any classroom.

wing college   Defunct term for a UK TRAINING COLLEGE designated by the then MINISTRY OF EDUCATION to provide specialist courses in the teaching of certain SECONDARY SCHOOL subjects and thus provide a special supplementary third-year course for some students.

Wing test of musical intelligence   Test designed by H D Wing to pick out musically promising children (eg those capable of learning an instrument) on the basis of their analysis of chords, pitch discrimination, appreciation of harmonies, etc.

Winnetka Plan   (US) An INDIVIDUALISED LEARNING scheme introduced into the schools of Winnetka near Chicago in 1919 by the SUPERINTENDENT OF SCHOOLS, Carleton W Washburne (who was influenced by the Pueblo Plan of PRESTON W SEARCH). The system involved clear definition of OBJECTIVES and the development of DIAGNOSTIC TESTS in the basic academic subjects, with children working on SELF-INSTRUCTIONAL MATERIALS, each at his own pace. The individual work was, however, leavened by daily group activities in subjects like music, art and physical education.

Winnicott, D W   (born 1896)   UK paediatrician and psychoanalyst who has been influential in creating awareness of the emotional and psychological needs of babies (and their mothers) leading to more relaxed child-care practices. For example, breast feeding is seen to be psychologically as well as nutritionally advantageous and early toilet training is seen as damaging if imposed too rigorously. He has also helped encourage respect for children's fantasy, dreams and art. See his *The Child, the Family and the Outside World* (1964).

WISC-R   The WESCHSLER INTELLIGENCE SCALE FOR CHILDREN (as revised in 1974).

Wiseman, Stephen   (1907–1971)   British psychologist and Director of the NATIONAL FOUNDATION FOR EDUCATIONAL RESEARCH, 1969–71. He is best known for his work on ASSESSMENT and EXAMINATIONS. See his *Examinations in English Education* (1961) and *Intelligence and Ability* (1967).

withdrawal unit   See SPECIAL UNITS.

WJEC   See WELSH JOINT EDUCATION COMMITTEE.

women's studies   Courses designed to highlight the economic and cultural contributions made to society by women (and so redress what is seen as the imbalance of a male-dominated CURRICULUM).

woodwork   A HANDICRAFT subject in the school CURRICULUM.

word-and-sentence method   Teaching a pupil to read by getting him to recognise whole words and sentences from the start. See LOOK AND SAY METHOD.

word association test   A type of PROJECTIVE TEST in which a series of unrelated words or phrases are shown or read out to a person (eg rich – horse – drunk – teenager) and he has to respond with the first word or phrase that comes into his head.

word blindness   See DYSLEXIA.

word method   Teaching a pupil to read by getting him to recognise whole words right from the start. See LOOK AND SAY METHOD.

word processor   A device in which a typewriter and a VISUAL DISPLAY UNIT are connected to a computer in such a way that 'pages' of material can be typed, inspected, edited and altered before being stored or reproduced on paper (perhaps with layout and pagination, etc, being decided by rules fed into the computer).

word recognition test   Test of a person's ability to recognise isolated words and read them aloud. The words are graded in difficulty and the test yields scores that can be converted into READING AGES.

word selection test   Any test in which a person makes his RESPONSE by selecting one of several words he is presented with (rather than providing a word of his own).

'Words in Colour'   The trade-name of an approach to the early stages of·the teaching of reading in which each of 48 sounds is given a colour to help a child recognise it, regardless of its spelling in a particular word. Introduced by Caleb Gattegno in *Words in Colour* (1962).

workcards   Cards containing individual exercises and assignments for pupils, usually prepared by their teacher and allowing pupils to work on their own.

Workers' Educational Association (WEA)   A UK organisation founded in 1903 to stimulate and satisfy the demand for EDUCATION among WORKING CLASS people (whom the UNIVERSITY EXTENSION MOVEMENT had not successfully reached). The WEA now arranges ADULT EDUCATION classes and courses throughout the UK (no longer primarily for working class people) in co-operation with trade unions, universities, and other organisations, and with financial help from the DEPARTMENT OF EDUCATION AND SCIENCE and from LOCAL EDUCATION AUTHORITIES.

work ethic   See PROTESTANT ETHIC.

work-experience   Part of the final year of the SECONDARY SCHOOL CURRICULUM for some pupils, in which they have some kind of part-time attachment to local firms or organisations in order to help their SOCIALISATION into the world of work they will shortly be joining full-time (local unemployment permitting).

working class   That class of people (the majority of the population) generally regarded as having lower social status than the MIDDLE CLASS; refers especially to those who work with their hands (rather than with their heads) and who earn wages (rather than salaries).

working men's colleges UK colleges the first of which was established in London in 1854 to embody the ideas of F D MAURICE (its first principal), who believed that EDUCATION for the WORKING CLASS should be not superficial and technical (as, for instance, in the MECHANICS' INSTITUTE) but liberal and humanising, with the kind of social life experienced in the universities. Only one or two of the colleges still survive but the distinction between TECHNICAL and LIBERAL EDUCATION has remained strong.

work loan program (US) An aid scheme whereby students may obtain payment and/or loans to finance their studies in college or university by undertaking domestic, laboratory or library duties, etc, in the institution.

work placement Matching students with suitable firms and organisations for WORK EXPERIENCE or SANDWICH COURSES.

work sample test A test of a person's likely ability to learn a particular job (his TRAINABILITY) by having him try his hand at some aspect of it after brief instruction.

workshop 1 A room or building equipped for practical HANDICRAFT work. 2 A discussion group in which the participants work on a common problem with a view to formulating solutions or at least to clarifying their understanding of it.

works schools School provided by an industrial firm to make some kind of education or training available to its employees (or their children), eg Robert Owen's NEW LANARK schools.

work study Techniques used in industry to analyse a job in order to determine faster or more effective ways of performing it.

work study program (or **course**) (US) 1 Scheme established by the Economic Opportunities Act of 1964 to provide part-time employment for full-time college students. The purpose is to help with expenses rather than to provide work-experience or to relate to the subjects being studied. The jobs may be on or off campus and the pay is subsidised from federal funds. 2 A HIGH SCHOOL scheme for providing WORK-EXPERIENCE. 3 College or university course in a programme of studies where CREDIT is given for work off-campus in social services, local government, and industrial or other organisations, rather as in a UK SANDWICH COURSE.

World Education Fellowship See NEW EDUCATION FELLOW-SHIP.

wpm Words per minute – a measure of a person's speed at typing or SHORTHAND.

world language 1 A language known to and spoken by people in many countries, eg English. 2 An artificial language created for international use, eg ESPERANTO, Ido, Interlingua, etc.

worship The EDUCATION ACT 1944 stipulated that every MAIN-TAINED SCHOOL must begin the day with a corporate act of worship (non-denominational except in certain VOLUNTARY SCHOOLS). Parents may withdraw their children from this if they wish. See also ASSEMBLY and RELIGIOUS EDUCATION.

WPPSI WECHSLER PRE-SCHOOL AND PRIMARY SCALE OF INTELLIGENCE.

wrangler Cambridge University graduate who has achieved first-class HONOURS in mathematics. (Quite different from its US association with horses, cattle and cowboys.)

wrong-answer frame See REMEDIAL FRAME.

X

xerography A photocopying (REPROGRAPHY) process whereby an electrostatic image is formed on a cylinder, which is then dusted with a resinous powder that adheres to the charged regions, allowing the image to be transferred to a sheet of paper where it is fixed by heating.

Xerox 1 The trademark of a particular company making XER-OGRAPHY machines. 2 A copy made by a Xerox machine or (by extension) by any XEROGRAPHY or similar reprographic machines. 3 (As a verb) to make such a copy.

Y

year book 1 A REFERENCE BOOK published annually and containing details of events (in general or in a particular field) during the previous twelve months, eg the *World Yearbook of Education*, edited jointly by colleagues from London University and Columbia University, New York and much respected as a source book of COMPARATIVE EDUCATION. **2** A publication prepared by the SENIOR class in US HIGH SCHOOLS and COLLEGES which records the event of the class throughout its previous three or four years.

year-group   The group of pupils, perhaps divided among several classes, who move up through the school together year by year, eg as in 'third year pupils' or 'fifth formers', etc.

year tutor/coordinator   Teacher responsible for planning the CURRICULUM and/or arranging PASTORAL care for all the pupils in a particular year of their school career.

Yehudi Menuhin School   INDEPENDENT BOARDING SCHOOL in Surrey, England, founded by the virtuoso violinist Yehudi Menuhin in 1963, to provide both general education and specialist musical training for musically gifted children between the ages of 8 and 15 years.

Yerkes-Dodson Law   A long-standing generalisation from experimental psychology to the effect that, in performing a task, a certain amount of anxiety is beneficial but the optimum amount decreases as the difficulty of the task increases.

YES   See YOUTH EMPLOYMENT SERVICE.

YOP   See YOUTH OPPORTUNITIES PROGRAMME.

Young Enterprise   A UK organisation formed in 1962 to give young people a grounding in the economics and organisation of business by enabling them to form and operate miniature companies with the advice of local businessmen.

young offender   Person convicted of an offence and who has reached the age of criminal responsibility but is not yet an adult.

youth club/or centre)   A leisure centre for young people, often associated with a school, church or community centre.

Youth Employment Service (YES)   CAREERS GUIDANCE service for school-leavers, established in 1948 and now called CAREERS ADVISORY SERVICE.

youth hostel   One of an international chain of cheap and basic lodging-places, intended primarily to accommodate young people wishing to explore the countryside at minimum cost.

youth leader   Person whose role is to facilitate productive relationships and activities among young people in a YOUTH CLUB or centre. A one-year training course is available for full-time youth leaders and there is a national pay scale, though many part-timers are voluntary workers.

Youth Opportunities Programme (**YOP**)   A UK five-year programme of training schemes and temporary WORK EXPERIENCE attachments, launched by the MANPOWER SERVICES COMMISSION in 1978 with a view to helping unemployed people between the ages of 16 and 19 to prepare for work and improve their chances of obtaining and keeping jobs.

Youth Service   A UK partnership between the LOCAL EDUCATION AUTHORITIES and the various voluntary bodies (eg churches, Boy Scouts, Girl Guides, etc) that operate YOUTH CLUBS and other educational, social and training facilities for young people. The service is under the general guidance of the DEPARTMENT OF EDUCATION AND SCIENCE from which it receives some funding.

youth treatment centre   A type of UK centre providing supervision for YOUNG OFFENDERS. (Operated by local authorities in cooperation with the Department of Health and Social Security.)

Z

zeitgeist   (German, 'time spirit'.) The spirit or general outlook of a particular period, especially as reflected in literature, philosophy, school CURRICULUM, etc.

zoning   Determining the CATCHMENT AREAS for the schools in a given district.

Z-scores   A form of STANDARDISED SCORE obtained by re-expressing the actual scores obtained on a test or examination in terms of how far each one is (in units of the STANDARD DEVIATION) above or below the MEAN score. Thus, an actual score that was bigger than the mean score by as much as two standard deviations would be quoted as a Z-score of $+2$; while an actual score that was one-and-a-half standard deviations less than the mean would give a Z-score of $-1\frac{1}{2}$.